Applied Equity Analysis

Stock Valuation Techniques
for Wall Street Professionals

James R. English

McGraw-Hill

New York Chicago San Francisco Lisbon London Madrid Mexico City
Milan New Delhi San Juan Seoul Singapore Sydney Toronto

Library of Congress Cataloging-in-Publication Data

English, James R.
   Applied equity analysis: stock valuation techniques for Wall Street professionals / by
James R. English.
     p. cm.
   ISBN 0-07-136051-4
   1. Corporations—Valuation.   2. Corporations—Finance.   I. Title.

HG4028.V3 E53 2001
658.15—dc21

                                               00-066232

McGraw-Hill

A Division of The McGraw·Hill Companies

      7 8 9 0 DOC/DOC 0 9 8 7 6

ISBN 0-07-136051-4

This book was set in Times Roman by Pro Image Corporation.

Printed and bound by R. R. Donnelley & Sons Company.

This publication is designed to provide accurate and authoritative information in regard to the subject
matter covered. It is sold with the understanding that the publisher is not engaged in rendering
legal, accounting, or other professional service. If legal advice or other expert assistance is required,
the services of a competent professional person should be sought.
> *—From a declaration of principles jointly adopted by a committee of the
> American Bar Association and a committee of publishers.*

 This book is printed on recycled, acid-free paper containing a
minimum of 50% recycled de-inked fiber.

Contents

Preface

In a 25-year career in finance, 20 of which were spent at J.P. Morgan & Company, I've practiced many of the field's subspecialties, from commercial banking and credit analysis, corporate treasury and foreign exchange, capital markets, mergers and acquisitions, and venture capital, as well as sell-side equity analysis covering the property/casualty insurance stocks. Over this period, I developed a working knowledge of each field, certainly enough to get along. In 1998 I began, as an adjunct assistant professor, to teach a securities analysis course to second-year MBA candidates at the Columbia Business School of Columbia University in New York. In preparation for the course, I tried to draw my ideas about competition, corporate strategy, and equity value into a coherent whole. This book grew out of that effort.

The book contains the collection of financial analytic techniques that I've found most useful in teaching the subject to students, and in actually doing the work of equity analysis myself. Others developed many of these techniques, and I've tried to acknowledge that where appropriate. The number of "war stories" is minimized because, after all, stories about the insurance industry, which I know best, probably have limited appeal, except to the insurance industry.

My objective in this book is to make the most powerful equity analysis techniques I've discovered, through experience, teaching and study, available to my professional colleagues. Although potentially useful as a text in equity analysis courses at the graduate level, the book remains a practitioners' guide to what works. Where academic opinions conflict or are absent, I propose my own views.

TWO LINES OF INQUIRY

It was in 1987, as a credit and corporate finance analyst at Morgan, that I first read Porter's books[1] on competitive strategy. It was clear after that reading that industry structure and competitive strategy have a profound impact upon the firm's financial performance. What wasn't clear, however, is how competitive forces can be seen to act directly upon financial results, and further, how those financial results drive stock valuation.

Valuation Multiples and Financial Performance

In 1991, when J.P. Morgan began its transformation to an investment and commercial banking hybrid, equity valuation assumed a prominence in our work with clients. Trained as a commercial banker, this sudden equity immersion set me on a search for a theoretical understanding of the subject. Having taken my MBA in 1974, I was woefully out of date. Not only that, but Wall Street's language of EPS and P/E ratios was a puzzle because I believed that discounted cash flow (DCF) was the only legitimate valuation technique. Valuation multiples seemed to me a slipshod shortcut around more rigorous techniques. The arrogance of youth.

An article by Hickman and Petry (H&P), who used industry cross-sectional regressions to tie observed price/earnings multiples to firms' beta, growth rate, and dividend payout ratios, provided my initial insight into the valuation multiple problem.[2] H&P found that such cross-sectional models outperformed traditional dividend discount and discounted-cash-flow techniques, observing, "Having noted the theoretical foundations of [dividend discount] models, some readers may be surprised at this outcome. . . ." H&P conclude:

> The problems inherent in capturing investor expectations by applying the [capital asset pricing model] to calculate required rates of return, as well as the difficulties in forecasting and discounting cash flows, are evident. . . . In contrast, market determined multiples and yields are reflective of market expectations and preferences, while firms within industries do share common components of value. Thus, the [market-based] models utilize observable data to capture implicitly that which is so difficult to explicitly quantify.

This certainly surprised me and was my first hint that the information inherent in stock prices could provide a more satisfactory valuation foundation than DCF techniques. I immediately began using cross-sectional regression in my own industry valuations. Eventually, I came to rely on Fuller, who demonstrated how regression models might be used to identify undervalued equities,[3] and upon Damodaran, who expanded the theoretical basis of the technique.[4]

Even though Wall Street's techniques now made much more sense, I still found some holes in the story:

- Although price/book value multiples behaved well in cross-sectional regression models, price/earnings multiples did not. This was fortunate for me since insurance, like many financial services industries, relied principally on the P/BV multiple in stock valuations. Still, my inability to explain P/E multiples using fundamental performance data was distressing.
- Competitive analysis and valuation remained relatively separate topics. I was unable to find an intuitive, quantitative connection between the two.

Focusing the Mind

The preparation for my 1998 Columbia course again focused my mind on these problems. It seemed clear, for example, that competitive analysis and valuation were required subjects in the course. And I strongly believed that the equity analysis process that I used and intended to teach was a relatively seamless whole. But making the connection between competitive processes and strategy, which determined a firm's financial returns, and valuation, which must in turn be driven by those returns, eluded me.

The breakthrough came as I searched for texts and cases for the course. I assigned White, Sondhi, and Fried (WSF) to support the course's financial statement analysis module.[5] In WSF for the first time, I saws the "abnormal" or residual earnings model of stock valuation and began to link strategy and value.

- Market value is added to a stock when the firm's abnormal income, defined as the difference between the return on and cost of equity, is positive.
- Successful strategies permit the firm to generate returns in excess of capital costs.
- Success attracts competition, which acts to force returns on equity toward equity capital costs in a mean reversion process.

■ Eventually, stock value is limited by the absence of profitable incremental investment opportunities.

The abnormal income formulation focuses on investment opportunities, which are directly affected by competitive actions, not on growth (so common in DCF valuations), where the competitive connections are less clear and the risk of "assumption drift" (away from reality) is much greater. Better still, the abnormal income model explained the behavior of valuation multiples, especially the P/E, under varying return and growth conditions, clearing up an issue that had puzzled me since the early 1990s.

Eventually, I discovered Palepu, Bernard, and Healy's (PBH) book, which I continue to use in my course.[6] PBH achieves the most important goal in equity analysis, which is to tie the disparate elements of the process into a logical whole. In fact, "equity analysis" may be misnamed since the effort is really not to take companies and stocks apart but to put investment stories together. We might better call it "equity synthesis." PBH helps students to achieve that synthesis.

The Laws of Nature

The sum of this intellectual journey is a set of personal "laws of nature" that guide my own analytical thinking. The book at many points reflects these views, which I hope readers find controversial:

■ *Accounting numbers are good things.* Contrary to what many accountants themselves now seem to believe, I think that the numbers produced by the GAAP financial accounting system, especially earnings measures, are the most useful single tool in equity analysis. Whether you believe this or not, earnings is what the market uses to value stocks, and you have to find a way to live with it.

■ *Accounting-based stock valuation is superior to cash flow.* A corollary of the first point, accounting-based equity valuation, especially in the abnormal earnings form, is more intuitive, compact, and convenient than discounted-cash-flow techniques. When used with observable stock price data, the combination is unbeatable. It is the expected earning power of the firm, not its cash flow, which drives stock value.

■ *The competitive process unavoidably constrains financial performance.* This is the hardest law for analysts to accept, in my view, because we all want the *bon temps* to *rouler* forever. The actions of competition and the underlying physical processes of the firm's business are absolute limitations on performance. Everything isn't possible, nothing lasts forever, and change is the rule.

ORGANIZATION OF THE BOOK

The book is organized into five distinct parts. The first part, "Getting Started," introduces the equity analysis world and lays the foundations for competitive and valuation discussions. Chapter 2 is a relatively complete presentation of the basic ideas of abnormal earnings valuation techniques.

Part Two, "The Basic Tools," focuses on reading financial statements, but with particular objectives. Reading financial statements effectively is a skill acquired through long practice, and it involves as much art as science. But any financial statement reading should attempt to determine (1) the accuracy, sustainability, and predictability of reported financial results; (2) the composition of the firm's returns on equity; and (3) the firm's capacity for continued investment. Chapter 10 presents the Stern Stewart EVA system as an alternative, and potentially useful, way of approaching financial statement information. EVA is also a precursor to Chapter 16's elaboration of the abnormal earnings model.

Part Three, "Financial Models," presents my personal views on designing financial models. Financial modeling is a common subject in security analysis texts but, unfortunately, is not handled well. Most analysts learn the subject on the job. These chapters present my on-the-job modeling experience. It may not seem like a lot, but it was hard won knowledge.

Part Four, "Valuation," is the book's heart because it attempts to present the argument for empirical, accounting-based valuation techniques. As a result, Chapter 14 on discounted-cash-flow valuation is purposefully much shorter than is usual in a treatment of valuation. Although DCF is the foundation of all other equity valuation methods, I simply never found the technique of much use as an equity analyst.

Finally, Part Five, "Getting It Down on Paper," consists of only one chapter on writing an equity analysis report. I hope that this book follows the chapter's suggestions. If it doesn't, shame on me.

A Note on the Use of Equations

Since it was one of my goals to establish a theoretical basis for valuation multiple techniques, some chapters make use of equations. Simple algebra and an understanding of the mathematics of discounting will carry the reader through these passages. For those who find equations confusing and distracting, I sympathize, but I don't agree.

ACKNOWLEDGMENTS

Through a career, there are only a few people from whom one learns the bulk of one's trade. For me, one of the most important was Roberto G. Mendoza, with whom I worked for many years at J.P. Morgan. Not just one of the most talented people in American finance, in my view, Roberto is one of the most principled. I thank him for teaching me not only the mechanics of finance, but also the primacy of integrity. I thank my tireless editor, Mary Sharkey, for her help from the very earliest stages of the project. Mary's reading shored up my writing when it faltered, and the book is much the better for it. Finally, very special thanks go to my friend and colleague, Ken Froewiss of the Stern School of Business at New York University, for his support, advice, and encouragement.

NOTES

[1] Michael E. Porter, *Competitive Strategy,* The Free Press, New York, 1980, and *Competitive Advantage,* The Free Press, New York, 1985.

[2] Kent Hickman and Glenn H. Petry, "A Comparison of Stock Price Predictions Using Court Accepted Formulas, Dividend Discount, and P/E Models," *Financial Management,* Summer 1990.

[3] Russell J. Fuller and James L. Farrell, Jr., *Modern Investments and Security Analysis,* McGraw-Hill, New York, 1987.

[4] Aswath Damodaran, *Damodaran on Valuation,* Wiley, New York, 1994.

[5] Gerald I. White, Ashwinpaul C. Sondhi, and Dov Fried, *The Analysis and Use of Financial Statements,* 2d ed., Wiley, New York, 1997.

[6] Krishna G. Palepu, Victor L. Bernard, and Paul M. Healy, *Introduction to Business Analysis & Valuation,* Cincinnati, Ohio: South-Western College Publishing, 1996.

PART ONE

Getting Started

CHAPTER 1

A Day in the Life

- The objective of the equity analysis process is the prediction of a future stock price, a *target price*. To find the target price, the equity analyst generally multiplies a projected measure of future financial performance, like earnings, by an estimated capitalization factor, like the price/earnings ratio. Such techniques, rather than being half-hearted attempts to short cut more rigorous valuation methods, are both theoretically sound and highly practical to the working analyst.

- The analyst must present point estimates of future stock performance, as difficult as that may be. Investors can then develop a range of possible outcomes from the opinions of a number of analysts. The individual analyst doesn't do anyone any favors with diffidence.

- Equity analysis is primarily advocacy, not description. The analyst's job is to present a position, supported by financial and nonfinancial evidence. Data unnecessary to the argument are, in a word, unnecessary. However, the analyst must understand the data, relevant or not.

- The ultimate goal of the equity analyst is to exploit any difference between a stock's price and its value.

Trained in the discounted-cash-flow world, I was unsettled when I was first exposed to Wall Street's equity analysis and valuation techniques as a junior sell-side equity analyst. Could a price/earnings ratio and predicted earnings per share really substitute for a rigorous analysis of future cash flows? Was the prediction of a stock target price, rather than a range of potential future values, a sound technique? These questions formed the basis of a personal investigation of the equity analytic process as currently practiced. To my surprise, it turns out that these techniques are not only theoretically sound but they are also substantially more practical to the working analyst than the more familiar cash flow techniques. But whatever one's personal analytic preferences, accounting earnings estimates, valuation multiples, target prices, and stock recommendations are the stock market's language, and an equity analyst must learn to speak it. I hope this book makes the process of acquiring that language a bit easier.

In spite of its shorthand, equity analysis must still be a disciplined process. The exploration of a firm's internal and external competitive environments is the foundation of the entire exercise. An understanding of the firm's competitive strengths and weaknesses permits the analyst to form basic expectations of future performance. No equity analysis can proceed without a competitive foundation, and no analyst should ignore it.

Reading the firm's financial statements is the next step in the process. Analysts need be concerned with three "numbers issues": (1) the accuracy, sustainability, and predictability of reported financial results; (2) the composition of the company's returns on equity; and (3) the company's capacity for continued investment.

Based upon these competitive and financial statement explorations, the analyst builds a model of the firm's future financial performance. This model provides the projections of earnings or cash flow upon which stock price estimates are based.

Finally, an equity analyst must understand what future performance is likely to be worth to investors. Equity valuation techniques are the final link in the analysis chain. Discounting future cash flows is the most familiar of these. But there are others, based on relative stock valuations or abnormal earnings analyses, which can speed the valuation process. Why is speed important? Because an equity analyst must be concerned with a large number of stocks, usually in a single industry. And, perhaps more importantly, the stock market moves quickly. Response time is of the essence.

TALKING THE TALK

Investors value most stocks as ongoing businesses, rather than collections of assets. In this view, a stock's value is the product of some future performance measure, like earnings, and a valuation multiple, like a price/earnings (P/E) ratio. Valuation multiples are frequently estimated by examining a group of "comparable" stocks. Price/earnings ratios are often compared to earnings growth rates as a measure of their appropriateness. The going-concern view focuses investors' attention on the firm's income statement, not its balance sheet. Many investors believe that stock price movement is caused by specific catalyst events, and investors are often highly trend oriented. Performance is measured quarterly against consensus earnings estimates, not historical periods. What management is saying often carries more weight with investors than reported financial results. And finally, sell-side equity analysts rarely recommend the sale of stocks.[1]

Meet the New Boss, Same As the Old Boss

Stock valuations are determined by, in Whitman's terms, *outside passive minority investors* (OPMIs) who can, by definition, exert little control over the firm's operations and strategy and who trade shares in quantities that do not amount to controlling blocks.[2] As a result, stock prices contain the embedded assumption, not surprisingly, that the company will continue to do pretty much the same thing with the same people. In other words, the market values companies as relatively unchanged ongoing businesses. Breakup value, private market value, value in a mergers and acquisitions (M&A) bidding contest, or the value of a changed strategy, for example, do not generally apply.

There are certainly exceptions to this rule. The fact or rumor of an M&A transaction will often cause both the buyer's and seller's stocks to revalue. To get to the expected M&A value, the stock price must have started somewhere. It started in fact at the OPMI price.

What's the P/E Ratio?

Investors think of stock value as the product of some future financial performance measure, such as earnings, and a valuation multiple, like the price/earnings ratio. This methodology seems, on its face, a less-than-satisfactory shortcut of more rigorous discounted-cash-flow methodologies. In truth, however, it is a relatively legitimate attempt to reason from the firm's earning power to its value. The notion here is that wealth is created when it is earned, rather than when cash is collected.[3] If there were any serious question about collectibility of cash, few investors would consider buying the stock anyway.

Balance Sheets? Who Needs Balance Sheets?

Investors' interest in earnings leads to a focus on the firm's income statement (and possibly statement of cash flows), rather than its balance sheet. Financial stability, like discounted cash flow, appears to receive short shrift. But this is stock investing, not commercial banking, and we are concerned with the firm's best prospects, not the possibility of failure. Again, if there were a legitimate concern about financial viability, equity investment would be questionable at best. Decisions about the company's cash flow, financial flexibility, solvency, and asset value need to be made before consideration of a stock purchase. It's not that investors ignore these issues, or if they do, they certainly shouldn't. It's that these issues are settled prior to equity valuation.

A Stock That Stays Cheap Is Not Cheap

It's the regular morning sales meeting, and you have just finished what you believe is a brilliant argument for the undervaluation of your favorite stock when a salesperson—usually the same one every time—raises his hand and says, "Yeah, but what's going to move the stock?"

Undervaluation, no matter how expertly asserted, is not a persuasive argument for the purchase of a stock. Investors want to know the specific catalysts that will cause the market to accept the analyst's view. Will a new contract be won? Will a drug be approved for sale? A new product offered for sale? A cost-cutting program implemented? A share buyback announced? Something has to happen, the stock's cheapness has to be generally acknowledged, and people need to be convinced.

I was surprised to find that often, investors would prefer to buy a stock that has moved from $20 to $40 than a stock with similar prospects that has fallen to $20 from $40. Valuation is not the critical variable. Catalysts and trends tip the investment decision.

"Milestones" work like catalysts. A set of publicly announced management objectives, laid out over months (or years), can move a stock as each, in turn, is reached (or not reached). For example, after its 1993 initial public offering, the management of Allstate Corporation (ALL), the nation's second-largest auto insurer, presented an "investor road map," a plan to eliminate a number of critical drags on the stock's value: to reduce its exposure to catastrophic loss; divest underperforming, non-strategic businesses; grow its profitable nonstandard auto insurance business; and deal with excess capital. Following the June 1995 Sears divestiture (with ALL at about $30), management vigorously attacked each objective. By November 1997, after substantially reducing its exposure to Florida hurricanes, selling its commercial insurance business, and announcing a $2 billion share buyback, the stock reached $85.

I know what you're thinking: If the analyst knows of catalysts and milestones, doesn't the rest of the market know of them too? And if the market knows, isn't the information already in the stock price? So how can an investor profit from a potentially catalyzing event, even if it does happen? All good questions, which we explore in the context of market efficiency in Chapter 5.

Hit the Number, or Hit the Road

Miss the quarterly consensus earnings estimate and suffer the consequences. Quarterly estimates may be the ultimate stock milestone. There are frequent examples of quarterly earnings per share (EPS) estimates that are $0.01 short of consensus, producing a shocking selloff in the stock. Investors focus intensely on the ability of companies to meet or exceed the estimated earnings consensus. This is probably, at least in part, as it should be. It is, of course, not the $0.01 of missed earnings that is important but the impact of the earnings shortfall on investors' expectations of future performance, or, perhaps, their confidence in management. Especially when growth expectations are very high, small reductions produce substantial changes in stock price. Not surprisingly, overpromising is one of the worst blunders management can make in its dealings with the Street. If you point to the center field fence when you step up to the plate, you'd better hit it out of the park.

Growth Rates, Absolute Value, and Other Dreams

It would be wonderful if there were an absolute standard for stock valuation—a number we could look at and say, this stock is overpriced, or underpriced. I don't believe it. Unfortunately, stock valuation is, at its base, a relative process. All valuation methods measure a stock's worth relative to other assets. Even discounted cash flow, a seemingly foolproof way of reaching "inherent value," is a relative valuation technique. According to the *capital asset pricing model* (CAPM), the cost of equity is measured relative to a broader market return. Exactly which broader market return is a subject of debate, but it is relative to some broader market return. Nevertheless, investors still search for absolute measures of value. One of the most frequently used is the ratio of the price/earnings multiple to the earnings growth rate. The notion is that a stock with a P/E ratio to growth ratio of less than 1 is undervalued and greater than 1, is overvalued. We will argue in Chapter 17 that P/E-to-growth is a considerably more complex measure than that. *PEG*

In the absence of absolute value measures, I'm afraid there is no easy way out in equity analysis. The reasonableness of a stock's (or the market's) valuation must finally be judged, it seems to me, by the future performance assumptions it contains. The investor must ask, if I pay the current stock price, what sort of performance must the company achieve if I am to earn a decent return? Can the company be expected to achieve such performance, given its competitive environment and management? Chapter 18 presents some analytic techniques to answer these questions.

Seats on Airplanes

It is often said that CEOs would prefer to believe a stranger they sat next to on an airplane than to believe someone from their own staffs. Investors are much the same. What management is saying is more important to investors, sometimes, than the financial results they are reporting. As an analyst, I often despaired that I was nothing more than a conduit for management pronouncements, rather than being an independent source of information. It would be simple to say that the truth is always in the numbers, and we ignore financial reports at our peril. In fact, the truth is in the numbers more frequently than not. But there is a legitimate purpose served in the dissemination of apparent hearsay. Knowing what management is saying helps investors to know what other investors are hearing, and that reduces everyone's uncertainty.[4] Knowing what information is incorporated into a stock's price is as important, I would argue, as knowing the truth. Maybe more important.

Sell Recommendations and Other Rarities

It is a fact that sell-side equity analysts rarely place a sell recommendation on any of the stocks they follow. There it is. Investors need to realize that sell-side analysis has more in common with journalism than with scientific research. Objectivity is important, but it is also important to preserve access to one's sources. And, unfortunately, management is a major source of information to analysts (although, in light of the SEC's recent adoption of Regulation FD, perhaps no longer such an exclusive source). Saying bad things about a company's stock is unlikely to endear one to its managers. And given the weight investors place upon management contact, loss of access can be crippling to an analyst.

Does this mean that sell-side research, because it often lacks impartiality, is useless? Hardly. Investors must realize that, in the end, the equity analyst is an advocate, not a neutral observer. It is the analyst's job to present a position. It is the investor's job to "diversify" by considering a variety of analysts' positions.

Target Prices Are, Well, the Target

The point of all this is the estimate of a future stock price. Using an earnings-per-share projection, for example, the analyst estimates the future earning power of the company. To that projection, the analyst applies an "appropriate" multiple, such as a P/E multiple. The result is a future stock price estimate, a *target price*. Seems simple enough.

Of course, it isn't simple at all. Earnings forecasts are almost certainly less accurate the longer the projection period. More than a year or so out, projections are more a statement of personal faith than a prediction of the future. Forecasting future valuation multiples may be more difficult. Even if a compelling argument about the proper current multiple can be made, the level of future interest rates and perhaps the overall level of the stock market will drive future multiples, at least partially.

Of course, no sensible investor should rely on equity analysts to accurately predict future stock prices. A target price is not a prophecy but an opinion based on a particular view of the firm's competitive prospects. It is the persuasiveness of the analyst's views, not the accuracy of his or her predictions, that is important.

Learning to Be Taller

Having said all this, the fact is that a large part—perhaps the bulk—of the equity analyst's time is spent selling, not analyzing. This is not a book about selling stock. I have always believed that trying to teach selling is like trying to teach someone to be taller. Sales skills are just not within the range of control of most analysts. It may be true, in the end, that selling skills make the difference between a successful and unsuccessful equity analyst. I believe firmly, however, that without the analytic horsepower, the sales engine will not run.

DOING THE WORK

The firm's competitive environment and strategy are the foundation of equity analysis and the starting point of the work.[5] Competitive strategy analysis generates the analyst's most basic ideas about the company's prospects. Those basic ideas—about future margins, sales growth, cash flow, and other financial variables—are grounded in an understanding of the company's historical performance. By reading the company's financial statements, the analyst can form judgments about three critical analytic issues: the accuracy of the financial information presented, the composition of the company's returns, and its capacity for continued investment. The accuracy of financial information is dependent on not only the economic reality of financial disclosure but also the sustainability and predictability of financial performance. An analysis of the firm's financial ratios, focusing on operating, investment, and financial decisions, produces an understanding of the components of the company's financial returns. The company's life cycle position and cash flow determine its ability to finance its investments, upon which future profitability depends. Basic competitive ideas and historical financial analysis supply the data for a financial projection model.

Having projected future financial performance, the analyst must decide what it is worth to investors (Figure 1–1). There are, in my view, at least three ways to do this. The traditional *discounted-cash-flow* (DCF) *methodology* uses cash flow projections (from the financial model) and a measure of capital or equity costs. *Relative valuation methods* determine valuation by examining trading and valuation patterns in closely related stocks called *comparables*. Finally, a hybrid methodology combines the DCF discounting process with measure of the company's performance in excess of capital costs to arrive at valuations.

Competitive Environment and Strategy Are the Foundation

It is the combination of the firm's internal competitive resources and its external environment that determines its potential for competitive

FIGURE 1–1

The objective of analysis is equity valuation.

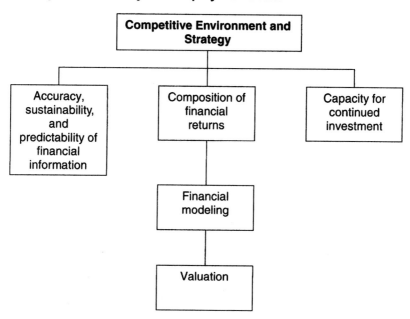

success. The company's internal resources form the "nature" side of this nature-nurture distinction. Internal resources and capabilities determine the company's competitive strengths and weaknesses. The firm's external environment, the "nurture" side of the debate, determines the strength of the competitive forces in action, the threats and opportunities present. The combination of these internal and external analyses forms the *SWOT process—strengths, weaknesses, opportunities, and threats—*a useful tool for competitive analysis.[6]

The basic question the analyst asks in competitive analysis is, what are the firm's investment opportunities and how profitable can they be? How are the firm's opportunities and profitability likely to be limited by the actions of competitors (or other actors) in its environment? Will the firm's own unique skills and resources be likely to resist those external competitive actions? The degree to which the actions of competitors—and there are always active competitors—can be identified and overcome is the principal determinant of future profitability.

Reading Financial Statements Is the Next Step

After taking a position on the firm's competitive prospects, the analyst needs to begin surrounding it with numbers. Numbers come out of the firm's historical financial statements. But financial statements have lots and lots of numbers. What do we do now? Students in my equity analysis course, although they have a solid grounding in both accounting and finance, are often frustrated by the detail of corporate financial reports. To serve as guideposts, I suggest that they explore three fundamental "numbers questions": the accuracy, sustainability, and predictability of the firm's financial information; the composition of its returns; and its capacity for continued investment.[7]

The Accuracy, Sustainability, and Predictability of Financial Information

The first numbers question the analyst should ask is, what is the accuracy, sustainability, and predictability of the financial information presented? If the firm's historical performance is not accurately depicted in its accounts, for whatever reason, forming a quantitative picture of its future performance prospects is difficult, and dangerous. Carrying accounting distortions into financial models leads to unsound projections, incorrect valuations, and bad stock recommendations. Distortions in accounting records can be caused by the rules of accounting themselves—the *generally accepted accounting principles* (GAAP). Management decisions and estimates, critical to the generation of financial statements, may prove inaccurate or they may be misleading. The company's operations themselves are never completely smooth and often contain one-time events, such as acquisitions. These one-time events, if carried inadvertently into projections, can distort valuations.

Accuracy is only one part of a larger analysis, often referred to as the *quality of earnings.* It is certainly important to know the impact of accounting presentation on the firm's reported results. It is equally important to understand the sustainability and predictability of the firm's income sources. Analysts must ask, is the company's financial disclosure adequate to determine the sources of earnings? Are income generators transparent, or are they buried in the numbers? Once income sources are identified, the sustainability and predictability of each tie the analyst right back to the company's fundamental competitive positioning.

The Composition of Returns

Equity value is created when a firm makes investments that produce returns in excess of its cost of capital. If the equity analyst learns nothing else about the company, he or she needs to know how the company earns these returns. So the second numbers question is, what is the composition of the firm's returns? How does the firm make money, if it does make money? Asking this question leads naturally to an examination of the firm's operational, investment, and financial decision making, the three basic components of financial return. Operational decisions drive the price and margin positioning of the company's products. Investment decisions involve the company's use of both current and capital assets. Finally, financial decisions determine the company's financial leverage and dividend policy, the third cornerstone of the return analysis process. (There is a fourth component of return, tax planning, which is well beyond our scope.) It ought to be, when the analysis of returns is finished, that the results are consistent with the analyst's basic notions about the firm's competitive position. Competitive positioning should be mirrored in return composition. If the numbers tell a different story than the competitive analysis, something is wrong.

One Key At a Time

One does not learn to play the piano by mastering one key at a time. The keys must work together to make music. Likewise, financial variables do not exist in isolation but are interdependent fundamentally. Financial statement analysis is a search for these relationships. Further, because there is a physical balance in business firms, financial possibilities are not unbounded. One needs manufacturing facilities and inventory to produce products; the more product one produces and sells, the more production capacity is needed, and so on. There is in fact a "scaling" process in financial performance. The parts of the organization move together, and the parts of financial statements move together. Sales are often the driver of this scaling process, but they don't have to be. Once these relationships are clear, financial performance can be modeled with as much assurance as is possible in a very uncertain process. Without these relationships, the process of change, inherent in projected performance, cannot be kept in the proper balance and will not accurately portray future possibilities. The logic works in the other direction as well.

Out-of-balance financial statements are very often an indicator of unbalanced operations. And that can mean trouble for investors.

The Capacity for Continued Investment

If profitable investments are the fundamental driver of equity value, how are these investments to be financed? The third numbers question that the analyst must ask is, what is the firm's capacity for continued investment? Study of the company's internal and external sources of cash is fundamental to an understanding of investment capacity. Sources of financing are often tied to the company's stage of development, and cash flow analysis reveals the firm's life cycle position more clearly than any other analytic process. Early-stage companies are dependent on external financing to continue the investment process. Established companies can generate substantial cash flow and finance dividend payments. As do operational and investment decisions, financial decisions must be kept in balance and in scale. Forecasting a capacity expansion without considering its cash flow consequences, and the costs of any additional financing, seriously misrepresents the firm's future opportunities.

Financial Modeling Is Opinion, Not Prophecy

The *financial model,* a projection of the firm's income statement, balance sheet, and statement of cash flow, provides point estimates of future financial performance, upon which valuation analysis is based. All the analysis to this point—competitive strategy and financial statement—had as its objective the building of a consistent picture of potential future financial results.

It is probably true that all financial projections are eventually proven wrong, to one extent or another. It is true, and it is unimportant. Financial modeling is not prophecy; it is opinion. The function of a financial model is to consistently present the potential consequences of the analyst's view of the future. If the model is wrong (barring the seemingly inevitable mathematical errors), it is because the analyst's view was wrong, not because modeling is an inherently empty exercise.

The complexity of financial models is often an issue of personal taste. The ideal, in my view, is to model all three of the company's principal financial statements—income statement, balance sheet, and statement of cash flows—in the form the company reports them. This requires building company financial models from scratch. But time pressures militate against such completeness, not because these models are too time-consuming to write (especially with the help of enthusiastic junior analysts) but because they are too time-consuming to use. Financial models must be complete, but they must also produce reasonable results quickly, especially when being updated on a day when five of the analyst's covered companies have reported earnings, 15 minutes before the market opens. In my own models, which I wrote from scratch, balance sheet and cash flow projections were sufficient to produce a credible income statement, the real focus of the exercise.

Valuation Is the Objective

The analyst's financial model presents a possible future, but he or she must now ask, what is that future worth? How much will equity investors pay for a stock with the predicted performance? These questions point out another necessary consistency in equity analysis. Not only must a company's growth be kept in financial balance, but ultimately its value must be a consequence of that performance. Discounted-cash-flow valuation methods achieve that balance by using the direct free-cash-flow output of a financial model. Whatever value the DCF produces, we can be sure that it is sensitive to predicted performance.

But what about valuation multiple methods? It often seems that valuation multiples are pulled out of the air. But in fact, P/E multiples and their cousins have a substantial theoretical underpinning. Understanding the drivers of multiples is essential to finding the right one, and thereby finding the right value. The principal driver of valuation multiples, and of value in general, is the level of abnormal earnings generated by the firm. *Abnormal earnings* are earnings in excess of the costs of the capital employed by the firm.

■ **Tip**   Abnormal earnings, whether they are supernormal or subnormal, are the most important concept in equity valuation.

TAKING A POSITION

When the analytic work is finished, the equity analyst is expected to take a firm position on a stock or an industry, as difficult as that may be. This means making *point estimates* of future performance of both the company and the stock under analysis, not presenting a range of possibilities. The final objective is the estimation of a future stock price, the *target price,* upon which an investment recommendation is based. That price is the product of some estimated future financial result, like earnings or book value, and a valuation multiple:

Target price = projected value driver (e.g., earnings or book value)
* estimated future valuation multiple

Point Estimates Are the Norm

Simply stated, the process is to estimate future earnings, book value, or other value driver, and then to apply a valuation multiple, arriving at a future target price.[8] Unfortunately, elaborate arguments about current under- or overvaluation of a stock are simply not convincing to investors. Investors want to know what potential price the stock might reach, and, more importantly, why.

Let me repeat: Equity analysis is not prophecy, and the analytic techniques used are inevitably imprecise. Estimation of future financial performance is difficult. Accurate projections are, in my view, more often accidental than intentional (nevertheless, always take credit if your projections prove correct). Projection of future valuation multiples is even more difficult, compounding the error. Not only do such multiples require an accurate picture of the firm's future performance but they also are driven by external fundamentals, interest rates in particular. In addition, stock prices may be influenced by market biases, trends, fads, "irrational exuberance," and other emotional factors that current financial theory does not adequately describe.

But this is not the analytical disaster it might seem. Stocks are ultimately valued on their potential, and it is the analyst's job to describe that potential. The description must be consistent with the company's competitive positioning, financial history, industry constraints, life cycle stage, and any number of other factors. Nonetheless, it is a description of potential, made as precise as possible.

Getting Stuck

Consider the following news story:

A well-known Internet analyst downgraded 11 of his 29 stocks. But "[t]he downgrades come after the issues have long since plunged in price from their 52-week highs, with two of them . . . having fallen about 90% from their highs. . . ."[9]

Taking firm positions on stocks is all very well, but unfortunately, the firmer the position, the more difficult it is to change. A substantial amount of inertia, a subject we will return to repeatedly, attaches to weighty analytic pronouncements. The sales staff, perhaps, has sold the stock to its most valued clients. The analyst himself or herself has invested his or her reputation. Even more significantly, maybe the company is an investment banking client. As a result, equity analysts will frequently hold on to a buy recommendation even as the stock enters free fall. I have done this myself. Ironically, the lower the stock falls, the greater the inertia. If you liked it at $60, you've got to love it at $35, right? A hot stock has become a cheap stock, and so we hold on.

If you do decide to upgrade or (especially) downgrade a stock, there is never a good time. If you move before strong evidence becomes available, your analytic position is weaker. If you move afterward, you're very likely too late to catch the stock's movement. Whenever you move, you'll be asked, "Why didn't you tell us this yesterday? What's so special about today?" Be prepared to answer it.

Does This Change Your Conclusions?

Somewhere on a computer worksheet, you've entered a wrong formula. The error goes unnoticed; the report is finished and distributed. Then the telephone rings. A client has found some numbers that just don't add up. A quick check shows he's right. The client asks, "Does this change your conclusions?"

Whoops. Not good. Mistakes are the curse of the analyst's existence, and, given the complexity of our computer-worksheet–based financial models, very likely increasingly common. I am not an apologist for mathematical sloppiness. I've made some nasty errors myself and know what trouble they can cause. Every analyst should check and recheck and recheck every number, especially those upon which critical elements of an investment argument rest.

But equity analysis is a game of speed and reaction as well as accuracy, and mistakes, in my view, are inevitable. Like golf, the trick is not to be error free but to limit the size of errors. A good analyst never stops scanning data for reasonableness. Are earnings or cash flow forecasts generally of the right size? Does the predicted growth make sense given the company's competitive position? Is it possible, at the product or divisional level, to meet sales forecasts? Do the numbers, in general, reflect your fundamental judgment of the firm? If your numbers are reasonable, any errors will probably be far less damaging. Of course, what is "reasonable" is itself a matter of analytic judgment, and that's where the real errors are made.

EQUITY ANALYSIS AND OBJECTIVITY

An unwillingness to issue sell recommendations isn't the only rap on equity analysts. For example, consider the following news stories:

- *The Wall Street Journal,* in a front-page article, reported the increasing overlap between brokerage firms' venture capital investments, investment banking and IPO relationships, and stock recommendations. The *Journal* cites the "widely held perception that some Wall Street analysts issue glowing reports on companies to help attract and keep those companies as investment banking clients. Now the phenomenon appears to have escalated. Banks are seeking opportunities to make pre-IPO investments with potential payoffs dwarfing ordinary Wall Street fees. And the bank's chances of landing those pre-IPO stakes are enhanced because technology start-ups are eager to associate with Wall Street institutions that can take them public and then publish positive analysts' reports about them." [10]
- A top sell-side analyst grouped 32 electronic commerce companies into winners and losers in the battle for survival. "Turns out, however, that each of the clear-cut winners, except one, also are banking clients. . . ." [11]
- An influential analyst was fined and censured by the New York Stock Exchange (NYSE) for violating an exchange rule barring members from circulating "a rumor . . . which was sensational in character . . . and could reasonably be expected to affect market conditions." NYSE officials reported concern "with the possibility that if left unchecked, analysts and other Wall Street players might look to spread rumors and drive up stock prices for their own personal gain." [12]

No analyst, present or past, is comfortable talking about these issues, and few would admit that their research is tainted. But one cannot write a book about the process of equity analysis without considering, however briefly, if such a process is actually ever used.

Neither a blanket condemnation nor total reprieve of the profession is wholly appropriate, but perhaps a better understanding of the analyst's position can help. The equity analyst, especially on the sell side, often stands in the center of a collection of strong forces, each pulling him or her in a separate direction. Each analyst must achieve some balance among these forces.

- *Deals are where the money is.* Investment banking fees, for IPOs or other equity transactions, and equity venture stakes are large profit sources for banks. Stock trading, the traditional avenue by which investors compensated banks for their services (including research), takes a secondary position. Traditional stock picking by sell-side equity analysts, in my opinion, is rapidly becoming an anachronism. Many large institutional investors now maintain their own research staffs.
- *One of the Street's favorite ways to sell its banking services is to demonstrate the importance of a well-known analyst's support.* Investment banks provide their sponsorship as a part of the deal package. An equity analyst breaks that implicit commitment at his or her peril. I have rarely seen an equity analyst condemned for bad stock calls, but I have seen them fired after conflicts with their firm's bankers.
- *Competition is vicious.* Sell-side equity analysts compete vigorously for recognition and influence. Sometimes it seems as valuable to make spectacular mistakes as to be spectacularly right.
- *The stakes are high.* Top analysts can earn substantially more than their lesser-known colleagues. And investment banks can profit hugely from venture capital and equity issuance fees.

If, as is frequently charged, equity analysts are increasingly cheerleaders for managements, investment bankers, or venture capitalists, the news is not all bad. As I say many times in the coming pages, equity analysis is not prophecy; it is opinion. It was never meant to be objective description, but it is strong advocacy. All analysis must reflect the positions of its author, whatever the source of those positions may be, or it is useless. Any user of the analytic product who loses sight of this fundamental bias is in for trouble.

Beyond advocacy, however, I suspect that the soaring stock markets of the 1990s exacerbated the pressures on equity analysts and contributed to the "bankerization" of the analytic profession. Although no one is happy in a down market, the substantial stock price corrections of 2000 may have one happy consequence: to permit equity analysts to return equity analysis. In addition, the SEC's new Regulation FD, which prohibits selective disclosure of material information to analysts or investors, may mean that analytic legwork, rather than management relationships, is once again central to formulating stock recommendations. It isn't clear that stock pickers will ever be the profession's stars, but it is something to hope for.

NOTES

[1] Martin J. Whitman, *Value Investing*, Wiley, New York, 1999, p. 82.

[2] Whitman, *Value Investing*, p. 4.

[3] Gerald I. White, Ashwinpaul C. Sondhi, and Dov Fried, *The Analysis and Use of Financial Statements*, 2d ed., Wiley, New York, 1997, p. 1069.

[4] Ray Ball, "The Theory of Stock Market Efficiency: Accomplishments and Limitations," in *The Revolution in Corporate Finance*, 3rd ed., edited by Joel M. Stern and Donald H. Chew, Jr., Blackwell Publishers, Malden, Mass., 1998.

[5] The structure of the equity analysis process, from competitive analysis to valuation, parallels that recommended by Krishna G. Palepu, Victor L. Bernard, and Paul M. Healy, *Introduction to Business Analysis and Valuation*, South-Western College Publishing, Cincinnati, Ohio, 1997.

[6] For an excellent discussion of the SWOT process and its relationship to strategy analysis, see Jay B. Barney, *Gaining and Sustaining Competitive Advantage*, Addison-Wesley Publishing Company, Reading, Mass., 1997.

[7] Palepu, Bernard, and Healy refer to these three processes as "accounting analysis" and "financial analysis," the latter of which combines financial ratio and cash flow analysis. I've chosen to separate cash flow analysis because of its importance in company life cycle analysis.

[8] Whitman, *Value Investing*, p. 85.

[9] "Merrill's Web Guru Changes His Mantra," *The Wall Street Journal*, August 8, 2000, p. C1.

[10] "Raising the Stakes: As Wall Street Seeks Pre-IPO Investments, Conflicts May Arise," *The Wall Street Journal*, July 24, 2000, p. A1.

[11] "Goldman's E-Commerce List Reduces Nonclients to Low Tiers," *The Wall Street Journal*, June 20, 2000, p. C1.

[12] "Analyst Hanley Is Censured, Fined for Wrong Forecast," *The Wall Street Journal*, June 29, 2000, p. C1.

CHAPTER 2

Fundamentals of Equity Valuation

- The *market value* of any firm is the sum of its capital and the present value of its future abnormal earnings. *Abnormal earnings* are calculated by subtracting *capital costs* (also called *normal earnings*) from the firm's *actual income.*

- Growth in earnings or book value, generated by investment in projects that produce only a normal return, can add no value to the firm, no matter how large that growth is or how long it continues. This is because such projects cover only their capital costs and provide no supernormal earnings.

- Only sustainable earnings should be considered in valuation. Transitory earnings are not capitalized because they have no persistent future earnings impact. Equity valuations that incorporate transitory earnings are likely to be flawed.

- Any valuation problem can be formulated either in terms of the growth of value drivers like dividends or free-cash flow or as a series of annual investment decisions. Growth is the more familiar starting point in a valuation analysis, but the investment formulation is conceptually useful because it connects the company's business opportunities and competitive position directly to the estimation of its value.

The late physicist and Nobel Prize winner Richard Feynman was fond of tormenting his colleagues with deceptively simple questions. Generally, these questions had simple answers, but they were phrased in an unusual and unfamiliar way. Often after hours or days of work, his unfortunate victims saw the trick. It amused Feynman to demonstrate that knowledge, especially expert knowledge, was deep but frequently not very broad.[1]

In this introductory chapter, I try (with a bit of presumption) to ask some Feynman-like questions about the value of equities, recognizing that valuation ultimately is at the heart of equity analysis. Through a series of simple examples, the chapter explores the relationships between earnings, free-cash flow, capital costs, and valuation multiples like the price/earnings and price/book value multiples. This exercise turns out to be surprisingly revealing (although Feynman would likely not have been surprised). The fundamental principles that emerge form the basis of more detailed treatments of equity valuation in later chapters. More importantly, this chapter lays the conceptual groundwork for much of the subsequent discussion of equity analysis by connecting valuation directly to the firm's business opportunities and competitive position. Simply put, firms with superior investment opportunities, perhaps forged through competitive advantage or gained as a first mover, have higher valuations. The equity analyst's job is to identify those investment opportunities and the firms that are positioned to exploit them.

GAAP-BASED FINANCIAL ACCOUNTING

Any measurement process needs measurement tools. Unfortunately, the tools of equity analysis, the firm's financial statements, are the subject of nearly endless controversy. In the United States, financial statements developed under generally accepted accounting principles (GAAP) are the starting point of the valuation process, but they have a poor reputation for accuracy. In frustration, some practitioners even recommend discarding GAAP concepts like net income or book value altogether, falling back upon cash flow as the bedrock of value. I acknowledge the problems, but I am in less of a hurry to abandon GAAP accounting with its advantages of convenience, compactness, and transparency.

THE PROBLEMS WITH GAAP ACCOUNTING

GAAP-based financial accounting is a persistent source of irritation. The potential distortions of economic reality are undeniable. Some practitioners recommend the abandonment of accrual accounting for cash flow–based valuation concepts, which are presumably less subject to error and manipulation. This view is unduly harsh. The use of cash flow analyses involves a tradeoff of GAAP distortions for a less compact, intuitive, and convenient system. Ultimately, a careful analyst can learn to live with and use GAAP accounting without substantial ill effects. Nevertheless, in deference to cash flow purists, it is possible to define a fully cash flow–compatible income concept, called *economic income,* which eliminates many of the current objections to GAAP. Subsequent examples test the usefulness of the economic income concept.

Accounting Distortions

Financial accounting based upon generally accepted accounting principles can distort economic reality in at least three ways.[2] First, accounting rules themselves, in an effort to conservatively measure income and asset values, can misrepresent the economic effects of transactions. Next, accrual accounting, by definition, must attempt to measure the future effects of current business transactions and can therefore contain forecasting errors. Finally, management's control of the accounting process can result in deliberate distortion or "earnings management."

Accounting Principles and Economic Reality

GAAP accounting is based upon a number of principles, such as conservatism, historical cost, and accrual, and perhaps the desire for ease in the auditing process, which may not be consistent with strict economic accuracy. Fundamentally, the business of accrual accounting is to conservatively present the economic result of historical business transactions. The firm's value, on the other hand, is based on its future earnings power. This basic incompatibility introduces a bias into financial accounts and can distort economic reality. Examples of such distortions abound— everyone has a favorite.

For example, the use of purchase or pooling-of-interests accounting methods for business combinations often strayed far from economic reality—so often, in fact, that GAAP rules governing such business combinations are under review and will probably soon change[3]:

■ Under the purchase accounting method, the target company purchase price is recorded on the acquirer's balance sheet. When the balance sheets of the target and acquirer are consolidated, however, the target's net asset value can—and usually does—differ from the recorded purchase price, requiring the introduction of "good-will" to balance debits and credits. *Goodwill* is the value of the target company in excess of the net assets recorded on its balance sheet (after any value adjustments) at the time of consolidation.

■ Under current rules, goodwill must be written off through the acquirer's earnings up to a 40-year period, thereby reducing the acquirer's future reported earnings.

Pooling of interests, on the other hand, views a business combination as a uniting of ownership interests through the exchange of equity securities.[4] No resources have been disbursed, so no purchase or sale has taken place. If the transaction can be structured as a pooling, the financial accounts of the target and acquiring firm are simply added together, avoiding the goodwill charge. Arguably, the economic effects of the actual business combination are precisely the same, and neither accounting system correctly portrays the deal.

The distortions may reach beyond the goodwill issue. For example, it isn't clear that goodwill ought to be amortized at all. If the goodwill of the target firm declines over time and represents a cost to the combined business, then the value of the acquiring company's customer relationships and reputation must also depreciate. Failure to include the acquiring firm's goodwill amortization understates the costs of the combined company, or of any company, for that matter. The problem here is that the value of the acquirer's goodwill has not been established for accounting purposes. The target's goodwill has been established by the purchase price.

Further, amortization of goodwill reduces the equity capital of the combined business, causing returns on equity (ROE) to rise, creating a distortion of actual returns on investment (ROI—which ought to be calculated on the target's purchase price, not its book value).

Another particularly dramatic example of this ROE distortion is the immediate write-off of acquired in-process research and development (R&D) costs, a practice now also under considerable fire from accounting authorities and the SEC. This practice, common in technology companies, has often resulted in the immediate deduction from equity of a substantial portion of the acquisition purchase price, reducing future goodwill charges to income, lowering equity, and generating a higher ROE. Interestingly, in 1999, the Financial Accounting Standards Board (FASB) delayed the adoption of a capitalization and amortization policy for in-process R&D costs. Their reasoning was that such a policy is at odds with the current practice of immediate expensing of regular R&D costs and could lead to investor confusion. An interesting conundrum, I think.

The expensing, rather than capitalization, of entire classes of expenditures, such as research and development, advertising, or marketing costs, that have an uncertain impact on future revenues is another potential misrepresentation of economic reality required by accounting principles. Again, the underlying motivation is conservatism. Since the future impact of R&D is indeterminate, expensing is the conservative treatment.

Forecasting Error

In an effort to capture the full impact of business transactions, accountants and management are forced to make estimates, and estimates can be wrong. Accounting estimates of the useful lives of fixed assets and assumptions underlying the accounting for pension and retirement costs are common examples. But the list goes on: estimates of bad debt reserve against receivables, warranty liabilities, and reserves for losses in insurance companies.

In the 1990s, restructuring and reengineering charge-offs became more common as companies strove for operational efficiency. These write-offs are essentially reestimates of asset values, or in some cases entire businesses. The sudden fall in the value of these businesses implied by restructuring write-offs is an economic distortion (one would have thought that the loss of value occurred over a period of time). Further, restructuring charges can contain provisions for future expenses (plant closings, rent, severance pay) that affect reported future earnings.

Management Decisions

Recognizing that management is in the best position to accurately portray the economic condition of the firm, accounting rules permit the exercise of considerable management judgment in the presentation of financial accounts. But the SEC and others increasingly worry that management discretion is being used for "earnings management" rather than fair representation of the company's condition. Monitoring financial statements for overaggressive accounting, overstatement of restructuring expenses, the use of special reserves (as alleged in the W. R. Grace case discussed in Chapter 6), or outright fraud introduces more tangles for analysts to hack through.

Forget Earnings; Use Cash

The difficulties of financial accounting have caused many analysts to abandon accounting earnings as a measure of periodic performance and to substitute free-cash flow. It is perfectly true that (1) cash flows are subject to substantially less (but not zero) distortion and manipulation than accounting earnings, and (2) discounted cash flow is the most rigorous and flexible method of valuation.

But the skeptics may have given up on GAAP accounting too soon. Cash flows present a number of practical problems to the analyst. First, cash flows do not attempt to represent the full economic impact of a business event in the period it happened. Instead, economic events are "spread out" over subsequent periods as cash flow is received or expended.[5] Cash flow analysis therefore often requires complex, multiperiod models to fully capture the effects of economic events. Of course there is nothing inherently wrong with complex, multiperiod models. But suppose an analyst were asked the following sort of question: "If Company A's return on equity were to rise from 15 to 20 percent, how does its value change?" How can the analyst answer this question rapidly and confidently using cash flow analysis?

This raises a second issue with cash flow analysis and valuation. Cash flows are certainly accurate—the company either generated the cash or it didn't. But cash flows are not a particularly intuitive or natural way of *thinking about value*. One prefers to think about value when it is created, rather than when cash is collected or dividends disbursed.[6] In other words, what the company earned, however difficult that is to determine, is an important indicator of its economic health. Further, cash flows are not immune to transitory elements that can hide underlying trends.

Finally, cash flow models do not provide a direct link to the competitive process. They rely instead upon detailed projections of sales growth, margins, and capital expenditures that potentially obscure the fundamental issue: What is the rate of return on investment?

Can Economic Earnings Save the Day?

If we expect to use a cash flow–based concept as a substitute for accounting earnings, we need to convert the discounted-cash-flow methodology to a measure of periodic income, because, as a boss of mine used to say, "Life is lived quarter to quarter." We adopt in the upcoming analysis "economic income" as the preferred cash flow–based earnings measurement.[7] Economic income in any period is simply the free-cash flow generated during the period plus the change in the firm's market value:

$$\text{Economic income}_i = \text{free-cash flow}_i + \text{change in market value}_i \quad (2.1)$$

Economic return, then, is economic income divided by beginning market value:

$$\text{Economic return}_i = \frac{\text{economic income}_i}{\text{market value}_{i-1}} \quad (2.2)$$

Because economic income is cash flow based, it eliminates many unreliable elements of accounting earnings. Economic income recognizes the current impact of future cash flows; accounting earnings contain only the estimated effects of historical events. Economic earnings properly account for the timing of cash flows; accounting earnings do not even consider some cash flows, like capital expenditures. Economic returns also eliminate accounting distortions. In fact, the use of beginning market value mirrors a DCF analysis in which the initial investment appears as the first cash flow.

All in all, it looks as though economic earnings can potentially solve our problems, providing a distortion-free measure of company performance. But let's see how it works in practice.

THE PRIMACY OF RETURN ON CAPITAL: HIGH TIMES AT CONSOLIDATED IMPORTS LTD.

When return on a company's capital exceeds its cost of capital, *abnormal earnings,* defined as the difference between actual earnings and the costs of employed capital, are positive. Under these conditions, the market value of the firm exceeds its capital, and its price/book value (P/BV) multiple exceeds 1.0. The P/BV multiple is a function of the present value of future abnormal earnings. But expected economic returns equals the cost of capital.

Consider the case of Consolidated Imports Ltd. (CIL). CIL purchases $10 of inventory at the beginning of each period and sells it all at the end of the same period. CIL has no debt, pays no taxes, makes no capital expenditures, and has no selling expenses. All free-cash flow is paid to shareholders as dividends. Suppose further that

- CIL generates a 20 percent return on its investments.
- Its cost of capital is 10 percent.

We can represent the first three periods of CIL's business in Table 2–1. The company sells its $10 inventory for $12 at the end of each period, generating a 20 percent return on its $10 investment. It then purchases another $10 of inventory and repeats the cycle. Since CIL has no debt, its $10 initial inventory investment is financed by equity capital. Earnings are calculated by subtracting, within each row, $10 of cost of goods sold from $12 in revenue, equaling $2 in each period.

Free-cash flow equals earnings less the increase in working capital (we assume no capital expenditures). Since working capital does not change in this example, because the company has a constant $10 inventory, free-cash flow also equals $2. Since all free-cash flow is paid to shareholders as dividends, dividends also equal $2.

TABLE 2–1

Consolidated imports earns 20 percent on investment.

Time	0	1	2	3
	(10.00)[a]	12.00		
		(10.00)	12.00	
			(10.00)	12.00
				(10.00)
	⋮	⋮	⋮	⋮
Capital	10.00	10.00	10.00	10.00
Actual earnings	—	2.00	2.00	2.00
Free-cash flow	—	2.00	2.00	2.00
Dividends		2.00	2.00	2.00

[a] Note that the initial investment in inventory is not part of operating cash flow.

expected

$r = riskfree\ rate + \beta(market\ return - riskfree\ rate)$

Because CIL is debt free, its value equals either the present value of future dividends or free-cash flow:

$$Value_0 = \sum_{i=1}^{\infty} \frac{dividend_i}{(1.00 + r)^i} = \sum_{i=1}^{\infty} \frac{free\text{-}cash\ flow_i}{(1.00 + r)^i} \quad (2.3)$$

where r is the cost of capital. Since dividends are unchanged through the entire example, *or discount rate of stock*

$$Value_0 = \frac{2.00}{1.10} + \frac{2.00}{(1.10)^2} + \frac{2.00}{(1.10)^3} + \cdots + \frac{2.00}{(1.10)^n} + \cdots$$

$$= \frac{2.00}{0.10}$$

$$= 20.00 \quad (2.4)$$

Notice that this value calculation looks a lot like terminal value assumptions often made in more elaborate DCF models. In the second step, dividing the $2.00 dividend by the 10 percent cost of capital is called *capitalization of the dividend.*

Since dividends don't change, value cannot change in subsequent periods. Knowing this, we can calculate economic income, which also turns out to be $2, the same as accounting income (Table 2–2). Notice in this case that the 20 percent return on capital exceeds the 10 percent cost of capital.

TABLE 2–2

CIL's economic return is 10 percent.

Time	0	1	2	3
Free-cash flow	—	2.00	2.00	2.00
Market value	20.00	20.00	20.00	20.00
Economic earnings	—	2.00	2.00	2.00
Return on capital	—	20%	20%	20%
Cost of capital	—	10%	10%	10%
Economic return	—	10%	10%	10%

The economic return is 10 percent ($2 of economic earnings divided by $20 market value), which is a more significant result than it seems. In fact, the expected economic return is *always* the cost of capital because economic return is market value based. The market value already contains the present value of any returns earned, including those in excess of capital costs, so-called economic rents. If you "pay" the market value, you must earn the cost of capital on the investment, which, of course, is the principal frustration of equity analysis. Investing at fair market value, provided that markets are efficient (a matter of some debate), will on average compensate an investor for risk, and nothing more. If an analyst expects to "add value," that is, produce returns in excess of capital costs, paying fair market value for investments won't work. Anybody can do that, and if anyone can do it, nobody ultimately makes money with the strategy. We need to think of another strategy—more on this in Chapter 4.

What does economic return tell us about CIL's performance? Virtually nothing. That's because the company itself does not "invest" its market value; it invests its capital and earnings. [In fact, market value accounting, upon which economic income and returns are based, is a special case of so-called unbiased accounting. Unbiased accounting is a system in which, when economic rents have been competed away (as they usually are), return on capital equals cost of capital. To the extent that an accounting system's quirks prevent this, the system is biased.[8]]

Let's follow the notion of economic rents for a moment. Consider the following modification of Equation 2.4. Simultaneously adding $10.00 and subtracting $10.00 from the firm's value does not affect the equation:

$$\text{Value}_0 = \frac{2.00}{1.10} + \frac{2.00}{(1.10)^2} + \frac{2.00}{(1.10)^3} + \frac{2.00}{(1.10)^n} + 10.00 - 10.00 \quad (2.5)$$

But $10.00 can be expressed as the present value of a $1.00 annuity:

$$10.00 = \sum_{i=1}^{\infty} \frac{1}{(1.00 + 0.10)^i} \quad (2.6)$$

Equation 2.5 can then be rewritten as

$$\text{Value}_0 = 10.00 + \frac{2.00 - 1.00}{1.10} + \frac{2.00 - 1.00}{(1.10)^2}$$

$$+ \cdots + \frac{2.00 - 1.00}{(1.10)^n} + \cdots$$

$$= 10.00 + \frac{1.00}{0.10}$$

$$= 20.00 \tag{2.7}$$

The actual earnings of the firm can be expressed as the product of the return on capital and the capital itself:

$$\text{Actual earnings} = \text{return on capital} * \text{capital}$$

$$= 20\% * \$10.00$$

$$= 2.00 \tag{2.8}$$

Let's call the product of the cost of capital and the capital itself the *normal earnings* of the firm:

$$\text{Normal earnings} = \text{cost of capital} * \text{capital}$$

$$= 10\% * \$10.00$$

$$= 1.00 \tag{2.9}$$

Then the "abnormal" earnings of the firm is the difference between the actual and normal earnings:

$$\text{Abnormal earnings} = \text{actual earnings} - \text{normal earnings}$$

$$= 2.00 - 1.00$$

$$= 1.00 \tag{2.10}$$

Equation 2.11 is the sum of the company's capital base and the present value of abnormal earnings:

$$\text{Value}_0 = \text{capital}_0 + \sum_{i=1}^{\infty} \frac{\text{abnormal earnings}_i}{(1.00 + r)^i}$$

$$= \text{capital}_0 + \sum_{i=1}^{\infty} \frac{(\text{return on capital}_i - \text{cost of capital}) * \text{capital}_{i-1}}{(1.00 + r)^i}$$

$$\tag{2.11}$$

But notice what has happened. The cash flow–based dividend discount model of Equation 2.3, or the equivalent free-cash flow model, has been converted to a valuation scheme based on accounting numbers, not cash. There is no specification of the timing of cash flows and no specific provision for cash investments, either in working capital or fixed assets. The value of the company, Equation 2.11 says, is equal to its capital plus the present value of abnormal earnings. Abnormal earnings are the surplus (or deficit) the firm earns over its cost of capital.

It is true that Equation 2.11 was suggested by a particularly well behaved example in which free-cash flow, dividends, and accounting earnings were all equal. This will certainly not always be the case, and this is not a rigorous proof. Nevertheless, given certain conditions, Equation 2.11 can be proven using both the firm's total return on capital or only returns on common equity. Table 2–3 summarizes these results.

Now that CIL's value and earnings are known for each period, we can look at the company's valuation multiples, as shown in Table 2–4. Note that since the company has no debt, capital and book value are the same, and the value of the company is the value of its equity.

The P/BV multiple is greater than 1.00 because the company has positive abnormal earnings. In fact, by rearranging Equation 2.11, we can derive a formal expression for the P/BV multiple[9]:

$$\frac{Price_0}{Book\ value_0} = 1.0 + \sum_{i=1}^{\infty} \frac{abnormal\ earnings_i / BV_0}{(1.00 + r)^i}$$

$$= 1.0 + \frac{1.0/10.0}{0.10}$$

$$= 1.00 + \frac{0.10}{0.10}$$

$$= 2.00 \qquad\qquad (2.12)$$

The P/BV multiple is a function of the level of future abnormal earnings. Clearly, if abnormal earnings are zero, the company's market value equals its book value. If, on the other hand, future abnormal earnings are negative, the market value falls below book value.

The price/earnings ratio, however, is not clearly specified in Equation 2.12. The P/E in this case equals the reciprocal of the cost of capital, $1/r$ or 10.0. Still, why the P/E should be 10.0 and not something else isn't clear.

TABLE 2–3

CIL's abnormal earnings are a constant $1.00.

Time	0	1	2	3
Actual earnings	—	2.00	2.00	2.00
Normal earnings	—	1.00	1.00	1.00
Abnormal earnings	—	1.00	1.00	1.00

TABLE 2–4

The P/BV and P/E ratios remain constant.

Time	0	1	2	3
Actual earnings	—	2.00	2.00	2.00
Book value	10.00	10.00	10.00	10.00
Market value	20.00	20.00	20.00	20.00
P/BV	2.00	2.00	2.00	2.00
P/E, LTM	—	10.0	10.0	10.0
P/E, NTM	10.0	10.0	10.0	10.0

Note: P/BV is the stock price/book value multiple; P/E is the stock price/earnings multiple; LTM is the last 12 months; and NTM is the next 12 months.

From this short example, we have learned the following:

- The expected economic return equals the cost of capital.
- When the return on capital exceeds the cost of capital, abnormal earnings are positive, the stock price exceeds capital, and the P/BV exceeds 1.00
- The P/BV multiple is a function of the present value of future abnormal earnings. The P/E, however, remains unspecified.

Suppose that a competitor to Consolidated Imports now appears, and the resulting price competition forces returns on capital down to 10 percent. This unfortunate situation is discussed in the next section.

COMPETITIVE EQUILIBRIUM: TROUBLES FOR CONSOLIDATED IMPORTS LTD.

When, as a result of competition, a firm's return on capital falls to the cost of capital, it reaches competitive equilibrium, or competitive parity. At competitive equilibrium, the firm can identify no incremental investment opportunities likely to generate returns in excess of capital costs. Competitive equilibrium is often defined as a condition in which new investment opportunities generate returns equal to capital costs, but existing investments continue to earn abnormal returns.[10] In CIL's case, neither existing nor incremental returns are supernormal. The market value equals capital, abnormal earnings are zero, and the P/BV multiple equals 1.0. The company's price/earnings multiple, on the other hand, continues to equal the reciprocal of the cost of capital.

CIL's aggressive competitor, United Goods, Inc., has cut pricing, forcing both companies' returns down to 10 percent, the cost of capital (Table 2–5). This situation is called *competitive equilibrium*, or *competitive parity*. What does *equilibrium* mean? When returns are forced down to capital costs, then economic rents and/or abnormal earnings disappear and no further incentive to enter the business exists.

Value here is relatively easy to determine. Since abnormal earnings have disappeared, we might guess that value will equal capital, which turns out to be the case:

TABLE 2–5

CIL's dividends fall to $1.00.

Time	0	1	2	3
	(10.00)	11.00		
		(10.00)	11.00	
			(10.00)	11.00
				(10.00)
Capital	10.00	10.00	10.00	10.00
Actual earnings	—	1.00	1.00	1.00
Free-cash flow	—	1.00	1.00	1.00
Dividends	—	1.00	1.00	1.00

$r = CoST oF Capital$

$$\text{Value}_0 = \sum_{i=1}^{\infty} \frac{\text{dividend}_i}{(1.00 + r)^i}$$

$$= \frac{1.00}{1.10} + \frac{1.00}{(1.10)^2} + \frac{1.00}{(1.10)^3} + \cdots + \frac{1.00}{(1.10)^n} + \cdots.$$

$$= \frac{1.00}{0.10}$$

$$= 10.00 \tag{2.13}$$

Since dividends do not change, value does not change in future periods. And, once again, economic returns equal the cost of capital, as shown in Table 2–6.

When CIL had 20 percent returns on capital, the economic return was 10 percent. When returns on capital were forced by competition down to 10 percent, economic returns were still 10 percent. Economic income does not distinguish between these two situations because it is concerned only with what an investor pays for the stock, not with what the company earns. An investor who pays fair value of CIL will earn an expected 10 percent return regardless of the company's own performance (within limits of course). But analysts need to be aware of CIL's operating success, and for that they must rely on internal, as well as external, performance measures, which, of course, returns us again to the problem of GAAP accounting.

The abnormal earnings (AE) formulation of the CIL value problem is very revealing of these issues. At competitive equilibrium, abnormal

TABLE 2–6

Economic return is unchanged at 10 percent.

Time	0	1	2	3
Free-cash flow	—	1.00	1.00	1.00
Market value	10.00	10.00	10.00	10.00
Economic earnings	—	1.00	1.00	1.00
Return on capital	—	10%	10%	10%
Cost of capital	—	10%	10%	10%
Economic return	—	10%	10%	10%

earnings fall to zero, as shown in Table 2–7. So CIL's valuation simplifies
substantially because the entire abnormal earnings summation drops out:

$$\text{Value}_0 = \text{capital}_0 + \sum_{i=1}^{\infty} \frac{\text{abnormal earnings}_i}{(1.00 + r)^i}$$

$$= 10.00 + \frac{1.00 - 1.00}{1.10} + \frac{1.00 - 1.00}{(1.10)^2}$$

$$+ \cdots + \frac{1.00 - 1.00}{(1.10)^n} + \cdots .$$

$$= 10.00 \tag{2.14}$$

Calculating the firm's valuation multiples produces some expected and
perhaps some unexpected results (Table 2–8). The P/BV multiple has
predictably fallen to 1.00 since abnormal earnings are zero in all future
periods. But the P/E ratio remains somewhat strangely at 10.00, even
though the company is clearly doing worse financially.

TABLE 2–7

Abnormal earnings fall to $0.00.

Time	0	1	2	3
Actual earnings	—	1.00	1.00	1.00
Normal earnings	—	1.00	1.00	1.00
Abnormal earnings	—	0.00	0.00	0.00

TABLE 2–8

P/BV is down, but P/E is still 10.00.

Time	0	1	2	3
Actual earnings	—	1.00	1.00	1.00
Capital/book value	10.00	10.00	10.00	10.00
Market value	10.00	10.00	10.00	10.00
P/BV	1.00	1.00	1.00	1.00
P/E, LTM	—	10.0	10.0	10.0
P/E, NTM	10.0	10.0	10.0	10.0

For the P/E ratio to remain unchanged, there must be common elements in CIL's performance, even though returns on capital have fallen to 10 percent from 20 percent. One possible common element is growth. In neither case do earnings, cash flow, or dividends grow.

With the competitive equilibrium example, we've peeled another layer from the equity valuation problem:

- When the return on capital equals the cost of capital, the firm reaches competitive equilibrium, in which further competitive entry is unlikely.

- At competitive equilibrium, the firm's market value equals its book value, abnormal earnings are zero, and the P/BV multiple equals 1.0.

- The P/E multiple, on the other hand, is not a function of the absolute level of future abnormal earnings. At this point, it's not clear what drives P/E.

GROWTH AND VALUE: HOPE RISES FROM THE ASHES AT CONSOLIDATED IMPORTS LTD.

The effect of growth on firm value depends on the associated returns on capital. In competitive equilibrium, when return on capital equals cost of capital, the prospect of future growth (of any size) does not add to current market value. Growth beyond competitive equilibrium can therefore be ignored for valuation purposes. On the other hand, reinvestment of free-cash flow when the return on capital exceeds the capital costs increases the value and produces abnormal earnings growth, resulting in valuation multiple expansion. As it turns out, the P/E multiple is a function of future abnormal earnings growth.

The chairman of Consolidated Imports is dejected. Competition has destroyed CIL's margins, his earnings are flat, Wall Street is unhappy, and the stock is dead in the water. His senior managers, who as a result of a progressive compensation system recommended by the company's management consultants, hold substantial CIL stock, are inconsolable. Something needs to be done. Consolidated's CFO has an idea. The company still generates a strong cash flow. Why not reinvest some of the cash in the business? Won't that produce growth and cheer up the Street? The chairman sees a ray of hope.

The chairman decides to allow the company's capital base to grow 5 percent per year by reinvesting a portion of the current dividend. He then calls the head of investor relations (IR), whom he suspects is partially responsible for the stock's malaise anyway, and he asks for some language explaining the company's new policy. The IR person, seeing a chance to redeem herself, writes a glowing press release which quotes the chairman: "CIL is aggressively identifying opportunities to grow our business and leveraging our core competencies to build shareholder value." Earnings growth returns. Things are definitely looking up (Table 2–9).

But has the value of the company really changed, even though it is now growing? Alas, no. Using the familiar simplification for a constantly growing annuity:

$$
\begin{aligned}
\text{Value}_0 &= \sum_{i=1}^{\infty} \frac{\text{dividend}_i}{(1.00 + r)^i} \\[2mm]
&= \frac{0.50}{1.10} + \frac{0.52}{(1.10)^2} + \frac{0.55}{(1.10)^3} + \cdots \\[2mm]
&= \frac{0.50}{1.10} + \frac{0.50 * (1 + 0.05)}{(1.10)^2} + \frac{0.50 * (1 + 0.05)^2}{(1.10)^3} \\[2mm]
&\quad + \cdots + \frac{0.50 * (1 + 0.05)^{n-1}}{(1.10)^n} + \cdots \\[2mm]
&= \frac{0.50}{0.10 - 0.05} \\[2mm]
&= 10.00
\end{aligned}
\tag{2.15}
$$

This seems very unfair. After all, the company has found a way to grow. Why has value not increased? In fact, the market value of the firm does increase (Table 2–10).

But notice that the market value of the company increases only enough to provide investors with a 10 percent return (including the dividend), which compensates them for their capital costs, but no more. For example, in period 1 the market value $10.50 plus the $0.50 dividend provides a 10 percent return on the $10.00 investment. The same is true in all subsequent periods.

A more telling clue to the mystery is provided by the AE formulation:

TABLE 2–9

Consolidated Imports grows capital at 5 percent.

Time	0	1	2	3
	(10.00)	11.00		
		(10.50)	11.55	
			(11.03)	12.13
				(11.58)
Capital	10.00	10.50	11.03	11.58
Actual earnings	—	1.00	1.05	1.10
Free-cash flow	—	0.50	0.52	0.55
Dividends		0.50	0.52	0.55

TABLE 2–10

Economic returns equal return on capital.

Time	0	1	2	3
Free-cash flow	—	0.50	0.52	0.55
Market value	10.00	10.50	11.03	11.58
Economic earnings	—	1.00	1.05	1.10
Return on capital	—	10%	10%	10%
Cost of capital	—	10%	10%	10%
Economic return	—	10%	10%	10%

$$\text{Value}_0 = \text{capital}_0 + \sum_{i=1}^{\infty} \frac{\text{abnormal earnings}_i}{(1.00 + r)^i}$$

$$= 10.00 + \frac{1.00 - 1.00}{1.10} + \frac{1.05 - 1.05}{(1.10)^2}$$

$$+ \cdots + \frac{(1.05 - 1.05)}{(1.10)^n} + \cdots .$$

$$= 10.00 \qquad\qquad\qquad (2.16)$$

As in the previous case, abnormal earnings are zero in every subsequent period (Table 2–11). The chairman's error here was to think about growth without thinking about the investment returns associated with that growth. As long as competition prevents incremental investments in the industry from earning more than 10 percent, the current cost of capital, no amount of prospective growth will add value to the company. In fact, the chairman would do well to think less about growth and more about his investment opportunities. The available returns on investment should tell him how much growth is worth, if anything. Growth turns out to be a slippery concept. Only profitable growth builds value.

Does this mean that reinvestment of free-cash flow at the company's capital cost is a bad thing? We'll look at this issue in more detail in Chapter 19. For now, what we're saying is that, although there may be good reasons for increasing the company's size through this sort of investment, building value is not one of them.

We may, however, have solved our P/E mystery because we finally have a case with earnings growth. But, unfortunately, the mystery only deepens (Table 2–12).

The P/E calculated with prospective earnings has not changed, in spite of the growth in earnings. The P/E, LTM, on the other hand, is now higher (because value grows ahead of last period's earnings). Can we conclude, from the higher P/E, LTM, that the company is now overvalued? Which P/E—LTM or NTM—is the right one?

Again, we learn a little more about valuation:

- When the return on capital equals the cost of capital, the prospect of future growth (of any size) does not add to the current value.

TABLE 2–11

Abnormal earnings are $0.00, in spite of growth.

Time	0	1	2	3
Actual earnings	—	1.00	1.05	1.10
Normal earnings	—	1.00	1.05	1.10
Abnormal earnings	—	0.00	0.00	0.00

TABLE 2–12

Prospective valuation multiples are unaltered.

Time	0	1	2	3
Actual earnings	—	1.00	1.05	1.10
Capital/book value	10	10.50	11.03	11.58
Market value	10	10.50	11.03	11.58
P/BV	1.00	1.00	1.00	1.00
P/E, LTM	—	10.5	10.5	10.5
P/E, NTM	10.0	10.0	10.0	10.0

- Since reinvestment at the cost of capital adds no value, growth beyond competitive equilibrium can be ignored for valuation purposes.
- The NTM and LTM P/E multiples can differ, but if the company's return on capital equals the cost of its capital, growth does not change the prospective P/E (calculated with the next 12 months' earnings).

We still do not seem to have found a variable that drives P/E.

TABLE 2–13

Consolidated Imports earns 20 percent on investment.

Time	0	1	2	3
	(10.00)	12.00		
		(10.50)	12.60	
			(11.03)	13.24
				(11.58)
Capital	10.00	10.50	11.03	11.58
Actual earnings	—	2.00	2.10	2.21
Free-cash flow	—	1.50	1.57	1.66
Dividends	—	1.50	1.57	1.66

CIL's chairman was on the right track, but his timing was bad. A better idea would have been to grow the company while profitable investment opportunities were still available. Suppose the chairman had reinvested in his business, allowing invested capital to grow 5 percent per year, while new investments were still producing a 20 percent return. What would happen to valuation then? (See Table 2–13.)

The company's abnormal earnings are positive, and, unlike previous cases, they grow at 5 percent per year (Table 2–14). Free-cash flow equals the funds management can pay to shareholders while maintaining the desired level of operations (in this case, 5 percent growth). The AE formulation now produces a $30 value, up from $20 in the no-growth case. It seems that growth that flows from investment at rates in excess of the capital costs adds value:

$$\text{Value}_0 = \text{capital}_0 + \sum_{i=1}^{\infty} \frac{\text{abnormal earnings}_i}{(1.00 + r)^i}$$

$$= 10.00 + \frac{2.00 - 1.00}{1.10} + \frac{2.10 - 1.05}{(1.10)^2} + \cdots$$

$$= 10.00 + \frac{1.00}{1.10} + 1.00 * \frac{(1.00 + 0.05)}{(1.10)^2} + 1.00$$

$$* \frac{(1.00 + 0.05)^2}{(1.10)^3} + \cdots + \frac{1.00 * (1.00 + 0.05)^{n-1}}{(1.10)^n} + \cdots$$

$$= 10.00 + \frac{1.00}{(0.10 - 0.05)}$$

$$= 30.00 \qquad\qquad (2.17)$$

Valuation multiples are also higher, even the P/E (see Table 2–15).

TABLE 2–14

Abnormal earnings grow at 5 percent annually.

Time	0	1	2	3
Actual earnings	—	2.00	2.10	2.21
Normal earnings	—	1.00	1.05	1.10
Abnormal earnings	—	1.00	1.05	1.10

TABLE 2–15

Finally, the P/E multiple rises, reaching 15.00.

Time	0	1	2	3
Actual earnings	—	2.00	2.10	2.21
Book value	10.00	10.50	11.03	11.58
Market value	30.00	31.50	33.08	34.73
P/BV	3.00	3.00	3.00	3.00
P/E, LTM	—	15.80	15.80	15.80
P/E, NTM	15.00	15.00	15.00	15.00

At last, the P/E has moved! In fact, unlike the P/BV, which is dependent on the level of prospective abnormal earnings, the P/E turns out to be a function of the prospective growth in abnormal earnings. Without deriving the equation, which we do in Chapter 16, the P/E is actually the following:

$$\frac{P_0}{E_1} = \frac{1}{r} + \frac{1}{E_1} \left[\sum_{i=1}^{\infty} \frac{\text{abnormal earnings}_i}{(1+r)^i} - \frac{\text{abnormal earnings}_1}{r} \right]$$

$$= 10.00 + \left(\frac{1.00}{2.00}\right) * (20.00 - 10.00)$$

$$= 15.00 \tag{2.18}$$

P/E, LTM, produces a completely different result of 15.80. This is, of course, a perfectly correct calculation, but somehow it is not as clean as the NTM calculation. Both forms are used frequently, but the NTM form is appealing for a number of reasons. First, it can be calculated at time 0, when no actual results are available. The use of beginning capital or value and subsequent results is intuitively satisfying; it mirrors the format of discounted-cash-flow analyses. Finally, it avoids major pitfalls when transitory elements are present in historical earnings, as discussed below.

The P/E is a substantially more complex measure of value than the P/BV:

■ Reinvestment of free-cash flow at rates of return in excess of capital costs creates growth in abnormal earnings, resulting in valuation multiple expansion.

- The P/E is a function of the prospective growth in future abnormal earnings, not in their level.
- Differences between the NTM and the LTM form of the P/E persist when earnings are growing.

TRANSITORY EARNINGS: AN UNEXPECTED 10 PERCENT PRICE INCREASE AT CONSOLIDATED IMPORTS LTD.

Unexpected and transitory earnings elements are not capitalized; only recurring ("sustainable") earnings affect firm value. Accounting earnings are frequently a mixture of recurring earnings, transitory earnings elements, and measurement errors.[11] Like accounting earnings, economic earnings are not always purely sustainable, and often they contain transitory components and even measurement errors. Valuation multiples, especially the P/E, can be distorted by transitory earnings.

Let's return to the preequilibrium case in which CIL still earns 20 percent on its investments. Suppose CIL were to experience an unanticipated, one-time, across-the-board price increase of 10 percent. How does this change our results? The key word here is "unanticipated." Since prices have risen, CIL must spend $11.00 in the second period to replace its inventory, but the company continues to earn a 20 percent return on investment (Table 2–16).

TABLE 2–16

Consolidated Imports experiences a 10 percent price increase.

Time	0	1	2	3
	(10.00)	13.20		
		(11.00)	13.20	
			(11.00)	13.20
Capital	10.00	11.00	11.00	11.00
Actual earnings	—	3.20	2.20	2.20
Free-cash flow	—	2.20	2.20	2.20
Dividends	—	2.20	2.20	2.20

Actual earnings reach $3.20 in period 1 and then fall to $2.20 in perpetuity. In fact, period 1 earnings consist of a one-time inventory holding gain of $1.00 (10 percent × $10.00) and $2.20 of *sustainable earnings,* usually defined as the level of earnings that can be maintained with the existing asset base. Clearly, the $1.00 holding gain is a transitory component of earnings; it appears once, and then disappears. Note that a similar "blip" does not appear in period 1 free-cash flow because of the $1.00 working capital increase needed to maintain an equivalent asset base. The question is, has the value of CIL risen at time 0?

This is a bit of a trick question. Because the price increase was not anticipated at time 0, anyone valuing the company at that point would have placed it at $20.00. Subsequently, the company's value rises to a constant $22.00 ($2.20/0.10). (See Table 2–17.)

Note that the economic income and return, although they are both cash flow–based concepts, are not immune to the transitory effects of the price increase. The transitory element in economic earnings is $2.00 ($4.20 − $2.20) rather than $1.00 because the variation impacts the $20.00 market price rather than the $10.00 initial capital base. Market value accounting will produce returns in excess of capital costs when actual earnings exceed expected earnings. This of course is one of the principal tricks of stock investing, to identify stocks where the full earnings potential is not contained in the purchase price. Earnings can exceed expectations for any number of reasons, price increases being only one possibility (and, admittedly, a somewhat artificial one in this example). The implication of this example, that stocks are a decent inflation hedge, is probably, in real life, true.

TABLE 2–17

Economic return, like return on capital, shows a period 1 blip.

Time	0	1	2	3
Free-cash flow	—	2.20	2.20	2.20
Market value	20.00	22.00	22.00	22.00
Economic earnings	—	4.20	2.20	2.20
Return on capital	—	32%	20%	20%
Cost of capital	—	10%	10%	10%
Economic return	—	21%	10%	10%

The presence of transitory earnings elements highlights the differences between NTM and LTM P/E multiple calculations (Table 2–18).

Notice that the P/BV multiple is unaffected by the earnings blip, provided the stock is correctly valued. Neither is the NTM P/E, even in period 1, since it relies upon estimated earnings rather than actual earnings.

But the behavior of the LTM P/E is anomalous. It drops to 6.90 in period 1 to reflect the $1.00 one-time holding gain and then returns to 10.00. Does this mean that the company was undervalued at time 1? Let's ask the question another way. Since there is no growth in abnormal earnings after time 1 (because there is no reinvestment of free-cash flow), our past experience suggests that the P/E at that point should be 10.00, the reciprocal of the firm's 10 percent cost of equity. Why then is the value of the company not $32.00 ($3.20 × 10.00) rather than $22.00?

The answer is that transitory earnings are not capitalized. Relying upon earnings, whether actual or projected, which contain transitory elements will result in misvaluation, or mistaken valuation multiples, or both. This is why equity analysts spend so much time seeking "sustainable earnings." Calculating sustainable earnings is greatly aided by removing from historical earnings any unsustainable elements. If we had done this with the LTM earnings of CIL, the resulting P/E would have risen from 6.90 to 10.00, which is arguably the right answer.

Unfortunately, historical GAAP accounting earnings will often contain not only transitory items but also the sort of measurement errors and distortions discussed earlier in this chapter. We know now that the true

TABLE 2–18

Transitory earnings do not disrupt prospective valuation multiples.

Time	0	1	2	3
Actual earnings	—	3.20	2.20	2.20
Capital (book value)	10.00	11.00	11.00	11.00
Market value	20.00	22.00	22.00	22.00
P/BV	2.00	2.00	2.00	2.00
P/E, LTM	—	6.9	10.0	10.0
P/E, NTM	10.0	10.0	10.0	10.0

P/E relationship is price to sustainable earnings. What we actually calculate is the ratio of price to actual earnings where

$$\text{Actual earnings} = \text{sustainable earnings} + \text{transitory elements} + \text{measurement errors} \qquad (2.19)$$

This problem is not only confined to actual results but can also carry into earnings projections. Projection of current transitory earnings forward is very likely to result in valuation errors. The analyst needs to exercise care to estimate as accurately as possible the firm's sustainable earnings. This is why one hears so much about a company's "earning power." It is literally the market's estimate of earning power that underlies the stock price, not the actual earnings. This is easy to understand from a practical standpoint. Investors simply will not pay for (capitalize) components of earnings that are unreliable.

We return to the issue of transitory earnings in more detail in Chapter 6. This section adds a bit more detail to our understanding of equity valuation.

- Transitory earnings elements are not capitalized; valuation should be based upon sustainable earnings.
- Accounting earnings contain transitory elements and measurement errors; in valuation problems, care must be taken to extract, to the extent possible, sustainable earnings elements.
- One does not escape the problem of transitory earnings by shifting to a cash flow concept like economic earnings; economic earnings also contain transitory elements.

THE EQUIVALENCE OF GROWTH AND INVESTMENT

Analysts frequently use the projected growth of free-cash flow or net income to drive equity valuations, but it is mathematically equivalent to think of total value as the sum of a series of individual annual investments. The growth formulation is familiar and can help explain the behavior of the P/E valuation multiple. On the other hand, the investment formulation focuses attention on the firm's available business opportunities and ties the analyst's thinking directly to competitive conditions in the firm's industry. The investment formulation also drives home the point that growth can continue to add to value only as long as profitable investment opportunities remain.

By focusing upon the AE formulation of value in this chapter, I have tried to suggest that valuation problems be structured in investment rather than growth terms, in order to draw attention to the relationship between investment returns and capital costs. It is that relationship which determines whether investment adds to firm value or not.

To see the growth/investment equivalence, let's return to the abnormal earnings formulation of value. For simplicity, we value only the equity capital, not the entire firm. ROE is return on equity, k is the cost of equity, BV is the book value of equity, and P is the equity market value:

$$P_0 = BV_0 + \sum_{i=1}^{\infty} (ROE_i - k) * \frac{BV_{i-1}}{(1 + k)^i}$$

$$= BV_0 + (ROE_1 - k) * \frac{BV_0}{(1 + k)} + (ROE_2 - k) * \frac{BV_1}{(1 + k)^2}$$

$$+ \cdots + (ROE_n - k) * \frac{BV_{n-1}}{(1 + k)^n} + \ldots \qquad (2.20)$$

To simplify this expression, notice that successive book values can be expressed in terms of the initial book value BV_0 and appropriate growth rates:

$$BV_1 = (1 + g_1) * BV_0$$

$$BV_2 = (1 + g_2) * BV_1 = (1 + g_2) * (1 + g_1) * BV_0$$

$$BV_3 = (1 + g_3) * BV_2 = (1 + g_3) * (1 + g_2) * (1 + g_1) * BV_0$$

$$BV_n = (1 + g_n) * BV_{n-1} = (1 + g_n) * \cdots (1 + g_1) * BV_0.$$

and so on. To simplify these expressions somewhat, let $A_i = (ROE_i - k) * BV_0$. Equation 2.20 becomes

$$P_0 = BV_0 + A_1 * \frac{1}{(1 + k)} + A_2 * \frac{(1 + g_1)}{(1 + k)^2} + A_3 * \frac{(1 + g_2)(1 + g_1)}{(1 + k)^2}$$

$$+ \cdots + A_n * \frac{(1 + g_{n-1}) \cdots (1 + g_1)}{(1 + k)^n} + \ldots \qquad (2.21)$$

The terms in Equation 2.21 can be rearranged into notional annual "investments," shown in the rows of Table 2–19. In each column, the top row is the sum of the elements below it. For example,

$$\frac{A_2 * (1 + g_1)}{(1 + k)^2} = \frac{A_2}{(1 + k)^2} + \frac{A_2 g_1}{(1 + k)^2} \qquad (2.22)$$

The first series, labeled 1 in Table 2–19, is the value of the abnormal income stream generated by the investment of the book value BV_0 itself:

$$A_1 = (ROE_1 - k) * BV_0$$

$$A_2 = (ROE_2 - k) * BV_0$$

$$A_n = (ROE_n - k) * BV_0$$

The second series is the value of the abnormal income produced by the investment of the incremental growth in book value during period 1, $g_1 * BV_0$:

$$A_2 g_1 = (ROE_2 - k) * (g_1 * BV_0)$$

$$A_3 g_1 = (ROE_3 - k) * (g_1 * BV_0)$$

$$A_n g_1 = (ROE_n - k) * (g_1 * BV_0)$$

The third investment series results from the investment of second-period book value growth, $BV_0 * (1 + g_1) g_2$, and so on. The value of the firm is built up from the reinvestment of incremental book value growth, fixing the connection between growth and investment. Both points of view have their uses.

Suppose growth lasts for some shorter period, say, two years, and then abnormal income levels remain constant. Assume further that returns on equity and growth rates are constants. Equation 2.20 then reduces to

$$P_0 = BV_0 + \frac{A}{(1 + k)} + \frac{A(1 + g)}{(1 + k)^2} + \frac{A(1 + g)^2}{(1 + k)^3} + \frac{A(1 + g)^2}{(1 + k)^4}$$

$$+ \cdots + \frac{A (1 + g)^2}{(1 + k)^n} + \cdots .$$

$$= BV_0 + \frac{A}{(1 + k)} + \frac{A(1 + g)}{(1 + k)^2} + \frac{A(1 + g)^2}{k(1 + k)^2} \qquad (2.23)$$

The final term is a simplification of the series expansion:

TABLE 2-19

Growth is the equivalent of a series of annual investments.

Investment	BV_0	$\dfrac{A_1}{(1+k)}$	$\dfrac{A_2(1+g_1)}{(1+k)^2}$	$\dfrac{A_3(1+g_2)(1+g_1)}{(1+k)^3}$	$\dfrac{A_n(1+g_{n-1})\cdots(1+g_1)}{(1+k)^n}$
1		$\dfrac{A_1}{(1+k)}$	$\dfrac{A_2}{(1+k)^2}$	$\dfrac{A_3}{(1+k)^3}$	$\dfrac{A_n}{(1+k)^n}$
2			$\dfrac{A_2 g_1}{(1+k)^2}$	$\dfrac{A_3 g_1}{(1+k)^3}$	$\dfrac{A_n g_1}{(1+k)^n}$
3				$\dfrac{A_3(1+g_2)g_1}{(1+k)^3}$	$\dfrac{A_n(1+g_2)\,g_1}{(1+k)^n}$
n				$\ldots$ and so on	$\dfrac{A_n(1+g_{n-1})\cdots(1+g_2)\,g_1}{(1+k)^n}$

$$\frac{A(1 + g)^2}{(1 + k)^3} + \frac{A(1 + g)^2}{(1 + k)^4} + \cdots + \frac{A(1 + g)^2}{(1 + k)^n} + \cdots$$

$$= \left[\frac{A(1 + g)^2}{(1 + k)^2}\right] * \sum_{i=1}^{\infty} \frac{1}{(1 + k)^i}$$

$$= \frac{A(1 + g)^2}{k(1 + k)^2}$$

By once again expanding each of the terms of this series successively, the two-year growth case breaks down into three distinct "investments." Because, after the second period, the numerator of each series member is the same, Equation 2.23 can generate only three sets of terms, three notional "investments." As in the full case, the investments are, in turn, of the book value BV_0, the first-period book value growth $g * BV_0$, and the second-period book value growth, $g * (1 + g) * BV_0$ (obviously, there is no growth after this because this is what we assumed). (See Table 2–20.)

In this example, the absence of abnormal earnings growth is equivalent to a zero value contribution from any incremental investment made after the second period; the original three investments continue to contribute to value in perpetuity. Precisely the same mathematical effect is achieved if incremental investments were able to earn only the cost of equity, causing the term ROE – k to be zero. Therefore, at the onset of competitive equilibrium, competitive forces eliminate abnormal income, and further growth (investment) cannot contribute to value and can be ignored.

The natural growth horizon of any valuation calculation is the onset of competitive equilibrium, after which further growth, associated with incremental investment, no longer can contribute to value. Rather than thinking about growth in isolation, an analyst can quite equivalently consider when the firm might exhaust its opportunities to invest profitably, that is, at a rate in excess of its capital costs. Once the firm reaches that horizon and competitive forces eliminate marginal profitable opportunities, further growth is irrelevant to value. This happy result simplifies the analyst's life considerably since in many valuations it is necessary to consider only near-term growth rather than contemplating the always difficult concept of long-term (perpetual) growth. There are examples of firms that seem to be able to sustain competitive advantages indefinitely. In those cases, a longer-term growth rate is relevant.

TABLE 2-20

Zero growth and the end of unprofitable investment are mathematically indistinguishable.

Investment	BV_0	$\dfrac{A}{(1+k)}$	$\dfrac{A(1+g)}{(1+k)^2}$	$\dfrac{A(1+g)^2}{(1+k)^3}$	$\dfrac{A(1+g)^2}{(1+k)^n}$
1	$\dfrac{A}{(1+k)}$		$\dfrac{A}{(1+k)^2}$	$\dfrac{A}{(1+k)^3}$	$\dfrac{A}{(1+k)^n}$
2			$\dfrac{Ag}{(1+k)^2}$	$\dfrac{Ag}{(1+k)^3}$	$\dfrac{Ag}{(1+k)^n}$
3				$\dfrac{A(1+g)/g}{(1+k)^3}$	$\dfrac{A*(1+g)*g}{(1+k)^n}$

GROWTH IN PERPETUITY

Another possibility for Equation 2.20 exists. Suppose ROE and g are constant and growth continues in perpetuity. Then Equation 2.20 reduces to

$$P_0 = BV_0 + \frac{A}{k - g}$$

$$= BV_0 + (ROE - k) * \frac{BV_0}{k - g}$$

$$= (ROE - g) * \frac{BV_0}{k - g} \qquad (2.24)$$

Equation 2.24 represents that highest possible stock price that is consistent with the parameters ROE, g, and k. A word of caution, however: Equation 2.24, although a wonderful valuation rule of thumb, can make it seem as if ROE, g, and k are sufficient to specify a firm's value. In fact, the expression contains an implicit assumption of growth persistence; specifically, that growth at the rate g continues *forever*. In reality, the period of profitable (or unprofitable) growth, coinciding with the presence of profitable investment opportunities, is necessary to fully specify a firm's value. More on growth persistency and value in Chapter 16.

So what have we learned in this section?

- Growth and investment provide equivalent ways to formulate a security valuation problem.

- Growth in value ends when incremental opportunities for profitable investment are exhausted, a condition called *competitive equilibrium.*

- Since value is no longer affected, growth extending beyond competitive equilibrium is irrelevant. In many cases, therefore, the analyst need contemplate only the firm's nearer-term growth prospects, rather than the more troublesome long-term growth expectation.

- Return on equity, growth, and the cost of equity are necessary but not sufficient to define a valuation problem; the additional ingredient is the persistency of profitable growth.

NOTES

[1] James Gleick, *Genius: The Life and Science of Richard Feynman,* Pantheon Books, New York, 1992.

[2] Krishna G. Palepu, Victor L. Bernard, and Paul M. Healy, *Introduction to Business Analysis and Valuation,* South-Western College Publishing, Cincinnati, Ohio, 1997, pp. 3–5.

[3] At this writing, the fate of business combination accounting remains undecided. Substantial public comment, in the wake of the Financial Accounting Standards Board (FASB) September 1999 *Exposure Draft on Business Combinations and Intangible Assets,* caused the board to redeliberate. The FASB is reconsidering the best ways for accounting for goodwill and other intangible assets, and, subsequently, whether to retain the pooling method. In December 2000, the FASB that purchased goodwill should not be amortized (as in current practice and the Exposure Draft), but it should be reviewed for impairment. The Board's reasoning here, briefly, included the notion that goodwill amortization "had little, if any, information value to most investors and that operating management was not held responsible internally for goodwill." ("Why Did the Board Change Its Mind on Goodwill Amortization?" Johnson, L. Todd, and Kimberley R. Petrone, FASB, December 2000.)

[4] Gerald I. White, Ashwinpaul C. Sondhi, and Dov Fried, *The Analysis and Use of Financial Statements,* 2d ed., Wiley, New York, 1997, p. 746.

[5] Palepu, Bernard, and Healy, *Introduction to Business Analysis,* pp. 7–16.

[6] White, Sondhi, and Fried, *Analysis and Use of Financial Statements,* p. 1076.

[7] I use the definition of *economic income* proposed by Alfred Rappaport, *Creating Shareholder Value: A Guide for Managers and Investors,* The Free Press, New York, 1998, p. 22.

[8] Palepu, Bernard, and Healy, *Introduction to Business Analysis,* pp. 7–16.

[9] I am playing a little fast and loose here. Strictly speaking, the P/BV and P/E are formed from the stock's current price, not its calculated value. For the example's purposes, I assume that price and value are the same.

[10] Palepu, Bernard, and Healy, *Introduction to Business Analysis,* pp. 6–11.

[11] White, Sondhi, and Fried, *The Analysis and Use of Financial Statements,* pp. 1056–1058.

CHAPTER 3

Strategy and Competition I: The Firm's External Environment

- Firms (or industries) earn superior returns by creating impediments to the natural leveling effects of competition. The more nearly efficient the firm's production markets are, the more difficult it is to exploit such competitive impediments.

- The analysis of any firm's potential competitive success is an interesting nature or nurture problem, a synthesis of influences from its external competitive environment (nurture) and its internal competitive resources (nature). An understanding of both external and internal competitive issues is the foundation of the entire equity analytic process. Nothing else happens without it.

- A strengths, weaknesses, opportunities, and threats (SWOT) analysis describes the firm's external environment in terms of the threats and opportunities presented.

- Porter's Five Forces methodology is our starting point for the analysis of the firm's external environmental threats. The relative strength of each of the Five Forces is a consequence of industry structure and drives average industry profitability. An individual firm's financial performance is determined, in turn, by its competitive positioning within the industry.

- The firm's life cycle position is a significant determinant of its competitive opportunities. Emergence, growth, and the transition to maturity are of particular interest to the equity analyst.

The economic return analysis of Chapter 2 demonstrates that buying a stock at its intrinsic value produces returns equal only to the cost of capital. In an efficient market, on average, stocks will be priced at their inherent value, so a diversified portfolio should be good enough to return capital costs, compensating investors (on average and in the longer run) for their risk, and no more. Equity analysts have to try to do better than that, by finding stocks whose prices do not fully reflect inherent value (Figure 3–1). But is this even possible? If production markets, the markets in which the firm offers its goods or services, operate efficiently, supernormal returns, for example, should be rare and unsustainable. Further, if the stock market itself operates efficiently, mispriced stocks, which do not reflect their inherent economic potential, should also be a rarity. In fact, in an efficient stock market, stocks are as likely to be overpriced as underpriced, and there is no objective means to decide which it is.

What drives assets to their inherent value, whether in production or trading (stock) markets, is competition, so a study of competition is the foundation of equity analysis. If a firm is to resist competitive forces, it must be able to construct impediments to competition. These impediments can exist in the firm's external industry environment, or they may arise from its own internal resources and capabilities. The SWOT technique, considering the firm's internal strengths and weaknesses, and its external opportunities and threats, is a useful foundation for competitive analysis. The standard for analysis of competitive threats and opportunities is Porter's Five Forces analysis. As an alternative to Porter, analysts might also use Value Net and Key Success Factor techniques.

GOOD COMPANIES = GOOD STOCKS?

Depending upon one's theoretical temperament, finding mispriced stocks may be an achievable challenge, or a fool's errand. But either way, it is

FIGURE 3–1

Equity analysis involves two markets.

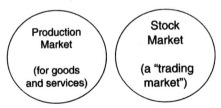

certainly true that expending time and effort in equity analysis isn't sensible unless it produces value in excess of its costs.

The goal of all equity portfolio management, regardless of investment style or technique, is to add value; that is, to exploit the differences between the current prices of stocks and their inherent or intrinsic value.[1]

If we are looking for stocks with above-average returns, we might begin by looking for companies that produce above-average performance in their production markets for goods or services. Even if we find such companies, and the market seems to be able to pretty adeptly identify them, there is no assurance that we can buy their stocks at a price below their inherent value. In fact, if both markets operate efficiently, we will be able, on average, to do neither.[2]

What we hope is that both production markets and stock markets have inefficiencies that we as analysts can exploit. As it turns out, production markets are the more likely to contain inefficiencies. We often refer to one such inefficiency, arguably the most important, as *sustainable competitive advantage*. So let's begin with production markets. Chapter 5 addresses the more controversial issue of stock market efficiency

MARKET EFFICIENCY AND COMPETITIVE IMPEDIMENTS

Extraordinary performance is not sustainable in an efficient market. But efficiency is the result of the operation of an unimpeded competitive process. If impediments exist, inefficiencies result.

Achieving Efficiency in Production Markets

Without putting too fine a point on it, efficient markets result when

- Entry and exit are unimpeded.
- Extraordinary profit opportunities are rapidly identified and dissipated.
- Prices (for goods and services) fall to cover marginal costs, including capital costs.

Opportunities for supernormal profit are quickly exploited by the entry of competitors (or exit, in the case of subnormal profits). Abnormal profits disappear rapidly, company returns fall to the cost of capital, and further earnings growth and investment activity add no value to the firm. The only way abnormal returns can be sustained is if somehow this "competitive fade"[3] is stopped, or slowed down.

The competitive process produces market efficiency when a number of conditions are met:

- The assets or activities producing the inefficiency can be bought and sold. This is easy to understand in the stock market, where stock mispricing can be corrected through astute stock trading. In a production market, competitors might offer a similar or substitute product.
- The winning strategy can be replicated. Imitation is another basic competitive technique.
- The profits produced by the imitative strategy exceed the strategy's cost.[4]

But maybe one or more of these conditions can be short-circuited, if only temporarily. Perhaps the assets or resources necessary are scarce or immobile, like a firm's reputation, and cannot easily be bought and sold. In a trading market, this condition is less likely to be violated because assets are freely exchanged. But in production markets, access to resources and skills is less fluid. As access to the necessary assets declines, the probability of inefficiency rises.[5]

Or even if competitors have access to the same skills and resources, duplicating the above-average firm's strategy might remain difficult. Perhaps competitors are unable to combine the resources correctly, or they are unable to determine exactly how the successful firm operates. Finally, competitors may be able to locate the necessary resources and combine them correctly, but it might be too expensive to do so.

Impeding Efficiency

There are a number of generic monkey wrenches we can throw into the competitive machinery, but consider the following three.[6]

Systemic Impediments

Firms may operate in a protected environment. Patent protection of new drugs, for example, is a substantial (though not insurmountable) competitive impediment. It limits entry and reduces competitive pressure.

Government regulation in general is a principal source of systemic impediments.

Entrepreneurial Impediments

Firms that are quick to move and exploit new opportunities can often steal a march on competitors and enjoy a period of reduced competitive pressure and extraordinary returns. This is often called the *first mover advantage,* and it frequently occurs early in the life cycle of an industry or product when demand far exceeds production capacity. Sometimes, if the first mover can establish a strong reputation or industry standards, this advantage can be extended well beyond the firm's startup stage. Microsoft is the principal example of a company's use of sustained first-mover advantage.

Sustainable Competitive Advantage

Firms can disrupt the competitive process even in nonprotected industries, and without a first-mover advantage, if they can establish some superiority over their existing competition. There are companies like General Electric, Proctor & Gamble, Coca-Cola, and Gillette that, at least until recently, seemed to be able to maintain such superiority over rivals perennially.

SWOT, NATURE, AND NURTURE

The nature-nurture debate rages in corporate strategy circles, just as it does in biology. And like biology, corporate performance is probably the result of a combination of the two forces. Study of the firm's external environment, industry structure, competitive opportunities, and threats is the nurture side of the debate. Examination of the firm's internal "assets, capabilities, competencies, organizational processes, firm attributes, information, knowledge" is the nature side, often called the *resource view* of the firm. The resource view focuses on the firm's strengths and weaknesses. The analytic examination of these two forces, nature and nurture, is called "SWOT analysis": strengths, weaknesses, opportunities and threats (Figure 3–2).[7]

   The opportunities and threats presented to the firm, combined with the firm's own internal strengths and weaknesses, determine the firm's available strategy options.

FIGURE 3-2

The SWOT technique focuses both on internal and external
stategic issues.

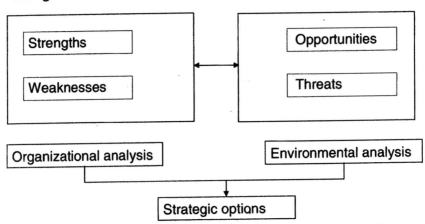

Equity analysts spend perhaps inordinate amounts of time studying
a firm's external competitive environment mainly because it is easier to
describe. This may seem like a classic search for lost keys under the
lamppost (because that's where the light is), but that might be an unfair
characterization. It is in fact a major competitive advantage to have internal skills and processes that are difficult to describe, and to imitate.
If it is difficult for competitors to get a handle on the successful firm's
"natural" advantages, it is also likely that analysts will have problems.

Dimensions of the Issue

The study of the external competitive environment proceeds in three dimensions.[8] First, there are horizontal and vertical product market boundaries (Figure 3-3). In the horizontal direction, companies decide how
big to be, how much market share to seek, and how to approach internal
industry competitive pressures. Vertically, companies determine how far
up and down the production and sales chain to extend their control. Do
we make or buy the components we need? Do we own our own distribution?

FIGURE 3–3

The firm has both horizontal and vertical dimensions along which strategy is pursued.

Economic Boundaries of the Firm

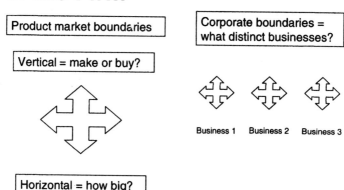

Product market boundaries

Corporate boundaries = what distinct businesses?

Vertical = make or buy?

Business 1   Business 2   Business 3

Horizontal = how big?

Source: David Besanko, David Dravove, and Mark Shanley, Economics of Strategy, Copyright © 1996. Reprinted by permission of John Wiley & Sons, Inc.

Finally, there is corporate strategy. How many and what kinds of product markets should the firm enter? The idea is that the skills built in one business can be applied to another, a "synergy" concept widely adopted in the age of the conglomerates of the 1960s and 1970s. The issue of corporate strategy is complex and beyond the scope of this book.

Notice that we are discussing here the external boundaries of the firm, the points at which the firm interacts with its competitors, suppliers, and customers. Chapter 4 considers the firm's internal resources—its assets, capabilities, and competencies.

The Five Forces

Porter's Five Forces are the basic tool of analysis of external competitive threats,[9] the first part of the SWOT technique we consider:

- Internal industry rivalry
- Threat of new entrants
- Threat of substitute products

■ Bargaining power of suppliers

■ Bargaining power of customers

I find it useful to divide the five forces into two sets. Internal industry rivalry, threats of new entrants, and substitute products are the first set, and they determine the profit potential of the industry. Industries with intense internal rivalry, large numbers of new entrants, or available substitutes are likely to have difficulty generating above-average returns (although there may be above-average firms within such an industry). The microeconomic concept of "perfect competition" is the template for such an industry. Competitors or new entrants rapidly identify and dissipate any extraordinary profit opportunities. Substitutes place limits on pricing and margins (Figure 3–4). On the other hand, in industries with little internal rivalry or new entry, profit potential is much higher. Unregulated monopolies are examples.

Once industry profit potential is determined, it must be divided among the industry's participants, their suppliers and their customers. Even if an industry's profit potential is high, powerful suppliers or customers can limit pricing or margins, and therefore industry profit. Powerful suppliers can keep input prices high, commanding a disproportionate share of the industry's potential return. Likewise, powerful

FIGURE 3–4

Porter's Five Forces produce both potential and actual industry profit.

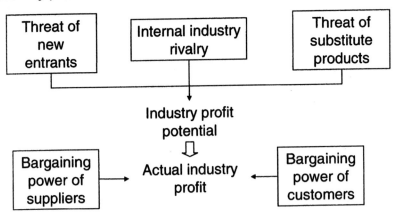

customers can force prices down, shifting return to themselves. It is not enough, unfortunately, to have a substantial internal competitive advantage. It is also necessary to be able to keep the resulting gains.

The Logic of the Porter System: Structure to Strategy

The logic of the Porter system flows from industry structure to competitive positioning to company product and market strategy. The idea at the heart of the system is that individual firm profitability, the driver of its stock valuation, arises from the interaction of

- Its industry's attractiveness
- The firm's relative position within the industry

Industry average profitability (attractiveness) is a consequence of industry structure. An industry's structure, its "underlying economic and technical characteristics," [10] determines the strength of each of the Five Forces. The relative importance of the forces can vary from industry to industry. The Five Forces, in turn, shape the industry's competitive battlefield and the opposing "order of battle." As shown in Figure 3–4, it is the interaction of the Five Forces that finally determines average industry profitability. Industry structure is "relatively stable," [11] but it can change over time, altering the impact of each of the Five Forces and influencing industry profitability.

The firm must take either offensive or defensive action to create a "defendable" [12] position on this battlefield (interesting that the objective of offensive action is to create a viable defense):

> Positioning determines whether a firm's profitability is above or below the industry average. A firm that can position itself well may earn high returns even though industry structure is unfavorable and the average profitability of the industry is therefore modest.[13]

The firm can take a number of courses[14] toward a defensible competitive position:

- Position itself so that its own strengths and weaknesses provide the best possible defense

- Alter the competitive landscape to its advantage
- Anticipate shifts in the direction of the battle and move ahead of its rivals to exploit them

But whatever general course of action it adopts, Porter identifies three generic strategies capable of establishing defendable competitive positions:

- Overall cost leadership
- Differentiation
- Focus

In the next chapter, we take up the issue of a firm's strengths, weaknesses, and competitive strategy in more detail.

Internal Rivalry

Equity analysts seem to spend most of their time on the issue of internal industry rivalry. This is, after all, where the light is. In fairness, the intensity of industry rivalry, industry structure, and growth in particular are important competitive indicators. Each internal industry characteristic raises a number of useful questions for the analyst:

- *Industry concentration:* Is the industry fragmented or concentrated? What are the market shares of the participating firms? Are there lots of small firms or a few big ones? Are all firms following the same strategy, or are they competing in different niches? Concentrated industries may be subject to less intense competitive pressure, whereas many competitors might produce destructive competition. Firms competing in different market segments reduce overall competitive intensity.

- *Growth rate:* Is the industry growing rapidly or slowly? What stage of its life cycle has it reached? If growth is high, competition may center on establishing standards for manufacturing processes or product design. Customer penetration is low (but increasing), and firms can grow without bumping into one another in the marketplace. As growth slows, however, increased sales often must come at the expense of an industry rival, and market share becomes the focus. Product standards are established, and customers are knowledgeable. Industry power shifts from the technological innovators to the marketers and distributors. The process is particularly obvious in the personal computer industry, where early technological innovators like IBM and Compaq have lost ground to distributors like Dell and Gateway. Of particular interest to the analyst are the transition points between these stages of growth. More about this in Chapter 8.

■ *Fixed costs:* Are fixed costs high or low? In high-fixed-cost industries, the battle for market share is more fierce and pricing pressure is greater as firms strive to maintain minimum capacity utilization. Lower-fixed-cost industries can more easily sustain production and sales volatility, lowering pricing pressure and competitive intensity. On the other hand, of course, lower-fixed-cost industries have less dramatic upsides in good times. Let's not be too quick to condemn fixed costs.

■ *Switching costs:* Is it expensive for customers to shift purchases among industry competitors? Are the industry's products highly differentiated, or are they commodities? Low switching costs are a likely limit on industry profitability.

■ *Scale issues:* Are capacity increments large or small? Large-capacity increments might involve substantial financial and business risk, intensifying competition for market share.

■ *Exit barriers:* An often overlooked subject, exit barriers can have a profound effect on internal industry competition and are at least (in my view) as important as the more familiar entry barriers. The fewer the alternative uses of an industry's assets and resources, the higher the barriers to exit and the more intense industry rivalry.

■ *Diversity of competitors:* Do industry participants all compete in the same niche, or in multiple niches? The more available niches, the less head-to-head competition.

Threat of Entry

The industry entry and exit is arguably the principal competitive process driving company returns on equity and ultimately stock values. But note that in the Porter system it is the *threat* of entry, not actual entry, which creates the competitive landscape. The interaction of existing "barriers to entry" and the expected reaction of incumbent firms determine the strength of this threat. If barriers are high and incumbent firms are expected to react aggressively, the threat of entry is low:

- *Economies of scale:* Entering firms may not be able to achieve sufficient scale to match existing firms' cost bases. If the minimum efficient scale (MES) is large relative to total industry productive capacity, it may be very difficult to negotiate a successful entry.

- *Product differentiation:* Companies with highly differentiated products may limit competitive entry because of the difficulty of imitating their strategies. On the other hand, highly specialized products of the incumbents may leave open niches for new entrants.

- *Capital requirements:* High capital requirements were once considered an entry barrier, although the substantial capital availability of the 1990s may have reduced the importance of this barrier. On the other hand, in an industry like silicon chip manufacture, where capacity increments are measured in billions of dollars, capital requirements likely still function to limit entry.

- *Switching costs:* Just as switching costs can affect the intensity of competition among existing firms, it can also impact new entry. High switching costs might limit a new entrant's ability to attract market share. However, in emerging industries, switching costs are less an issue because, although existing customers may have high switching costs, new ones (and there are a lot of new ones) do not.

- *Access to distribution:* If existing competitors control distribution channels, entry is discouraged, although certainly not prevented.

- *Cost disadvantages independent of scale:* Porter discusses a number of these entry barriers, such as proprietary technology; favorable access to raw materials; favorable locations; government subsidies; the learning curve; the threat of retaliation; and an entry-deterring pricing structure.

- *Government policy:* Regulation may be a significant entry barrier. Federal requirements for the approval of new pharmaceutical products likely have a significant impact upon industry entry, for example.

An alternative formulation of the entry problem reduces the issue to just three points.[15] First, entry is deterred by the prospect of falling prices, either because of the aggressive reputation of existing competitors or because of scale and/or capacity issues. Note again that it is not actual retaliation but the expectations of potential new entrants that is important in deterring entry. Second, entry is discouraged by advantages of the existing incumbents, such as licenses, patents, or the learning-curve effect. Finally, entry is deterred, interestingly, by exit costs. In industries with high exit costs, new entrants make difficult-to-reverse investments with the prospect of aggressive responses by existing players, who also have limited alternatives (Figure 3–5).

It may also be that a reputation for speed of execution creates an entry barrier, especially in rapidly changing technology industries.[16] The faster the response of an incumbent firm to a competitive challenge, the less time new entrants have to exploit product or marketing innovations.

Power of Buyers

In the Porter system, the power of buyers is driven by (1) their bargaining leverage and (2) their price sensitivity. Buyers have strong bargaining leverage if

- They are few in number versus sellers.
- They buy a relatively large amount from the seller, but the seller represents a small part of the buyer's product's cost or quality.
- They can shift to other suppliers without excessive cost or disruption.
- They are knowledgeable.
- They are capable of backward integration.
- There are available substitute products.

Power of Suppliers

Not surprisingly, the power of suppliers is a rough mirror image of buyer power. Suppliers are powerful when

FIGURE 3–5

Barriers to entry flow from the potential actions of
incumbent firms.

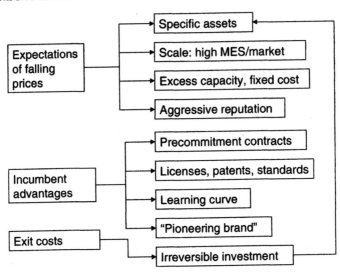

- They are few in number versus buyers.
- They sell a relatively large amount to the buyer or are a large part of the buyer's cost or his or her product's quality, but the buyer's purchases are small relative to the supplier's total volume.
- The costs of shifting to other suppliers are high.
- They are capable of forward integration.
- Substitute inputs are few.

The Holdup Problem

The "holdup problem" can be a significant driver of the division of advantage between buyers and sellers.[17] Some transactions between buyers and sellers require investment in relationship-specific assets. For example, to limit transportation costs and speed delivery, suppliers may be forced to locate plants near their customers. Or the supplier may need to purchase special equipment, dedicate assets to his or her customer, or train personnel in the skills necessary to service the buyer. These investments can have substantial consequences upon the bargaining positions of both buyer and seller.

One party to the transaction may now attempt to exploit the vulnerability of the other created by the investment in relationship-specific assets, the classic "holdup problem." When a seller has made a relationship-specific investment, the revenue level that induced him or her to enter the transaction (the one that provides him or her with his or her required return) may be above the level that just barely induces him or her to not exit the transaction (redeploying a relationship-specific asset in some other use). This so-called quasi-rent is created by the limited value of the relationship-specific asset in uses other than servicing the current buyer. The seller is now economically vulnerable because the buyer may opportunistically attempt to hold up the seller for the quasi-rent.

The threat of a holdup can raise an industry's costs by, for example, increasing the difficulty of buyer-seller bargaining or by causing buyers to keep standby supply capacity in reserve to prevent a holdup by primary suppliers.

THE GENERIC OPPORTUNITIES: EMERGING TO MATURE INDUSTRIES

The Five Forces are our principal tool for analyzing the competitive threats facing the firm. But there are also competitive opportunities presented by industry structure, especially as the industry evolves through newly emerging to mature and finally to declining stages.

The portion of the industry life cycle from startup to maturity is of particular interest to equity analysts and is covered in some detail in Chapters 9 and 18. There we distinguish five industry development stages: startup, emerging growth, established growth, mature, and declining. (Porter combines the startup and emerging-growth phase into an "introduction" period.) In general, each stage of development has unique competitive characteristics and opportunities. Porter has a considerable amount to teach us about these earlier industry stages (Figure 3–6).

Opportunities in Emerging Industries

The essential characteristic of an emerging industry from the viewpoint of formulating strategy is that there are no rules of the game.[18]

FIGURE 3-6

The firm's life cycle extends from startup to decline.

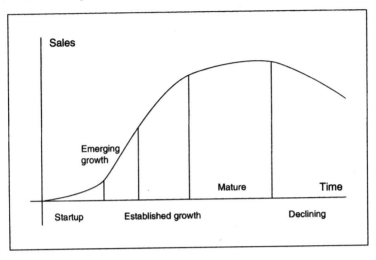

The structure of emerging industries is driven by the absence of "rules of the game" and by the small size and newness of the participating firms.

- *Technological uncertainty:* What form the industry's products and production processes take is still to be determined.
- *Strategic uncertainty:* In Internet parlance, there is no established business model in emerging industries.
- *High but steeply falling costs:* As production levels grow, efficiencies rise rapidly.
- *Large numbers of newly formed companies.*
- *First-time buyers:* Buyers are not knowledgeable about the product and must be educated about its features and advantages.
- *Altered entry barriers:* Entry barriers are centered on technology and cumulative experience rather than "the need to command massive resources."[19]

The rapidly changing, vaguely defined nature of emerging industries produces specific strategic opportunities:

- A firm may be able to establish product standards or define the winning business model, both of which should convey first-mover competitive advantages.
- Early commitments to suppliers and customers can produce loyalty and favored treatment as competition grows.

Opportunities in Late-Stage Growth and Transition to Maturity

In a mature, slow-growing industry, the assumptions required to justify investing new cash in order to build market share are often heroic. Maturity of an industry works against increasing or maintaining margins long enough to recoup cash investments down the road. . . .[20]

If emerging companies possess a wide range of competitive opportunities, those nearing the transition to maturity face constricting possibilities. Much of equity analysis is focused on large capitalization growth stocks, and equity analysts must, reluctantly, anticipate these stocks' eventual transition. Nevertheless, late-stage growth companies do have some interesting strategic alternatives.

As firms near the end of their rapid growth phases, their external competitive environments become generally more difficult:

- As product and market penetration increases, competition necessarily focuses more on market share. Large performance improvements now come increasingly at the expense of competitors.
- Customers are knowledgeable. Competition focuses less on technology and product features and more on cost and service.
- Needs for personnel and productive capacity growth wane. Management faces a risk of "overshoot,"[21] overinvestment in staff and plant, if it fails to recognize the change.
- New product and process development opportunities constrict.
- International competition increases.
- Head-to-head competition, knowledgeable customers, and increased emphasis on cost and service can put downward pressure on profit margins.

■ Distributors' power increases as the sales process focuses increasingly upon price.

In spite of the difficulties of the transition, late-stage growth companies still have strategic alternatives:

■ An increased "financial consciousness"[22] can produce an advantage in an increasingly price-sensitive market. Driving more deliberately toward operational efficiency can convey an advantage, if only temporarily.

■ Raising customers' "scope of purchases,"[23] or cross selling, can be a cost-effective way of maintaining growth. It is also, in my view, an extraordinarily difficult task. In the financial services, cross selling is the Grand Vision of most managements.

■ As profit pressures rise in an industry's later growth stages, attractive acquisition candidates may appear among more distressed competitors. However, as argued in Chapter 19, it isn't clear that mergers and acquisitions ultimately add much value to the buyer.

■ Finally, as domestic markets mature and margin pressure rises, international markets may continue to offer opportunities.

BEYOND PORTER

Porter's Five Forces are a highly useful method of analyzing industry attractiveness in order to forecast average industry profitability.[24] In the so-called *structure-conduct-performance* (SCP) *model,* industry average profitability is viewed as a consequence of industry structure, the industry's basic technological and economic logic. There are at least three directions in which the Porter method has been extended.

In the Porter system, industry structure is exogenous and relatively static. But suppose competitive actions alter an industry's basic economic and/or technological logic, making structure a moving target? This is unlikely to happen often or in every industry, but where it does, an industry analysis system focusing on competitive innovation might be more helpful. The Schumpeterian idea of "creative destruction" is useful in such rapidly changing industries.[25] We use the computer graphics accelerator industry below as an example of an innovation-driven competitive environment. Even in less volatile industries, some sense of the dynamics of competition—the action and counteraction of industry rivals—extends the static Porter analysis. We discuss such a dynamic analytic method in Chapter 4.

The Porter system is essentially enterprise based, adversarial, and focused upon rivalries and bargaining. But companies may compete intensely in some activities, and, on the other hand, cooperate or partner in others. An analytic system called *the Value Net* accounts for such mixed competitive-cooperative industry interactions. In a broader sense, the value net concept is a reaction to the blurring of industry and company boundaries, driven at least partially by advances in information technology. In the Porter world, the boundary between the company and its external environment is more distinct, and the creation of economic value can be fruitfully examined through the firm's own internal value chain, or through sets of value chains ("value systems") of multiple firms. In newer, integrated, networked, and convergent markets, value is created by "sets of economic players which, while remaining legally and strategically distinguishable, operate jointly as elements of a single integrated organism." [26]

Porter's Five Forces are threat based, focusing on the threats of entry and substitution and the relative economic mass of industry participants and their customers and/or suppliers. The "Key Success Factors" methodology, often associated with the McKinsey & Co. consulting firm, on the other hand, concentrates instead upon opportunities to improve profitability embedded in industry economics. The Key Success Factors method searches for the industry's principal profitability levers and examines the impact of company competitive actions in those arenas. [27]

Innovation As a Driver of Industry Structural Change

An innovation-based industry analysis system relies upon the *law of nemesis,* another of my favorite laws of nature, which holds that every situation contains the seeds of its own reversal. [28] The very competitive success of some industry participants encourages others to attack established positions. [29] When the attack comes in the form of technological innovation, industry structure and the current rules of the game are likely to change rapidly, sweeping aside established firms and strategies. This is the Schumpeterian idea of "creative destruction," which is particularly applicable to many newer technological industries such as the personal computers, the Internet, and telecommunications (Example 3–1).

EXAMPLE 3-1

CREATIVE DESTRUCTION IN COMPUTER GRAPHICS ACCELERATOR INDUSTRY

Personal computer graphics accelerators are an excellent example of an innovation-driven industry. Since the mid-1990s, the intense popularity of computer-based gaming has created a small war in the 3D graphic accelerator business. Don't underestimate the importance of personal computer gaming; computer games account for an incredible 40 percent of unit sales and 20 to 25 percent of revenue in the personal computer software market.[30] Graphic accelerators are computer components designed to process the complex calculations necessary to present a three-dimensional gaming experience on standard computer monitors.

The growing graphic intensity of newer game software drove manufacturers to produce increasingly faster graphics boards. Defying Moore's law (which holds that semiconductor chip processing power can be expected to double every 18 months), 3D graphic chip speeds have risen about three times that fast since 1996.[31] As each new accelerator generation has swept away the previous industry leaders, product life cycles have declined to months rather than years. The industry lead in the United States now seesaws back and forth among several manufacturers. With its proprietary *Glide*™ technology, 3dfx Interactive, Inc. was the long-time performance leader, selling primarily through retail outlets. Other manufacturers concentrated upon OEM channels (3dfx has now also joined the OEM channel through its purchase of STB Systems, Inc.). In its fifth generation, 3dfx's *Voodoo*™ product line is being challenged by nVidia Corporation's *GeForce*™ architecture. Computer graphics technology standards remain in flux. *Glide*™, the early industry leader, did not establish an unchallenged position among gaming software writers. Other graphics systems, such as Microsoft's *Direct 3D*™, are gaining popularity. The very successful *Quake* game series, for example, is written in the Open GL™ format, a graphics system developed by Silicon Graphics, Inc., primarily for very high quality technical and industrial imaging.[32]

Graphic accelerator speeds have grown so great, in fact, that they frequently outrun the demands of current gaming software, and their performance can be limited by slower operating speeds in the remainder of the computer system. As a result, competition has recently focused on each technology's capability to render the complex color and textural information necessary for higher-quality graphic presentations. Accelerator functions such as *full-screen antialiasing* (FSSA), which eliminates the

EXAMPLE 3–1 (Continued)

CREATIVE DESTRUCTION IN COMPUTER GRAPHICS ACCELERATOR INDUSTRY

familiar jagged edges in many graphic images, are increasingly competitive features.[33] *DirectX 8*®, Microsoft's latest *Windows*-based graphics software protocol update, will enable newer technologies that permit complex lighting and surface texture effects.[34] Although years away, the industry continues to drive for photorealism in 3D games.

In the meantime, however, videogame console technology, in which single-purpose processors connect directly to television monitors, is itself undergoing rapid improvement. Console gaming is the larger business, producing $4 billion in 1999 software revenue versus $2 billion for PC-based games.[35] Companies like Nintendo, Sega, and Sony have (or will soon) introduced new, high-performance generations of console gaming devices. Even Microsoft, not known as a hardware producer (although it does a sizeable business in gaming devices such as joysticks and game-pads), intends to offer a dedicated gaming device called the *Xbox*®. Because of the exceptional images produced by these console systems (and their vast software libraries), the image-quality battle among computer accelerators is likely to accelerate, so to speak. NVidia has already partnered with Microsoft to provide the graphics chip technology for the Xbox.[36]

Rapidly improving console gaming hardware presents a serious challenge to PC graphics accelerator manufacturers partly because consoles are cheap, costing perhaps $200 to 300, about as much as a top-end graphics accelerator alone (to which one must add a PC, of course, itself costing $800 to $1000 at a minimum). Consoles are a classic "razorblades and razors" business, in which console manufacturers lose money or break even on hardware sales but make substantial profits on subsequent game software purchases. In addition, competitive strategies of console manufacturers, particularly Sony with its Playstation 2 (released in the United States in late 2000), embrace the evolution of gaming consoles into broader consumer electronics devices. Such devices might incorporate Internet connectivity, DVD, telecommunications capabilities, cable video technology, or high-quality audio, all for a couple hundred bucks.

It would be difficult to characterize the "structure" of the graphic accelerator industry because of the constant swirl of technological innovation, the absence of product standards, and the shifting competitive strategies of industry players. It is difficult even to name competitors and potential entrants. For example, Microsoft, heretofore principally a com-

EXAMPLE 3–1 (Continued)

**CREATIVE DESTRUCTION IN COMPUTER GRAPHICS
ACCELERATOR INDUSTRY**

puter game publisher, will enter the video console business opposite Sega,
Nintendo, and Sony. To ensure at least a base of Xbox game software,
Microsoft in 2000 purchased well-known game developer, Bungie. Nvidia,
primarily a PC platform specialist, will support the Microsoft console effort. In the meantime, Sony's new Playstation 2 may be the opening push
to create game consoles with broad consumer electronics functions. The
potential competitive threat of the Playstation 2 to established software
platforms (maybe even *Windows* itself) perhaps encouraged Microsoft's
entry.

The Value Net and Mixed Business Relationships

In their fascinating book *Co-opetition,* Brandenburger and Nalebuff (BN)
suggest an alternative to the competitive, adversarial relationships of the
Five Forces methodology.[37] Proposing a more complex view, the BN
enterprise interacts with four basic "players": customers, suppliers, competitors, and "complementors."

- You are a complementor if customers value your product more
  when they have the other player's product than when they have
  your product alone.
- You are a competitor if customers value your product less
  when they have the other player's product than when they have
  your product alone.[38]

Examples are rife. Ford and General Motors are competitors; you value
a Ford less once you have purchased a Chevrolet. On the other hand,
catalogs and overnight delivery services are complementors.[39] One values
the catalog more in the presence of overnight delivery than in its absence.

But the world is even more complicated. Players may have multiple
roles, acting at times as suppliers, customers, competitors, and complementors. For example, BN note the tendency of competing enterprises,
such as antique dealers or art galleries, to cluster together geographically.
Although this may seem foolish, the clustered dealers together form a

FIGURE 3-7

The BN Value Net presents the friend-foe nature of business relationships.

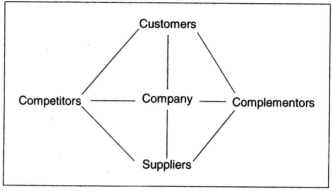

Source: Adam M. Brandenburger and Barry J. Nalebuff, Co-opetition, copyright © 1996 by Adam M. Brandenburger and Barry J. Nalebuff. Used by permission of Doubleday, a division of Random House, Inc.

FIGURE 3-8

The Value Net is a powerful tool in analysis of the computer graphics accelerator market.

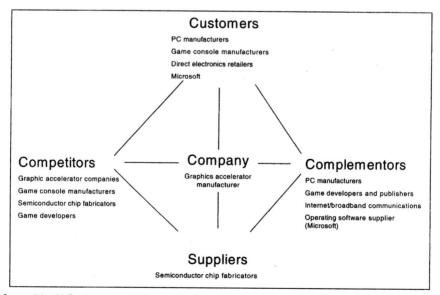

Source: Adam M. Brandenburger and Barry J. Nalebuff, Co-opetition, copyright © 1996 by Adam M. Brandenburger and Barry J. Nalebuff. Used by permission of Doubleday, a division of Random House, Inc.

EXAMPLE 3-2

THE GRAPHICS ACCELERATOR VALUE NET

Our previous example of the computer graphics accelerator industy (Box 3-1) is particularly suited to a Value Net analysis because of the complexity of its interrelationships and dependencies. Graphic accelerator manufacturers clearly compete with one another and with the console game industry. But, in at least one case, nVidia, an accelerator manufacturer will supply graphics hardware to Microsoft's new Xbox console. The accelerator companies' other principal customers are the PC manufacturers themselves; on the other hand, the PC clearly enhances the value of the accelerator, which isn't much good on its own (unlike the game console). Many accelerator companies act as design shops only and outsource their chip and board manufacture to independent chip "fabs." But a chip fabricator is also a potential competitor in the design and manufacture of graphics boards, and it might very well have a cost advantage over the accelerator company.

A vigorous game development industry is a strong complement to the accelerator companies. Nevertheless, developers who produce games written in nonproprietary protocols might be seen as competitors; this is especially true of 3dfx's proprietary *Glide*™ system. Improved operating system functionality, which supports more complex graphics, strongly complements the accelerator industry. Microsoft has in fact made steady improvement in the *Windows* graphic environment. Finally, the Internet and telecommunications industry supports the very popular online multiplayer gaming experience, a driving factor in many game purchases.

larger draw to customers, who value the convenience and the likely competitive prices encouraged by the close proximity of other dealers.[40] In addition, dealers are likely to buy and sell among themselves.

In fact, no player in the BN universe plays a pure role.

> Whether it be customer, supplier, complementor, or competitor, no one can be cast purely as friend or foe. There is a duality in every relationship—the simultaneous elements of win-win and win-lose.[41]

This complex array of relationships can be visualized in BN's "Value Net," which depicts the players in business situations and their interrelationships. Contrast the Value Net in Figure 3-7 (page 77) to the Five Forces view.

EXAMPLE 3–3

KEY SUCCESS FACTORS IN THE GRAPHICS ACCELERATOR BUSINESS

Like the PC business itself, the graphics accelerator industry is intensely technology and price competitive (particularly, one assumes, the OEM segment). nVidia and 3dfx are "fabless" operators, meaning that their graphics chips are manufactured and assembled by third parties, freeing the accelerator companies of the risks of owning and operating semiconductor chip manufacturing facilities (3dfx does assemble and market its own branded graphics boards). As a result, their competitive success revolves around nonmanufacturing issues.

Advanced Technology

Like the chipmakers Intel and AMD, the accelerator companies are under relentless pressure to incorporate the latest technological capabilities into their products, requiring a substantial R&D effort. R&D expenses in the most recent fiscal year amounted to 18.3 and 12.7 percent of revenue at 3dfx and nVidia, respectively. Graphics technology must respond to the simultaneous, and somewhat conflicting, demands of both frame rate and fill rate. *Frame rate* refers to the sheer processing speed of the graphics chip. The higher the frame rate, the smoother is the displayed graphics action on the computer monitor. *Fill rate,* on the other hand, refers to the quality of the graphic image, the amount of textual and lighting information displayed. The higher the fill rate, the more realistic the graphics image. Clearly, less detailed images may be displayed at a higher frame rate (all else being equal), leading to the technological tradeoff. As mentioned above, the current race seems to be centered on the fill rate, as companies compete to introduce technology that can produce more nearly photo-realistic images.

Rapid Product Introduction

Great technology is no good if it is late. The accelerator companies must introduce upgraded technology rapidly. Because this requires working ahead several chip generations, companies must anticipate the demand for advanced features (and the actions of competing firms). Graphics chip development is so rapid, in fact, that it frequently outruns graphics software, which often does not exploit the hardware's advanced capabilities. By the time the software catches up, graphics chips have taken another leap forward.

EXAMPLE 3–3 (Continued)

KEY SUCCESS FACTORS IN THE GRAPHICS ACCELERATOR BUSINESS

Large PC OEMs and add-in graphics board producers often introduce two model upgrades per year. Accelerator companies must be prepared with the latest technology to ensure their inclusion in new systems, keeping accelerator product life cycles short, at least in the higher-end, cutting edge of the market.[44]

Affordable Price

Graphics accelerator hardware is price competitive in both the retail and OEM markets. An add-in graphics board can retail at \$100 to \$200, a significant percentage of perhaps a \$1000 to \$2000 computer purchase. OEMs like Dell and Gateway typically operate under substantial profit margin constraint, especially as average system prices (ASPs) have fallen, and this pricing pressure is no doubt communicated to graphics accelerator suppliers.

The "value" in the Value Net refers to the process by which firms complement one another in the building of markets and compete in their division.[42] To analyze how value is created and divided among industry players, BN use game theory (Example 3–2, page 78).

Key Success Factors in Opportunities to Improve Profitability

Rather than viewing the industry environment in terms of threats and bargaining, the Key Success Factors methodology focuses upon the important variables in the company's return equation.[43]

$$\text{Return on equity} = \text{net profit margin} \times \text{asset turnover} \times \text{financial leverage}$$

Chapter 7 presents a complete discussion of the return equation and its components. But, leaving aside the corporate financial issues raised by the financial leverage variable, the management of company operations, driver of the net profit margin, and the management of assets and investment, the driver of asset turnover, start the analyst's search for key success factors. Within the net margin, issues of cost control, manufacturing scale, pricing and product mix, marketing and development expense, and revenue and unit growth may all be important to the company's ultimate profitability. The efficiency of asset management, working capital turnover, and capital investment are the principal issues in asset turnover (Example 3–3, pages 79–80).

NOTES

[1] Steven Pisarkiewicz and Mark R. Gordon, "Quantitative Tools in Equity Valuation and Portfolio Management: Applying the DDM," in *Applied Equity Valuation,* edited by T. Daniel Coggin and Frank J. Fabozzi, Frank J. Fabozzi Associates, New Hope, Penna., 1999.

[2] For excellent discussions of the efficient market hypothesis, see Sharon M. Oster, *Modern Competitive Analysis,* Oxford University Press, New York, 1999, p. 29; and Robert M. Grant, *Contemporary Strategy Analysis,* 3rd ed., Blackwell Publishers, Malden, Mass., 1998, pp. 185–192.

[3] Bartley J. Madden, *CFROI Valuation: A Total System Approach to Valuing the Firm,* Butterworth-Heinemann, Oxford, England, 1999, p. 163.

[4] Aswath Damodaran, *Investment Valuation,* Wiley, New York, 1996, p. 149.

[5] Ibid., p. 149.

[6] Oster, *Modern Competitive Analysis,* p. 29.

[7] Barney's description of the SWOT process and its relationship to the rest of strategy analysis is excellent; Jay B. Barney, *Gaining and Sustaining Competitive Advantage,* Addison-Wesley Publishing Company, Reading, Mass., 1997, p. 22.

[8] David Besanko, David Dranove, and Mark Shanley, *Economics of Strategy,* Wiley, New York, 1996, pp. 1–7.

[9] The Five Forces discussion is drawn from Michael E. Porter, *Competitive Strategy,* The Free Press, New York, 1980, and Michael E. Porter, *Competitive Advantage,* The Free Press, New York, 1985.

[10] Porter, *Competitive Advantage,* p. 5.

[11] Ibid., p. 7.

[12] Porter, *Competitive Strategy,* p. 34.

[13] Porter, *Competitive Advantage,* p. 11.

[14] Porter, *Competitive Strategy,* p. 29.

[15] Oster, *Modern Competitive Analysis,* p. 78.

[16] Vincent M. Occhipinti, "Startup Essentials," *Upside,* August 2000, p. 44.

[17] Besanko, Dranove, and Shanley, *Economics of Strategy,* pp. 111–132.

[18] Porter, *Competitive Strategy,* p. 215.

[19] Ibid., p. 220.

[20] Ibid., p. 247.

[21] Ibid., p. 239.

[22] Ibid., p. 243.

[23] Ibid.

[24] Robert M. Grant, *Contemporary Strategy Analysis,* Blackwell Publishers, Malden, Mass., 1998, p. 75.

[25] Ibid., p. 71.

[26] Cinzia Parolini, *The Value Net,* Wiley, New York, 1999, p. xxi.

[27] Grant, *Contemporary Strategy Analysis,* p. 76.

[28] George S. Day and David J. Reibstein, eds., *Wharton on Dynamic Competitive Strategy,* Wiley, New York, 1997, p. 49.

[29] Grant, *Contemporary Strategy Analysis,* p. 71.

[30] Eriq Gardner, "Video Might Kill the PC Star," *Upside,* October 2000, p. 192.

[31] "The Future of 3D," *Computer Gaming World,* Ziff-Davis, November 2000, p. 124.

[32] For the technically minded, *Glide, Direct3D,* and *OpenGL* are known as *APIs,* or *application programming interfaces.* APIs are the instruction sets that connect 3D graphics applications (like computer games) to the underlying hardware functions of the graphics chip.

[33] "Videocard Smackdown," *Maximum PC,* August 2000, p. 40.

[34] "The Future of 3D," p. 127.

[35] Gardner, "Video Might Kill the PC Star," p. 196.

[36] John F. Ince, "The Graphic Truth: Silicon Is Out There," *Upside,* October 2000, p. 164.

[37] Adam M. Brandenburger, and Barry J. Nalebuff, *Co-opetition,* Doubleday, New York, 1996.

[38] Ibid., p. 18.

[39] Ibid., p. 12.

[40] Ibid., p. 33.

[41] Ibid., p. 39.

[42] Ibid., p. 34.

[43] Grant, *Contemporary Strategy Analysis,* pp. 77–80.

[44] nVidia Corporation, form 10-K filed with the SEC on March 13, 2000.

CHAPTER 4

Strategy and Competition II: The Firm's Internal Competitive Resources

- "A firm can outperform its rivals only if it can establish a difference it can preserve."[1] The preservation of difference underlies sustainable competitive advantage. Advantage cannot be sustained unless the firm can create impediments to competitors.

- In the Porter view, firms achieve and sustain differences through three basic strategies: cost leadership, differentiation, and focus. These generic strategies are archetypal and probably occur rarely in pure form. They do, however, represent mutually exclusive competitive styles.

- "Operational effectiveness is not strategy."[2] Operational effectiveness is necessary regardless of the firm's competitive strategy. But the pursuit of operational effectiveness, especially on an industry-wide basis, can lead to competitive convergence and the stagnation of financial returns.

- The "resource view" of the firm, an alternative to Porter, holds that companies sustain competitive advantage by developing resources and capabilities that are valuable, rare, costly to imitate, and effectively implemented. Such competitive advantages often involve interlocking systems of functions that are difficult to duplicate.

- The Porter and resource views are neatly reconciled when competitive advantage is viewed as a dynamic process. The firm's resources permit it to create advantageous competitive positions that are protected by entry and/or mobility barriers, eroded by rivals, and renewed by investment.

To paraphrase legendary investor Warren Buffet, when an industry with a reputation for difficulty meets a manager with a reputation for brilliance, it is usually the industry that emerges with its reputation intact. Industry structure, and the threats and opportunities it presents, is an undeniably major driver of firm financial performance. Tough industries make superior performance difficult. But even in the toughest industries, some firms are highly successful. Why should this be? This question lies at the heart of the nature side of the nature-nurture debate on competitive advantage. What is it about individual companies that makes them successful, aside from the issue of industry structure? How do they create competitive advantage?

Porter's approach to this question focuses on corporate strategy. He explores three mutually exclusive generic corporate strategies: cost leadership, differentiation, and focus. Each style requires a radically different arrangement of resources. Cost leadership relies on discipline and tight control of the production process. Creativity, marketing, and brand image, on the other hand, drive differentiation. Focus involves achieving a local, versus an industry-wide, advantage.

The "resource view" of the firm backs up one step from corporate strategy and searches for "assets, capabilities, competencies, organizational processes, firm attributes, information, or knowledge,"[3] which can convey and sustain a competitive advantage. Firms are free to choose a corporate strategy. But in the resource view, corporate strategy cannot be executed successfully unless the firm has necessary "assets," both tangible and intangible.

Probably both Porter and the resource view proponents would agree on the key to sustainable competitive advantage:

A company can outperform its rivals only if it can establish a difference it can preserve.

First, outperformance requires that a company establish that their products or services are different from their rivals. Sustainable advantage requires a company to do different things, or to do things differently, from its competitors.[4] Then that difference, once established, must be preserved.

THE PORTER APPROACH: COST LEADERSHIP, DIFFERENTIATION, AND FOCUS

Porter presents three generic strategies for establishing competitive difference:

■ Cost leadership
■ Differentiation
■ Focus[5]

A cost leader strives to be the lowest-cost producer while selling its product at or near the industry average price. In a differentiation strategy, on the other hand, the firm seeks to be unique in its industry, allowing it to charge premium prices in excess of the extra costs of uniqueness. Finally, a focused strategy requires the firm to concentrate on a narrow competitive segment to the exclusion of others, in the hope of achieving a local, rather than industry-wide, competitive advantage. A cost focuser seeks a local cost advantage over rivals, and a differentiation focuser a local difference.

Cost Leadership: The World of Metal Desks

Upon first reading Porter's *Competitive Strategy*, I was struck by his description of the harsh discipline imposed by a cost leadership strategy. Real cost leadership requires an in-the-trenches, slug-it-out-for-every-penny mentality. On Wall Street such a cost focus is sometimes known, perhaps a bit arrogantly, as a "metal-desk strategy." The drive for scale and efficiency must be relentless. Organizations built around cost efficiency must minimize agency and influence costs, requiring tighter controls and a narrower field of play for management. Investments in product design, process, and manufacturing efficiency are continuous. Marketing must be ruthless, unprofitable customers eliminated, and distribution costs controlled.

Cost leadership is often driven by efficiencies of firm size, scale, scope, and cumulative experience ("learning curve") although factors independent of size may be at work (Figure 4–1). Achieving cost advantages through economies of scale may require the firm to capture significant market share,[6] yielding not only production but also purchasing economies. Extending the firm's scope by serving more than one industry segment or customer group can build volume and efficiency.[7]

In addition to the more familiar size, scope, and experience strategy, Porter discusses other principal "cost drivers," a partial list of which appears below:

■ *Linkages:* Relationships between the firm's functional areas, or between the firm and its customers and/or suppliers, may be

FIGURE 4–1

Cost leadership arises from both scale- and non-scale-related factors.

Source: David Besanko, David Dravove, and Mark Shanley, Economics of Strategy, Copyright © 1996. Reprinted by permission of John Wiley & Sons, Inc.

exploited to increase cost efficiency. For example, higher precision parts from a supplier may reduce the need for after-production inspection and adjustment. Or a just-in-time delivery program may reduce inventory costs. In addition, such linkages may enhance the sustainability of cost leadership because "competitors often fail to recognize their presence or are incapable of harnessing them."[8]

- *Timing:* Firms may be able to build volume and brand more cheaply by early market entry simply because of the absence of significant competitors. On the other hand, later movers can purchase the latest equipment and perhaps avoid heavy development costs borne by first movers.[9]

- *Policy choices:* It certainly makes sense for an aspiring cost leader to develop product designs, manufacturing processes, and a distribution system with a strong attention to cost. But more than that, the firm's culture—its physical environment, employee amenities and compensation, and administrative procedures—can be built around cost consciousness. To quote Porter, "Such policy choices not only reduce costs in their own right but also seem to have important symbolic value."[10]

Cost leadership is not a choice for every product and industry. In fact, it lends itself best only under particular economic conditions[11]:

- Economies of scale or experience are significant but unexploited. Clearly, if these economies are already exploited, volume must be built in the face of larger competitors.
- The potential for the enhancement of product benefits is minimal. This is probably a good description of a "commodity product." On the other hand, the product must be seen as "comparable or acceptable by buyers."[12]
- Buyers are price sensitive.
- The product is a "search" rather than an "experience" good. A *search good* has features that are obvious to the buyer at purchase, such as basic commodities. An *experience good*, usually a more complex product, must be used for its features to be obvious.

Differentiation: Valuable Distinctions

A firm differentiates itself from its competitors if it can be unique at something valuable to buyers.[13]

With a differentiation strategy, the seller attempts to enhance his or her products' benefits versus those of his or her rivals. Differentiation is usually costly[14] because the firm incurs expense to achieve a unique position. A differentiator does not ignore these costs; they are simply not its primary strategic focus.[15] The strategy can be successful if the value perceived by buyers exceeds the costs of differentiation.[16]

Differentiation might be expressed in product, service, or sales and/or delivery features (Figure 4–2). Or benefit enhancement may be subtler, aimed at the buyers' expectations and perceptions—for example, the manufacturer's reputation for quality, service, or financial strength. Alternatively, the subjective image of the product can be enhanced through advertising, packaging, or the quality of its retailers.[17]

Differentiation works better in the following circumstances[18]:

- Buyers are willing to pay a premium price for differences. Differences will be valuable to buyers if they (1) lower the buyers' costs, or (2) raise performance.[19]
- Scale economies are minimal, or they exist but are already exploited.

FIGURE 4-2

Differentiation flows from both tangible and
subjective strategies.

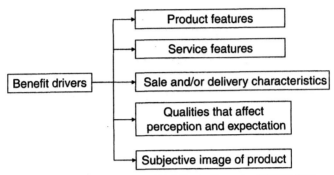

Source: David Besanko, David Dravove, and Mark Shanley, Economics of Strategy, Copyright © 1996. Reprinted by permission of John Wiley & Sons, Inc.

■ The product is an experience good. To differentiate a search
good, one is forced to change characteristics that are obvious
at purchase, to both buyer and competitors. Preventing
imitation is difficult. But with an experience good, subtle
differences of reputation, image, and reliability are much more
difficult to copy.

Everything to Everybody

"But cost leadership and differentiation are not really distinct strategies,
are they?" This is a comment I hear often from my MBA classes. Porter
argues that the two strategies require such different organizational styles
and objectives that, if adopted concurrently, they would likely undermine
one another (Figure 4–3). He calls this practice strategic "straddling" or
being "caught in the middle," unable to effectively respond to competitive challenges from more focused competitors.

He might also argue that a cost leadership strategy should be dis-
tinguished from a drive for operational effectiveness. Cost leadership is
an organizational style that runs right to the bones of a company. Operational effectiveness, on the other hand, needs to be an objective of
every company—cost leader, differentiator, or focuser, metal desks or
not.

FIGURE 4-3

Cost leadership and differentiation are mutually exclusive strategies.

Cost Leadership   Differentiation

Cost Leadership	Differentiation
• Tight controls • Intense supervision • Efficiency in size, process, or experience • Low-cost distribution; no marginal customers	• Creativity • Intense marketing • Unique technology, process, service, quality • Brand image

THE RESOURCE VIEW: WHAT ABOUT INTERNAL RESOURCES?

The resource view of the firm digs a layer below Porter's generic strategies to address the firm's internal strengths and weaknesses, its capabilities, resources, and skills. In the resource view, the firm's tangible and intangible assets, combined with its experience, produce distinctive capabilities. If the firm can then prevent rivals from imitating its capabilities, it can create persistent resource asymmetries, leading to a sustainable competitive advantage.[20] (See Figure 4-4.)

By "resources" we mean the full range of the firm's assets from its processes, technologies, or locations and more intangible characteristics, like brand names, reputation, and personal relationships. The company's experience with these resources, over time, produces its distinctive capabilities, functions that the firm does better than its competition. If the firm can successfully create impediments to imitation of these capabilities by rivals, it can establish sustainable competitive advantage. Persistent "resource heterogeneity" is therefore a fundamental precursor of sustainable competitive advantage.

SUSTAINING RESOURCE HETEROGENEITY

How can the firm discourage its rivals from imitating a winning strategy? The firm might, for example, base its strategy upon competitive resources

FIGURE 4-4

In the resource view, advantage results from
distinctive capabilities.

Resource View of the Firm

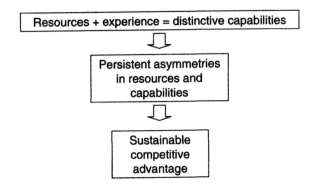

that are scarce, making it difficult for rivals to obtain the means to compete. Examples of these resources might be

- Prime retail store locations
- Skilled workforce (a particular problem in high-tech industries)

Or perhaps the successful firm's resources are "immobile," that is, difficult to package and sell (and therefore difficult to buy), like reputation.

Finally, there may be other "isolating mechanisms"[21] at work. An
isolating mechanism is the resource-level analog of the industry-level
barrier-to-entry concept. But why, if resources are scarce and immobile,
are isolating mechanisms necessary? Because rivals may not need to
imitate a successful firm's resources exactly in order to compete. There
are two primary isolating mechanisms: impediments to imitation and
first-mover advantages.

Impediments to Imitation

A successful firm may be able to sustain advantage through the scarcity
and immobility of its competitive resources, but additional impediments

to imitation can help enormously. Some of these impediments may be tangible:

■ Legal barriers like patents, copyrights, and trademarks.
■ Favorable access to inputs like raw materials, information, or customers.
■ Scale and market share—existing firms may have substantial market share, or the minimum efficient scale for a new entrant might be large relative to market size, or both.

Frankly, in my experience, these tangible impediments themselves are relatively scarce. Certainly, proprietary technologies or patented drugs for pharmaceutical companies qualify as impediments. But what if there are no such barriers? Is it still possible to create impediments for rivals?

There are intangible impediments that can operate as powerfully as their more tangible cousins.[22]

■ *Ambiguity:* It may be difficult for rivals, or even its own management, to reduce the successful firm's advantages to an algorithm, formula, or set of rules.
■ *Historical circumstances:* A firm's advantage may have arisen because of the unique set of competitive circumstances it faced. Rival may find it difficult to imitate the success, out of the context of the successful firm's particular history.
■ *Social complexity:* The successful firm may have developed particularly advantageous relationships, internally among employees and management, or externally with customers and suppliers. Even if rivals are aware of such relationships, it may be difficult to disrupt or reproduce them. Social complexity is, for example, probably one of the principal competitive impediments in the securities and investment banking industries.

First-Mover Advantage

The "first-mover advantage" was batted around frequently in the 1990s venture capital and Internet boom. But what advantage exactly does being the first mover convey? Perhaps there are costs to buyers who switch from the first mover's product to that of a new entrant. This may be true of the first mover's existing customers, but it isn't true of new customers. And there are a lot of new customers in new markets. In fact, a first mover may be reluctant to cede its higher margins to new entrants because it jeopardizes the profitability of its existing customer base, leaving an opening for "second movers." Worse, second movers may wait for a technology or business model to be proven, avoiding a first mover's development costs, and then copy it. Pioneering is, unfortunately, risky business.

But there are other potential advantages of the first mover:

- The learning-curve effect can function as a first-mover advantage. The greater the cumulative experience of the pioneering firm, the greater its potential cost and efficiency advantages over newer firms operating at smaller initial scale. The first mover's lower cost base makes it a formidable pricing threat to would-be competitors and likely discourages imitation.
- With a strong reputation, for quality or service for example, a first mover may discourage customer desertion to new entrants.

Finally, there is my personal favorite, "network externalities." The presence of the first mover's existing installed base may, in itself, make the future purchase of its products much more attractive to new customers. If the use of a word processor is widespread, there are substantial advantages in ease of communication if you use it too. The classic example of a network externality is the fax machine. One fax machine is useless, but if there are many, it makes sense to buy one. This sort of advantage is often called "establishing a standard."

OPERATIONAL EFFECTIVENESS IS NOT STRATEGY

Both the Porter and the resource view require that firms establish a difference between themselves and their rivals. But differences are risky. They may mean departing from standard industry practices and traditions. They require management to gamble on an unproved system. Instead, shouldn't management concentrate on improving what it is already doing? In fact, isn't all this strategy stuff really for dreamers who can't run their businesses? Why not do what everyone else does, but do it better?[23]

A considerable industry has arisen around the notion of doing it better—rather than differently—and achieving operational efficiency, giving rise, for example, to the "best-practices" culture. But, to quote Porter, "operational efficiency is not strategy." Operational efficiency is a necessity for any firm, regardless of its strategy. It is a necessary but insufficient condition for competitive advantage.

What's wrong with operational efficiency as a competitive strategy?

- Best practices diffuse rapidly through an industry. In fact, there are armies of professional consultants who are paid handsomely for spreading best practices throughout an industry.

- Best practices need to be highly specific and focused, so that they can be implemented efficiently. Whoops! Doesn't this mean that competitors can imitate your best practices?

- The best-practices mentality begins, eventually, to make all competitors look alike, a process Porter calls "competitive convergence." Competition becomes more head to head, and customers begin to focus on price as the prime difference among increasingly similar competitors. Margins come under pressure, and returns move toward normal levels in a classic competitive fade.

If everyone runs the same race, nobody wins in the end. In the long run, the pursuit of competitive dominance through operational effectiveness is both unwinnable—because everyone can do it—and destructive of industry profitability to boot. Successful companies need instead to run their own race. Do things differently or do different things:

> Strategy is the creation of a unique and valuable position, involving a different set of activities.[24]

Strategy Runs Deep

Strategy runs deep into a firm's operations. It informs the firm's activities at every level. Strategy tailors the firm to achieve the competitive position it chooses. Because it is bred in the bone, a successful strategy is tough for competitors to imitate. But it is also tough to change. Strategy requires commitment, a limitation of choice, a reduction in flexibility. Strategy is choosing what not to do:

> Strategy is the conscious loss of business.

No wonder it is more comfortable for management to adopt operational efficiency in place of true competitive strategy.

Interlocking Activities

Strategies are far more difficult to imitate if they involve systems of interlocking activities throughout the firm. Operational effectiveness is the achievement of excellence in an individual activity. Strategy is achieving excellence in combining activities.[25]

THE VRIO SYSTEM

Barney's VRIO system tests the power of a firm's resources to achieve sustainable competitive advantage by concentrating upon four issues[26]:

- *Value:* Does the resource allow the firm to respond to external threats and opportunities? If the firm's assets do not ultimately provide value to the buyer, they can produce no sustainable advantage.
- *Rarity:* Do competing firms have the same or similar resources? "Valuable but common (that is, not rare) resources

FIGURE 4–5

Only valuable, rare, costly-to-imitate capabilities can sustain competitive advantage.

Valuable?	Rare?	Costly to imitate?	Exploited by firm?	Competitive implications	Economic performance
No			Yes	Competitive disadvantage	Below normal
Yes	No			Competitive parity	Normal
Yes	Yes	No		Temporary competitive advantage	Temporarily above normal
Yes	Yes	Yes	Yes	Sustainable advantage	Above normal

Source: Jay B. Barney, *Gaining and Sustaining Competitive Advantage,* © 1996. Reprinted by permission of Prentice-Hall, Inc., Upper Saddle River, NJ.

EXAMPLE 4-1

SUSTAINING A COST ADVANTAGE

The VRIO system is wonderful for testing the relative sustainability of the drivers of both cost leadership and differentiation. Assuming that, at least initially, cost advantages are valuable and exploited by the firm, the issue becomes, are they also rare and costly to imitate? If advantages are costly to imitate, what is the source of the cost? Consider a few of the Porter cost leadership drivers in Figure 4-1:

- *Size and scope:* Size- and scope-related advantages are probably the least defensible cost advantages. Information on efficient productive scale is generally well known within an industry. It is not a rare resource. There is nothing inherent about size that prevents competitors from achieving it, although rivals may risk retaliation from incumbents if they should try. Finally, although it may be costly, there is nothing about achieving scale that necessarily puts rivals at a disadvantage to leaders. Scale efficiencies are difficult to hide and to protect.

- *Hard technology:* Hard advantages may be more robust than scale advantages. Although not particularly rare, competitors may take some time to imitate hardware advantages, like new machines or processes. The principal impediments to imitation are ambiguity (competitors may not know exactly how a particular process works) and social complexity (competitors' organizations may be ill suited to adopt new hardware because, for example, of established work rules).

- *Soft technology:* "Values, beliefs, culture, and teamwork" are much more hardy sources of advantage. Not only are culture-based advantages rarer than either scale or hardware, but also they may have arisen from the firm's unique historical experience.

As an analyst, I attended a presentation by Sandy Weill, now the chairman of Citigroup, explaining his acquisition of the Travelers Insurance Company. He and his managers became most animated when relating their discovery at Travelers of a closet full of operational but unused cell phones. The insurer's claims adjustors used these phones when they were deployed to the field during natural disasters like hurricanes. When not in use, the phones could have been—but were not—deactivated, resulting in excess telephone cost. So deeply was attention to cost embedded in the company that everyone, right up to the chairman, was committed. From

EXAMPLE 4–1 (Continued)

SUSTAINING A COST ADVANTAGE

his initial acquisition of Commercial Credit in the mid-1980s, Weill built
a unique management team focused on acquisition and attention to cost.
Even knowing this, however, could a competitor efficiently duplicate this
culture? Could the values necessary, or the personal relationships required,
be copied and imposed upon a rival's own corporate culture? Tough to
do. In Porter's words, "More often than not, cost leaders have a culture
emanating from senior management that reinforces such behavior." [29]

---

and capabilities are sources of competitive parity, not
competitive advantage." [27]

- *Imitation:* Do firms without this resource face a cost
  disadvantage in acquiring it, versus those firms who already
  have it? Such cost disadvantages accrue because the "have"
  firm's advantages arose out of unique historical circumstances;
  the "have-not" firms cannot determine exactly how the
  capability works ("casual ambiguity"); the have nots cannot
  reproduce the required corporate culture ("social complexity");
  or the have firms possess protective patents.
- *Organization:* Is the firm organized correctly to exploit this
  valuable resource? The firm's reporting structure, management
  control systems, and compensation policies must be geared to
  complement its competitive capabilities. [28]

If a firm's resources can produce nothing of value, even if they are fully
exploited, the firm is at a competitive disadvantage and will achieve
below-normal returns (Figure 4–5, page 94).

The firm that has valuable resources that are not rare will likely
reach competitive parity with its rivals and produce normal returns. On
the other hand, firms with valuable, rare, but imitatible resources will
likely achieve only a temporary competitive advantage until rivals acquire similar resources. This firm's returns will initially, but only temporarily, be above normal. Finally, a firm with valuable, rare,
costly-to-imitate, and properly exploited resources can achieve competitive advantage (Examples 4–1 and 4–2; see pages 95–96 and 97).

EXAMPLE 4–2

SUSTAINING DIFFERENTIATION

Like cost leadership, some of the drivers of a successful differentiation strategy, even if they are valuable and exploited by the firm, are likely more sustainable than others (see Figure 4–2).

- *Product features:* If product features are clear to buyers, and they have to be, they are also clear to competitors, and are unlikely to be rare for very long. On the other hand, if the differentiator has a cost advantage in the creation of product features, competitors may still be deterred.[30]

- *Qualities that affect perception and/or expectation:* Firms can build unique marketing positions for products that are more difficult to challenge than product features alone. The most important impediment to imitation of these more intangible features is probably ambiguity. It is not always clear why marketing plans work or how to copy them. Still, there is nothing inherent in these perceptual qualities that discourages long-term competitive attack. And differentiation based on "signaling" like advertising is vulnerable to increasing buyer sophistication.[31]

- *Reputation:* Reputation is clearly a rare commodity, attaching as it does to a particular firm. But it is also a costly resource to imitate. First, reputation often grows out of the firm's particular historical circumstances, making it difficult to reproduce overnight. For example, the great London custom shotgun makers Purdey's and Holland and Holland build reputations for workmanship by supplying only the finest quality products since the nineteenth century. But even if it could be imitated, what do you imitate, exactly? Rivals must be able define the exact nature of the reputational advantage. Then, all the complex relationships, with customers and employees, bound up in the firm's reputation, must somehow be duplicated.

In general, the sustainability of a differentiation strategy depends on how many coordinated sources of uniqueness it has. "Differentiation that results from coordinated actions in many value activities will be more durable, since it requires wholesale changes in competitor behavior to imitate."[32]

FIGURE 4–6

The dynamic competitive view reconciles the nature-nurture
conflict in strategy analysis.

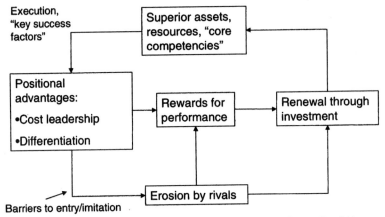

Barriers to entry/imitation

Source: George S. Day and David J. Reibstein, *Wharton on Dynamic Competitive Strategy,* Copyright
© 1997. Reprinted by permission of John Wiley & Sons, Inc.

A DYNAMIC VIEW: RENEWAL AND EROSION
OF ADVANTAGE

The Porter view, based upon strategic positioning, and the resource view,
driven by internal firm competencies, are neatly reconciled by a dynamic
view of competitive advantage. In the dynamic view, sustaining competitive advantage is a long-run, iterative process placing on the firm
continuing demands for investment, management energy, and foresight.[33]
(See Figure 4–6.)

In the dynamic view of the competitive process, the firm's superior
assets, resources, and capabilities are the sources of positional advantages. Positional advantages erode because of efforts by competitors to
imitate the firm's success, they are sustained by the barriers to entry and/
or impediments to imitation available, and they are renewed by investment.

In spite of the best competitive efforts, however, sustainable advantage is probably a temporary condition. The easiest advantages to imitate,
price and product innovation and/or features, are quickly copied. Even
knowledge of advantageous internal processes and relationships eventually diffuses into the industry. If there is a key to competitive success, it

is to break out of the iterative cycle, change the game's rules, and do something differently.[34]

NOTES

[1] Michael E. Porter, *On Competition,* Harvard Business Review Books, Boston, 1998, p. 40.

[2] Ibid., p. 39.

[3] Jay B. Barney, *Gaining and Sustaining Competitive Advantage,* Addison-Wesley Publishing Company, Reading, Mass., 1997, p. 142.

[4] Porter, *On Competition,* p. 40.

[5] The discussion of generic corporate strategies is drawn from Michael E. Porter, *Competitive Strategy,* The Free Press, New York, 1980.

[6] Ibid., p. 36.

[7] David Besanko, David Dranove, and Mark Shanley, *Economics of Strategy,* Wiley, New York, 1996, p. 505.

[8] Porter, *Competitive Strategy,* p. 76.

[9] Ibid., p. 80.

[10] Ibid., p. 105.

[11] Besanko, Dranove, and Shanley, *Economics of Strategy,* p. 471.

[12] Porter, *Competitive Advantage,* p. 13.

[13] Ibid., p. 119.

[14] Ibid., p. 127.

[15] Porter, *Competitive Strategy,* p. 37.

[16] Porter, *Competitive Advantage,* p. 153.

[17] Besanko, Dranove, and Shanley, *Economics of Strategy,* p. 522.

[18] Ibid., p. 472.

[19] Porter, *Competitive Advantage,* p. 131.

[20] This discussion is drawn largely from Besanko, Dranove, and Shanley, *Economics of Strategy.*

[21] Ibid., *Economics of Strategy,* p. 546.

[22] Ibid., p. 552.

[23] The discussion on operational effectiveness is drawn from Porter's *On Competition* and an unpublished speech to J.P. Morgan management in January 1998.

[24] Porter, *On Competition,* p. 55.

[25] Ibid., p. 63.

[26] The VRIO discussion is drawn from Barney, *Gaining and Sustaining Competitive Advantage,* pp. 145–173.

[27] Ibid., p. 148.

[28] Ibid., p. 160.

[29] Porter, *Competitive Advantage*, p. 99.

[30] Ibid., p. 159.

[31] Ibid.

[32] Ibid.

[33] George S. Day, "Maintaining the Competitive Edge: Creating and Sustaining Advantages in Dynamic Competitive Environments," in *Wharton on Dynamic Competitive Strategy*, by George S. Day and David J. Reibstein, Wiley, New York, 1997, p. 53.

CHAPTER 5

Fundamentals of Stock Behavior

- In an efficient stock market, no investor can consistently exploit differences between stock price and value. Although in such a market, a stock's price can and frequently does differ from its value, differences are small and short-lived. There are no systematic means to determine the timing, extent, or direction of such differences. In an efficient market, overvaluation is as likely as undervaluation.

- The efficiency of the stock market is the subject of seemingly endless academic debate, and a full treatment of this debate is beyond the scope of this book. There is evidence, however, that over the longer run, the market systematically overestimates the persistence of financial returns.

- In such an overly persistent market, stocks carrying the highest investor expectations tend, on average, to underperform when compared to those with the lowest expectations.

- Investment styles have arisen in an attempt to exploit potential biases in the market. The *value style* focuses on stocks that carry low investor expectations. The *growth style* centers on stocks with high investor expectations. The *momentum style* attempts to exploit the market's stock buying and selling behavior.

If it is the goal of equity analysts to exploit the difference between a stock's price and its value, then such differences had better exist, be reasonably persistent, and be discoverable by our analytic techniques, or we, as a profession, are out of luck. These issues are at the core of the debate over the *efficient market hypothesis* (EMH) that rages incessantly in the academic media. In spite of what appear to be recent serious challenges to the theory, researchers have reached no definitive conclusion on the EMH. That said, it is beyond the scope of this book, not to mention the author's knowledge, to present the details of this struggle. Nevertheless, based on years of staring at stock quotes, it is my unscientific belief that persistent departures of stock prices from value do exist. This chapter provides a conceptual framework for understanding such departures.

In an efficient stock market, competitive forces are so strong and arbitrage so effective that price-value differences, resulting perhaps from new information, are very rapidly dissipated. There is no information or technique available that can provide reliable insight into the fairness of any stock's valuation (*fairness* in this case meaning that value and price are equal). Efficient markets are also *unbiased,* meaning that stock price is an unbiased indicator of value. Why are efficient markets unbiased? Because investors rapidly discover and bid away any systematic bias in stock pricing.[1] This doesn't mean that stocks in an efficient market are at all times fairly valued. It means, rather, that competition tends to restrict stock price in a corridor around fair value, and, within that corridor, stocks are as likely to be overvalued as undervalued.

If this is true, it isn't good news for equity analysts. In efficient markets, investment strategies cannot, in the long run, consistently outperform the market return. Again, this doesn't mean that some investment strategies will not outperform others, or even outperform the market. It means that there is no reliable way, a priori, to tell a successful from an unsuccessful investment strategy.

But suppose there was evidence that pricing biases do persist in the stock market? Then, the EMH may not apply, and, happily:

- Stock prices may very well move significantly away from value for long periods of time.
- There ought to be analytic techniques capable of revealing these misvaluations.
- Some investment strategies may be better than others.

Researchers think they have found evidences of such persistent biases, like overreaction, weekend and January effects, too much volatility (or too little), and other so-called anomalies. In the long run, of course, researchers are speaking in front of the children, and the children are listening. Biases, once discovered, should disappear through the action of competitive forces.

Bear in mind, however, that even if systematic departures from fair value do exist, and can be identified, it may still be very difficult to profit from this knowledge. Why this difficulty exists is discussed below.

A THOUGHT EXPERIMENT: THE HAUGEN METHODOLOGY

Haugen provides a wonderfully vivid method for visualizing potential stock pricing biases.[2] Better still, this method predicts the outcome of stock price research under conditions of bias.

The Growth Horizon

We argued in Chapter 2 that a stock's value is a function of the length of time it produces investment returns in excess of (or less than) its cost of equity, the "normal" return. Once available returns on incremental investments reach a normal level, further company growth cannot add to the value of its stock. The Haugen method refers to this profitable period as the "true growth horizon." The value of the stock is a function of its true growth horizon.

The stock price, on the other hand, contains the market's best estimate of the true growth horizon, called the "perceived growth horizon." In an efficient stock market, arbitrage should, on average, confine the perceived growth horizon to a region around the true. The stock's price, driven by the perceived growth horizon, should then be an unbiased indicator of its value, containing the true growth horizon. Figure 5–1 presents a (slightly modified) Haugen view of the true growth horizon as a sharp cut-off, beyond which further growth cannot add to value.

The graph pictures two firms, one of which produces returns on capital at relative rates above the average, the second below the average. Both stocks revert suddenly to normal returns at the same future time. For the above-average performer, the "growth stock," we expect competitive processes to gradually eliminate profitable investment opportunities, driving returns to the average at competitive equilibrium. For the below-average performer, the "value stock," competition should permit incremental profitable investment—because below-average returns cause

FIGURE 5-1

Stock prices contain a perceived growth horizon.

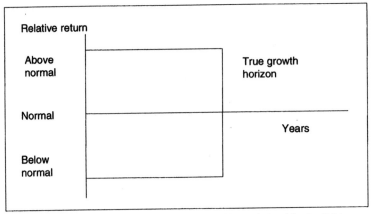

Source: Robert A. Haugen, *The New Finance,* © 1995. Reprinted by permission of Prentice-Hall, Inc., Upper Saddle River, NJ.

competitors to depart—again driving growth to the average. Undoubtedly the process is somewhat more gradual than Figure 5–1 implies, with abnormal growth approaching normal levels over a number of years.

The distinction between growth and value stocks is important. Growth stocks are the market's current high performers. They have good-looking financial statements, good press, and are producing substantial value. Their stock prices are often rising, and expectations for future performance are high. Many growth stocks are larger companies. Value stocks, on the other hand, are the market's laggards. Recent financial performance has been poor and press comments negative. The stocks have often fallen, producing nasty-looking charts. Frequently, value stocks are smaller companies, financial services, consumer cyclicals, or utilities.

In this graphical representation of an efficient market, departures of price from value are random and unexploitable. But suppose that the perceived growth horizon were to depart systematically from the true? Suppose that over long periods of time the market were to hold expectations for profitable growth that were biased, either too high or too low? How would returns on our hypothetical growth and value stocks be likely to differ?

Zero Perceived Growth Horizon: The Graham and Dodd View

Suppose we were to attribute no profitable growth potential to a stock? If the market accepted this assertion, stock prices would be based solely upon the existing level of profitability, ignoring even current growth trends. This is the viewpoint espoused in the original Graham and Dodd (G&D) formulation:

> The analyst's philosophy must still compel him to base his investment valuation on an assumed earnings power no larger than the company has already achieved in some year of normal business. Investment value can be related only to demonstrated performance.[3]

Consider the consequences of this no-growth philosophy. If the true growth horizon were anything greater than zero, and that's certainly been a good guess historically, the value of stocks with positive growth potential would consistently exceed their stock prices. G&D call this difference the "margin of safety," the amount by which (intrinsic) stock value exceeds the stock's market price. Investment in these stocks would, on average, produce superior returns. Investment in value stocks with a below average return, on the other hand, would be very disappointing since their performance would continue to deteriorate well beyond the zero perceived growth horizon.[4]

True Growth Exceeds Perceived: Growth Stocks Prosper

In fact, as long as the perceived growth horizon is lower than the true, growth stock investment is likely to produce superior returns, and value stock investment inferior returns (Figure 5–2):

- If the market underestimates the length of the true growth horizon, superior growth continues for longer than expected, and growth stock prices lag their values. Growth stocks prices, in this case, do not express their actual growth potential. Growth stocks are relative bargains, and growth stock investment produces above-average returns.

FIGURE 5-2

When true growth potential exceeds that contained in stock
prices, growth stocks produce superior returns.

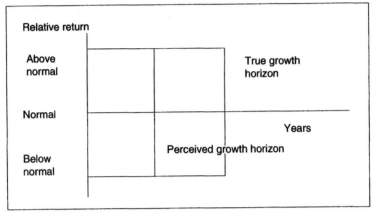

Source: Robert A. Haugen, *The New Finance,* © 1995. Reprinted by permission of Prentice-Hall, Inc.,
Upper Saddle River, NJ.

■ At the same time, the market underestimates the persistence of
inferior performance, and value stock prices exceed their
values. Value stocks are generally overpriced in this market,
and value stock investment produces below-average returns.

Perceived Growth Exceeds True Growth: Value Stocks Prosper

Let's consider the opposite market bias, in which perceived growth horizons consistently exceed true. How will growth and value stocks
behave?

In this case, the market believes that both good performance and
poor performance will persist for longer than it actually will (Figure
5-3):

■ The market will tend to overprice growth stocks in the
mistaken belief that strong performance will persist.
Investments in growth stocks will produce inferior returns.

■ In the value stock case, the market's belief in the persistence
of poor performance leads to underpricing of value stocks.
Investments in value stocks will produce superior returns.

FIGURE 5-3

When perceived growth exceeds true growth potential, growth stocks produce disappointing returns.

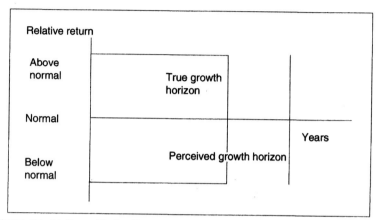

Source: Robert A. Haugen, The New Finance, © 1995. Reprinted by permission of Prentice-Hall, Inc., Upper Saddle River, NJ.

The Theory's Predictions

Like all legitimate scientific inquiries, we now have a theory of stock market behavior that produces testable predictions.

If markets are efficient, the perceived growth horizon is an unbiased indicator of the true horizon. Competitive forces confine perceived horizons in a range around the true. Deviations of stock price from value are random and unsystematic. No analytic methods can consistently identify underpriced stocks. Returns on stock investment should then be ordered according to risk, as measured by beta in the capital asset pricing model (CAPM), with higher-risk investments producing higher returns.

But if the stock market is biased, then perceived growth horizons may differ systematically from true growth horizons and stock prices may persistently differ from values. It should be possible to identify stocks likely to produce superior investment results. Also, some investment styles may be more effective than others.

If the market's bias is to underestimate true growth potential, stock prices will indicate underreaction. Investment in growth stocks should produce superior returns because prices will not initially reflect the growth stock's true performance potential. Value stocks, on the other hand, will be consistently overpriced and produce inferior investment returns.

On the other hand, if the market persistently overestimates growth potential, stock prices will show evidence of overreaction. Growth stocks will be overpriced and produce inferior returns. Value stocks will be underpriced and are likely to produce superior investment returns.

If the market is biased, the CAPM, in its current form, will produce poor estimates of actual equity returns. Risk, as expressed by beta, will not be the sole driver of equity costs. Other factors could have equal or greater performance.

THE EVIDENCE SUGGESTS MARKET BIAS IS REAL, MAYBE

With the caveat that controversy persists over these points, there is research evidence which suggests the following:

- The market can accurately distinguish value from growth stocks through stock pricing. Further, both value and growth stock financial performance tends to approach normal levels ("revert to the mean"), consistent with the Haugen growth horizon model.
- Contrary to the behavior of the stock market in the late 1990s, longer-term studies show that value stocks have outperformed growth stocks. Differences in performance are not explained by the stocks' betas.
- Valuations based upon the CAPM are relatively poor predictors of investment performance. Predictive power is substantially enhanced by other stock attributes.

This evidence is consistent with the presence of market bias. Specifically, although the market can differentiate between value and growth stocks and is aware of mean reversion, it may nevertheless tend to overestimate true growth horizons, leading to overpricing of growth stocks and poor growth stock investment performance. The market's initial (erroneous) perceptions are borne out by strong near-term financial performance of growth stocks, but eventually, growth stock earnings disappoint, leading to poor subsequent investment returns.

Mean Reversion Is Real: The Christmas Tree

We've argued that competition drives financial performance toward a normal return, a process called *mean reversion*. In fact, the Haugen growth horizon methodology presumes mean reversion. Fortunately, mean reversion is real. Further, the market is skilled at identifying potential good and poor performers.

The Fuller, Huberts, and Levinson (FHL) "Christmas tree" is graphic evidence of mean reversion.[5] In the FHL study,

- At the end of March in each year from 1973 through 1990, FHL ranked firms by their previous year's earnings/price ratio. The E/P ratio is the reciprocal of the more familiar P/E. A low E/P ratio is associated with a more richly priced stock. The FHL presumption is that, if the market price is high relative to current earnings, that the market expects strong future earnings growth. Market valuation is used here as a proxy for the market's financial performance expectations, which, as Haugen points out, aren't published anywhere— more's the pity.

- The 20 percent of companies with the largest E/P go into the first group, the next 20 percent in the second, and so on.

- FHL then follow the relative rates of earnings growth in all groups for the next eight years.

The result is the "Christmas tree" graph, as shown in Figure 5–4. We move into the future as we move up the tree. The horizontal presents the growth in earnings per share relative to the middle quint.

High growers ("growth" stocks) with low E/P ratios (high valuations) are to the right. Low growers ("value" stocks) with high E/P ratios are to the left. Clearly, the stocks the market identifies initially as growth stocks do outperform value stocks, but by a steadily declining margin. By the fifth or sixth year, the growth performances of both growth and value stocks have reverted to more normal levels.

FHL makes clear that financial performance does revert to normal, in this case over 5 to 6 years.

Current stock prices are, in general, decent indicators of future financial performance. Stock prices of growth stocks are relatively higher than stock prices of value stocks.

But as Haugen points out, distinguishing growth from value stocks is not the issue. We want to know whether the market has priced subsequent growth and mean reversion *correctly.* Or does the market make systematic errors in its estimate of growth horizons, leading to mispricing of stocks?

FIGURE 5-4

The Christmas tree demonstrates the stock market's skill in
picking superior performers.

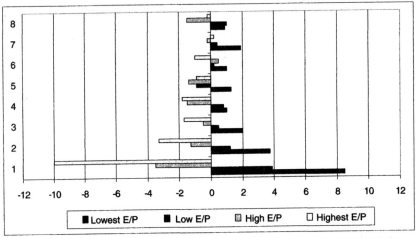

Source: R. J. Fuller, L. C. Huberts, and M. J. Levinson, "Returns to E/P Strategies: Higgledy-Piggledy Growth; Analysts' Forecast Errors; and Omitted Risk Factors," Exhibit 6, *Journal of Portfolio Management,* Winter 1993.

Fama and French Strike a Blow:
The Case for Overreaction

In their now-famous 1992 *Journal of Finance* paper, Fama and French
(F&F) strike the unbiased market hypothesis a nasty blow.[6] In the F&F
study, investments in value stocks, which (according to the Christmas
tree) the market can accurately identify as having lower future earnings
power, produce higher returns than similar growth stock investments
(Figure 5–5). This result is consistent with the overreaction hypothesis:
The market's growth horizon expectations may simply exceed reality, at
least over the period of the study. Growth stock prices are therefore bid
up to levels above what can be justified by their true performance potential. Value stock prices, in the meantime, reflect too negative a view
of future performance.[7]

What is worse for the market-efficiency folks is that these return
differences are not explained by differences in risk as measured by the
stocks' betas. In fact, F&F's value stocks, which have initial lower valuations evidenced by higher book value to price multiples, actually have
lower composite betas (Figure 5–6).

FIGURE 5–5

Fama and French's results indicate superior value stock returns.

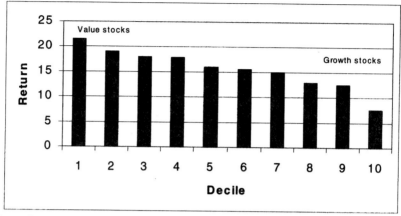

Source: E. Fama and K. French, "The Cross-section of Expected Stock Returns," *The Journal of Finance,* V. 47 (1992). © American Finance Association.

FIGURE 5–6

Value stocks, the superior performers, actually have lower betas.

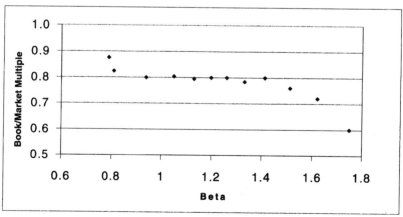

Source: E. Fama and K. French, "The Cross-section of Expected Stock Returns," *The Journal of Finance,* V. 47 (1992). © American Finance Association.

A portfolios of value stocks, according to F&F, generated superior returns without a consequent increase in risk, as measured by CAPM's beta, another disturbing conclusion for EMH advocates. But if beta isn't the determinant of return differences, as it should be under CAPM, then perhaps there are other factors that contribute.

Jacobs and Levy: Other Equity Attributes

Jacobs and Levy (J&L) suggest that other "equity attributes," besides a traditional value measure like the dividend discount model (DDM), have substantial explanatory power in stock returns.[8]

Using a multiple regression technique, J&L tested a variety of equity attributes gathered from 1183 large capitalization stocks from June 1982 to June 1987, including:

- Valuation measures like low P/E
- Simple ratios like cash flow to stock price and sales to stock price
- Dividend yield
- Beta, sigma (unsystematic risk), and skewness of return distribution
- Size
- Momentum-like measures like downward earnings estimate revisions, estimate controversy, trends in earnings estimates, and number of analysts following the stock

Regression analysis against actual returns shows the surprisingly strong explanatory power of attributes other than DDM value. As surprising as the power of other equity attributes is the weakness of DDM measures in explaining stock returns, consistent with F&F's findings on beta.[9] (See Table 5–1.)

Robert Shiller, in his book *Irrational Exuberance*,[10] presents more disturbing, and hence persuasive, evidence of the DDM model's weak predictive power. Shiller calculates the real value of dividends paid subsequent to each year from 1871 to 1979 by stocks in the S&P Composite Stock Price Index, after making an assumption about dividends after the last actual year. According to the EMH, the stock price is "supposed to be the optimal prediction, using the information available in that year,

TABLE 5–1

Traditional value measures like DDM explain little of
return variation

	Adjusted Average R^2
Value (DDM) alone	0.37
Value and low P/E	3.38
Value and simple ratios	8.94
Value and all attributes	43.93

of the dividend present value shown for the same year."[11] In fact, stock prices appear exceptionally bad at predicting subsequent dividend flows. As Shiller says, "We see no such tendency of stock price to forecast the dividend present value; the dividend present value is not doing anything exceptionally dramatic, whereas the stock price is jumping around a great deal."[12] Now, it may be that, over the past century, investors were simply wrong, that they expected long-run dividend fluctuations that did not in fact occur. Or, it may be that there are powerful forces driving stock prices outside of the DDM. Interestingly, by Shiller's method, the most spectacular overvaluation of stocks in the past century, compared to a realistic forecast of future dividend trends, occurred in the late 1990s. The bubble burst in 2000.

IMPLICATIONS FOR INVESTMENT STYLES

If the stock market's apparent tendency to overestimate the persistence of profitable growth is real, investment styles that exploit this bias should produce superior returns. But exactly how? Again, Haugen's formulation can be of substantial help.[13]

Instead of the growth-horizon thought experiment, consider Figure 5–7 with two axes: perceived future abnormal profit on the horizontal and true future abnormal profit on the vertical. Perceived abnormal profit is incorporated into a stock's price and measures the market's expectation for future superior—or inferior—financial performance. True abnormal profit is the company's real profit potential and determines its value:

FIGURE 5-7

Along the 45 degree line, stocks are fairly valued.

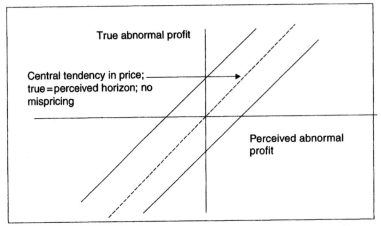

Source: Robert A. Haugen, "The Effects of Imprecision-Bias on the Abilities of Growth and Value Managers to Outperform their Respective Benchmarks," *The Handbook of Equity Style Management, P. D. Coggin, F. J. Fabozzi, and R. D. Arnott (eds). © 1997 Frank J. Fabozzi Associates.

■ Along the 45 degree line, true and abnormal profit are equal, and stock price equals stock value. There is no mispricing.

■ In an efficient market, actual stock prices would be confined to a region around the 45 degree line, depicted by the solid lines in Figure 5–7. Haugen refers to this market as "unbiased but imprecise."

■ In the pricing region above the 45 degree line, true profit exceeds perceived. Growth stocks are underpriced, and value stocks are overpriced.

■ In the pricing region below the 45 degree line, perceived profit exceeds true profit, and growth stocks are overpriced.

Even in this unbiased market it is possible to pick stocks that fall above the central 45 degree line (but within the pricing corridor) and earn superior returns. But it is not possible to pick them consistently. Nevertheless, some investors will probably succeed in doing so.

In a market biased toward overreaction, on the other hand, the central pricing tendency does not lead to equal true and perceived abnormal profit.

Market Bias: Overreaction

Consider, for example, the market in Figure 5–8, in which the central tendency is shifted downward. Stocks with positive perceived abnormal

FIGURE 5-8

An overreaction bias favors the value investment style.

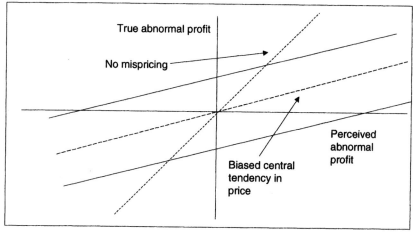

True abnormal profit

No mispricing

Perceived abnormal profit

Biased central tendency in price

profits—growth stocks—lie for the most part below the 45 degree line, meaning that perceived abnormal profit exceeds true profit and the stocks are generally overpriced. Investors and analysts' efforts to pick growth stocks with superior returns will on average result in overpayment and poor returns. The higher the stocks' valuation, given by the perceived abnormal profit, the bigger the potential overpayment. The exception is the small region near the origin, where some growth stocks fall above the central line and will be favorably priced. In fact, strategies to exploit this loophole in the market's bias, called *growth at a reasonable price* (GARP) *strategies,* could be successful when "pure" growth strategies have not:

- A "pure" growth investor is willing to buy a stock at a high price provided he or she believes that the stock's price does not fully reflect its profit and growth potential.

- A GARP investor, on the other hand, is more price sensitive and searches for growth stocks with somewhat lower valuations.

The story is different for value stocks lying to the left of the graph's center line. For the most part these stocks will fall above the 45 degree line, and in this market they will be, on average, underpriced. A "pure" value investor, who will consider value stocks that are substantially out of market favor, will on average produce superior returns.

The Psychology of Overreaction

If the stock market does systematically overreact, exaggerating the persistence of both good and bad financial performance, what can explain such apparent irrationality? Perhaps, as Tvede suggests,[14] investor behavior is just a special case of more general psychological tendencies, and stock prices have more to do with the way we process information and make decisions than with our perceptions of long-term value. Or perhaps not. At any rate, the implications are fun:

- We are more persuaded by a credible source than by a credible argument ("persuasion effect"). The movement of real stock prices is one heck of a lot more convincing than any analyst's calculation of value. This is the "strangers on airplanes" phenomenon of Chapter 1.

- We think that trends we observe are likely to continue ("representativeness effect"). This tendency seems to me to have strong survival value when aiming a spear at fleeing game, but in the stock market it may be less useful.

- We use the behavior of others as our source of information about a subject we find difficult to interpret ("social comparison"). "I don't know why this stock is going up, but it must be a good stock because someone is buying it."

- We avoid or distort information that shows that our assumptions were wrong ("cognitive dissonance"). Tech stocks continued to rise in 1999 in spite of repeated commentary, some of it by respected academics, on their overvaluation. Add to this our misinterpretation of information in a way that confirms our behavior and attitudes ("selective perception").

- "Magical thinking": "We think that certain behavior leads to a desired effect, even when we know of no explanation and when there is in fact none." The trend is your friend, for whatever reason.

- We overestimate the likelihood that we could have predicted the outcome of a past series of events ("hindsight bias"). As Tvede points out, news does not make stock prices; stock prices make the news. Much business news, and analyst commentary, consists of after-the-fact explanations of stock price movements. If the market goes up, the news is good. Simple.

Market Bias: Underreaction

Suppose bias shifts the market's central pricing tendency upward rather than downward, producing an underreaction bias in which the market has systematically underestimated stocks' true abnormal profit potential. In such a market, most growth stocks would lie above the 45 degree center line, making them on average underpriced. Many value stocks, on the other hand, lie below the center line and are overpriced (Figure 5–9).

Investment results in such a market would be the opposite of those in the F&F study. Growth stocks would tend to outperform value stocks, and pure growth strategies would be highly successful. More conservative GARP strategies would falter.

Because of human psychological and analytic inertia, my guess is that the overreactive market is likely to be the more common bias. Projecting trends for longer than they deserve, believing that good stocks

FIGURE 5–9

An underreaction bias, on the other hand, favors growth stock investment.

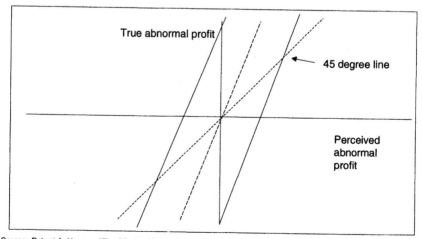

Source: Robert A. Haugen, "The Effects of Imprecision-Bias on the Abilities of Growth and Value Managers to Outperform their Respective Benchmarks," *The Handbook of Equity Style Management,* P. D. Coggin, F. J. Fabozzi, and R. D. Arnott (eds). © 1997 Frank J. Fabozzi Associates.

will stay good and successful investments will remain successful, sticking with stock recommendations longer than is prudent, all seem, to me, to be basic human nature. But perhaps the boom in technology and Internet stocks in the 1990s, and the simultaneous lag in value stock investment performance, was partial evidence of the market's initial failure to appreciate the impact of new technologies. Once that potential was perceived, and initial technology investment returns were so high, the market's bias may have quickly reverted to overreaction. Sharp corrections in technology stock prices in early 2000 could have been the result.

There is in fact evidence that, over periods of 6 to 12 months, the stock market underreacts to information and is slow to incorporate it into stock prices.[15] Jegadeesh and Titman find evidence that over a 6-month time horizon, stock returns are positively autocorrelated. That is, good returns are followed by further good returns, and poor returns by poor.[16]

EFFICIENT AND INEFFICIENT MARKETS

Even if, in spite of this evidence, you believe it, the EMH requires a curious kind of doublethink. On the one hand, according to the EMH, efficient market prices are, at all times, unbiased indicators of true value, and, in the strongest EMH form, no available information can confer an investment advantage. On the other hand, unbiased prices must be maintained by the arbitrage actions of investors "sensing a bargain and putting into effect schemes to beat the market."[17] Sensing a bargain? Beating the market? How do investors "sense a bargain" when no amount of analysis can reliably reveal price deviations from true value? In fact, why would they even try? This inherent contradiction in the EMH is resolved by viewing an efficient market as "a self-correcting mechanism, where inefficiencies appear at regular intervals but disappear almost instantaneously as investors find them and trade on them."[18] In other words, efficient markets must, in order to remain efficient, be periodically inefficient.

Echoing Chapter 3's discussion of trade and production markets, things can go wrong with these self-corrective mechanisms. For example, investors may not rapidly recognize inefficiencies. Or they recognize the inefficiencies but cannot (or will not) trade on them. Or they trade on the inefficiencies, but the trading is insufficient to eliminate price deviations from true value. Under those circumstances, inefficiencies might be persistent and not "disappear almost instantaneously."

If inefficiencies exist, corrective arbitrage methods must fail, at least for a while. Why should this be so? The new field of "behavioral finance" suggests that, in contrast to the tenets of the EMH, real-world arbitrage is risky and therefore limited.[19] There are two potential sources of risk: (1) basis risk and (2) noise trader risk.

In the EMH, arbitrage can be virtually riskless because investors have ready access to close substitutes for the securities they trade. If, for example, a large block of stock A is offered, investors are happy to purchase it at little if any price concession and adjust their portfolios by selling stock B, a close substitute for A, thereby keeping constant the risk of their portfolios. A "close substitute" security has very similar cash flows under all potential scenarios.[20] But if stock B is not a close substitute for A, investors cannot be certain the stock B for A "hedge" will work, and therefore they will have more limited interest in the trade.

Beyond the issue of close substitutes, arbitrageurs with limited time horizons run the risk that any potential stock mispricing gets worse before it gets better, perhaps forcing them to liquidate trades while they are in a loss position. This risk arises from the presence of irrational "noise traders," who trade for reasons other than new information and who make systematic errors, sometimes being too optimistic and sometimes too pessimistic.[21] In the presence of the shifting sentiments of noise traders, risk-averse rational investors may avoid "aggressive arbitrage strategies,"[22] thereby permitting substantial inefficiencies to persist:

- Smithers and Wright cite evidence of the presence of noise traders, noting that there is a strong association between trading volume and changes in stock prices.[23] In an efficient market, the authors point out, such an association should not exist because prices change only on new information, and the timing of new information has no necessary correlation with stock trading volume.

- Thaler notes that persistent differences between the values of closed-end mutual funds and their underlying assets may be evidence of noise trading and the failure of arbitrage mechanisms.[24] The actions of noise traders mean that "the demand for securities can influence the price, even if that demand is based on irrational beliefs."

IF YOU'RE SO SMART, WHY AREN'T YOU RICH?

In my mind, one of the most serious indictments of the market bias hypothesis is the underperformance of professional investment management. Why, if biases exist, do professionals not discover them and consistently outperform market averages?

Haugen suggests that professional investment managers underperform because, in short, value investing is unattractive.[25] Value investment returns may require more time to mature than the one- to three-year time horizon of many managers and, more particularly, investment management consultants. Value stocks are ugly, and clients may be uncomfortable with them. And, finally, professional managers are concerned with their relative, not absolute, performance. If a growth stock manager does well versus other growth stock managers, he or she will keep his or her job, in spite of long-term underperformance of the strategy.

J&L suggest some other reasons:

- *Reliance on the "home run":* Many managers rely on picking a relatively few big winners, ignoring the singles and doubles investments. Such a strategy is unlikely to provide sufficient return to outperform the market simply because no manager can hit that many homers.

- *Cognitive bias:* Perhaps professional managers are as susceptible to market biases as everyone else, and they are at risk of becoming noise traders themselves. Investment fads, a tendency to accept company managements' pronouncements, or overconfidence could all lead to poor stock selections.

- *Lack of discipline:* Often called "style drift," managers move away from their original investment objections in search of return, often placing risk in a secondary position.[26]

Essentially, the indictment of the market bias hypothesis is this: If in an efficient market no investor can consistently outperform, then in an inefficient market, some investors, especially smart professional investors, should consistently outperform. If they do not, the market is likely efficient. But what if this is not true? What if stock markets are both inefficient and, nevertheless, tough to make money in? How could this be?

One answer to this dilemma is that, given the imperfection of available arbitrage methods that we previously discussed, simply identifying market inefficiency does not mean it can be successfully exploited. Mispricing can only be exploited if it is corrected reasonably quickly (meaning within the practical time horizon of the arbitrageur). If amplified by noisy markets, mispricing can worsen, fooling even the smart investor who is "right" about underlying value. This uncertainty limits the professional's ability to profit from the market's misperceptions of value.[27] To paraphrase an old highway safety commercial, a smart investor may be right—dead right—about value.

MAYBE KEYNES WAS RIGHT

If stock market bias is real, perhaps Keynes was right to characterize it as a "beauty contest":

> [I]nvestment based upon genuine long term expectations is so. . . difficult as to be scarcely practical. He who attempts it must surely. . . run greater risks than he who tries to guess better than the crowd how the crowd will behave.[28]

The idea, then, is not to pick the best stock, based upon long-term valuation techniques, but to pick the stock that the market is likely to think is best. Or to avoid that stock when it becomes too popular.

Shliefer points out that the Keynesian investor, exploiting behavior of noise traders, could adopt "positive feedback investment strategies," buying when prices rise and selling when they fall. Aware that noise traders chasing a trend can sustain a stock price rise, the positive feedback investor buys, assisting the price rise and further encouraging the noise traders. In such a case, the smart money, rather than "leaning against" noise traders, actually exacerbates stock price inefficiencies. Such a mechanism may underlie stock price bubbles.[29]

NOTES

[1] Aswath Damodaran, *On Valuation,* Wiley, New York, 1997.

[2] Robert A. Haugen, *The New Finance: The Case Against Efficient Markets,* Prentice-Hall, Englewood Cliffs, N.J., 1995.

[3] Haugen, *The New Finance,* quoting from B. Graham and D. Dodd, *Security Analysis,* 3rd ed., McGraw-Hill, New York, 1951, pp. 422–423.

[4] Cottle Sidney, Roger F. Murray, and Frank E. Block, *Graham and Dodd's Security Analysis,* 5th ed., McGraw-Hill, New York, 1988. By the Fifth Edition, the authors

had backed off the original no-growth philosophy. They admit that, if analysis projected an EPS no higher than the company had already achieved, investors might be forced "to remain on the sidelines with their funds uninvested for extended periods, if the market itself is priced on a basis of expectations of future earnings that do exceed previous peak earnings." The authors attribute this change to higher modern rates of inflation and earnings growth.

[5] Presented in Haugen, *The New Finance*, p. 51, from the paper by R. J. Fuller, L. C. Huberts, and M. J. Levinson, "Returns to E/P Strategies; Higgledy Piggledy Growth; Analysts' Forecast Errors; and Omitted Risk Factors," *Journal of Portfolio Management*, Winter 1993, Exhibit 6.

[6] E. Fama, and K. French, "The Cross-section of Expected Stock Returns," *The Journal of Finance*, June 1992.

[7] Haugen, *The New Finance*, fig. 1.1, p. 4.

[8] Bruce I. Jacobs and Kenneth N. Levy, *Equity Management: Quantitative Analysis for Stock Selection*, McGraw-Hill, New York, 2000, pp. 103–133.

[9] Ibid., p. 121.

[10] Robert J. Shiller, *Irrational Exuberance*, Princeton University Press, 2000.

[11] Ibid., p. 185.

[12] Ibid., p. 186.

[13] Robert A. Haugen, *The Inefficient Stock Market*, Prentice-Hall, Englewood Cliffs, N.J., 1999, pp. 95–109; and Robert A. Haugen, "The Effects of Imprecision and Bias on the Abilities of Growth and Value Managers to Out-perform Their Respective Benchmarks," in *The Handbook of Equity Style Management*, 2d ed., edited by T. Daniel Coggin, Frank J. Fabozzi, and Robert D. Arnott, Frank J. Fabozzi Associates, New Hope, Penn., 1997.

[14] Lars Tvede, *The Psychology of Finance*, Wiley, New York, 1999, pp. 94–96.

[15] Andrei Schliefer, *Inefficient Markets: An Introduction to Behavioral Finance*, Oxford University Press, New York, 2000, pp. 114–120.

[16] N. Jegadeesh and S. Titman, "Returns to Buying Winners and Selling Losers: Implications for Stock Market Efficiency," *Journal of Finance*, 48 (1993):65–91. See, for example, Haugen, *The Inefficient Stock Market*, or Schliefer, *Inefficient Markets*, for discussions of the Jegadeesh and Titman results.

[17] Damodaran, *On Valuation*, p. 149.

[18] Ibid.

[19] Schliefer, *Inefficient Markets*, p. 13.

[20] Ibid., p. 8.

[21] Richard H. Thaler, *The Winner's Curse*, Princeton University Press, Princeton, N.J., 1992, p. 178.

[22] Ibid., p. 179.

[23] Andrew Smithers and Stephen Wright, *Valuing Wall Street*, McGraw-Hill, New York, 2000, p. 298.

[24] Thaler, *The Winner's Curse*, pp. 179–181.

[25] Haugen, *The New Finance,* pp. 111–114.

[26] Jacobs and Levy, *Equity Management,* pp. 4–8.

[27] Andrei Shliefer, "Are Markets Efficient? No, Arbitrage Is Inherently Risky," *The Wall Street Journal,* December 28, 2000, p. A10.

[28] J. M. Keynes, *The General Theory of Employment, Interest, and Money,* Harcourt, U.K., 1936. Quoted in Tvede, *Psychology of Finance.*

[29] Schliefer, *Inefficient Markets,* p. 156.

PART TWO

The Basic Tools

Reading a Financial Statement: The Accuracy, Sustainability, and Predictability of Financial Information

- Reading a financial statement is the analyst's basic art. And like any art, there are as many methods as there are analysts. But, regardless of the method, there ought to be three distinct issues addressed in any financial statement analysis: the accuracy, sustainability, and predictability of the financial information itself, the composition of the company's returns, and the capacity of the company for continued investment.

- The quality of financial information has a direct impact on stock valuation. Equity analysts generally prefer financial results that are accurate, sustainable, and predictable.

- Accurate financial information reflects a firm's true underlying economic reality. The GAAP accounting system controls the presentation of financial information and can itself distort business reality. Management estimates and judgments, combined with the impulse to "manage earnings," are second serious sources of distortion. These distortions cannot be permitted into financial models or stock valuation estimates will suffer.

- There are other dimensions of financial information quality beyond unintentional or intentional distortions of financial disclosure. Financial performance of higher quality is sustainable and contains few nonrecurring items. Not only are nonrecurring items not capitalized in valuation but they also introduce an element of uncertainty into the analysis, lowering analysts' confidence.

■ Financial results often fail to meet market or analyst
expectations. These "earnings surprises" can have substantial
impacts—both positive and negative—on stock valuations. The
lower the potential for surprise in financial information, the
higher the predictability of financial performance, and the
higher the quality of the information to the analyst.

Equity analysts hate surprises. After all, analysts trade on their understanding of and insight into the companies they follow. Analysts' credibility lies in their ability to anticipate financial and business developments reliably. They like companies to produce accurate, sustainable, and predictable financial results. With such results, analysts can be more confident in their earnings projections and investment recommendations. Higher confidence probably translates into higher stock valuations. But few businesses are actually so well behaved. Management's efforts to shoehorn unpredictable businesses into predictable forms can lead to manipulation of physical operations, aggressive financial reporting, and even fraud.

Very few corporate events destroy investors' confidence more surely than the misreporting—inadvertent or otherwise—of financial results. Stocks can take months or years to recover from the blow. Knowing this—and everyone knows this—these events ought to be relatively rare. Unfortunately, in my experience, they are not. Perhaps management considers reporting earnings disappointments to be even more unpalatable. Equity analysts need to be keenly aware of the potential for accounting-related problems in financial reports; nothing can torpedo a stock recommendation faster.

Even without misreporting and deliberate manipulation, financial reports can still contain nasty surprises arising, interestingly, from changing business fundamentals. That equity analysts, whose lifeblood is business fundamentals, should be surprised when they change, is puzzling in itself and probably arises from the natural inertia of the equity analysis process. We often permit our financial models to continue indefinitely in one direction until knocked off course by reality. There is probably a mirror image of this inertia on the management side, where an unwillingness to disclose bad news delays its recognition—both psychological and accounting. Everyone wants to believe.

FINANCIAL MISREPORTING: THE SEVEN SHENANIGANS

Shilit's highly entertaining and useful book proposes "seven shenanigans," common accounting techniques—or outright fraud—used to manipulate financial reporting.[1] The first five techniques permit reported earnings to increase. The last two, shifting income to later or expense to earlier periods, reduce current reported earnings and are often used to create "reserves" for a future earnings increase, should it be needed:

- Recording revenue before it is earned
- Inventing revenue
- Boosting profits with nonrecurring items (NRIs)
- Shifting expenses to later periods
- Failing to disclose and/or record liabilities
- Shifting income to later periods
- Shifting expense to earlier periods

Recording Revenue before It Is Earned

Because of the wide variety of businesses to which accounting rules must be applied, revenue recognition remains subject to judgment, and therein lies the problem. Current earnings can be inflated if revenue can be shifted forward from later periods. Essentially, to recognize revenue, three conditions should be met:

- The earning process is complete. All services have been rendered, products delivered, and obligations fulfilled. If, for example, the seller has remaining obligations to the buyer, some portion of the revenue should be deferred.
- The "exchange of value" is determined. That is, a valid claim for payment, in a specific amount, exists.
- The likelihood of collection can be determined. It isn't necessary that all revenue be collected at the sale. But if receivables are created, the collectible portion should be reasonably determinable. If it isn't, then perhaps a valid sale didn't take place after all.

The SEC's Staff Accounting Bulletin (SAB) 101, issued in 1999 and most recently revised in June 2000, requires companies to inform investors of the Staff's revenue recognition guidelines (which essentialy mirror those above) before those guidelines must be adopted. For most calendar-year reporters, the adoption occurs in the 2000 fourth quarter, although few companies have mentioned the guidelines in their financial reports thus far. The SEC expects up to 300 companies to change their revenue recognition procedures to comply with SAB 101. Most likely to change their procedures are biotechnology, health care, computers, semiconductor equipment, and telecom companies.[2]

Inventing Revenue

If one is intent upon manipulating earnings, then one can ignore revenue recognition problems altogether and simply invent revenue.

■ **McKesson HBOC**   The May 26, 1999, *New York Times* reported that McKesson, the nation's largest drug wholesaler, would make revisions to its annual and quarterly earnings because of improperly recorded revenue at HBO & Company, a software maker acquired in January 1999 for $12 billion.[3] The announcement came on the heels of a similar action in April 1999, in which McKesson reversed $42.2 million in HBO sales transactions that had not been fully completed, because sales were reported before contracts had been signed.

By July 1999, the details of the problem began to emerge. *The Wall Street Journal* reported July 15, 1999, that HBO managers had allegedly:

■ Booked sales subject to undisclosed "side letters" that stated conditions that had to be met before sales could be completed. The letters were "stashed away" and kept separate from sales contracts.

■ Recognized sales prematurely because of backdated contracts.

■ Booked the sale of future software upgrades as current sales and counted as sold upgrades that were not yet available.[4]

The misreporting occurred in concert with intense sales pressure. HBO managers were "desperate for dollars" in order to make the company "prime for a takeover," according to the *Journal*'s sources.

Boosting Profits with Nonrecurring Items

Nonrecurring revenues and/or earnings can be a legitimate source of current income under accounting rules, but they raise "quality-of-earnings" issues. Nonrecurring earnings cannot support stock valuation because they are not, as pointed out in Chapter 2, capitalized. They also contribute to a climate of analytic uncertainty, which can call into question the value of core businesses:

- Nonrecurring earnings may include sources of earnings that do actually recur but are highly unpredictable. Securities trading gains of brokerage houses, banks, and insurance companies are a regular source of income, for example, but they have little predictability. Analysts tend to ignore—or "haircut"— potential value contributions from such income sources. Management complains loudly about this practice when booking securities gains, but it is often curiously silent when gains turn to losses.

- Substantial nonrecurring earnings contributions raise questions about the health of the company's sustainable businesses. Does the presence of so much nonrecurring income mean, for example, that the earnings potential of core businesses has fallen?

■ **Overfunded Pension Plan Income**   *The Wall Street Journal* reported on June 15, 1999, that some large companies, including GE, Bell Atlantic, GTE, Northrop-Grumman, and USX-US Steel Group, produced substantial 1998 earnings from income from overfunded pension plans.[5] Accounting rules provide that, if investment returns on pension assets exceed the plan's current costs, the difference can be reported as current income. In GE's case, $1 billion of $13 billion 1998 pretax income came from the company's pension plans.

The earnings windfall resulted as the rising stock market, in which many large-company pension funds invested heavily, pushed up the value of pension plan assets. Cutting pension liabilities, often by converting defined benefit to "cash balance plans," also contributed, in some cases, to the overfunding.

Shifting Current Expenses to Later Periods

Shifting expenses to later periods increases current earnings and reduces future earnings. Management can shift expenses to later periods by delaying spending, on advertising or research for example. Or financial reporting can be changed.

■ **Depreciation Expenses**   Changes in accounting estimates, such as the useful life of productive assets, need not be separately disclosed in a reported income statement, although notice of such changes does appear in the notes to the financial statements. An increase in useful-life estimates will reduce current, and increase future, depreciation expense, effectively shifting cost to future time periods.

■ **America Online, Inc., Advertising Expenses**   *The Wall Street Journal* reported on May 16, 2000, that America Online, Inc., agreed to pay $3.5 million in penalties to the SEC in settlement of allegations surrounding its accounting for mid-1990s advertising and marketing expenses.[6] The SEC alleged that AOL's practice of capitalizing subscriber advertising expenses, and amortizing the balance over two years, violated accounting rules because recovery of these costs was not reasonably supported by past experience. The effect of the capitalization was to shift current marketing expenses to future years, allowing AOL to report profits rather than losses in six of the eight quarters of fiscal 1995 and 1996.

Richard Walker, the SEC's director of enforcement, noted that the AOL case should "serve as a warning to others not to stretch the rules with aggressive accounting."

Failing to Disclose and/or Record Liabilities

Failure to record liabilities can understate costs or overstate revenues, both resulting in higher current income. In the McKesson case above, for example, the company's failure to record sales contingencies produced an inflated current revenue figure.

■ **Unrecorded Trade Payables**   Unrecorded trade payables reduce purchases for the period, thereby increasing earnings, via the following formula:

$$\text{Cost of goods sold} = \text{beginning inventory} + \text{purchases} - \text{ending inventory}$$

If beginning and ending inventories are both $100, and purchases during the period were $200, then the cost of goods sold (COGS) is also $200. But if $100 in purchases went unrecorded, then the COGS is apparently $100, and pretax income is seemingly $100 higher.

■ **Rite Aid Corporation**   *The Wall Street Journal* reported on June 2, 2000, that Rite Aid admitted to raising earnings incorrectly by reducing trade payables by $11 million in fiscal 1999, related to discounts Rite Aid felt it was due from suppliers, but had not deducted from the suppliers' bills nor discussed with them.[7] The company reversed another $7 million in earnings because of credit card billings, which had been rejected by the issuing bank but had not been written off or reserved by Rite Aid in the hope it could eventually collect.

Shifting Current Income to Later Periods

Sometimes accounting manipulation is meant to reduce rather than increase earnings, allowing management to store away excess earnings for a rainy day. In the property-casualty insurance industry, many analysts believe that, in periods of particularly low loss experience, insurers continue to add aggressively to loss reserves, creating excess costs and storing away, rather than recognizing, current earnings. As loss experience worsens, excess reserves can be reduced and rolled into future earnings, bolstering a bottom line under increasing pressure.

■ **W. R. Grace**   In a relatively controversial action, the SEC in April 1999 accused executives of W. R. Grace's National Medical Care, Inc., unit of fraudulently manipulating earnings, as reported by *The Wall Street Journal*.[8] The Grace unit managers, apparently concerned that a 30 percent growth rate was unsustainable, stored excess earnings in an all-purpose reserve, which they could later tap if earnings growth slowed.

According to Richard Walker, the SEC enforcement chief, as quoted by the *Journal,* such earnings management "is not an isolated phenomenon."

Shifting Future Expenses to Earlier Periods

Management can shift future expenses forward to earlier periods by accelerating expenditures, creating prepaid expenses, or by manipulating the books of account. A common expense shift is the "big bath."

■ **The "Big Bath"**   The write-off of unproductive assets or businesses, with the accompanying reserves for expenses like employee severance, is a perfectly legitimate—even essential—accounting action. When such expense acceleration becomes a big bath is a matter of opinion, but analysts should be suspicious when write-offs are very large relative to current income, or when they occur in otherwise poor operating conditions. Management may reason, since business is bad anyway, that increasing losses by dumping write-offs into the current year won't make things much worse, and it can increase future income.

The difficulty for equity analysts is that big-bath accounting destroys financial trends. Assets and businesses are worth their carrying values on one day, and zero on the next. Losses associated with the big bath likely occurred over a number of previous years, effectively reducing earnings. But previous years' results are not restated, unless the analyst does it himself or herself. In addition, acceleration of expenses increases future earnings. So, with the exception of the big-bath year itself, earnings can appear substantially more consistent than they actually were, had expenses been recognized in the correct years.

A Shenanigan Self-Defense Plan

If accounting shenanigans were easy to detect, investors and analysts would rarely be surprised when earnings and stock prices are torpedoed. Unfortunately, aggressive accounting and fraud often go undetected, as recent cases like Cendant, Waste Management, Inc., Sunbeam Corp., and Rite Aid make clear. As an analyst, I too have had my share of nasty accounting surprises.

Many accounting texts do a good job illustrating the financial effects of shenanigans, and I highly recommend reading several. But often, even staring right at the evidence, analysts still miss the implications. Management often has plausible-sounding explanations for odd-looking results and, as investors, we want to believe management. We want to believe that strong growth will continue. We want to believe that the competition is held at bay. We want to think that the bad times are behind us and that the bon tons will always roullez. In my experience, one's only defense against these "want-tos" is to repeat, as many times a day as necessary, that the laws of economics are never violated for long:

- Companies must stay in balance as they grow, and financial results should generally scale upward with productive capacity and sales. If, for example, inventory or accounts receivable grows faster than sales, something is out of balance, and trouble may be brewing—even if the imbalance appears in a single quarter.
- In the real world, things do not always go smoothly. Excessive smoothness in earnings could very likely signal earnings management. Earnings management can lead to accounting surprises.

■ If financial results seem too good for too long, they probably are. Trees do not grow to the sky, and companies do not forever move in one direction. Growth eventually slows, returns are forced toward normal levels, competition grabs share, and companies and products make transitions from higher to lower growth life stages. This is the hardest lesson for analysts to learn, given their attachment to sustainability and predictability in financial results.

FACING REALITY: EARNINGS SURPRISES AND ANALYTIC INERTIA

Aggressive accounting and fraud, perhaps of the types outlined in the seven shenanigans, are not the only sources—maybe not even the principal sources—of earnings surprises. Changing business fundamentals are also a major contributor, according to some very interesting work by Mulford and Comisky (M&C).[9] That this should be is, to me, very curious, since as analysts we should not be surprised by changing fundamentals. Change, in fact, should be our principal focus. As usual, Graham and Dodd said it best:

> Because the detection of change is such a key element in security analysis, the analyst devotes a great deal of time to thinking about change and its causes.[10]

So why don't analysts focus enough on change? Because, for one thing, change is hard, and analysts have a far easier time with predictability and sustainability. This preoccupation with continuity creates substantial analytic inertia, giving our thinking and projections a tendency to continue in one direction until knocked off course. We might call this the *first law of financial motion*. In addition, when growth has been relatively continuous and in one direction, there is no evidence of the coming change in the historical record. It's hard for analysts to predict change without evidence of, well, change, and then it's often too late. You can see the problem.

The Sources of Earnings Surprises

M&C's work on earnings surprises suggests that unexpected change in gross and operating margins, as well as nonrecurring items, are the principal financial sources of change. The M&C study built a database of "trend-based" and "analyst-based" earnings surprises:

- Trend-based surprises are represented by the 100 companies, which, in 1980 to 1993, after four years of earnings increases, showed the largest percentage earnings decline, averaging about 55 percent. Data were drawn from the Standard & Poor's *Compustat* database.

- Analyst-based surprises consist of the 100 companies in 1981 to 1989 that showed the largest negative deviation in income from continuing operations from mean forecasts drawn from the Institutional Brokerage Estimate System (I/B/E/S). The average earnings decline in the sample was 25.3 percent.

Once the companies were identified, M&C used public financial statements to determine the source of the surprise. In both trend- and analyst-based surprises, unexpected behavior of operating margins played a substantial role (Table 6–1).

Trend-Based Surprises

Trend-based surprises, especially those that are margin related, show strong evidence of changing business fundamentals. Of the 100 companies displaying trend-based surprises, 90 experienced declining operating margins. Of the 90, 76 showed declining gross margins, although clear explanations were available for only 63 companies. Again of the 90, 75 suffered increases in selling, general, and administrative (SGA) expense margins, although explanations for only 62 of these were available. In addition, 45 of the 100 companies also booked nonrecurring losses in the year of the margin decline. M&C found explanations for all 45 nonrecurring events.

TABLE 6–1

Declining operating margins and nonrecurring items explain most earnings surprises.

	Declining Operating Margin			
	Operating Margin	Gross Margin	Selling, General, and Administrative Margin	Nonrecurring Loss
Trend based	90	76	75	45
Analyst based	73	58	56	41

Competitive pressures could well explain lower selling prices, shifts to lower-margin products, and excess capacity. The restructurings and asset write-offs that underlie nonrecurring losses could also be strongly driven by changing competitive conditions, as companies shed unproductive businesses and assets. Table 6–2 shows the top four reasons for declining gross margins, rising SGA expenses, and nonrecurring losses, which explain 78, 82, and 67 percent, respectively, of the trend-based incidents (for which explanations were found).

Analyst-Based Surprises

Like trend-based, analyst-based earnings surprises show strong evidence of changing business fundamentals. Table 6–3 shows the top four reasons for analyst-based surprises that account for 74, 93, and 77 percent of declining gross margin, rising SGA expenses, and nonrecurring losses, respectively.

Again, changing product mix, excess capacity, increased advertising expenses, and write-downs and restructuring, all play a strong role in analyst-based surprises.

PREDICTING PERFORMANCE: NONRECURRING ITEMS

Because nonrecurring items (NRIs) play such a large role in earnings surprises and can wreak havoc on financial models, they are worth a

TABLE 6–2

Changed competitive conditions explain both margin decline and NRIs in trend-based earnings surprises.

Gross Margin Decline	Rising SGA Expenses	Nonrecurring Losses
Decreased revenue due to lower selling prices	Increased marketing and advertising expenses	Restructuring events
Changing product mix to products with lower gross margins	Increased administrative and miscellaneous expenses	Write-downs of PPE and intangibles
Excess capacity due to declining revenue volume	Decreased revenue due to lower prices or volume	Write-down of inventory
Increased costs associated with general cost increases	Costs of expansion ahead of sales growth	Write-down of accounts receivable

TABLE 6–3

Competitive conditions also underlie analyst-based
earnings surprises.

Gross Margin Decline	Rising SGA Expenses	Nonrecurring Losses
Increased costs associated with general cost increases	Increased marketing and advertising expenses	Write-downs of PPE and intangibles
Changing product mix to products with lower gross margins	Increased administrative and miscellaneous expenses	Restructuring events
Excess capacity due to declining revenue volume	Increased customer service expenses	Write-down of inventory
Lower gross margin of an acquired company	Unfavorable foreign currency movements	Other events

closer look. A complete discussion of accounting for NRIs is outside the
scope of this book, not to mention my expertise. But it is worth noting
that NRIs are one of the most difficult challenges we face in financial
analysis. This challenge arises not only because NRIs are sometimes
difficult to find but also because they are often difficult—or impractical—to reverse. If undetected and unreversed, NRIs find their way into
financial models, distorting projected results.

Finding NRIs

M&C report that only 25 percent of NRIs in their study were separately
disclosed in company income statements, a disconcerting result.[11] Evidence of and explanations for NRIs then need to be found in other financial statements and disclosures, such as the balance sheet, statement
of cash flows, notes to the financial statements, or management's discussion and analysis (MD&A).

   If NRIs are separated, they can be placed "above" or "below" the
line; that is, they can be part of continuing operations or not. Not surprisingly, research suggests that most above-the-line disclosures are
gains, and most below the line are losses.[12] (See Table 6–4.)

   Some NRIs above the line appear separately, such as gains (losses)
from the sale of fixed assets, restructuring charges, write-downs of receivables, inventory, or other impaired values. But other items, like LIFO

TABLE 6-4

Nonrecurring items can be presented both above and below the continuing operations line.

Net sales	
Cost of goods sold	
Gross profit	
Selling, general, and administrative expenses	
Research and development	
Operating income	
Other income (expense)	Above the line
Unusual or infrequent item	
Equity in earnings of unconsolidated subsidiary	
Pretax income	
Tax provision	
Income from continuing operations	
Discontinued operations, net of tax	
Discontinued operations, net of tax	
Extraordinary items, net of tax	
Cumulative effects of accounting changes	Below the line
Net income	
Minority interest	
Net income net of minority interest	

liquidations (roll-out of inventory carried at low cost into earnings, re-sulting in a gross margin spike), changes in tax assumptions, or changes in accounting estimates (like the useful life of productive assets), are not. If not, we need to search elsewhere.

Operational NRIs

Nonrecurring events are not solely accounting driven. It is possible for management to manipulate operations to change reported results. For example,

- Offering special credit and/or payment incentives for preorders can accelerate revenue.
- Delaying or accelerating discretionary expenditures like advertising, marketing, or R&D.

This sort of thing can be difficult to detect, but monitoring imbalances is probably the analyst's best bet. For example, a rise in accounts receivable growth in excess of sales can suggest a change in sales terms.

AN NRI ANALYSIS OF GATEWAY

Gateway's 1997 income statement provides an interesting nonrecurring item problem. Appendix 6–1 contains summary gateway financial statements of the company's 1998 annual report. Let's move through the NRI analysis step by step.

■ **Step 1. Locate the NRIs**   With a quick examination of the 1996 to 1998 GTW income statements, we see the $113.8 million 1997 nonrecurring expenses, which certainly contributed to the sharp drop in 1997 net income to $109.8 million from $250.7 million the year before. Without further research, it's difficult to say what's going on here, but I notice two things:

- Sales trends seem relatively steady, moving from $5.0 billion to $6.3 billion to $7.5 billion over the three years.

- But the 1996 to 1997 gross profit growth was only about $140 million versus the $470 million in 1998. Did something else bad happen in 1997? Are there other nonrecurring elements in 1997 income?

■ **Step 2. Identify the NRIs**   Fortunately, note 9 of GTW's financial statements provides an explanation of the $113.8 million (see Table 6–5).

TABLE 6–5

Gateway's note 9 presents NRI detail (in $ millions).

Write-off of in-process R&D	$59.7
Abandonment of software project	45.2
Severance, office closing	8.6
Other (not identified)	0.3
	$113.8

In-Process R&D Write-Off

The $59.7 million in-process R&D write-off is associated with GTW's third-quarter $196.4 million 1997 acquisition of Advanced Logic Research. Accounting rules permit the immediate write-off of that portion of the purchase price attributed to research and development values. This type of write-off has come under considerable regulatory scrutiny, but it is consistent with the regular income statement treatment of R&D expense. It certainly seems that this charge is nonrecurring.

Suppose, however, the write-off had not been made, increasing the acquisition's resulting goodwill by the $59.7 million. GTW reports that it uses a 3- to 10-year write-off period for such intangibles. The immediate write-off therefore increases future reported income by roughly $6 to $20 million ($59.7 million divided by 3 and 10 years).

Abandonment of Software Project

GTW notes tell us that the company, in accordance with GAAP, capitalizes the cost of internal software development, amortizing the capitalized cost generally over 3 to 5 years once the software enters service. In this case, clearly, the software never reached service and was written off.

In retrospect, it is apparent that previous years' earnings were overstated by $45.2 million, which could in fact have been expensed. These expenses were, in effect, shifted forward to 1997. Was there anything special about 1997? No way to tell, really, but note that 1997 was otherwise a very tough year for GTW. The management discussion and analysis (MD&A) reports that the company's gross profit margin contracted to 17.1 percent from 18.6 percent the previous year because of the adverse impact of excess inventory. Average computer unit prices fell 8 percent. Collapsing unit prices led GTW, in 1998, to aggressively diversify its revenue sources.

Severance and Office Closing

The company recorded an $8.6 million write-off for employee severance and closing of a foreign office, probably also rightly identified as a nonrecurring item. The effect of the write-off is to shift expenses, which might have been booked in future periods, into 1997.

■ **Step 3. Adjust for NRIs**   Pulling the NRIs out of 1997 income is straightforward, as shown in Table 6–6. Pretax recurring income of $317.5 million, offset by the $113.8 million, produces the $203.6 million reported 1997 reported pretax income.

Adjusting taxes is a bit more complicated. Note 5 reports that the 1997 tax provision contained the components shown in Table 6–7. To assign these components to the recurring and nonrecurring columns in Table 6–6, try the following procedure:

■ Apply the statutory 35 percent rate to both recurring and nonrecurring operating income. The sum of the $39.8 million nonrecurring and the $111.1 million recurring provision equals the $71.3 million net statutory provision.

TABLE 6–6

Gateway's 1997 net income contains both recurring and nonrecurring items (in $000).

	As Reported	Recurring	Nonrecurring
Operating income before nonrecurring items	290,273	290,273	
Nonrecurring items			
In-process R&D	(59,700)		(59,700)
Abandonment of software project	(45,200)		(45,200)
Closing costs	(8,600)		(8,600)
Other	(342)		(342)
Subtotal	(113,842)		(113,842)
Operating Income	176,431	290,273	(113,842)
Other income	27,189	27,189	
Income before tax	203,620	317,462	(113,842)
Tax			
At statutory rate (35%)	(71,267)	(111,112)	39,845
Nondeductible items	(20,704)		(20,704)
Other, net	(1,852)	(1,852)	
Subtotal	(93,823)	(112,964)	19,141
Net income	109,797	204,498	(94,701)

TABLE 6-7

Tax provision details contained in note 5 of GTW financial statements (in $000).

Federal tax at statutory rate (35%)	$71,267
Nondeductible purchased R&D costs	20,704
Other, net	1,852
Provision for taxes	93,823

■ Assign the $20.7 million nondeductible element to the nonrecurring column.

■ Assign the $1.8 million in other tax expense to the recurring column, for want of a better place.

The 1997 reported net income of $109.8 million now consists of a $204.5 million recurring and $(94.7) million nonrecurring element. GTW now shows much clearer recurring net income behavior. As we suspected, 1997 was a nasty year even without the nonrecurring items, as shown in Table 6–8.

We've adjusted 1997 income, eliminating nonrecurring items. But NRIs can't just disappear, can they? And if not, where do they go? The $59.7 million was part of the ALR purchase price and is now in the hands of ALR's former shareholders. The $45.2 million represents costs expended in earlier years on the development of an internal software system. That cash is out the door as well, whether or not the system

TABLE 6-8

GTW's net margin from recurring income declined in 1997 (in $000).

	1996	1997	1998
Net sales	5,035,228	6,293,680	7,467,925
Recurring net income	250,679	204,498	346,399
Net margin (%)	5.0	3.2	4.6

TABLE 6–9

With NRIs replaced, Gateway's 1997 prospective ROE declines (in $000).

	1997 Book Value	1998 Net Income	Prospective Return on 1997 Book Value
Unadjusted	930,044	346,399	37.2%
NRI	94,701		
Adjusted	1,024,745	346,399	33.8%

succeeded. The $94.7 million nonrecurring loss was, for the most part, invested in GTW's business. Suppose we add it back to the company's book value. This adjustment can make an important difference in return calculations, especially in the prospective return on book value so important in equity valuation, as shown in Table 6–9. The difference between a 37 percent return and a 33 percent return is pretty significant. In Chapter 10, we discuss economic value added (EVA) analysis techniques in which such add-backs are common.

NOTES

[1] Howard M. Schilit, *Financial Shenanigans: How to Detect Accounting Gimmicks and Fraud in Financial Reports,* McGraw-Hill, New York, 1993.

[2] "Many Companies Fail to Heed the SEC on Its Revenue Recognition Guidelines," Heard on the Street, *The Wall Street Journal,* December 14, 2000, page C1.

[3] "Once Again, McKesson Is Revising Its Earnings," *The New York Times,* May 26, 1999, p. C-2.

[4] "McKesson Restates Income Again as Probe of Accounting Widens," *The Wall Street Journal,* July 15, 1999, p. A-1.

[5] "Companies Reap a Gain Off Fat Pension Plans: Fattened Earnings," *The Wall Street Journal,* June 15, 1999, p. A-1.

[6] "AOL Settles SEC Charges Over Its Costs," *The Wall Street Journal,* May 6, 2000, p. A-3.

[7] "Rite Aid Restates Year Net Downward, Reversing Some Accounting Maneuvers," *The Wall Street Journal,* June 2, 1999, p. A-3.

[8] "SEC Case Claims Profit 'Management' by Grace." *The Wall Street Journal,* April 7, 1999, p. C-1.

[9] Charles W. Mulford, and Eugene E. Comiskey, *Financial Warnings,* Wiley, New York, 1996.

[10] Sidney Cottle, Roger F. Murray, and Frank E. Block, *Graham and Dodd's Security Analyses* (5th ed.), McGraw-Hill, New York, 1988, page 541.

[11] H. Choi, "Analysis and Valuation Implications of Persistence and Cash Content Dimensions of Earnings Components Based on Extent of Analyst Following," unpublished Ph.D. thesis, Georgia Institute of Technology, October 1994, p. 80; quoted in Mulford and Comiskey, *Financial Warnings,* p. 90.

[12] Gerald I. White, Ashwinpaul C. Sandhi, and Dov Fried, *The Analysis and Use of Financial Statements* (2nd ed.), Wiley, New York, 1998.

Gateway Financial Statements

Income Statement	1994	1995	1996	1997	1998
Net Sales	2,701.2	3,676.3	5,035.2	6,293.7	7,467.9
Cost of goods sold	2,343.7	3,070.2	4,099.1	5,217.2	5,921.7
Gross profit	357.5	606.1	936.2	1,076.4	1,546.3
Selling gen & admin	216.5	357.1	580.1	786.2	1,052.0
Nonrecurring expenses				113.8	
Operating Income	141.0	249.0	356.1	176.4	494.2
Other income, net	5.1	13.1	26.6	27.2	47.0
Income before taxes	146.1	262.1	382.7	203.6	541.2
Provision for income taxes	50.1	89.1	132.1	93.8	194.8
Net income	96.0	173.0	250.7	109.8	346.4
EPS					
Basic		$ 1.19	$ 1.64	$ 0.71	$ 2.23
Diluted		$ 1.09	$ 1.60	$ 0.70	$ 2.18
Weighted average shares					
Basic		145.3	152.7	153.8	155.5
Diluted		158.0	156.2	156.2	158.9
EBITDA	159.0	287.1	417.9	263.2	599.8
Cash interest expense	1.1	2.1	0.7	0.7	0.9

Statement of Cash Flows	1994	1995	1996	1997	1998
Net Income	96.0	173.0	250.7	109.8	346.4
Adjustments to reconcile net income to net cash					
Depreciation and amortization	18.0	38.1	61.8	86.8	105.5
Provision for uncollectible receivables	11.7	7.8	20.8	5.7	4.0
Deferred income taxes	(1.1)	(23.8)	(13.4)	(63.2)	(58.4)
Other, net	1.5	0.5	2.0	0.0	0.8
Nonrecurring expenses				113.8	—
Interest expense less interest income, net	0.7	1.4	0.4	0.5	0.6
Subtotal	30.9	24.0	71.6	143.6	52.5
Cash flow before working capital, interest	126.9	197.0	322.3	253.4	398.9
Cash flow effects of working capital					
Accounts receivable	(94.4)	(158.0)	(66.1)	(42.0)	(52.2)
Inventory	44.1	(103.2)	(54.3)	59.5	81.3
Other current assets	(8.3)	(10.8)	(13.3)	(54.5)	0.5
Accounts payable	57.0	51.8	176.7	66.3	228.9
Accrued liabilities	32.8	20.7	51.4	48.4	144.9
Accrued royalties	34.1	37.6	1.9	34.1	8.5
Income taxes payable	1.7	50.5	42.9	8.3	
Other current liabilities	(2.6)	(7.3)	0.2	27.5	76.3
Other liabilities	11.5	12.9	22.7	42.3	21.3
Subtotal	75.9	(105.8)	162.1	189.9	509.4
Cash flow before interest	202.8	91.1	484.4	443.3	908.3
Interest expense, net	(0.7)	(1.4)	(0.4)	(0.5)	(0.6)
Cash flow from operations	202.1	89.8	484.0	442.8	907.7
Cash flow effects of long-term assets					
Capital expenditures	(29.0)	(95.8)	(112.2)	(162.0)	(235.4)
Internal use of software	(26.6)	(39.0)	(31.6)	(13.6)	
Purchases of AFS securities	(172.3)	(10.7)		(49.6)	(169.0)
Purchases of HTM securities	(8.0)	(1.7)			
Proceeds from HTM securities	3.0	5.0			
Proceeds from AFS securities	164.0	33.0	3.0	11.0	48.9
Acquisitions, net of cash acquired		(3.6)		(142.3)	
Other, net		(13.2)	2.7	(4.1)	(1.0)
Subtotal	(69.0)	(126.0)	(138.0)	(360.7)	(356.4)
Free cash flow	133.1	(36.2)	345.9	82.1	551.2
Dividends	(28.4)	—	—	—	—
Free cash flow after dividends	104.7	(36.2)	345.9	82.1	551.2
Cash flow effects of financing					
Proceeds from issuance of notes		5.0	10.0	10.0	
Principal payments on LTD, notes	(4.6)	(24.6)	(14.0)	(15.6)	(13.2)
Stock options exercised	0.0	8.1	9.5	5.7	36.2
Subtotal	(4.6)	(11.5)	5.5	0.2	23.0
Foreign exchange effects	—	0.1	(1.5)	(5.0)	2.0
Net Change in Cash	100.1	(47.6)	350.0	77.2	576.2
Tax rate applied to interest	35%	35%	35%	35%	35%

Balance Sheet	1994	1995	1996	1997	1998
Current assets					
Cash	214.0	166.4	516.4	593.6	1,169.8
Marketable securities	29.9	3.0		38.6	158.7
Accounts receivable	252.9	405.3	449.7	510.7	558.9
Inventory	120.2	224.9	278.0	249.2	167.9
Other	17.4	66.6	74.2	152.5	172.9
Subtotal	649.2	866.2	1,318.3	1,544.7	2,228.2
Property, plant, and equipment, net	89.3	170.3	242.4	336.5	531.0
Internal use software cost, net	27.1	58.5	77.1	40.0	
Intangibles, net			9.9	82.6	65.9
Other assets	5.0	29.1	25.8	35.5	65.3
Total assets	770.6	1,124.0	1,673.4	2,039.3	2,890.4
Current liabilities					
Notes payable	3.8	13.6	15.0	14.0	11.4
Accounts payable	183.3	235.1	411.8	488.7	718.1
Accrued liabilities	57.8	109.0	190.8	271.3	415.3
Accrued royalties	85.8	123.4	125.3	159.4	167.9
Income taxes payable	0.2	16.4	40.3	26.5	
Other current liabilities	18.0	27.9	16.6	44.0	117.1
Subtotal	348.9	525.3	799.8	1,003.9	1,429.7
Long-term obligations	27.1	10.8	7.2	7.2	3.4
Warranty and other liabilities	18.5	32.4	50.9	98.1	113.0
Total liabilities	394.5	568.5	857.9	1,109.2	1,546.0
Shareholders equity					
Preferred stock					
Class A common					
Common stock	0.7	0.7	1.5	1.5	1.6
Additional paid in capital	274.4	280.4	288.7	299.5	366.0
Retained earnings	101.1	274.0	524.7	634.5	980.9
Other	−0.1	0.3	0.5	(5.5)	(4.1)
Total shareholders equity	376.0	555.5	815.5	930.0	1,344.4

Source: Gateway financial reports and author's calculations.

CHAPTER 7

Reading a Financial Statement: The Composition of Returns

- Financial ratio analysis is the fundamental tool for examining the composition of the company's returns, the second objective in reading a financial statement. Since returns on equity are the driver of common stock value, return analysis is central to our understanding of equity performance.

- Financial ratios do not exist in a vacuum. Rather, they are part of distinct families, such as revenue and expense management or current/capital investment management. Each of these families contributes to the analyst's insight into the composition of the company's returns.

- In addition to the composition of returns, financial ratios reveal underlying regularities in financial data. Understanding such regularities is the basis of financial statement modeling. Ratios are the basic fodder of modeling.

- Ratio analysis connects the company's investment returns, financial reports, and management decisions to its competitive strategies, forming a direct line from strategy to performance to value.

- There are only three dimensions to ratio analysis: time series analysis of financial performance within a single company or group of companies, cross-sectional comparison of performance of a group of companies at a point in time, and standard or benchmark analysis, in which a ratio is compared to a standard. Often benchmark analysis occurs in a legal or regulatory context.

Financial ratios are not dull. I know that sounds implausible, but it's true. They very often seem dull, I think, because they are presented without structure and seemingly without objective, except to fill up pages at the end of equity analysis reports in endless columns of numbers. But if we focus ratio analysis on the composition of the company's returns, the columns of numbers suddenly acquire an organization and can be forced to tell a story. The story is about the return consequences of the company's basic operational, investment, and financing decisions. Much of this discussion draws heavily upon Palepu, Bernard, and Healy's excellent treatment of the subject.[1]

THE FOCUS OF RATIO ANALYSIS IS ROE

Determining the composition of the company's returns is a principal objective of reading a financial statement, and financial ratios are the natural tool for pulling apart the components of return. ROE has three components: net margin, asset turnover, and balance sheet leverage. Each component is associated with a family of financial ratios:[2]

$$\text{ROE} = \text{net margin} * \text{asset turnover} * \text{balance sheet leverage} \quad (7.1)$$

The net margin ratio family consists of familiar ratios like gross margin; selling, general, and administrative (SGA) expense percentages; and net margin on sales. This family is most conveniently generated by a "common-sized" historical income statement, in which each income statement component is divided by a common variable, usually sales. Common-sized statements illustrate the financial consequences of the company's basic competitive strategy, pricing, product positioning, and expense control—essentially the basic operational decisions of the business.

Asset turnover, on the other hand, is concerned with the company's investment decisions, both shorter-term working capital and longer-term capital expenditures. The turnover family includes working capital concepts like inventory and receivables turnover, and perhaps the less familiar cash conversion cycle. Turnover ratios focus on the physical basis of the business—the structures of production and the movement of materials through them. Efficiency in the use of physical assets and the collection of cash can have a strong effect on the company's returns.

Balance sheet leverage forces the analyst to consider the company's corporate financial decisions. The company's financing decisions, although not directly connected to the production and marketing process, are fundamental to its success. The balance sheet leverage family includes not only the familiar debt/equity ratio but more generally coverage ratios like interest and cash flow. The leverage ratio analysis tells the analyst about the composition of the company's capital structure and the ability of the company to service that capital structure.

The Connection Between Growth and ROE

The ROE approach is, as we have argued in Chapter 2, equivalent to a focus on growth. The connection between the two viewpoints in ratio analysis is the sustainable growth calculation.

$$\text{Sustainable growth} = \text{ROE} * (1 - \text{dividend payout}) \qquad (7.2)$$

Sustainable growth refers to shareholders' equity growth, not earnings. This can be demonstrated simply through the clean surplus relationship:

$$BV_0 + E_1 - D_1 = BV_1$$
$$BV_1 - BV_0 = E_1 - D_1 \qquad (7.3)$$

Dividing both sides of Equation 7.3 by BV_0,

$$\frac{BV_1 - BV_0}{BV_0} = \frac{E_1 - D_1}{BV_0} \qquad (7.4)$$

But the expression $(BV_1 - BV_0)/BV_0$ is simply the book value growth g. And the dividend can be expressed as the dividend payout b times the period earnings E_1:

$$D_1 = E_1 \times b$$

$$g = E_1 * \frac{(1 - b)}{BV_0}$$
$$g = \text{ROE} * (1 - b) \qquad (7.5)$$

$$ROE = \frac{E_1}{BV_0}$$

A Three-Dimensional Problem

The news gets better. As equity analysts, I believe we need to focus primarily on three families of ratios: margins, turnover, and leverage. There are, in turn, only three ways to analyze these families (Figure 7–1). We can examine the development of ratios over time within a single company or group of companies—time series analysis. We can examine several companies' ratios at one particular time—cross-sectional analysis. Finally, we can compare ratios to some standard or benchmark.

FIGURE 7-1

There are three possible ratio analysis techniques.

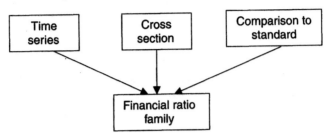

Analysis of ratios versus a standard is common, for example, in regulatory and legal processes. We will focus on time series and cross-sectional analyses.

MARGINS REVEAL OPERATIONAL DECISIONS

The net margin component of return suggests a whole line of inquiry into the company's revenue and expense decisions (Figure 7–2):

- What is the composition of earnings? What are the sources of income?
- What is the composition of sales? How fast have its components grown? What is the logic of product decisions?

FIGURE 7-2

Revenue and expense decisions form one dimension of return on equity.

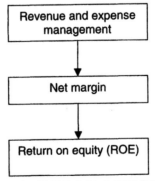

- What is the profitability of sales? How is it changing? What about the cost of inputs? What are the components of cost?

Margin analysis is best performed through a common-sized income statement. A common-sized income statement is formed by dividing each income statement line into net sales (most commonly). Common-sized income statements are, quite literally, starting points of financial statement analysis. They should be the first thing an analyst does with company financial data:

- Common-sized statements immediately reveal the company's margins, which is critical in the analysis of return.
- The procedure also eases cross-sectional comparisons by placing all income statement accounts in the same scale, by dollar of sales.
- Finally, common-sized statements reveal margin trends. Understanding operational trends is the basis of financial forecasting.

Appendix 6–1 contains a sales-based, common-sized income statement for Gateway. We will present a detailed example of financial ratio analysis using Gateway later in the chapter.

TURNOVERS DESCRIBE INVESTMENT DECISIONS

The asset turnover leads the analyst to a consideration of management's short- and long-term investment decisions (Figure 7–3):

FIGURE 7–3

Investment decisions are the second analytic dimension of equity return.

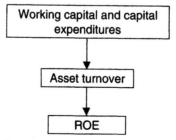

Source: From K. G. Palepu, V. L. Bernard, and P. M. Healy, *Introduction to Business Analysis and Valuation*, 1st ed., © 1997. Reprinted with permission of South-Western College Publishing, a division of Thomson Learning.

- What is the relationship between the company, its suppliers, and its customers?
- How does the company manage its working capital? Is it efficient? Are investments in working capital consistent with the sales growth and profitability evidence revealed by margin analysis? Is working capital management changing?
- In what fixed assets does the company invest? Is growth in fixed assets consistent with sales growth?

Structure of Turnovers

Dividing a financial flow (i.e., sales or cost of goods sold) by a financial stock measure (i.e., receivables or inventory) forms a turnover ratio. I like to think of turnovers as a measure of the asset or liability stock necessary to support a level of operational activity. A turnover also represents the number of times the asset or liability "runs through" the operations.

$$\text{Sales-based turnover} = \frac{\text{sales}}{\text{ending asset or liability}} \quad (7.6)$$

$$\text{Cost-based turnover} = \frac{\text{cost of goods sold}}{\text{ending asset or liability}} \quad (7.7)$$

$$\text{Purchase-based turnover} = \frac{\text{purchases}}{\text{ending asset or liability}} \quad (7.8)$$

Sales-based turnovers, like sales and accounts receivable, are very familiar. But sales turnovers can be calculated with fixed assets, other assets, liability accounts, or almost any balance sheet measure. Since sales is also the most common driver of financial forecasts, sales-based turnovers can be very helpful in modeling.

The asset turnover in the ROE calculation is sales based:

$$\text{Asset turnover} = \frac{\text{net sales}}{\text{total assets}} \quad (7.9)$$

A note about the denominators of the turnover calculations. Many finance texts recommend that turnovers be calculated with an average asset or liability. This is perfectly correct, but I don't recommend it. In the first place, turnovers formed with ending assets are just as valid as those with averages, provided the analyst is consistent in their use. Second, ending asset turnovers make the projection of balance sheet accounts far easier. To project a year-end balance sheet, one need forecast only the flow account and the turnover, without unraveling an average asset level. Turnovers calculated with averages also introduce a potential circularity, in that one can't calculate the turnover without the ending asset level (to form the average), but one can't calculate the ending asset level without the turnover. Looking forward to financial modeling in Chapter 12, the ending asset form is much simpler.

■ **Trick**   Consistently use ending asset or liability values to calculate turnover ratios. Ending values ease the use of turnover ratios in financial modeling.

The most familiar cost-based turnover is the inventory turnover, cost of goods sold/inventory. A payables turnover—cost of goods sold/ accounts payable—is also possible, but the payables turnover is also often calculated with purchases:

$$\text{Beginning inventory} + \text{purchases} - \text{cost of goods sold}$$
$$= \text{ending inventory} \qquad (7.10)$$
$$\text{Purchases} = \text{cost of goods sold}$$
$$+ (\text{ending inventory} - \text{beginning inventory})$$

Once again, simpler is better. Stick with the cost-of-goods-sold form of payables turnover. It's just as valid as the more complex purchases form, and it doesn't tangle the analyst up with ending inventory.

The Cash Conversion Cycle

Operational turnovers can be converted to the "days-in" form and then expressed conveniently as a "cash conversion cycle":

$$\text{Days in an asset or liability account} = \frac{365}{\text{turnover}} \qquad (7.11)$$

For example, days in inventory is

$$\text{Days in inventory} = \frac{365}{\text{inventory turnover}} \qquad (7.12)$$

If turnover is a measure of the number of times per year that an asset or liability account "runs through" the company's operations, then the days-in calculation produces the number of days required for each run-through. I use 365 days in a notional year. Other authors use 360 days. Once again, the number itself isn't important, provided that it is used consistently.

Converting inventory, receivables, and accounts payable turnovers to days-in form allows us to construct a cash conversion cycle.

$$\text{Cash conversion cycle} = \text{days in inventory}$$
$$+ \text{ days in accounts receivable}$$
$$- \text{ days in accounts payable} \qquad (7.13)$$

The cash conversion cycle is a rough measure of the time it takes for a company's operations to produce cash, beginning with the initial inventory investment. It is a wonderful way to summarize the efficiency.

LEVERAGE IS THE RETURN AMPLIFIER

Balance sheet leverage is the third component of the ROE calculation and draws the analyst into the firm's corporate financial management (Figure 7–4). It is the habit of most equity analysts to ignore—or down-play—corporate financial issues, focusing instead upon margins and growth. This may be partially because corporate financial decisions are slowly changing, compared with the volatility of the stock market. However, financial management issues, although often submerged, are never far from the surface. It is outside of the scope of this book to consider

FIGURE 7–4

Corporate finance is the final dimension of equity returns.

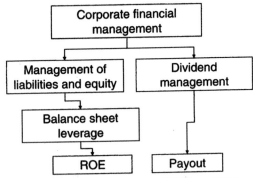

Source: From K. G. Palepu, V. L. Bernard, and P. M. Healy, *Introduction to Business Analysis and Valuation*, 1st ed., © 1997. Reprinted with permission of South-Western College Publishing, a division of Thomson Learning.

corporate finance issues in detail. But the return amplification provided by balance sheet leverage, and the tangible risks involved, are certainly of concern to the equity analyst.

The Leverage Ratio

Balance sheet leverage in the ROE calculation is a total leverage concept:

$$\text{Balance sheet leverage} = \frac{\text{total assets}}{\text{equity book value}} \qquad (7.14)$$

All else being equal, increasing balance sheet leverage is positive to ROE, but increasing leverage clearly involves increased risk. To get more directly at the risk issue, calculate a cash flow coverage ratio:

$$\text{Cash flow coverage} = \frac{\text{cash flow from operations}}{\text{total liabilities or debt}} \qquad (7.15)$$

Cash flow coverage looks a little like a turnover ratio. The idea is to measure how the cash flow-generating capacity of the company compares to its total obligations. The lower the cash flow coverage, the higher the company's potential financial risks.

Other Coverage Ratios

The equity analyst ought to be concerned about the company's ability to service debt. I find that interest and cash flow coverage ratios are helpful in determining that ability:

$$\text{Interest coverage} = \frac{\text{net income} + \text{after-tax interest expense}}{\text{after-tax interest}} \qquad (7.16)$$

The after-tax (AT) interest is determined by multiplying by $(1 - \text{tax rate})$:

$$\begin{aligned}
\text{After-tax interest expense} \\
= \text{pretax interest expense} * (1 - \text{tax rate}) \qquad (7.17)
\end{aligned}$$

What tax rate are we talking about? I don't think there's a right or wrong way to answer. The issue is to be consistent. The marginal statutory corporate tax rate of 35 percent is a decent compromise, or, at least, it is the choice I usually make.

I also like a cash flow interest coverage ratio in which cash flow from operations replaces net income. Net income can have a variety of noncash elements. Cash flow interest coverage measures the actual cash resources versus the required interest payments (more on cash flow coverage ratios in Chapter 13).

$$\text{Cash flow interest coverage} = \frac{\text{cash flow from operations} + \text{AT interest}}{\text{AT interest}} \quad (7.18)$$

In general, it's possible to substitute cash flow from operations into any ratio containing net income, such as coverage ratios or returns discussed below. Sometimes cash flow ratios can illustrate interesting—or distressing—differences between earnings and cash flow.

SOME OTHER RATIO ISSUES

Liquidity Ratios Used in Credit Analysis

There is an entire class of financial ratios, the liquidity ratios, that are used in credit analysis. The current ratio is an example of a liquidity ratio:

$$\text{Current ratio} = \frac{\text{current assets}}{\text{current liabilities}} \quad (7.19)$$

The presumption in liquidity ratios is, well, liquidation. These ratios attempt to test whether, if company operations were to stop, assets would be adequate to liquidate liabilities. It isn't clear of course that the results of an actual liquidation would mirror those of a liquidity analysis. Nevertheless, this is an essential question for lenders to ask. It is not the equity analyst's focus. This doesn't mean liquidity and solvency aren't important, but, if a serious solvency issue exists, an equity analyst's job is probably finished. The answer is, don't buy the stock (you might consider buying the debt, however). The company must be a going concern for equity analysis to make any sense at all. It's not that credit analysis isn't important; it's that credit analysis does not advance the equity analysis.

My Campaign against Tangible Net Worth

I have a personal prejudice against tangible net worth (TNW). Chapter 10 on economic value added returns to this subject, but for the moment let me assert that tangible net worth is of no real use to the equity analyst. TNW is a common concept in credit agreements, and it is often found in ratio form:

$$\text{Leverage} = \frac{\text{funded debt}}{\text{tangible net worth}} \qquad (7.20)$$

The idea here is to determine if physical assets, when liquidated, are sufficient to repay debt. But the ratio, based upon historical cost accounting, tells us nothing about the cash resources potentially available to the company. In addition, tangible net worth understates the actual stockholder investment in the company by, for one thing, the amounts paid for acquisitions in excess of book value, and is therefore unsuitable for return calculations. And finally, it is not a going-concern concept. If tangible net worth is a serious issue, I advise once again, consider another stock.

Potential Inconsistencies in Some Ratios

Logical inconsistencies in financial ratios arise most often in return calculations, which combine an earnings measure in the numerator with an asset or liability in the denominator. The inconsistency occurs when the earnings measure used is inappropriate to the balance sheet account.

■ **Trap**   Return ratios, which combine earnings inappropriate to the asset or liability account used, result in an inconsistency, such as in the following examples:

$$\text{Return on assets} = \frac{\text{net income}}{\text{assets}}$$

$$\text{Return on capital} = \frac{\text{net income}}{\text{total capital}}$$

Net income accrues to shareholders' equity only, not to total assets or the entire capital base of the company. To correct these inconsistencies, the analyst must remove interest expense from net income, resulting in an earnings measure that matches each ratio's denominator.

$$\text{Return on capital} = \frac{\text{net income} + \text{after-tax interest expense}}{\text{total capital}} \qquad (7.21)$$

Another corrective approach is to use EBITDA—earnings before interest, taxes, depreciation, and amortization—in place of net earnings, forming a pretax return:

$$\text{Pretax return on capital} = \frac{\text{EBITDA}}{\text{total capital}} \qquad (7.22)$$

CONNECTING STRATEGY TO VALUE

Financial ratio analysis is the bridge between common stock valuation, driven by the return on equity, and management's competitive strategy. The management choices that arise from its strategy flow into operational and investment decisions and produce, along with financial policy, the company's returns. Analysts ought to be looking for the evidence of competitive strategy in financial returns (Figure 7–5). This should be a way of confirming his or her understanding of the company's strategies; the evidence must be in the numbers. If it isn't, or if the numbers tell some different story, then he or she needs to reexamine his or her understanding of company strategy.[3]

THE COMPOSITION OF RETURNS

Consider, for example, the three hypothetical companies in Table 7–1. Without knowing anything about their industries or strategies, what can we say about their relative competitive positioning?

Company A's business generates a relatively low 4 percent after-tax margin, but 2.5 times asset turnover drives its returns to a respectable

FIGURE 7–5

Competitive strategies must ultimately emerge in equity returns.

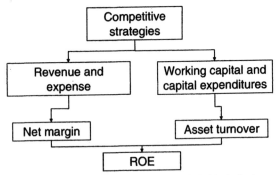

Source: From K. G. Palepu, V. L. Bernard, and P. M. Healy, *Introduction to Business Analysis and Valuation*, 1st ed., © 1997. Reprinted with permission of South-Western College Publishing, a division of Thomson Learning.

TABLE 7-1

Return composition can reveal strategic decisions.

	Net Margin	Asset Turnover	Balance Sheet Leverage	Return on Equity
Company A	4%	2.5	1.5	15%
Company B	15%	1.5	1.5	34%
Company C	2%	1.0	2.5	5%

15 percent. Perhaps Company A is a cost leader in a highly competitive market (low net margins) that, because of its efficiency (high asset turnover), is able to achieve target returns without excessive financial leverage.

On the other hand, Company B has far lower asset efficiency (asset turnover 1.5) than Company A, but substantially higher margins, leading to its very strong 34 percent return on equity. Maybe Company B is a differentiator with special reputational advantages, allowing it to charge higher prices (high net margin) than its competition. Or, Company B may be a first mover enjoying a period of high product demand and low competitive challenge, leading to superior returns.

Company C is a laggard, with neither the high margins nor efficiency of the others. Its low profitability and turnover suggest poor competitive positioning. Higher leverage may also be a symptom of cash flow distress. Alternatively, Company C may participate in a declining industry. Low product demand could cause cash flow difficulties (higher leverage) and excess asset buildup (low turnover). Such a company would need, perhaps, to shrink its asset base and thereby free cash and build operational efficiency.

GATEWAY TIME SERIES ANALYSIS

Appendixes 6–1 and 7–1 contain financial statements and analysis of GTW for the years 1994 to 1998 and are the sources for discussion of financial ratio analysis. These are also, by the way, useful financial model formats for any company and translate well into Excel spreadsheets.

Although the spreadsheets contains additional ratios, what follows is a brief analysis of the company's financial statements using the return analysis format. Return analysis provides structure for the study of financial ratios, but alone it doesn't make them interesting. To be interesting to the investor, and useful to the analyst, ratios analysis must ultimately tell us the story of the company's strategy. The analyst has to put this information into a context. Without a narrative, the writing devolves into "this went up and that went down," which, in my view, is a shameful waste of time, paper, and energy.

■ **Trick**   Use ratio analysis to connect the company's equity returns to its competitive strategy. Tell the company's story.

Gateway and the Personal Computer Industry

Gateway is a direct seller of personal computers, ranking number 3 in the United States and 6 in the world at the time of these financials. The company's business is divided 53 percent to consumer and 47 percent to business markets. Personal computer industry unit sales growth was 10 to 15 percent in 1997 to 1998, although the company's unit sales grew in the 35 to 37 percent range in the same period. Some analysts believed that the personal computer industry was beginning to show signs of maturity. Substantial pricing pressure was developing in the United States. GTW noted that its average price per unit (APU) declined 8 percent in 1997 and 14 percent in 1998. Personal computers selling for under $1000 were gaining popularity.

Turnover Driven Returns

Gateway's 37.2 percent 1998 return on equity resulted from a sharp recovery in net margin versus 1997 and a slight rise in financial leverage, offset by a slight decline in 1998 asset turnover (Table 7–2).

Recovery of the Company's Margins

Dividing each element of the income statement by the year's net sales converts the income statement to common-sized form. In this form, the income statement can be used as the basis of time series analysis of Gateway's own margins, as well as the basis of the cross-sectional analysis later on in this chapter.

One's eye is immediately drawn to GTW's gross margin performance. Gross margin increased from 13.2 percent in 1994 to 18.6 percent

TABLE 7–2

Declining margins and turnovers underlie Gateway's 1997 return decline.

	1996	1997	1998
Net margin	5.0%	1.7%	4.6%
Asset turnover	4.48	3.76	3.66
Leverage	2.02	2.05	2.19
Return	45.1%	13.5%	37.2%

in 1996 before dropping sharply to 17.1 percent in 1997. The company's 1998 annual report notes that an excessive buildup of high-cost inventory, combined with pressure on the APU, explained the decline. But in 1998, gross margin recovered to 20.7 percent after aggressive management corrective action. The company diversified its revenue stream to include Internet access and a product financing and trade-in scheme, and it took aggressive pricing and supplier control actions. Declining component costs also helped margins. But even with corrective action, GTW's income before taxes did not return to its 7.6 percent 1996 high, reaching only 7.2 percent. Why?

Ignoring small fluctuations in other income, the company's steadily rising selling, general, and administrative expense (SGA) explains the reduced pretax profit. The SGA rose from 8.0 percent in 1994 to 14.1 percent in 1998, quite a dramatic increase. Rising infrastructure, personnel, advertising, and marketing expenses explain the increase. It clearly takes a more intensive marketing and administrative effort to support the company's sales growth and margins.

In spite of rising SGA expenses, strong increases in gross margin drove the company's operating margin from 5.2 percent in 1994 to 7.1 percent in 1996. But the 1997 gross margin decline, as well as nonrecurring charges of 1.8 percent, dropped the operating margin to 2.8 percent. The recovering 1998 gross margin of 20.7 percent, even though greater than the 17.1 percent 1996 level, was insufficient to fully restore the 1998 operating margin, which reached only 6.6 percent. Slight increases in other income brought the 1998 4.6 percent net margin back close to the 5.0 percent 1996 high.

Remarkably Improved Working Capital Management

GTW, through a combination of rising inventory and slowing payables turnover, aggressively reduced its cash conversion cycle from 39 days in 1995 to negative 7 in 1998 (Table 7–3).

Nevertheless, asset turnover in the return calculation actually slowed to 3.66 in 1998 from 4.48 in 1996. Does this make sense? Actually it does, if we refer to the GTW statement of cash flows. Working capital management produced a remarkable $509.4 million cash inflow in 1998, in keeping with the sharp fall in the cash conversion cycle, much larger than the $189.9 million 1997 level. Strong cash generation from working capital pushed cash flow from operations to $907.7 million from $484.0 million and $442.8 million in 1996 and 1997, respectively. But the company's capital investment needs remained relatively constant, permitting 1998 year-end cash to rise by $576.2 million. It is this substantial rise in cash that explains slower asset turnover. Given the success of the company's working capital management efforts, if management can find a productive use for this cash, it's reasonable to expect asset turnover to begin to recover.

Rising Leverage

Interestingly, rising asset levels produced by increased cash and marketable securities, rather than increased debt, explain GTW's increased leverage (measured by the ratio of total assets to stockholders' equity) to 2.19 times from 2.02 in 1996. Declining debt/equity ratios and increasing cash flow coverage confirm the asset-driven leverage increase. On the other hand, the 58.7 percent 1998 cash flow from operations to total liabilities ratio seems unsustainable since it relies on the release of large amounts of cash from working capital.

TABLE 7–3

Gateway's cash conversion dramatically improved in 1998.

Days in	1995	1996	1997	1998
Accounts receivable	40	33	30	27
Inventory	27	25	17	10
Payables	28	37	34	44
Cash conversion cycle	39	21	13	(7)

It is unusual for working capital to be a source, rather than a use, of cash in a company growing as rapidly as GTW, although it was in four of the five years between 1994 and 1998. The power of GTW's made-to-order, direct-sales strategy, which permits inventories and receivables to be minimized, and the company's considerable buying power, which allows extension of payables, is clear.

DELL COMPUTER IN ITS INDUSTRY CONTEXT

Gateway provided an example of financial ratio time series analysis founded on the components of the return on equity. In this section, Dell Computer Corporation (DELL), a GTW competitor, is the focus of a cross-sectional analysis of the personal computer industry. DELL will also be our example of financial model building in the next section. In the meantime, Appendix 7–1 presents a comparative ratio analysis of DELL, GTW, and six other industry participants.

Margins

Let's begin the cross-sectional analysis where the time series analysis began, with the return on equity found in the "Value Drivers" section of Appendix 7–1. Dell produces an astounding ROE, reaching 112.9 percent in 1998. Only GTW and Sun Microsystems come close. But the company's net margins, which fall in the 6 to 8 percent range in the 1997 to 1999 period, do not seem unreasonably high. For example, IBM, Sun, and HP all have margins in this range.

DELL's margins have improved substantially, from 6.7 percent in 1997 to 8.0 percent in 1999, while GTW's have remained about the same, as we have already discussed. Why? The common-sized income statements indicate that DELL's gross profit, which fell in the 21 to 23 percent range over the period, is lower than its competitors. GTW's own gross profit margin reached 20.7 percent in 1998, and Compaq, HP, Sun, IBM, and Silicon Graphics all generate higher gross margins. However, DELL's SGA expenses are low relative to its competitors, and they have improved from 10.6 percent of sales in 1997 to 9.8 percent in 1999, while GTW's increased from 11.5 to 14.1 percent over the same period. When we reach the operating profit line, then, in spite of an average gross profit performance, DELL's profitability equals or exceeds most of its competition, especially its closest rivals GTW and Micron.

Even if we knew nothing else about DELL, the cross-sectional analysis suggests the following:

- DELL sells a low margin product relative to companies like Sun Microsystems and HP, but its SGA overhead is low enough to keep its operating profitability in line with higher margin producers. In fact, the bulk of SGA expenses are research and development at many of DELL's rivals, suggesting that DELL carries a low research burden. This is in fact true. As primarily an assembler and marketer of computer products, DELL carries on relatively little independent R&D, relying upon component suppliers for product and technology development.

- DELL is weathering increased competitive pressure better than its rivals. From the GTW time series analysis, we know that personal computer manufacturers have seen increased pricing pressure in a maturing market. DELL's own sales growth has slipped a bit from 58.9 percent in 1998 to 48.0 percent in 1999. DELL's margin improvement in the face of industry-wide pressure suggests a number of followup questions for the analyst. For example, has DELL maintained its margins through a changing mix of products or new product development? Does it have input cost advantages? Does a stronger brand reduce the company's marketing overhead?

Asset Turnover

DELL's asset turnover, which reached 4.27 times in 1999, far exceeds any of its rivals, especially the nondirect sellers like Compaq, Sun, and HP. The power of the direct-sales strategy is even more graphically illustrated by the cash conversion cycle. DELL's cycle reached a negative 13 days in 1999. Only GTW and Micron, the other two direct sellers, even came close.

High Leverage, High Risks?

Does DELL achieve this remarkable performance at the expense of higher financial risk? The company's high balance sheet leverage 3.30

in 1999 exceeds all other industry participants but IBM. A quick check of the "leverage and coverage" section reveals that, once again with the exception of IBM, DELL's 22.1 percent 1999 debt/capital ratio does exceed that of its rivals. But 79 times interest coverage and 53.5 percent cash flow coverage certainly raise no concerns with debt service. In fact, the company's high balance sheet leverage probably arises not from excessive borrowing but from its ability to minimize the equity base employed in its business. In other words, high leverage can suggest risky financial management practices, but it can also mean high (equity) capital efficiency. The difference between the two situations is coverage—that is, the ability of the company to comfortably service its obligations.

DIRECT SELLERS HAVE THE EDGE

This cross-sectional industry analysis leads the analyst in very clear directions, and is very revealing of industry competitive conditions:

- Direct sellers, like DELL and GTW, have the clear financial edge at this point in the personal computer industry's development. Adequate margins, helped by low research and marketing overheads, combined with powerful asset efficiencies, allow the direct sellers to substantially outperform the competition.

- The very fact that the industry's most successful companies do the least research indicates that the industry may be approaching maturity. Product standards have been set. The shakeout of nonstandard technologies is apparently finished.

- Slowing sales growth and margin pressure indicate a shift in the nature of the personal computer itself, from an experience good to a search good. Companies like DELL and GTW have established sufficient reputations for quality that competition now often comes down to price—interesting in a high-technology field. Product technology, features, and performance are now secondary in differentiating one company from the next. Cramming the most performance into the cheapest box may even be a passing strategy. Producing the cheapest box may be the new personal computer competitive game.

NOTES

[1] Krishna G. Palepu, Victor L. Bernard, and Paul M. Healy, *Introduction to Business Analysis and Valuation,* South-Western College Publishing, 1997, pp. 4–1 through 4–29.

[2] ROE = (net income/sales) * (sales/total assets) * (total assets/shareholders' equity) = net income/shareholders' equity.

[3] Palepu, Bernard, and Healy, *Business Analysis and Valuation,* p. 4–2.

Comparative Financial Analysis: Personal Computer Industry

	Dell (1)			Gateway			1998 Fiscal Year					
	1997	1998	1999	1996	1997	1998	Micron	Compaq	HP	Sun (2)	IBM	Silicon Graphics (3)
Common-sized income statement												
Net sales	100.0%	100.0%	100.0%	100.0%	100.0%	100.0%	100.0%	100.0%	100.0%	100.0%	100.0%	100.0%
Cost of good sold	78.5%	77.9%	77.5%	81.4%	82.9%	79.3%	87.2%	76.9%	68.1%	48.0%	62.2%	58.3%
Gross profit	21.5%	22.1%	22.5%	18.6%	17.1%	20.7%	12.8%	23.1%	31.9%	52.0%	37.8%	41.7%
Selling gen & admin	10.6%	9.8%	9.8%	11.5%	12.5%	14.1%	16.4%	16.0%	16.6%	27.2%	20.4%	33.0%
Other expenses	1.6%	1.7%	1.5%	0.0%	1.8%	0.0%	0.6%	4.3%	7.1%	10.8%	6.2%	13.3%
Operating income	12.3%	11.4%	11.3%	7.1%	2.8%	6.6%	-4.8%	2.8%	8.2%	12.9%	11.2%	-4.6%
Other income, net	0.4%	0.4%	0.2%	0.5%	0.4%	0.6%	0.8%	11.3%	0.5%	0.7%	-0.2%	-0.7%
Income before taxes	9.6%	11.1%	11.4%	7.6%	3.2%	7.2%	5.0%	-8.5%	8.7%	13.6%	11.1%	-5.3%
Provision for income taxes	2.8%	3.4%	3.4%	2.6%	1.5%	2.6%	2.2%	0.3%	2.4%	4.9%	3.3%	-1.2%
Net income	6.8%	7.7%	8.0%	5.0%	1.7%	4.6%	2.8%	-8.8%	6.3%	8.7%	7.7%	-4.2%
Returns												
Return on average equity	58.2%	89.9%	80.8%	36.6%	12.6%	30.5%	12.3%	-26.4%	17.8%	24.6%	32.2%	-8.0%
Return on beginning equity	53.2%	117.1%	112.9%	45.1%	13.5%	37.2%	13.1%	-29.1%	18.2%	29.3%	31.9%	-7.9%
Return on beginning assets (unadjusted)	24.1%	31.5%	34.2%	22.3%	6.6%	17.0%	6.3%	-18.7%	9.3%	18.0%	7.8%	-3.9%
Pretax operating return on beg assets	33.2%	44.0%	47.9%	31.7%	10.5%	24.2%	-11.1%	5.9%	12.1%	26.6%	11.2%	-4.3%
Return on beginning total capital (adjusted)	49.3%	114.8%	112.7%	43.2%	13.1%	36.4%	11.9%	-27.3%	15.1%	28.7%	14.5%	-4.9%
EBITDA/beginning total capital	70.1%	167.8%	164.0%	72.1%	31.4%	63.0%	-11.1%	18.6%	27.8%	59.9%	29.2%	5.0%
Growth												
Net sales	46.5%	58.9%	48.0%	37.0%	25.0%	18.7%	-11.4%	26.8%	9.7%	19.7%	4.0%	-11.3%
Operating income	89.4%	84.3%	55.5%	43.0%	-50.5%	180.1%	-161.5%	-71.3%	-11.5%	36.4%	0.7%	-78.7%
Net income	95.2%	77.8%	54.7%	44.9%	-56.2%	215.5%	-45.0%	-247.9%	-5.5%	36.4%	3.9%	-75.0%
Total assets	39.3%	42.6%	61.1%	48.9%	21.9%	41.7%	-8.7%	57.5%	6.1%	48.8%	5.6%	-6.0%
Shareholder's equity	-17.2%	60.4%	79.5%	46.8%	14.0%	44.5%	14.0%	20.4%	4.7%	38.5%	-1.9%	-2.8%

	Dell (1)			Gateway			1998 Fiscal Year					
	1997	1998	1999	1996	1997	1998	Micron	Compaq	HP	Sun (2)	IBM	Silicon Graphics (3)
Value Drivers (not adjusted for interest expense)												
Net profit margin	6.7%	7.7%	8.0%	5.0%	1.7%	4.6%	2.8%	-8.8%	6.3%	8.7%	7.7%	-4.2%
× Asset turnover	3.61	4.12	4.27	4.48	3.76	3.66	2.29	2.13	1.48	2.07	1.00	0.93
= Return on assets	24.1%	31.5%	34.2%	22.3%	6.6%	17.0%	6.3%	-18.7%	9.3%	18.0%	7.7%	-3.9%
× Balance sheet leverage	2.21	3.71	3.30	2.02	2.05	2.19	2.07	1.55	1.97	1.63	4.11	2.02
= Return on equity	53.2%	117.1%	112.9%	45.1%	13.5%	37.2%	13.1%	-29.1%	18.2%	29.3%	31.8%	-7.9%
Asset turnover												
Current asset turnover	2.8	3.2	2.9	6.3	6.9	8.3	3.2	2.1	2.2	1.9	1.9	0.7
Working capital turnover	7.1	10.1	6.9	291.8	(81.2)	(14.4)	6.0	7.0	5.8	4.0	14.8	3.2
Accounts receivable turnover	8.6	8.3	8.7	11.2	12.3	13.4	13.5	4.5	6.1	5.1	3.0	4.7
Inventory turnover	24.3	41.2	51.8	14.7	20.9	35.3	49.0	12.0	5.2	18.4	9.8	6.2
Accounts payable turnover	5.9	5.8	5.9	10.0	10.7	8.2	7.0	5.7	10.0	7.5	8.1	6.2
Days in receivables	42	44	42	33	30	27	27	82	60	71	120	77
Days in inventories	15	9	7	25	17	10	7	31	70	20	37	59
Days in payables	62	62	62	37	34	44	52	64	36	49	45	59
Cash conversion cycle	(5)	(10)	(13)	21	13	(7)	(17)	48	94	43	112	78
PPE turnover	33.0	36.0	34.9	20.8	18.7	14.1	11.7	10.7	7.4	7.3	4.2	
Leverage and coverage												
Liabilities to equity	236.7%	230.1%	196.3%	105.2%	119.3%	115.0%	66.1%	103.1%	99.0%	74.6%	343.1%	95.8%
Debt to capital	2.2%	1.4%	22.1%	2.7%	2.3%	1.1%	6.8%	0.0%	19.6%	3.9%	151.4%	0.0%
Warranty liabilities/equity	2.2%	1.3%	18.1%	2.7%	2.2%	1.1%	6.4%	0.0%	16.4%	3.8%	60.2%	0.0%
Interest coverage	27.2%	17.4%	15.0%	6.2%	10.5%	8.4%	0.0%	0.0%	0.0%	0.0%	0.0%	0.0%
Operating cash flow/total liabilities	102.0	438.7	78.7	535.5	246.4	531.4	—	3.3	16.3	NM	12.9	-563.5%
	71.4%	53.5%	53.5%	56.4%	39.9%	58.7%	-0.9%	5.5%	32.5%	69.1%	13.9%	10.7%
Cash flow characteristics												
Net income/cash flow from operations	0.38	0.59	0.60	0.52	0.25	0.38	(19.41)	(4.26)	0.54	0.41	0.68	(0.79)
CFO/fixed investment	11.95	8.51	8.23	3.51	1.23	2.55	0.02	(0.35)	6.85	3.39	1.51	0.99
Depreciation/capital expenditures	0.41	0.36	0.35	0.55	0.54	0.45	0.58	1.49	0.94	0.85	0.69	1.50
Sustainable growth rate												
ROE	53.2%	117.1%	112.9%	45.1%	13.5%	37.2%	13.1%	-29.1%	18.2%	29.3%	31.9%	-7.9%
Dividend payout	0.0%	0.1%	0.0%	0.0%	0.0%	0.0%	0.0%	0.0%	21.2%	0.0%	13.2%	0.0%
Sustainable growth rate	53.2%	117.0%	112.9%	45.1%	13.5%	37.2%	13.1%	-29.1%	14.4%	29.3%	27.7%	-7.9%

(1) Dell fiscal year ends at January month end
(2) Fiscal year ending June 30; 6/30/99 figures shown
(3) Fiscal year ends June 30; 6/30/99 figures shown

CHAPTER 8

Reading a Financial Statement: Early-Stage Companies and Investment Capacity

- The capacity of a firm for continued investment is the third principal issue in reading a financial statement. Investment capacity focuses the analyst on the statement of cash flows (SOCF). There are recurring patterns in the SOCF related to a firm's stage of development. Each development stage has unique growth, return, and cash flow characteristics.[1]

- Startup and emerging growth are the earliest stages of company development. A startup company is engaged in organizing itself and in developing and introducing products. Sales begin gradually to build, earnings are elusive and likely negative, and the company is probably dependent on outside finance. In the startup stage, managers are searching for financing, and investors are searching for market potential and first-mover advantage.

- Emerging growth companies, the next stage in company development, are experiencing accelerating sales growth. Products begin to penetrate the market, and revenues begin to build. The competitive struggle in this stage focuses on technology and business models, as firms strive to establish product standards and develop efficient production processes. Emerging growth companies often remain fragile, dependent on outside funding. The analyst's problems in emerging growth companies are much the same as in startup companies since at this stage companies do have products, but their products have not yet achieved market dominance.

■ Near the end of the emerging growth phase, an industry "shakeout" is likely, as particular products and business models are successful in the market and begin to capture increased share, and production moves toward an efficient scale. Unsuccessful business models experience increasing financial pressure, and many fail. The market transforms from emerging to established growth, where successful products and processes achieve a dominant market position.

Assessing a firm's capacity for continued investment is the third and final stage in reading financial statements. The most conspicuous influence on a firm's capacity for profitable investment is, in my view, its stage of development. Each development stage has a recognizable pattern and offers distinct challenges to the equity analyst. New companies, in the startup or emerging growth stages, have investment opportunities but few internal financial resources. Established growth companies have achieved competitive success, and they have begun to produce substantial earnings and cash. Mature companies experience a flattening of demand, often producing even stronger cash flow—because of reduced productive capacity needs—but lagging profit growth. Declining companies suffer a drop in the physical demand for their products, and they must manage the shrinkage of their productive resources.

As important as the stages themselves are to equity analysts, the transitions between them are even more critical. Stage transitions are the boundaries between stock valuation regimes. Values of early-stage companies contain a substantial speculative component, in the absence of operating history, proven products or proven markets, and business models. "Projections, conjecture, extrapolation, hopes, and even dreams" drive their values.[2] The equity analysis of early-stage companies focuses on the abundance of potential, and the power of the companies' business models and managements to exploit it. In later stages, companies may have proven products and markets but declining investment potential. The transitions, from wide-open to limited possibilities, from accelerating to decelerating growth, from expanding to steady—or declining— valuation multiples, are the crucial points for equity analysis. The equity analyst must recognize change and overcome his or her reluctance to forecast the continuation of a dying trend. Sounds easy, but it isn't. It is of some comfort to realize that change always occurs.

STAGES OF COMPANY DEVELOPMENT

Company life cycles are often divided into five stages. The two earliest stages, startup and emerging growth, are our focus in this chapter. I'll make no attempt to scientifically define these stages; in fact, I'm not sure that they can be precisely defined, especially in quantitative terms. Nevertheless, the stage of development model is a useful conceptual tool.

To avoid the issues of inflation and changing product pricing, I like to think of the "Sales" axis of Figure 8–1 in physical, rather than annual dollar, terms.

Financial evidence of a company's development stage can be found in all of its financial statements. But the SOCF is the most revealing because it presents the cash flow and investment trends that are so central to the development process.

STARTUP: THE COMPANY DEFINES ITSELF

In the startup phase, a company organizes itself and develops its products. Sales are slow as the company struggles for recognition and begins

FIGURE 8–1

Company development begins with startup and ends with decline stage.

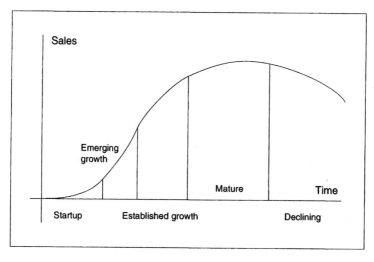

its marketing. Revenue is low, and operating losses are likely. Expenses and capital expenditures are high because the company is building administrative and production infrastructure. The company is very likely dependent on outside finance.

eToys, Inc.

eToys in 1997–1998 provides an excellent example of a firm in the start-up phase. The financials in Table 8–1 for the nine months ending December 31 of 1997 and 1998 are drawn from the company's S-1 filed in February 1999.

The company experienced a growing operating loss in 1998, up to $15.3 million from $1.1 million one year earlier. Cash outflows before working capital grew to $13.5 million from $1.1 million.

Interestingly, a buildup of accounts payable permitted eToys to actually generate cash from working capital, which reached $8.3 million in 1998 from $0.1 million in 1997. As an Internet toy seller, the company may be able, through minimizing its inventory investment, to sustain working capital cash flow generation. We saw the same phenomenon with direct computer sellers Dell and Gateway.

In spite of the cash from working capital, the company's operating cash outflow is accelerating, to $4.9 million in 1998 from about $1.0 million in 1997. Capital exenditures are modest at $1.9 million in 1998, but they contribute to the firm's negative free cash flow of $7.9 million.

External financing, from a $5.0 million bridge loan and $22.0 million in convertible preferred stock, makes up the cash shortfall. The resulting $17.0 million cash increase equals about two years of cash needs at the current $7.9 million free-cash "burn" rate, but, as the company ramps up its growth, burn rates will probably accelerate. More outside financing, in this case the upcoming public offering, is likely.

Focus on Potential

A detailed description of the financial analysis of early-stage companies is beyond the scope of this book but it can be found in many texts on venture capital investing. However, some general principles guide any analysis of very early-stage investments:

- As illustrated by eToys, early-stage companies have large cash appetites, and managements must spend substantial time

TABLE 8-1

eToys financials show characteristics of a startup company (in thousands of dollars, nine months ending December 31).

	1997	1998
Operating activities		
Net loss	(1,127)	(15,258)
Adjustments to reconcile to net cash		
Noncash interest	15	38
Nonemployee stock compensation		
Amortization of deferred compensation		1,621
Depreciation	7	246
Amortization		122
Other interest expense, net of tax	—	3
Interest income, net of tax	—	(315)
Subtotal	22	1,715
Net cash before working capital, interest expense	(1,105)	(13,543)
Changes in operating assets and liabilities		
Inventories	(105)	(4,747)
Prepaid expenses	(147)	(359)
Accounts payable	387	11,968
Accrued expenses	6	1,446
Subtotal	141	8,308
Net cash before interest	(964)	(5,235)
Cash interest expense, net of tax (35%)	—	312
Net cash provided by operating activities	(964)	(4,923)
Investment activities		
Expenditures for PPE	(102)	(1,913)
Acquisition	—	—
Other	—	(1,022)
Net cash (used for) provided by investing	(102)	(2,935)
Free-cash flow	(1,066)	(7,858)
Dividends	—	—
Free cash after dividends	(1,066)	(7,858)
Financing activities		
Proceeds from bridge loan	—	5,000
Payments on bridge loan	—	(2,238)
Proceeds from issuance of common stock	224	4
Exercise of stock options	1	—
Proceeds from redeemable convertible preferred stock	3,007	22,047
Proceeds from convertible notes	895	—
Payments on capital leases	—	(15)
Proceeds from receivables from stockholders	—	23
Proceeds from exercise of warrants	—	30
Net cash from financing activities	4,127	24,851
Net increase in cash and cash equivalents	3,061	16,993

searching for outside financing. The abundance of venture
capital eased that search (until recently), but financing remains
a management distraction from the business of, well, building
a business.

- Analysts and investors must focus on the company's potential
  since there is little else to go on. This means that the
  competitive analysis of the firm is of primary importance.
  Financial analytic techniques and even financial modeling are
  secondary. All the techniques presented in Chapters 3 and 4
  can be useful.

- The place to start in the analysis of early-stage companies is
  management.[3] This sounds like a cliché, but it isn't. The
  reason is simply that no war plan survives first contact with
  the enemy. Few business plans are executed exactly as written.
  It is the ability of the management to make adjustments and
  control the business as it changes direction that is critical to
  success. I have often heard venture capitalists say that they
  completely ignore most of the company's business plan. The
  management is the reality.

- If potential is a startup's best quality, then the size of the
  market is the best indicator of potential—not because investors
  believe management's market share projections (they usually
  don't) but because, if market share projections are wrong, there
  is at least room for error. Suppose the startup fails to capture
  the planned 10 percent market share—it's often 10 percent, by
  the way. Will 2 percent still produce a reasonable investment
  return? Many venture investors look for startups that can
  potentially achieve a $1 billion equity market capitalization and
  "hundreds of millions" in revenue.[4]

- The problem with big markets is that they attract big
  competitors and big investment. As in the VRIO technique,
  venture capitalists want to know if the startup has any
  sustainable advantages over its competition, current or future.
  Will the startup be a first mover? Does it have unique,
  difficult-to-imitate technology, patents, or copyrights? The key
  here is to try to guess whether the startup has the power to
  carve out profits. I recall sitting in a meeting with a well-
  known Internet startup company as they explained their ability

to ramp up volume on their Web site by increasing advertising and marketing expenditures. Unfortunately, when the spending stopped, so did the volume growth. One wonders if such a business model ever reaches sustainable profitability.

eToys Confronts a Critical Christmas

Sadly, Christmas 2000 proved to be a significant disappointment to eToys. Since its May 1999 IPO, eToys (ETYS) established itself as the leading online toy merchandiser, but struggled to establish profitability. In the wake of the 2000 shakeout in e-retailing and Internet stocks, ETYS fell more than 90 percent, from its $86 12-month high to $4 per share. The company faced stiffening competition from the newly formed partnership of Toysrus.com, the Toys R Us toy merchandising Web site, and Amazon.com. Company officials acknowledged that the 2000 Christmas buying season would be crucial to the company's ultimate success. ETYS expected to more than double holiday quarter sales to $240 million, to provide satisfactory customer service, and to demonstrate rising margins in order to secure an additional $100 million in financing before its expected break into profitability in 2002.[5]

Unfortunately, Christmas 2000 sales appear to have reached only $120 to $130 million, well off management's expectation.[6] In January 2001, eToys announced the layoff of 70 percent of its workforce and said it did not expect to achieve profitability by its previously announced March 31, 2003 goal.[7]

Driven both by rapid sales growth and expanding operating losses, the company's continued need for external finance is illustrated by the abbreviated SOCF in Table 8–2.

EMERGING GROWTH: THE BATTLE IS JOINED

In the emerging growth stage, the battle between competing business models, products, and production processes is joined. Markets are often new, and penetration is low. Sales ramp up quickly. Investment in productive capacity accelerates as companies strive to meet demand. Standards are not fixed, and many different product features compete for acceptance. Continued infrastructure spending may keep emerging growth companies unprofitable and keep their investment needs at a high

TABLE 8–2

ETYS continues to need external financing (in thousands of
dollars, years ending March 31).

	1999	2000
Net cash from operations	(23,930)	(174,435)
Net cash used in investing activities	(2,720)	(26,842)
Initial public offering of common stock		178,821
Convertible subordinated notes		150,000
Redeemable convertible preferred and exercise of warrants	42,469	
Other	2,802	(7,928)
Net cash provided by financing	45,271	320,893
Change in cash and cash equivalents	18,621	119,454
Note: Net sales	29,959	151,036

Source: ETYS financial reports.

level and dependent on external financing. Dividends are a rarity in this
explosive growth phase.

Amazon.com

Between 1996 and 1998, Amazon.com (AMZN) entered the emerging
growth stage of its development. Sales grew from $15.7 million in 1996
to $610.0 million in 1998, an astounding 523 percent annual rate. But
as shown in Table 8–3, loss also accelerated, reaching $124.5 million in
1998. Cumulative cash outflows over the three years reached $82.1 mil-
lion before working capital.

Once again, as in eToys, working capital acted as a source rather
than a use of cash. Cash generated by working capital equaled $103.3
million, exceeding the operating outflow. In fact, in spite of the 1998
$124 million net loss, the company actually generated $31.0 million in
cash flow from operations, thanks to $72.5 million produced by working
capital, mostly from a buildup of payables. The power of the Internet
sales model was demonstrated once again.

TABLE 8–3

Amazon.com illustrates the behavior of an emerging growth company (in thousands of dollars).

	1996	1997	1998	Total
Operating activities				
Net loss	(6,246)	(31,020)	(124,546)	(161,812)
Adjustments to reconcile to net cash				
Depreciation and amortization	296	3,442	9,692	13,430
Amortization of deferred compensation		1,354	2,386	3,740
Noncash merger and acquisition costs			47,065	47,065
Noncash interest expense		64	23,970	24,034
Cash interest expense, net of tax (35%)	3	170	1,735	1,908
Interest income, net of tax (35%)	(131)	(1,236)	(9,134)	(10,501)
Subtotal	168	3,795	75,713	79,676
Net cash before working capital, interest expense	(6,078)	(27,225)	(48,833)	(82,136)
Changes in operating assets and liabilities				
Inventories	(554)	(8,400)	(20,513)	(29,467)
Prepaid expenses	(315)	(3,034)	(16,465)	(19,814)
Deposits and other	(148)	(21)	(293)	(462)
Accounts payable	2,756	30,172	78,674	111,602
Accrued advertising	598	2,856	9,617	13,071
Other liabilities and accrued expenses	1,603	5,274	21,448	28,325
Subtotal	3,940	26,847	72,468	103,255
Net cash before interest	(2,138)	(378)	23,635	21,119
Cash interest expense, net of tax (35%)	(3)	(170)	(1,735)	(1,908)
Interest income, net of tax (35%)	131	1,236	9,134	10,501
Net cash provided by operating activities	(2,010)	687	31,035	29,712
Investment activities				
Maturities of marketable securities		4,311	332,084	336,395
Purchases of marketable securities	(5,233)	(122,385)	(546,509)	(674,127)
Purchases of fixed assets	(1,335)	(7,603)	(28,333)	(37,271)
Acquisitions, dispositions, and investments			(19,019)	(19,019)
Net cash (used for) provided by investing	(6,568)	(125,677)	(261,777)	(394,022)
Free-cash flow	(8,578)	(124,990)	(230,742)	(364,310)
Dividends	—	—	—	—
Free cash after dividends	(8,578)	(124,990)	(230,742)	(364,310)

TABLE 8–3

Amazon.com illustrates the behavior of an emerging growth company (in thousands of dollars). *(Continued)*

	1996	1997	1998	Total
Financing activities				
Proceeds from issuance of common stock	—	49,103	—	49,103
Proceeds from stock options	195	509	5,983	6,687
Proceeds from issuance of capital stock	8,443	3,746	8,383	20,572
Proceeds from long-term debt	—	75,000	325,987	400,987
Repayment of long-term debt	—	(47)	(78,108)	(78,155)
Financing costs	—	(2,309)	(7,783)	(10,092)
Net cash from financing activities	8,638	126,002	254,462	389,102
Effect of exchange rate changes	—	—	(35)	(35)
Net increase in cash and cash equivalents	60	1,012	23,685	24,757

Purchases of fixed assets accelerated rapidly, from $1.3 million in 1996 to $28.3 million in 1998. The company also spent a net $19.0 million on net acquisitions in 1998. But the bulk of the cumulative $394.3 million in spending over the three-year period was the $674.1 million purchase of marketable securities, offset by securities' maturities and fixed asset spending. Excluding marketable securities, free-cash outflow of $364.3 million was reduced to $26.6 million. AMZN paid no common dividends during the three years shown.

Unlike eToys, which financed its cash needs through equity sales, AMZN added $401 million in long-term debt over the period, as well as selling $49.1 million in common stock, a sign of a somewhat more mature company. But like eToys, much of the company's additional financing found its way into a cash and marketable securities "war chest" equaling $373.4 million at year end 1998. Since AMZN actually generated positive operational cash flow, the analyst might ask the purpose of this financing build-up. Accelerated capital spending or acquisitions is each a good bet. Or perhaps an inventory buildup, like the warehouse building program the company began in 1999, might be anticipated, turning working capital into a cash user.

Focus on the Business Model

Still, AMZN's business model remains to be proven. Rapidly accelerating sales have not produced positive operating profits. True, the company generates positive operating cash flow, surprising in such an early stage with its rapidly growing business. But its operating cash is principally the result of an Internet business model—low inventories and receivables combined with high payables—which is still being tested.

AMZN remains reliant on external financing. Because its business model is more developed, AMZN's situation is somewhat clearer than that of eToys. The questions facing the analyst are similar, however:

- The company's basic book sales business produces cash. But marketing and administrative costs are very heavy, generating an operating loss. Can the company find a way to leverage its marketing expenses by piling more revenue on top? AMZN has added music and electronics sales to its original book business, and it collects fee revenue from small retailers who piggyback on its systems. Or will these new product areas demand even heavier overhead spending, perpetuating the cycle of growth and losses?

- Can working capital remain such a critical source of cash? Or will the company need to incorporate a more cash-intensive bricks-and-mortar strategy, with warehouses and retail outlets?

- Are the company's considerable brand recognition and first-mover advantages sufficient to sustain it against the competition? Many large bricks-and-mortar retailers have yet to develop adequate Internet strategies. What happens to AMZN when they do?

- How will rapid technological change impact AMZN's competitive position? Will broadband and wireless access to the Internet bring more intense competition, or will it cement the positions of pioneers like Amazon?

AMZN Stays Young

Amazon's rapid growth continued in 1999, accompanied by accelerating losses and external financing needs. The company aggressively expanded its business offerings, adding online auctions, electronics, toys, zShops

(individual retailers using AMZN's Web technology), home improvement, software, video games, and international operations in the United
Kingdom and Germany. Through its Amazon.com Commerce Network,
AMZN entered strategic partnerships with companies like Sotheby's,
drugstore.com, NextCard Inc., and Toys R Us to promote their products
on its site. In addition, the company, in a somewhat unusual move, added
4 million square feet of warehouse space in eight separate locations
worldwide to improve its product delivery services. These substantial
efforts more than doubled sales to $1.6 billion in 1999 from $609.8
million in 1998, but profitability remained elusive as the net loss rose to
$720.0 million from $124.5 million the previous year (Table 8–4).

Gross profit expanded in 1999 in dollar terms but fell as a percentage of sales because of new product line introductions and excess
inventories. The company expects the 2000 gross margin to recover to
the 20 percent range. Marketing and sales expenses, AMZN's largest
overhead expense category, expanded dramatically to 25.2 percent of
1999 sales with the added expenses of the new warehousing system.
Management hopes these expenses in the future will decline as a percentage of sales.

As in the previous years shown in Table 8–5, AMZN's 1999 cash
flow statement shows the pattern of operational deficits and external financing typical of early-stage enterprises. The company's online business
model provided cash from working capital of $230.1 million, but these
flows were insufficient to offset accelerating operating cash uses, causing

TABLE 8–4

AMZN expands rapidly, but profitability remains elusive.

	1998		1999	
	$, Millions	%	$, Millions	%
Net sales	609.8	100.0	1,639.8	100.0
Gross profit	133.7	21.9	290.6	17.7
Marketing and sales expenses	132.6	21.8	413.1	25.2
Net loss	(124.5)	(20.4)	(720.0)	(43.9)

Source: Company financial reports.

TABLE 8–5

AMZN's SOCF shows early development stage pattern.

	1998	1999
Net loss	(124.5)	(720.0)
Cash flows from working capital	72.5	230.1
Net cash from operations	31.0	(90.9)
Net cash used in investing	(261.8)	(922.3)
Net cash provided by financing	254.5	1,104.1
Change in cash balances	23.7	91.4

Source: Company financial reports.

a CFO deficit of $90.9 million. Larger investments of $922.3 million, consisting of acquisitions and increased bricks-and-mortar construction, far exceeded the previous year's $261.8 million. As a result, AMZN's external financing was particularly heavy in 1999 with the addition of $1.3 billion of long-term debt.

In spite of the increasing clamor for profitability from Wall Street, AMZN persists in its aggressive investment and marketing strategy, thereby extending the early development stage characteristics of its financial statements.

Unlike the eToys experience, AMZN ended the Christmas 2000 quarter with estimated sales of $960 million, up 42 percent from 1999 but at the bottom of its $950 million to $1.05 billion target range.[8] In keeping with the current gloomy Wall Street atmosphere, analysts were distinctly underwhelmed by the result, and worried that continued high marketing expenses, as well holiday discounting, could have depressed profit margins.

NOTES

[1] This approach was suggested by the work of Martin S. Fridson, *Financial Statement Analysis: A Practitioner's Guide,* 2d ed., Wiley, New York, 1997, ch. 4, "The Statement of Cash Flows."

[2] Sidney Cottle, Roger F. Murray, and Frank E. Block, *Graham and Dodd's Security Analysis,* 5th ed., McGraw-Hill, New York, 1988, p. 545.

[3] William A. Sahlman, "Some Thoughts on Business Plans," in *The Entrepreneurial Venture*, 2d ed., edited by William A. Sahlman, Howard H. Stevenson, Michael J. Roberts, and Amar Bhide, Harvard Business School Press, Boston, 1999.

[4] Jon Callaghan, interview in *Upside,* August 2000, p. 135.

[5] "Toy Wars II: Holiday Cyber Battle Begins," *The Wall Street Journal,* September 25, 2000, p. B1.

[6] Etoys Warns of Weak Revenue in Critical Christmas Season," *The Wall Street Journal* Interactive Edition, December 15, 2000.

[7] Etoys to Lay Off 70% of Workers, Close Two Warehouse Operations," *The Wall Street Journal* Interactive Edition, January 5, 2001.

[8] "Amazon Sees Revenue up 42% for Its Crucial Fourth Quarter," *The Wall Street Journal* Interactive Edition, January 9, 2001.

CHAPTER 9

Reading a Financial Statement: Later-Stage Companies and the Transition to Maturity

- In the established growth phase, product and process features are standardized. Sales likely continue to grow at above-average rates, although at a decelerated pace compared with the emerging growth phase.

- High returns of successful firms may begin to attract imitators, and the competitive environment can remain ferocious. Market power shifts from companies with a technological and/or product focus, to marketers and distributors. Customers are increasingly sophisticated, demanding higher levels of quality, service, and product choice. The cash needs of established growth companies can often be met internally. Such companies may use excess cash for dividends, debt repayment, or acquisitions.

- The transition from established growth to maturity carries substantial risk for equity analysts. Growth companies come under intense pressure to maintain earnings growth rates, in an attempt to convince the stock market that they can postpone product and market maturity. Excess cash may begin to burn holes in management's pockets, leading to ill-advised acquisitions and investments—all in the name of maintaining growth. Accounting difficulties may arise. Analysts themselves can fall into this cycle of denial, hoping that, just this once, the laws of economics can be broken.

- Mature companies exhibit sales and earnings growth rates closer to the underlying economy-wide rates. Managements of mature companies often try to increase or reenergize growth through diversification, acquisition, or globalization or through cost reengineering. The analyst's principal problem is to decide whether any of these efforts is worth paying a premium for the stock.

■ Companies in decline experience absolute reductions in demand for their products, and often mirror, financially, their early-stage cousins. In its effort to raise finance, management may sell assets or borrow heavily. Profits may be insufficient to finance replacement of productive capacity, causing company or industry shrinkage.

Early-stage companies are mostly potential, but with unproven values. Later-stage companies, on the other hand, often have more certain valuations but shrinking potential for profitable investment. Growth rates, which have already decelerated from their highs in the emerging stage, may have held steady at respectable levels for years in the established growth stage. With the beginning of maturity, however, growth declines to levels closer to underlying broad economic growth. As products reach the end of their lives and are replaced, physical sales levels decrease and the company enters decline.

This transition from steady to decelerating growth, from established growth to maturity, is, in my view, the most dangerous stage of company development for the equity analyst. Management comes under intense pressure to maintain growth expectations, in defiance of the laws of economics. Ill-advised acquisitions, aggressive accounting, and other abuses can be the result.

ESTABLISHED GROWTH: PAST THE SHAKEOUT

Companies in the established growth phase have successfully negotiated the industry "shakeout." They have developed a business model, product design, and production processes that have proven successful in the marketplace. Weaker competitors, with unsuccessful business models, have fallen away. Competition has shifted from basic technology toward satisfying increasingly sophisticated customers who demand better quality, more advanced product features, higher service levels, and greater product choice. Growth rates remain above normal, but market share has become an issue since many new sales must often come at the expense of competitors. The marketers within companies begin to gain political ground against the technologists because what competitors are doing is now much more important.

Intel Corporation

Intel in the late 1990s was a good example of a growth company, showing strong sales expansion, cash flow, and earnings (Table 9–1). Company sales grew at a 12 percent average annual pace between 1996 and 1998, reaching $26.3 billion. Although sales rose only about 5 percent in 1998, sales grew over 20 percent in 1997.

Net earnings declined to $6.1 billion in 1998 from $6.9 billion in 1997, but cash flow before working capital increased slightly to $8.9 billion from $8.8 billion, aided by the add-back of substantially increased depreciation charges. Working capital was a net source of $1.9 billion in cash over the period, but it did use $208 million in 1998, in contrast with the two previous years. Cash flow from operations was strongly positive in all three years, totaling $27.9 billion for the period.

Operation cash flow is more than sufficient to fund the period's $11.1 billion in capital expenditures. The purchase of a net $7.2 billion in "available-for-sale" (AFS) investments still left $15.9 billion in free-cash flow before common dividends. Here, for the first time among our life cycle examples, we see nonzero common dividends of $545 million for the period. Common dividends are a marker for more established companies.

Another prominent characteristic of more established companies, the $11.5 billion repurchase of common stock over the period, appears in the SOCF financing section. The company funded $217 million in short-term and $300 billion in long-term debt repayments with an additional $658 million in long-term debt financing.

■ **Tip**   Common dividends and the repurchase of common stock are markers of more established companies.

THE TRANSITION TO MATURITY: MAXIMUM ANALYTIC RISK

The transition from established growth to maturity produces the highest analytic risk of any stage transition simply because no one wants to believe it. Toward the end of a company's established growth phase, investment opportunities are becoming more limited. Intense pressure

TABLE 9–1

Intel Corporation is a strong example of established growth (in millions of dollars).

	1996	1997	1998	Total
Operating activities				
Net earnings	5,157	6,945	6,068	18,170
Adjustments to reconcile to net cash				
Depreciation	1,888	2,192	2,807	6,887
Net loss on retirements of PPE	120	130	282	532
Deferred federal income tax	179	6	77	262
Purchased in-process R&D	—	—	165	165
Net interest expense, net of tax (35%)	(248)	(502)	(493)	(1,242)
Subtotal	1,939	1,826	2,838	6,604
Net cash before working capital, interest expense	7,096	8,771	8,906	24,774
Changes in operating assets and liabilities				
Receivables	(607)	285	(38)	(360)
Inventories	711	(404)	167	474
Accounts payable	105	438	(180)	363
Accrued compensation	370	140	17	527
Income taxes payable	185	179	(211)	153
Tax benefit from employee stock plans	196	224	415	835
Other	439	(127)	(378)	(66)
Subtotal	1,399	735	(208)	1,926
Net cash before interest	8,495	9,506	8,698	26,700
Net interest expense, net of tax (35%)	248	502	493	1,242
Net cash provided by operating activities	8,743	10,008	9,191	27,942

	1996	1997	1998	Total
Investment activities				
Additions to PPE	(3,024)	(4,501)	(3,557)	(11,082)
Purchase of company			(321)	(321)
Purchase of business			(585)	(585)
Purchase of AFS investments	(4,683)	(9,224)	(10,925)	(24,832)
Sale of AFS investments	225	153	201	579
Maturities and/or changes in AFS investments	2,214	6,713	8,681	17,608
Net cash (used for) provided by investing	(5,268)	(6,859)	(6,506)	(18,633)
Free-cash flow	3,475	3,149	2,685	9,309
Free-cash flow, including net AFS purchases	5,719	5,507	4,728	15,954
Common dividends	(148)	(180)	(217)	(545)
Free cash after dividends	3,327	2,969	2,468	8,764
Financing activities				
Increase in ST debt	43	(177)	(83)	(217)
Additions to LT debt	317	172	169	658
Retirement of LT debt		(300)		(300)
Proceeds from employee stock plans	257	317	507	1,081
Proceeds from warrant exercise	4	40	1,620	1,664
Proceeds from sale of put warrants	56	288	40	384
Repurchase and/or retirement of common stock	(1,302)	(3,372)	(6,785)	(11,459)
Net cash from financing activities	(625)	(3,032)	(4,532)	(8,189)
Net increase in cash and cash equivalents	2,702	(63)	(2,064)	575

builds to maintain growth expectations. An earnings dance sometimes begins, with analysts following management's lead. These are telltale indicators of the onset of a mature market:

- ■ "This quarter's numbers are misleading because. . ." Maybe, but there's a good chance of many "misleading" quarters ahead.
- ■ "New products will maintain growth." Meaning, of course, that existing products will not. New products may sustain a growth phase, but analytic risks have certainly risen. In many ways, this situation returns the analyst to the problems of the emerging growth company.
- ■ "We are restructuring our sales force for higher growth." The market is still growing, but the competition is hammering us. Maybe this will work, but again the risks have risen.
- ■ "We will cut distribution costs." The marketplace is still changing, but we've been too slow to keep up. It is interesting to ask how distribution costs will decline as physical growth rekindles.
- ■ "We are considering strategic acquisitions to leverage our industry expertise." Hold on to your wallets, investors! Of all corporate initiatives in this critical transition, acquisitions are the most problematic and should create the highest analytic skepticism. Buying more sales may revitalize sales growth, but it isn't clear that it revitalizes value growth. More on acquisitions in Chapter 19.

Since established growth companies are strong cash generators, like Intel, management has substantial opportunities for reinvestment. But, as maturity approaches, traditional investment opportunities begin to disappear, driving management further afield. Reinvestment risks rise substantially, and ill-advised acquisitions and diversifications become much more likely. In my own industry, the property and casualty insurers, company valuations were punished for excess cash because investors often lacked the confidence that management could deploy the funds profitably.

Analysts, too, have a strong incentive to deny the onset of maturity since they so often find themselves committed to well-performing, successful growth companies. Earnings forecasts in this period begin to face higher risks, as proven income sources play out. Financial models, based upon extrapolation of existing trends, begin to misbehave, showing slowing growth and lagging profitability:

- Cash buildup might raise the percentage of income from interest earnings, creating a quality-of-earnings issue and highlighting the reinvestment issue.
- Aggressive sales projections become harder to justify as sales growth slows.
- Margins show signs of pressure as competition builds and imitators enter the market. This is one of the toughest problems to explain away because it is the company's very success, on which the analyst depends, that must inevitably attract competitors, resulting in margin pressure. It is hard to have success without growing competitive pressure, unless one suspends the laws of economics.
- The stock might begin to behave erratically, as faster money notes signs of trouble ahead. An erratic stock places even more pressure on forecasts that assume the status quo. Someone doesn't believe it and is voting with his or her feet.

In extreme cases, the pressure to maintain growth can lead to overly aggressive accounting or even fraud. Analysts should begin to search for accounting shenanigans especially vigorously as companies approach the maturity transformation.[1]

MATURE COMPANIES: THE OLD— BUT GOOD—ECONOMY

Many successful companies are mature in the sense that their growth rates have declined to a level more in line with that of the underlying broader economy. Mature companies face more modest productive capacity demands. Management may begin to pare away less viable businesses and replace them with newly acquired companies.

A mature company's management usually tries to revitalize growth and improve margins, which have come under competitive pressure:

- "We will diversify, building upon core competencies."
- "We will globalize." If the business isn't growing domestically, maybe it is internationally.

- "We will downsize/right-size/restructure/reengineer." Let's try to fix the margins we have rather than fly to margins we know not of.

The analyst's principal problem with mature companies is to decide whether investors should pay for any of these efforts. In a truly declining industry, management may waste stockholders' resources in vain efforts to stop the tides. On the other hand, deft managements may be able to craft highly successful companies from more modestly growing markets.

Emerson Electric

Emerson Electric is such a company, successfully fashioning a strong, steadily growing business out of slower-growing markets like industry and commercial control systems, motors, and automation systems, through a combination of internal investment and acquisition (Table 9–2). Its sales growth rate averaged 10 percent in the 1993 to 1998 period, and its 1998 return on equity was a respectable 21.9 percent.

The company's SOCF shows steady growth in earnings and operating cash flow. Cumulative operating cash flow reached $4.5 billion over the 1996 to 1998 period, in spite of an increase of $440 million in working capital.

The SOCF investment section reveals some of the company's strategy. Emerson purchased a cumulative $1.2 billion in businesses in the three-year period while investing $1.7 billion internally. It also sold businesses totaling $382.5 billion. Still, even after $1.4 billion in dividends, the company generated about $526 million in free-cash flow.

Interestingly, the company repurchased $996 million of common stock over the period, requiring $588 million in additional debt financing. Because Emerson is a stable company, the resulting increased leverage has had an amplifying effect upon returns without substantially increasing risk.

DECLINING COMPANIES: DEMAND SHRINKS

Declining companies experience a fall in physical demand for their products. Falling demand often means that the company, and its industry, must shrink to match productive capacity with demand. Profits may still be insufficient to meet capital replacement needs, requiring substantial

TABLE 9-2

Emerson Electric maintains strong returns with mature businesses (in millions of dollars).

	1996	1997	1998	Total
Operating activities				
Net earnings	1,018.5	1,121.9	1,228.6	3,369.0
Adjustments to reconcile to net cash				
Depreciation and amortization	464.6	511.6	562.5	1,538.7
Interest expense, net of tax (35%)	82.5	78.6	98.6	259.7
Subtotal	547.1	590.2	661.1	1,798.4
Net cash before working capital, interest expense	1,565.6	1,712.1	1,889.7	5,167.4
Changes in operating assets and liabilities				
Changes in operating working capital	(131.6)	(42.6)	(81.0)	(255.2)
Other	(34.2)	(92.3)	(58.5)	(185.0)
Subtotal	(165.8)	(134.9)	(139.5)	(440.2)
Net cash before interest	1,399.8	1,577.2	1,750.2	4,727.2
Interest expense, net of tax (35%)	(82.5)	(78.6)	(98.6)	(259.7)
Net cash provided by operating activities	1,317.3	1,498.6	1,651.6	4,467.5
Investment activities				
Capital expenditures	(513.5)	(575.4)	(602.6)	(1,691.5)
Purchases of businesses, net of cash acquired	(299.8)	(319.2)	(572.9)	(1,191.9)
Divestiture of businesses, interests, other	272.3	34.0	76.2	382.5
Net cash (used for) provided by investing	(541.0)	(860.6)	(1,099.3)	(2,500.9)
Free-cash flow	776.3	638.0	552.3	1,966.6
Dividends paid	(439.1)	(480.7)	(521.0)	(1,440.8)
Free cash after dividends	337.2	157.3	31.3	525.8

TABLE 9-2

Emerson Electric maintains strong returns with mature businesses (in millions of dollars). (Continued)

	1996	1997	1998	Total
Financing activities				
Net increase in ST borrowings	(363.8)	321.8	145.4	103.4
Proceeds from LT debt	249.9	5.8	452.0	707.7
Repayments of LT debt	(77.0)	(13.1)	(132.5)	(222.6)
Net purchases of treasury stock	(120.3)	(376.6)	(499.4)	(996.3)
Net cash from financing activities	(311.2)	(62.1)	(34.5)	(407.8)
Effect of exchange rate changes	5.7	(23.1)	(8.2)	(25.6)
Net increase in cash and cash equivalents	31.7	72.1	(11.4)	92.4

TABLE 9-3

Lockheed Martin has faced declining product demand (in millions of dollars.)

	1996	1997	1998	Total
Operating activities				
Net earnings	1,347	1,300	1,001	3,648
Adjustments to reconcile to net cash				
Depreciation and amortization	732	606	569	1,907
Amortization of intangibles	402	446	436	1,284
Deferred federal income tax	(251)	155	203	107
Large transaction A		(311)		(311)
Large transaction B	(365)			(365)
Merger-related and consolidation payments	(244)	(68)		(312)
Interest expense, net of tax (35%)	455	547	560	1,562
Interest income, net of tax (35%)	(39)	(26)	(25)	(90)
Subtotal	690	1,349	1,743	3,782
Net cash before working capital, interest expense	2,037	2,649	2,744	7,430
Changes in operating assets and liabilities				
Receivables	(328)	(572)	809	(91)
Inventories	(125)	(687)	(1,183)	(1,995)
Customer advances	544	1,048	329	1,921
Income taxes	(158)	(560)	189	(529)
Other	82	(149)	(322)	(389)
Subtotal	15	(920)	(178)	(1,083)
Net cash before interest	2,052	1,729	2,566	6,347
Interest expense, net of tax (35%)	(455)	(547)	(560)	(1,562)
Interest income, net of tax (35%)	39	26	25	90
Net cash provided by operating activities	1,636	1,208	2,031	4,875

TABLE 9–3

Lockheed Martin has faced declining product demand (in millions of dollars.) (Continued)

	1996	1997	1998	Total
Investment activities				
Expenditures for PPE	(737)	(750)	(697)	(2,184)
Acquisition	(7,344)			(7,344)
Divestiture of Division C		464		464
Divestiture of Division D		450		450
Other acquisition and divestiture activities		12	134	146
Other	52	9	108	169
Net cash (used for) provided by investing	(8,029)	185	(455)	(8,299)
Free-cash flow	(6,393)	1,393	1,576	(3,424)
Preferred dividends	(60)	(53)	—	(113)
Common dividends	(302)	(299)	(310)	(911)
Free cash after dividends	(6,755)	1,041	1,266	(4,448)
Financing activities				
Net increase in ST borrowings	1,110	(866)	(151)	93
Increases in LT debt	7,000	1,505	266	8,771
Repayments of LT debt	(2,105)	(219)	(1,136)	(3,460)
Issuance of common stock	97	110	91	298
Redemptions of preferred stock	—	(1,571)	(51)	(1,622)
Net cash from financing activities	6,102	(1,041)	(981)	4,080
Net increase in cash and cash equivalents	(653)	—	285	(368)

outside financing. Large blocks of assets might be sold to partially finance remaining productive needs. The often-precarious financial state of companies in decline may mirror that of startup companies. Declining companies often become cash users.

Lockheed Martin

Declining aerospace and military expenditures in the wake of the cold war's end forced a consolidation and shrinkage of the aerospace industry (Table 9–3). Lockheed Martin's sales grew 3.5 percent in 1994 to 1998, but this growth included the substantial Loral acquisition in 1996. Earnings have been erratic for much of the 1990s, settling at about $1.0 billion in 1998, down from $1.3 billion one year earlier.

Lockheed's 1996 to 1998 operational cash flow reached a positive $4.9 billion, although it must carry considerable burdens of $1.6 billion after-tax interest and $1.0 billion working capital increase. But even with a cumulative $1.1 billion ($464 + $450 + $146) in cash raised by asset divestitures, cash flow was inadequate to pay for $2.2 billion in capital expenditures and the $7.3 billion Loral acquisition. As a result, the company has been dependent on external financing. It borrowed an additional $8.8 billion in the three-year period.

NOTES

[1] See Michael E. Porter, *Competitive Strategy*, The Free Press, New York, 1980, chap. 11, "The Transition to Industry Maturity," for a discussion of the strategic issues raised by the approach of maturity.

CHAPTER 10

Economic Value Added: An Alternative to Traditional Analysis Techniques

- Unlike either accrual or cash flow–based financial reporting methodologies, Economic Value Added™ (EVA™) makes explicit the connection between investment returns, growth, and market value and therefore can be of great assistance in determining the value implications of corporate strategy.[1]

- EVA is neither a pure accrual nor cash flow concept. The system was developed to measure managerial performance,[2] using elements of both accrual and cash flow accounting, in an effort to create incentives for profitable investment and "changed management behavior."

- In practice, the EVA system can be complex, potentially involving substantial numbers of adjustments to reported accounting numbers. For the working analyst who is implementing EVA, materiality and consistency of application are more important than high precision.

- EVA is not yet a standard tool for intercompany comparative analysis because there remains no standard definition of "economic value added."

A central (perhaps *the* central) theme of this book is that companies can build their market values only through *profitable* growth. In equity analysis, *profitable* means something very special. It means that growth results from the investment of capital at rates of return in excess of capital costs, generating positive abnormal earnings. Unlike GAAP net income or free-cash flow, the Stern Stewart Economic Value Added technique makes explicit the connection between return, growth, and value.

In fact, if GAAP strays further from cash-based reality (with concepts like comprehensive income and market value accounting), hybrid concepts like EVA may be more broadly used. In practice, EVA can be complex, involving large numbers of adjustments to reported income statement and balance sheet numbers. A numerical example, using Gateway 2000, Inc., stresses that materiality considerations should prevail over high precision.

THE FOUNDATIONS OF EVA

EVA is the Stern Stewart & Co. (SSC) formalization of a concept introduced earlier in this text, the abnormal earnings of the firm, and is a restatement of the "economic rents" reasoning familiar to microeconomics students. The idea is simply that, before any business activity can add market value, it must first cover its costs. Those costs include not only the expenses necessary to produce revenue but also capital costs, which are opportunity costs measuring the rate of return available from alternative investments of the same risk. Firms whose investment returns exceed capital costs add market value; in contrast, those who fail to meet capital costs destroy value.

SSC actually set out to find a satisfactory measure of corporate and managerial performance, and they were very unhappy with their discoveries. GAAP accounting measures, like earnings per share (EPS), contained biases, introduced by accounting rules themselves that did not reflect economic reality. Discounted cash flow reflects reality, but, as we saw in Chapter 2, it does not easily generate periodic performance measures. The EVA solution is to formulate performance in terms of abnormal earnings generation, after a considerable number of adjustments (up to 120 to 160 are possible, according to SSC[3]) to GAAP accounting statements. I will not, and in fact cannot, present all the details of the EVA system as it is applied by SSC. My purpose rather is to show, through my own interpretation of the SSC system, one way that abnormal earnings, used up to now as a theoretical construct, can actually be put to some analytic use.

The EVA system is designed primarily to make sense to management, not to its accountants. The EVA, with its myriad potential adjustments, is generally tailored to individual company needs, not to standard rules like GAAP.[4] Furthermore, its underlying intent is to provide the correct incentives to management, not to strive for theoretical purity.

Nevertheless, the absence of common definitions limits the system's usefulness as a comparative tool. Chapter 17 presents a reformulation of economic rent reasoning, using reported GAAP results, which may be of more immediate practical use to the equity analyst.

SSC defines EVA as the difference between the adjusted <u>net operating profit after tax (NOPAT)</u> and the capital costs, which equal the product of the firm's cost of capital and capital (also an adjusted amount):

$$EVA = NOPAT - \text{capital costs}$$
$$= NOPAT - \text{cost of capital} * \text{capital} \quad (10.1)$$

As discussed below, EVA is neither a pure accrual nor net cash flow concept, but it contains elements of both.

THE FIRM AS A SAVINGS ACCOUNT

To measure the returns and the costs of capital, we need to know what "returns" and "capital" are. SSC mean something very unique by "capital":

> Capital is the measure of all cash that has been deposited into a company over its life without regard to financing form, accounting name, or business purpose—much as if the company were a savings account.[5]

I very much like the "savings account" metaphor. It means that once capital is invested, it stays invested until it is returned to capital providers (in the form of dividends, share buybacks, interest expense, or debt repayment) or lost in operations. How GAAP accounting chooses to value the resulting assets once capital is invested in the firm is irrelevant to SSC. If an investor "makes a deposit" by injecting capital, in debt or equity form, that deposit adds to the base of capital at risk.

This viewpoint requires that the traditional measure of a firm's capital—usually consisting of the sum of common and preferred equity, funded debt, and minority interest—be supplemented by what SSC labels "equity equivalents"[6]:

> Book value of common equity
> + funded debt (including leases)
> + preferred stock
> + minority interest
> + equity equivalents
> = capital

Equity Equivalents

Equity equivalents are amounts, either recorded in financial statements or not, that should, in SSC's view, be considered part of investors' "deposits" in the company but, because of GAAP accounting treatment, are not. We'll discuss three of the more common equity equivalents: intangible assets, balance sheet reserves, and special charges to income.

Capitalized Intangibles: Pfizer Research and Development Expense

Accounting rules often require expensing the cost of activities, like research and development (R&D) or marketing, that have an uncertain future earnings impact. SSC views such accounting as overly conservative and advocates the capitalization of these expenses, creating a new class of intangible assets. Capitalized expenses are then amortized over an appropriate period. Such intangible assets are not likely to benefit investors, particularly lenders, if the company were to fail. What, for example, is the value of a failed retailer's new store preopening marketing costs if the store never opens? However, investors do not expect companies to fail, or they would not invest in the first place. A going-concern view is therefore more appropriate to measure investment returns.

The technique for capitalizing R&D expense is illustrated in Table 10–1, using 10 years of data provided in the 1998 Pfizer, Inc., annual report:

- First, R&D expense is accumulated by adding each successive year of the 10-year period, producing total 10-year cumulative R&D expenses of $11,732 million by 1998.
- Next, assuming a 5-year amortization period, each year's expenses are amortized over the subsequent 5 years, and the total amortization in each year is calculated by summing each column. For example, in 1998, $1,605 million of R&D expense, consisting of amounts from the 1994 to 1998 period, is amortized.
- The capitalized R&D amount is the difference between accumulated expenses and accumulated amortization. In 1998, cumulative R&D expense of $11,732 million less cumulative R&D amortization of $7,931 million equals the $3,801 million capitalized balance.

TABLE 10-1

Capitalization of Pfizer research and development costs alters income substantially. Amortization period is 5. (in $ millions)

	1988	1989	1990	1991	1992	1993	1994	1995	1996	1997	1998
R&D expense	401.0	449.0	545.0	654.0	776.0	880.0	1,036.0	1,340.0	1,567.0	1,805.0	2,279.0
Cumulative R&D	401.0	850.0	1,395.0	2,049.0	2,825.0	3,705.0	4,741.0	6,081.0	7,648.0	9,453.0	11,732.0
	80.2	80.2	80.2	80.2	80.2	89.8	109.0	130.8	155.2	176.0	207.2
		89.8	89.8	89.8	89.8	109.0	130.8	155.2	176.0	207.2	268.0
			109.0	109.0	109.0	130.8	155.2	176.0	207.2	268.0	313.4
				130.8	130.8	155.2	176.0	207.2	268.0	313.4	361.0
					155.2	176.0	207.2	268.0	313.4	361.0	455.8
Annual amortization	80.2	170.0	279.0	409.8	565.0	660.8	778.2	937.2	1,119.8	1,325.6	1,605.4
Cumulative amortization	80.2	250.2	529.2	939.0	1,504.0	2,164.8	2,943.0	3,880.2	5,000.0	6,325.6	7,931.0
Capitalized balance	320.8	599.8	865.8	1,110.0	1,321.0	1,540.2	1,798.0	2,200.8	2,648.0	3,127.4	3,801.0
Change in balance		279.0	266.0	244.2	211.0	219.2	257.8	402.8	447.2	479.4	673.6

■ As a part of the NOPAT calculation discussed below, the
change in the capitalized balance is added back to income. In
1998, $673.6 million (pretax) would be added to net income.
The net income effect of this add-back is to replace R&D
expense with R&D amortization.

Note in the Pfizer calculation that 1992 is the first year in which
capitalized R&D is fully accumulated. This is because years before 1988,
when the data series begins, are by then fully amortized and can no
longer affect the calculation. From a practical standpoint, still assuming
a 5-year amortization, the analyst need gather only 5 years of expense
history to fully specify the capitalized expense in the most current year
(clearly, changing the amortization period changes the data requirements).

Persistent Reserves: The Boeing Company

SSC advocates adding back to capital many persistent balance sheet reserves. Deferred taxes, bad debt reserves, warranty reserves, and other
balance sheet amounts that, if the company remains a growing and viable
concern, will never actually decline or be liquidated are included in equity equivalents. Creation of these reserves serves, in SSC's view, the
need for conservatism in the accounting presentation of shareholders'
equity and measurement of net income, but it is again more appropriate
to a liquidation view. As SSC says, accountants are rarely sued for un-
derstating income. Other reserves, which do not show smooth growth,
remain outside the firm's capital.

It is interesting to consider the proper EVA capital impact of specialized reserves such as accrued retiree health care, as booked in the
Boeing 1998 annual report (Table 10–2). Given the size of retiree health

TABLE 10–2

Boeing retiree health care reserves are substantial compared to
shareholders' equity. (in $ billions)

	1997	1998
Accrued retiree health care	4,796	4,831
Total shareholders' equity	12,953	12,316

obligations compared to shareholders' equity, the issue is of some significance.

It is not clear, for example, that large industrials like Boeing with aging workforces will not experience a decline in accrued retiree benefits (because of growing benefit payments), should the retiree base grow sufficiently large. If these benefits have a substantial chance of actual liquidation, SSC does not recommend the capital add-back. On the other hand, changes in actuarial assumptions underlying pension and other postretirement plans can have substantial income statement and balance sheet effects, and inclusion of these accounts in EVA calculations might avoid material distortions in year-to-year results. Judgments about such reserves need to be made on a company-by-company basis.

M&A Accounting: MCI WorldCom

Mergers and acquisitions and corporate restructuring spin out lots of accounting detail, much of it inconsistent with the SSC view of capital (although consistency may increase as business combination accounting changes, as discussed in Chapter 2). The SSC notion is, once again, that capital invested in the firm is still there unless it is returned or lost through a negative operating return. This view produces a variety of adjustments to both capital and earnings, only a few examples of which can be mentioned here:

- *Cumulative goodwill.* If a company purchases another for $100, it has invested $100 in the new venture, regardless of the accounting for the deal. The amortization of goodwill, which reduces both GAAP income and capital, is therefore reversed cumulatively in EVA calculations. The usual reason for reversing goodwill amortization in discounted cash-flow (DCF) calculations, that goodwill is not cash, is not the issue here; EVA attempts to incorporate into capital the full cost of acquisitions. For these purposes the concept of "tangible net worth" is truly not useful because it represents a liquidation viewpoint not appropriate to the measurement of investment returns.

- *"Hidden goodwill."* The pooling-of-interests accounting method for business combinations (currently under scrutiny by the Financial Accounting Standards Board) hides invested amounts and must be adjusted in EVA analyses. Hidden

goodwill, the amount spent for the acquisition in excess of the
net book value of assets acquired, is added to EVA capital.
Reconstructing pooled acquisitions may not be particularly
easy since it requires valuation of the acquiring company's
stock at the deal's closing.

■ *Restructuring and other unusual charges.* In our $100
acquisition example, suppose at some future point the
acquisition should be deemed a failure. GAAP accounting
requires a write-down of the acquired assets (including
goodwill) to fair value, reducing current net income and
invested capital. EVA, on the other hand, takes a "successful-
efforts-to-full-cost" position. That is, regardless of the project's
success or failure, the company still invested the $100. The
$100 should be considered part of the investment in those
projects that do eventually succeed. A number of dry holes are
often drilled before oil is struck. Restructuring and other
unusual charges are added back to income and capital in the
EVA system.

It would be difficult to find a more active acquirer in 1998 than
MCI WorldCom (WCOM), the telecommunications giant, which made
roughly $44 billion of acquisitions including the mergers with MCI,
Brooks Fiber Properties (BPF), Embratel (a Brazilian telecommunications provider), CompuServe, and ANS Communications (the "AOL
transaction"). These transactions generated an estimated $7.5 billion in
adjustments to transform WCOM's GAAP capital to the EVA format, a
significant adjustment on a $45.0 billion reported shareholders' equity
base. The adjustments involve in-process research and development
(IPR&D) charges, special merger-related charge-offs, goodwill amortization, and hidden goodwill. (See Table 10–3.)

WCOM took a number of special charges associated with its 1998
acquisitions, as outlined in the MD&A section and footnotes to the financial statements. Charge-off of in-process R&D, under GAAP accounting, recognizes that some portion of purchase price of a technology
acquisition is attributable to the potential, but uncertain, future value of
ongoing research efforts. In the EVA system, the eventual success of
R&D projects is not the issue; the investment in these projects was a
real use of resources and must be recognized as part of the total capital
deployed in the firm. (See Table 10–4.)

TABLE 10-3

MCI acquisitions produce numerous adjustments. (in $ millions)

	Pretax	Tax Effect (35%)	After Tax
In-process R&D	3,529	—	3,529
Other charges	196	69	127
	3,725	69	3,656
Cumulative goodwill amortization	1,547	—	1,547
Hidden goodwill	2,200	—	2,200
	7,472	69	7,403

TABLE 10-4

WCOM took significant in-process R&D development and other charges in 1996 and 1997. (in $ millions)

	1996	1998
In-process R&D	2,140	3,529
Provision to reduce the carrying value of certain assets	402	49
Severance	58	21
BFP direct merger costs	—	17
Alignment and other exit activities	140	109
	2,740	3,725

The 1998 $3,529 million IPR&D charge represents the immediate write-off of a portion of the MCI and CompuServe/ANS purchase prices and is, under full-cost-to-successful-efforts accounting, added back to EVA capital. The IPR&D charge-off carries no tax effect (the purchase price of target company stock is not tax deductible):

> In connection with the recent business combinations, the Company made allocations of the purchase price to acquired in-process research & development totaling $429 million in the first quarter of 1998 related to the CompuServe Merger and the AOL transaction and $3.1 billion in the third quarter of 1998 related to the MCI Merger.

The other $196 million charges in the $3725 write-off look like nonre-curring but taxable expenses and therefore I tax effected them before their add-back to capital.

Fortunately, WCOM provides substantial footnote disclosure of goodwill and other intangible assets, so reconstruction of cumulative goodwill amortization (by adding historical goodwill expenses) is un-necessary. (See Table 10–5.) Like IPR&D, goodwill is added to capital without tax effect.

Hidden goodwill likely arose in WCOM's 1998 $2.5 billion acqui-sition of BFP, which was accounted for as a pooling of interest. Unfor-tunately, quantifying the amount of hidden goodwill, if any, is a challenge because BFP's preconsolidation balance sheet is not disclosed. But since pooling-of-interest accounting requires the restatement of past financial reports, it is perhaps possible to compare the 1997 restated and original balance sheets to determine the impact of the BFP combination. (See Table 10–6.)

According to this technique, BFP appears to have been very highly leveraged, with $889 million of longer-term liabilities and only $291 million of net worth, and to have operated, at least in 1997, at a $137 million loss. Of the $2.5 billion (7.2 million MCI shares issued times $34.98 price) purchase price, an estimated $2.2 billion is goodwill or other intangibles. The precise goodwill amount cannot be determined without knowing the adjustments necessary to move BFP's assets to fair value. The best we can do is guess.

TABLE 10–5

WCOM footnote disclosure of goodwill is extensive.
(in $ millions)

	Amortization Period	1997	1998
Goodwill	5–40 years	13,336	44,076
Trade name	40 years		1,100
Developed technology	5–10 years	400	2,100
Other intangibles	5–10 years	951	1,290
		14,687	48,566
Less: Accumulated amortization		805	1,547
		13,882	47,018

TABLE 10–6

Hidden goodwill emerges from comparison of 1997 original and restated MCI financial statements. (in $ millions)

	1997 Original	1997 Restated	Difference
Total assets	22,390	23,596	1,206
Liabilities and net worth			
Current liabilities	2,048	2,074	26
Long-term liabilities	6,832	7,721	889
Net worth	13,510	13,801	291
Net income (before extraordinary items)	384	247	(137)

Special Charges: Bristol-Myers Squibb Company

The Bristol-Myers Squibb (BMY) 1998 annual report provides excellent disclosure on special charges from 1989. As shown in Table 10–7, cumulative special charges since 1989 reached $3,345.0 million after tax, or $3,619 million excluding the gain on sale of businesses, the bulk of which were generated by product litigation and business restructuring charges. EVA methods suggest the addition to capital of these amounts, excluding the gains on sale. Unfortunately, litigation and restructuring costs fall under the full-cost-to-successful-efforts principle discussed above, under which the cost of business failures are a part of the capital investment in the company's successes. The gain or loss on the sale of a business, on the other hand, is a realized amount that already has the appropriate impact on capital and should not, in my view, be reversed.

NOPAT IS THE POOL OF PROFITS

Following the savings account analogy, the net operating profit after tax (NOPAT) is the "yield" on invested capital:

> [NOPAT is] a savings account equivalent, after-tax, cash-on-cash yield earned in the business. . . [It] is the total pool of profits available to provide a cash return to all financial providers of capital to the firm.[7]

NOPAT is built from the company's reported GAAP net income:

TABLE 10-7

Product litigation and business restructuring produced the bulk of Bristol-Myers special charges. (in $ millions)

	1989	1990	1991	1992	1993	1994	1995	1996	1997	1998
Pretax										
Gain on sale of business									225.0	201.0
Special charge for prescription pricing litigation										(100.0)
Special charge for product liability claims					(500.0)	(750.0)	(950.0)			(700.0)
Provision for restructuring				(890.0)			(310.0)		(225.0)	(201.0)
Provision for integrating businesses	(855.0)	—	—		(500.0)	(750.0)	(1,260.0)			(800.0)
Total	(855.0)	—	—	(890.0)	(500.0)	(750.0)	(1,260.0)	—	—	(800.0)
Cumulative	(855.0)	(855.0)	(855.0)	(1,745.0)	(2,245.0)	(2,995.0)	(4,255.0)	(4,255.0)	(4,255.0)	(5,055.0)
After tax										
Gain on sale of business									140.0	125.0
Special charge for prescription pricing litigation										(62.0)
Special charge for product liability claims					(310.0)	(488.0)	(590.0)			(443.0)
Provision for restructuring				(570.0)			(198.0)		(140.0)	(125.0)
Provision for integrating businesses	(693.0)	—	—		(310.0)	(488.0)	(788.0)			(505.0)
Total	(693.0)	—	—	(570.0)	(310.0)	(488.0)	(788.0)	—	—	(505.0)
Cumulative	(693.0)	(693.0)	(693.0)	(1,263.0)	(1,573.0)	(2,061.0)	(2,849.0)	(2,849.0)	(2,849.0)	(3,354.0)
Total without gain on sale	(693.0)	—	—	(570.0)	(310.0)	(488.0)	(788.0)	—	(140.0)	(630.0)
Cumulative	(693.0)	(693.0)	(693.0)	(1,263.0)	(1,573.0)	(2,061.0)	(2,849.0)	(2,849.0)	(2,989.0)	(3,619.0)

GAAP net income available to common stock
   + after-tax interest expense
   + preferred dividends
   + minority interest
   + goodwill amortization
   + unusual charges, gains, or losses
   + increase in certain equity equivalents
= NOPAT

Much of the NOPAT calculation is familiar and self-explanatory, but the treatment of equity equivalents is something of an issue.

Since SSC advocates adding certain balance sheet reserves to invested capital, any increases in these reserves must simultaneously be added back to income. For example, increases in a warranty reserve, deducted from income under GAAP rules, are added back to NOPAT. Again, the motivation here is not to eliminate noncash items. Reserve increases are added back in order to correctly measure the "yield" on the capital base that now includes the corresponding balance sheet amounts.

A Foolish Consistency

Notice that NOPAT is not exactly a "cash-on-cash yield" on invested capital. In fact, NOPAT is not a cash flow concept at all but a hybrid of accrual and cash ideas. The EVA system certainly does make adjustments to GAAP income that move it closer to cash flow:

- *Add-back of goodwill amortization:* Goodwill amortization is added back to net income both in the calculation of net cash flow from operations and NOPAT.

- *Add-back of restructuring charges:* Often representing an unrealized fall in asset value or discounted future expenses of discontinued operations, restructuring charges are added to net income in cash flow calculations and NOPAT.

- *Reversal of reserve increases:* Treatment of changes in balance sheet reserves is identical in cash flow and NOPAT calculations. The effect in both cases is to transform the expense incorporated into net income into current cash payments through the formula:

Beginning reserve + incurred expense − payments = ending reserve

The addition of reserve increases to incurred expenses produces the amount of cash payment outflow, "−payments" shown below:

−Payments = −incurred expense + increase in reserve

On the other hand, there are some decidedly noncash ideas in NOPAT:

- The capitalization and/or amortization of research and development costs: The creation of a new class of intangible assets moves NOPAT further from pure cash flow thinking. The notion is to measure "economic reality," not cash flow. In fact, in keeping with the savings account analogy, one wonders why R&D and other development costs might not be considered discretionary capital additions, rather than expenses, and permanently added back to the company's capital base. Does R&D amortization mean that the knowledge gained is somehow lost (or forgotten) over time? Can knowledge be used up? The resolution of this dilemma is purely practical. R&D expenses are amortized into NOPAT to maintain an incentive to control expenses, but not enough incentive to tempt management to earnings manipulation. The same reasoning applies to depreciation and amortization, discussed in the next point. Depreciation expense provides control, albeit indirect, over the capital expenditure process. Both the treatment of R&D costs and depreciation have more to do with management incentives than with theoretical consistency.
- Unlike net cash flow from operations, NOPAT includes asset depreciation and amortization (but not goodwill amortization). In SSC's view, these charges measure a true loss of capital over time and must be considered. Another way of thinking about this might be that depreciation charges are a periodic recognition of the opportunity cost of replacing productive assets. Still, this isn't cash.
- For performance measurement purposes, SSC advocates the use of a "suspension account" for strategic investment.[8] Investments that are strategic to the firm but unlikely to generate near-term NOPAT for middle managers are placed to the side until they become productive. This treatment prevents

managers from being penalized for long-term strategic investment, but, again, this isn't cash.

SSC seems aware that EVA is hybrid, neither completely cash flow nor accrual oriented. For the equity analyst interested in cross-company comparisons, how one calculates EVA is probably less important than that it is done consistently for all companies. Like many other equity analysis techniques, EVA is essentially a comparative tool. What economic value added "really" is for a particular company in a particular year is as elusive as the company's "real" net income:

> The purpose, after all, isn't to arrive at some theoretically pristine measure of profits. Rather, it is to change the behavior of managers and workers in ways that will maximize shareholder wealth, and the effectiveness of any measure in shaping behavior will diminish as it becomes more complex and difficult to understand.[9]

We might add that EVA can help analysts to see which managements are actually successful at the task of wealth maximization.

A Mirror of Abnormal Earnings

The EVA methodology mirrors the abnormal earnings formulations derived in Chapter 2. Economic value added, as defined by SSC, is the residual profit remaining after capital costs are deducted from reported profit:

$$\text{Reported profit} = \text{normal profit} + \text{residual profit} \tag{10.2}$$

$$\text{Residual profit} = \text{EVA} = \text{reported profit} - \text{normal profit}$$

where normal profit equals the costs of capital use.

Let r be the reported return on capital and c the normal return on capital. Then,

$$\text{Reported profit} = r * \text{capital} \tag{10.3}$$

$$\text{Normal profit} = c * \text{capital} \tag{10.4}$$

Substituting 10.3 and 10.4, Equation 10.2 can be written:

$$\begin{aligned}\text{EVA} &= \text{reported profit} - \text{normal profit}\\ &= r * \text{capital} - c * \text{capital}\\ &= (r - c) * \text{capital}\end{aligned} \tag{10.5}$$

Equation 10.5 is the same as the Chapter 2 formulation of abnormal earnings. Adding a series of equations in the form of Equation 10.5, representing future years, each discounted by the appropriate factor, demonstrates that the SSC concept of "market value added" equals the present value of the expected annual economic value added by the firm:

$$\frac{\sum_{i=1}^{\infty} EVA_i}{(1 + c)^i} = \frac{\sum_{i=1}^{\infty} r_i * capital_i}{(1 + c)^i} - \frac{\sum_{i=1}^{\infty} c * capital_i}{(1 + c)^i} \qquad (10.6)$$

Equation 10.6 can be restated as:

PV (EVA) = market value − capital = market value added

where PV (EVA) is the present value of the firm's future expected economic value added.

The power of the EVA concept, tying market value to financial performance, is demonstrated in Figure 10–1, which presents data from the 1998 Stern Stewart market-value-added (MVA) rankings appearing in *Fortune* magazine. In excess of 53 percent of the variation in the market value of the first 100 largest MVA generators in 1998 is explained by the ratio of return on capital to the cost of capital, a rough measure of excess profitability. The missing variable, which we'll discuss in greater depth in Chapter 17, is the sustainability of excess profits. It is likely, for example, that for companies lying well above the 1998 trend

FIGURE 10–1

In recent Stern-Stewart rankings, the market value to capital ratio is a strong function of company returns.

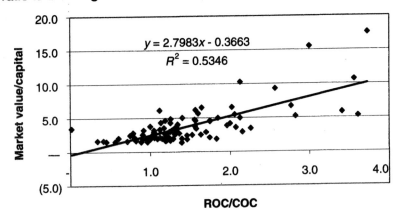

line, like Microsoft and Coca-Cola, the market then expected a substantially longer-than-average period of excess profitability. Given the dominant competitive positions of those companies (at least at that time), this seemed a reasonable expectation.

GATEWAY: EVA IN PRACTICE

A calculation for Gateway 2000, Inc. (GTW), illustrates that, in spite of the many adjustments to reported capital and earnings, the EVA technique produces worthwhile financial performance insights. In 1998 Gateway generated economic value added of $241.3 million on an adjusted capital base of $619.5 million, which excludes estimated excess cash of $1,169.8 million. The 1998 EVA rose 33 percent from the 1997 $180.8 million result. A principal driver in the EVA rise was higher NOPAT, which grew to $306.4 million from $258.6 million because of operating improvements, driven both by higher sales and improved profit margins. In addition, declining interest rates dropped the company's cost of capital from 11.2 to 10.5 percent. But perhaps most significantly, the company's powerful cash generation pushed estimated excess cash up $576.2 million to $1,169.8 million, helping to reduce the capital employed in the business from $695.0 million to $619.5 million. The capital was released by an aggressive reduction of the company's operating cycle (days in inventory and receivables less days in accounts payable) from 13 days to negative 7 days.

Both reported net income and net cash from operations are considerably more choppy. Reported net income rose 215 percent during the same period to $346.4 million in 1998 because of substantial nonrecurring expenses in 1997 (which are added back in the EVA calculation). Net cash provided by operations also jumped sharply to $907.7 million, up 105 percent over 1997 because of the company's working capital management. Appendix 6–1 presents the company's balance sheet, income statement, and statement of cash flows.

Gateway Capital Calculation

GTW's $619.5 million 1998 capital base consists of a $1,516.1 million shareholders' equity, funded debt, and lease base, plus $273.2 million in equity equivalents, less $1,169.8 million in excess cash. Gateway's equity equivalents are principally warranty and royalty reserves, the cumulative goodwill write-off, and an add-back of 1997 nonrecurring expenses related to the acquisition of Advanced Logic Research, Inc., a manufacturer of network servers and personal computers. The level of excess cash is set, somewhat arbitrarily, at the company's "cash and cash equivalents" account balance because its $576.2 million 1998 increase is roughly equal to the company's free-cash flow (net operating cash flow less capital expenditures).

Unexpectedly, the $619.5 million 1998 capital actually fell from the $695.0 million 1997 level, due principally to the company's remarkable cash generation. Although excess cash remains on the balance sheet, it is, notionally at least, no longer invested in the business (because it is excess), and it is treated as if it had been returned to shareholders. This treatment, although theoretically sound, may not always correctly capture the market's attitude toward excess cash. For example, if the market were to anticipate the eventual deployment of excess cash at returns less than the cost of capital, it may well apply a discount to the cash face amount. (See Table 10–8.)

Such a harsh judgment is more likely in maturing companies and industries than in a company growing as rapidly as GTW at this time. In a maturing company, the market may conclude that management's concern (or desperation) about maintaining growth will lead to suboptimal investment policies. One reason that stock prices often rise in the wake of a share repurchase announcement may be a step-up in the market's valuation of excess cash.

TABLE 10–8

Gateway's capital contains adjustments for debt, equity equivalents, and excess cash. (in $ thousands)

	1997	1998
Book value of shareholders' equity	930,044	1,344,375
+ Funded debt, including leases	66,907	171,725
+ Equity equivalents	291,618	273,184
− Excess cash	(593,601)	(1,169,810)
= Capital	694,968	619,474

Book Value of Shareholders' Equity

Gateway presents common shareholders' equity balances in 1997 and 1998 of $930.0 million and $1,344.4 million, respectively. The company has no preferred stock, minority interests, or other adjustments to the common equity amount.

Funded Debt, Including Operating Leases

The 1997 and 1998 GTW funded debt and lease balance consists of contributions from current and noncurrent maturities of long-term debt and notes payable, plus an estimate of the present value of operating leases. (See Table 10–9.)

Estimates of the present value of operating leases usually involve a certain amount of analytic fiddling. Footnote disclosure in the 1998 GTW annual report provides substantial, but not unambiguous, information on capital and operating leases. (See Table 10–10.)

The reported 1998 present value of GTW capital implies an embedded interest rate of 3.3 percent, and indeed the company reports that capital lease rates range from 3.3 to 15.3 percent. Since 3.3 percent seems an unlikely medium-term borrowing rate, we chose 5.17 percent, the embedded rate applied to the company's 1998 average notes payable, as the operating lease discount rate. We also follow the SSC convention of discounting only the first five years' payments. The implied interest expense generated by operating leases, an amount required in the NOPAT calculation, is the product of the average lease balance and the 5.17 percent discount rate. (See Table 10–11.)

TABLE 10–9

Total debt adjustment contains capitalized leases.
(in $ thousands)

	1997	1998
Current maturities of notes payable	13,969	11,415
Long-term obligations	7,240	3,360
Present value of operating leases	45,698	156,950
Total	66,907	171,725

TABLE 10-10

GTW's annual report presents helpful disclosure on both capital
and operating leases. (in $ thousands)

	Capital Leases	Operating Leases
1996	—	11,873
1997	—	16,105
1998	—	25,713
1999	330	39,400
2000	38	39,695
2001	12	38,794
2002	1	36,256
2003	—	26,523
Thereafter	—	25,910
Total minimum lease payments	381	206,578
Present value of net minimum lease payments	367	

TABLE 10-11

Implied interest rates apply to capitalized leases.
(in $ thousands)

	1996	1997	1998
Beginning capitalized leases	22,278	58,765	173,684
Ending capitalized leases	11,557	45,698	156,950
Implied interest rate (%)	—	5.17%	5.17%

Equity Equivalents

The reversal of cumulative goodwill amortization, add-back of special
charges, addition of warranty and royalty reserves, and deduction of deferred tax assets are the principal components of the GTW equity equivalents calculation. Goodwill amortization is not separately disclosed in
GTW accounts, but it can be inferred from the behavior of the balance
sheet intangibles account. Because there were minimal (if any) additions
to the account in 1998, the assumed 1998 amortization is just the account's $16.6 million decline, the equivalent of about a 5-year write-off

period (consistent with the 3- to 10-year footnote disclosure). Since the ALR acquisition occurred in the 1997 third quarter, 1997 amortization is 25 percent of the 1998 amount, or about $4.2 million. (See Table 10–12.)

The $113.8 million nonrecurring charge to 1997 income consisted, according to footnote disclosure, of a $59.7 million write-off of in-process ALR research and development, a $45.2 million write-off of GTW capitalized software development and hardware costs, and $8.6 million of severance from the closing of foreign offices. Following the full-cost-to-successful-efforts principle, these amounts are added back to capital. Royalty and warranty reserves should continue to grow as the business expands and to represent true liabilities, in the EVA system, only in the event of bankruptcy.

As an aside, the in-process R&D write-off, used frequently in technology acquisitions, has come under increasing fire in recent years. Clearly, the larger the in-process write-off, the lower the goodwill balance and the resulting future earnings pressure from goodwill amortization. The SEC's concern is that the write-off, in some cases, has not been well supported and could amount to "earnings management." EVA is free from potential distortions from either goodwill or the in-process R&D write-off because of its full-cost-to-successful-efforts view. If a company purchases another with in-process R&D, the subsequent write-off has no effect on the original purchase price, which remains part of EVA capital and upon which the acquirer must now earn a return. EVA capital can therefore come to consist of the book value of the company,

TABLE 10–12

GTW's equity equivalents dominated by reserves and nonrecurring charges. (in $ thousands)

	1997	1998
Cumulative goodwill	4,161	20,807
Nonrecurring charges	113,800	113,800
Royalty reserve	159,418	167,873
Warranty reserve	98,081	112,971
Deferred tax assets	(83,842)	(142,267)
Total	291,618	273,184

at historical cost, and the market values of any acquired companies. Although this sounds like a hopeless mishmash of accounting concepts, the justification is straightforward. Quite reasonably, EVA assumes that each year a firm invests the book value of its beginning capital plus the purchase prices of any company it acquires. This is true even if acquisitions are financed with excess cash since reductions in excess cash increase, mathematically at least, the effective capital deployed in the business.

Deferred tax assets, on the other hand, pose a greater analytic challenge. In the EVA scheme, adding back reserves (including deferred tax liabilities) to capital recognizes that such amounts are unlikely to ever be liquidated, staying permanently invested in the company. GTW's deferred tax assets may be truly temporary. Nevertheless, for the sake of consistency, deferred tax assets are deducted in the Gateway equity equivalents section.

The company does not separately disclose research and development expenditures, but there is reason to think that, as a computer assembler rather than a technology developer, it does not spend materially on R&D. The equity equivalents calculation therefore ignores the capitalized R&D.

Gateway NOPAT Calculation

Gateway's 1998 NOPAT reached $306.4 million, up 18 percent from $258.6 million in 1997 because of stronger gross profit performance. The principal differences between the GTW NOPAT and reported net income fall into 1997, where substantial reported charges, related to the ALR acquisition and abandonment of an internal software project, are reversed in the NOPAT. Large increases in royalty and warranty reserves, added back to the NOPAT, are offset by increases in the net deferred tax asset, which is deducted from the NOPAT—consistent with the treatment of deferred tax assets in the GTW capital calculation. (See Table 10–13.)

Net After-Tax Interest Expense

Given GTW's minimal funded debt, most of the company's interest expense is imputed from the capitalization of operating leases. Offsetting this expense is interest income from excess cash holdings, which, since excess cash was eliminated from capital, must be deducted from the NOPAT. The company does not disclose interest expense directly (probably because of materiality), but it does provide cash interest payments,

TABLE 10–13

The GTW NOPAT shows more gradual 1997 to 1998 rise than reported net income. (in $ thousands)

	1997	1998
Reported net income	109,797	346,399
+ Net AT interest expense	(14,479)	(21,590)
+ Goodwill amortization	4,161	16,646
+ Unusual gains and losses	113,842	—
+ Increase in other equity equivalents	45,282	(35,080)
= NOPAT	258,603	306,375

which are used in Table 10–14. A 35 percent tax rate is used in the tax shield calculation.

Imputed interest from operating leases and excess cash is the product of the embedded interest rates and beginning balances presented in Table 10–15. The embedded interest rate in operating leases is simply the 5.17 percent discount rate used in the present value calculation above. The interest rate on excess funds is derived assuming that reported 1997 and 1998 "other income, net" consists entirely of interest expense and interest income, a reasonable assumption given the size of the company's cash balances and necessary since separate components are not disclosed.

The GTW capital calculation added back to capital royalty and warranty reserves, and deducted deferred tax assets; therefore, the

TABLE 10–14

Interest expense must be adjusted for leases and excess cash. (in $ thousands)

	1997	1998
Cash interest paid	716	930
Imputed operating lease interest	3,038	8,979
Interest income on excess cash	(26,030)	(43,125)
Subtotal	(22,276)	(33,216)
Tax shield	7,797	11,626
After-tax interest expense, net	(14,479)	(21,590)

TABLE 10–15

Interest on leases and excess cash flow from estimated
balances. (in $ thousands)

	1997	1998
Average excess cash	535,656	881,705
Imputed interest rate	4.9%	4.9%
Interest income on excess cash	26,030	43,125
Operating lease balance	58,765	173,684
Discount rate	5.17%	5.17%
Imputed interest expense on operating leases	3,038	8,979

NOPAT calculation must also add back changes in those balances, shown
in Table 10–16. Normally, these changes can be calculated either directly
from the company's balance sheet or drawn from the statement of cash
flows (not shown). Perversely, in this case the two calculations will not
agree. This is because changes in balance sheet operating accounts associated with the 1997 ALR acquisition will, under GAAP rules (SFAS
95), be booked in the investment section of the 1997 statement of cash
flows, not in the cash flow from operations section. Changes in reported
1997 balance sheet accounts (which include the acquired assets) will
therefore not match the changes listed in the operating section of the
cash flow statement (which does not include the acquisition). Here we
use the balance sheet changes since the balance sheet amounts were
included in the capital.

TABLE 10–16

Changes in other equity equivalents dominated by deferred
taxes (in thousands of dollars).

	1997	1998
Accrued royalties	34,148	8,455
Warranty liabilities	47,224	14,890
Deferred tax asset	(36,090)	(58,425)
Total	45,282	(35,080)

In light of the company's 1998 profit margin improvement, notice that both the royalty and warranty accruals fell as a percentage of sales, suggesting a reduced expense burden. On the other hand, such reductions could represent more rapid payment of warranty and royalty costs. Reasons for the declines are not disclosed in the company's financials, but the changes are not seriously troubling. Substantial reductions in warranty expense accruals, however, could constitute "borrowing" from future earnings and would therefore need scrutiny. (See Table 10–17.)

Gateway Economic Value Added

GTW's remarkable 49.5 percent 1998 return on capital generated a $241.3 million EVA, in excess of the $180.8 million 1997 result. The 1998 result is partially driven by a fall in the capital charge from $77.8 million in 1997 to $65.0 million, both because of a drop in the cost of capital and the jump in the company's excess cash generation, related to growing working capital efficiency. Appendix 10–1 presents GTW's cost-of-capital calculation. (See Table 10–18.)

The company's 1998 market value added, the difference between the market and book value of its capital, increased nearly 71 percent to $7.6 billion from $4.4 billion in 1997, as shown in Table 10–19.

Comparison to Net Income and Cash Flow

The EVA process clearly does smooth some of the fluctuations to which both reported net income and net cash flow are subject, as shown in Table 10–20. EVA grew 33 percent to $241.3 million in 1998. The 215 percent substantial leap in net income to $346.4 million in 1998, on the

TABLE 10–17

Both warranty and royalty reserves fell as a percentage of sales in 1998, in spite of substantial sales growth. (in $ millions)

	1997	1998
Net sales	6,293.7	7,467.9
Accrued royalties	159.4	167.9
Warranty and other liabilities	98.1	113.0
As a % of sales		
Accrued royalties	2.5%	2.2%
Warranty and other liabilities	1.6%	1.5%

TABLE 10–18

GTW generated significant economic value added in both 1997
and 1998. (in $ thousands)

	1997	1998
NOPAT	258,603	306,375
Return on capital	37.2%	49.5%
Capital	694,968	619,474
Capital charge	77,836	65,045
Cost of capital	11.2%	10.5%
EVA	180,767	241,330

TABLE 10–19

GTW added considerable market value in both 1997 and 1998.
(in $ millions)

	1997	1998
Market value	5,115.0	8,186.0
Capital	695.0	619.5
Market value added	4,420.0	7,566.5

TABLE 10–20

EVA is considerably smoother than either income or cash flow
measures. (in $ thousands)

	1997	1998
NOPAT	258,603	306,375
Net income	109,797	346,399
Net cash flow from operations	442,797	907,651
Cash flow from earnings	252,896	398,259
Cash flow from working capital	189,901	509,392

TABLE 10–21

GTW's operating efficiencies improved remarkably over 1996 to 1998.

	1996	1997	1998
Days in accounts receivable	33	30	27
Days in inventory	25	17	10
Days in accounts payable	37	34	44
Operating cycle	21	13	(7)

other hand, was due partly to the $113.8 million nonrecurring charge in 1997, and partly to pretax gross profit, which reached $1,546.3 million from $1,076.4 million in the same period.

Net cash flow from operations also jumped 105 percent to $907.7 million in 1998 following management's focus on more efficient use of working capital, as shown in Table 10–21. In fact, the company's operating cycle (total days in inventory and accounts receivable minus days in accounts payable) fell from 13 days in 1997 to a negative 7 days in 1998. GTW actually generated cash from working capital in 1998, even in the face of its 19 percent annual sales growth.

The EVA capital calculation recognizes that Gateway's working capital efforts produced a one-time cash benefit that was effectively removed from the business.

NOTES

[1] Much of the material in this chapter is drawn from G. Bennett Stewart, *The Quest for Value*, Harper Collins Publishers, New York, 1991.

[2] "Stern Stewart EVA® Roundtable, Johnson & Johnson Headquarters, New Brunswick, New Jersey," June 1, 1994, reprinted in *The Revolution in Corporate Finance*, 3rd ed., edited by Joel M. Stern and Donald H. Chew, Jr., Blackwell Publishers, Ltd., 1998, p. 490. The higher 160 figure appears in Al Ehrbar, *Stern Stewart's EVA: The Real Key to Creating Wealth*, Wiley, New York, 1998.

[3] "The EVA® Financial Management System," reprinted in *The Revolution in Corporate Finance*, 3rd ed., edited by Joel M. Stern and Donald H. Chew, Jr., Blackwell Publishers, Ltd., 1998, p. 483.

[4] Ibid.

[5] Stewart, *The Quest for Value*, p. 70.

[6] Ibid., p. 91.
[7] Ibid., p. 86.
[8] Ehrbar, *Stern Stewart's EVA,* 170.
[9] Ibid., p. 166.

Gateway's Cost of Capital

Gateway's 1998 estimated weighted-average cost of capital falls to 10.5 percent from 11.2 percent in 1997 because of a lower risk-free rate assumption. Given the company's very low financial leverage (roughly 2 percent debt to capital), the bulk of capital costs are equity related. (See Table 10–1–1.)

COST OF EQUITY

GTW's estimated cost of equity drops slightly to 10.6 percent in 1998 from 11.4 percent in the previous year because of a fall in the long government bond rate to 5.08 percent from 5.93 percent. Since the company's predicted *Barra* beta varies from 1.30 to 1.40 in 1997 to 1998, 1.35 is chosen as representative of the period. Using the familiar capital asset pricing model format,

$Co\,E$

Cost of equity = risk-free rate + β * market premium

To adjust for the risk premium inherent in the 30-year government bond, we normally deduct 125 basis points. The market premium is always a subject of controversy. Recognizing that the future market premium is likely to be below 7 percent to 9 percent historical levels, 5 percent seems about as high as is comfortable:

TABLE 10-1-1

GTW's capital structure changes in 1997 and 1998.

	1997	1998
Equity		
Share price	$32.75	$51.19
Number of shares outstanding	154.1	156.6
Market capitalization	5,048.0	8,014.0
Book value of debt including operating leases	66.9	171.7
Total capital	5,114.9	8,185.7
Capital structure		
Equity percentage	98.7	97.9
Debt percentage	1.3	2.1

$$\text{Cost of 1997 equity} = (5.93\% - 1.25\%) + 1.35 * 5.00\%$$
$$= 11.40\%$$
$$\text{Cost of 1998 equity} = (5.08\% - 1.25\%) + 1.35 * 5.00\%$$
$$= 10.60\%$$

WEIGHTED-AVERAGE COST OF CAPITAL

GTW's cost of capital is very heavily weighted toward equity costs because of the company's very large equity market capitalization compared to its funded debt (including leases). Following convention, even though it is theoretically unsound, the book value, rather than market value, of debt is used in the weighted-average cost-of-capital (WACC) calculation.

For convenience in the WACC calculation, we chose a 2 percent debt to capital percentage, a 5.17 percent implied cost of borrowing (derived above), and a 35 percent corporate tax rate:

$$\text{WACC 1997} = 98.00\% * 11.40\% + 2.00\% * (1.00 - 0.35) * 5.17\%$$
$$= 11.20\%$$

$$\text{WACC 1998} = 98\% * 10.60\% + 2.00\% * (1.00 - 0.35) * 5.17\%$$
$$= 10.50\%$$

Financial Models

CHAPTER 11

Financial Modeling: Base Case Assumptions and Model Design

- The most important parts of a financial model are its base case assumptions. The rest of the process is, essentially, mechanical.

- Before setting base case assumptions, the analyst should examine both the firm's strategic and/or competitive position and its financial statements. These preliminary analyses proceed without any preconceptions. After completing these steps, the analyst should know the company's "story."[1] If he or she does not, then he or she should postpone modeling and return to the analysis.

- Financial modeling is not prophecy, it is opinion. In making base case assumptions, the analyst takes a position on the company's future prospects. This position needs to be consistent with his or her understanding of the firm's strategy and competitive challenges. It also must be consistent with the company's historical performance and with economic reality.

- No business has available to it an infinite range of financial possibilities. The art of financial modeling is defining the possibilities that do exist.

- In addition to consistency with strategy, competitive conditions, and historical performance, financial models need to conform to "natural laws." Growth does not continue forever, returns eventually revert to a normal level, and sales increases and productive capacity scale together.

- Financial model format is important. Not because neatness counts—although maybe it does—but because it is efficient.

Equity analysts typically follow more than one company. Sloppy models, without a common format, quickly become unwieldy, slowing down decisions and reaction time, which are the analyst's principal competitive advantage.

One does not learn to play the piano by mastering one key at a time. The keys must work together to create music. In financial modeling, torturing the metaphor a bit, we don't project one income statement or balance sheet account at a time but all of them at once. This would be a daunting process indeed if companies actually had an unlimited range of financial possibilities. Fortunately, their basic physical processes, strategy, and competition, and the laws of economics limit the possible future outcomes of any company. Projecting financial statements is, in my view, a three-step process, each step assuring consistency with these fundamental physical, strategic, and economic constraints.

First, we need to know how the financial accounts "scale," that is, how they grow or shrink as the company's operations change. Each account moves in a predictable way relative to some scale factor, usually net sales, which is a proxy for the company's overall activity level. Why this is so is best understood not by looking at financial statements but by looking at actual physical operations.

For example, to increase sales, more raw materials are purchased, increasing the cost of goods sold, and perhaps accounts payable and inventory. Adding sales might mean building additional productive capacity, causing capital expenditures and fixed assets to rise. Selling more physical goods may require a larger sales force, more advertising, additional distribution centers, and more managers, all of which could force selling, general, and administrative expenses upward. Each of these elements must ultimately remain in physical balance, or growth simply will not be successful. Without balance, plants would reach capacity, sales forces would become overextended, and financial and production control lost, resulting in physical breakdown of the system. It is the basic physical processes of the business that prevent sharp operational—and financial—discontinuities. Financial statement analysis—particularly ratio analysis—reveals many of these financial scaling factors and shows the basic financial continuity (discontinuities may be signs of financial or operational distress). Any financial forecast must be fundamentally consistent with this historical record.

But continuity with the historical record does not tell the analyst where the company is headed, only how it is likely to get there. At this point, the analyst must decide what he or she thinks about the company's prospects. Those prospects need to be consistent with the company's operational strategy and with the competitive challenges it is likely to face. The company's historical competitive positioning should become apparent in the financial statement analysis. If that strategy is to continue, forecasted financial statements must play out the likely consequences. If the analyst believes the company may change its operating strategy, financial expectations need to adjust to reflect the change. Whatever choices the analyst makes, he or she must remember that successful corporate strategies are deeply embedded, and difficult to change. If the analyst does predict a strategic discontinuity—and there's no rule against that—he or she needs to understand why.

"Playing out" the forecasted strategic choices might itself be very difficult were it not that the likely outcomes of competitive strategies are themselves bounded and subject to the laws of economics, a set of fundamental, generic financial constraints. Competitive processes have, unfortunately, an inevitable leveling effect. Eventually, margins shrink, returns on equity decline, sales growth moderates, and operations move toward the average. As much as we analysts and investors would prefer successful strategies to last forever, they will not. Some companies can sustain their competitive successes for long periods, periods well beyond an analyst's typical five-year horizon. But trees do not grow to the sky, and eventually, painfully, economic law reasserts itself. Does this mean that all financial models should predict competitive deterioration and reversion to mean returns? Not at all. But an analyst must consider why this company, among all others, can successfully resist competitive challenge, at least over the time horizon being forecast. So, once again, the analytic process leads us back to the basic competitive facts.

CONSISTENCY AND CONTINUITY IN FINANCIAL MODELS

The basic physical processes of the firm—producing, selling, planning, and controlling—assure a fundamental continuity in its financial performance. Research indicates, for example, that the best predictor of next period's sales and earnings is this period's[2]:

$$\text{Sales}_T = \text{sales}_{T-1} + \text{drift} \qquad (11.1)$$

$$\text{Earning}_T = \text{earning}_{T-1} + \text{drift} \qquad (11.2)$$

where *drift* is a function of the average change in the series over previous periods. All else being equal, sales and earnings ought to change smoothly from period to period. Any forecast that predicts sharp, discontinuous change in either variable needs to be carefully thought out. How can such sharp changes be physically brought about? Is there sufficient productive capacity? How can additional production be sold through existing distribution systems? What marketing and advertising issues are raised? Can margins be maintained and sales leap simultaneously?

The exception to the continuity rule is in quarterly accounts, which, if seasonal, may be more driven by the same quarter last year rather than last quarter.

THOSE PESKY QUARTERLY EARNINGS FORECASTS

Some of these consistency and continuity issues are raised by the following example. Consider the issue of a one-year quarterly earnings forecast (Table 11–1). How do consistency and continuity constrain the forecast?

Since physical constraints, presumably, limit the amount by which EPS can grow quarter over quarter, perhaps we should continue the $0.01 quarterly EPS increase (Table 11–2). But this forecast predicts declining quarterly and annual growth. Is this what we really expect? What explanation does the analyst offer to investors, especially those who own the

TABLE 11–1

With 1999 quarterly history, there are many possible projections for 2000.

	1Q	2Q	3Q	4Q	Year	Growth
1999	0.10	0.11	0.12	0.13	0.46	50%
Growth	?	?	?	?	?	?
2000	?	?	?	?	?	?

TABLE 11-2

The $0.01 quarterly increase can carry forward.

	1Q	2Q	3Q	4Q	Year	Growth
1999	0.10	0.11	0.12	0.13	0.46	50%
Growth	40%	36%	33%	31%		
2000	0.14	0.15	0.16	0.17	0.62	35%

stock? Does this signal to the market a decline in the analyst's enthusiasm for the stock?

To correct this impression of deceleration, suppose instead that we predict a 50 percent growth rate in each quarter of 2000, as shown in Table 11–3. Now year-over-year quarterly growth is continuous. But how does the company grow earnings by $0.02 in 1Q 2000 over 4Q 1999, especially since growth of $0.01 seems to be the norm? Doesn't this require some step-up in the rate of production and sales growth? How is that step-up accomplished? What does it cost?

Let's try another alternative, in which growth is ramped up to allow physical operations to adjust, as shown in Table 11–4. This kind of quarterly forecast is pretty common. It preserves the annual 50 percent earnings growth rate, but it requires growth to accelerate during the year. Is there some reason to believe this will happen, and why?

Accommodating our expectations of the impact of company strategy, while at the same time maintaining both consistency with historical performance and the period-to-period continuity of financial forecasts,

TABLE 11-3

Or, quarterly growth could be constant.

	1Q	2Q	3Q	4Q	Year	Growth
1999	0.10	0.11	0.12	0.13	0.46	50%
Growth	50%	50%	50%	50%		
2000	0.15	0.16	0.18	0.20	0.62	50%

TABLE 11-4

Perhaps growth should accelerate in 2000.

	1Q	2Q	3Q	4Q	Year	Growth
1999	0.10	0.11	0.12	0.13	0.46	50%
Growth	40%	45%	50%	62%		
2000	0.14	0.16	0.18	0.21	0.62	50%

can lead to these sorts of quandaries. The key to resolving these issues is a clear vision of the company's capabilities and competitive position on a physical level—in short, understanding the business, not just the finances.

■ **Tip**   Period-to-period consistency can be a good test of a forecast. Be aware of predicted quarter-over-quarter changes as well as year-over-year changes. Make sure that annual growth forecasts can actually be achieved without straining credulity. If you're having trouble, it may be a signal of underlying problems with your basic performance expectations.

■ **Trick**   Think of physical as well as financial growth. If, for example, you grow sales by a percentage, how can the growth be physically accomplished? New customers? Market share increases? Did you expand the sales force, or do you expect sales productivity to increase? How do you increase sales productivity? Training? Better supervision? How much does that cost and how quickly can it be done? Or is there excess capacity in both production and sales systems? Can output be increased quickly enough to produce the quarterly growth you're predicting? What will that cost, and what is the effect on margins? What is the likely competitive response to this growth?

■ **Trap**   Be aware that maintaining annual forecasts by "back-ending" earnings into later quarters accelerates growth in those quarters.

THE LAWS OF ECONOMICS AND OTHER DISAPPOINTMENTS

Sales and earnings may grow (or shrink) period to period, but returns on investment do not behave this way. The leveling effects of competition drive returns toward a normal level. In many cases, this means reversion is accomplished through changes in operating margins. In any financial model, the predicted changes in ROE are a valuable indicator of the reasonableness of forecast assumptions. Again, this doesn't mean that all financial models must predict the mean reversion of returns, especially relatively short term models. It does mean, however, that the analyst needs to know why he or she is predicting something else, leading, once more, to the basic understanding he or she has formed of the company's strategy and competitive challenges.

Mean Reversion of ROE

Suppose the ROE of the firm is built up of N separate capital projects, with individual dollar investments of I_i. Competition places each successive project under greater profit pressure. It becomes progressively harder to find projects that produce returns in excess of capital costs. As more projects are added, the firm's aggregate ROE is forced downward:

$$\text{Aggregate ROE} = \frac{\sum_{i=1}^{N} I_i * \text{ROE}_i}{\sum_{i=1}^{N} I_i} \qquad (11.3)$$

Aggregate ROE does not decline because of cash buildup, although accumulation of excess cash can depress ROE, but because of competitive forces.

Normal Margins

If ROE gradually declines, because of competitive forces, toward the firm's equity capital costs, then other performance measures must naturally follow[3]:

$$\text{ROE} = \text{net margin} * \text{asset turnover} * \text{balance sheet leverage} \qquad (11.4)$$

Competition might certainly reduce asset turnovers if, for example, slowing sales volume were accompanied by working capital, probably inventory, buildup. But probably there is a natural level of assets that is necessary, in any industry, to accomplish basic production. Oil companies need refineries, microchip makers need fabrication plants, and retailers need stores (at least for the moment).

Balance sheet leverage is often a matter of corporate policy rather than competitive pressure. Relative asset levels can change as competitive pressure rises and falls. But balance sheet structure is, to some extent, a matter of design.

On the other hand, net margin is likely to be highly sensitive to the firm's competitive environment, and it is the element of the ROE most likely to change as returns approach normal levels. The "normal" margin level, however, is a function of the other ROE elements. In Table 11–5, the same normal ROE of 10 percent can produce substantially different net margin performance, depending on asset turnover and leverage. In the second row, the firm's normal net margin is 5 percent, rather than 10 percent, because its higher turnover permits it to operate at lower profitability.

■ **Trap**   Failure to maintain consistency between all elements of a forecast can produce faulty financial models. Mean reversion of returns forces changes throughout a model, particularly in net margins.

■ **Trick**   Before you begin a financial model, consider whether the company's returns are above or below normal levels. This will suggest a direction in which net margins, particularly, will eventually move.

The Back-of-the-Envelope Forecast

Consider Perpetual Motion Ltd. (PML), a company generating $400 in sales at a 15 percent net margin, for $60 in net income. Suppose we want a simple financial projection model of PML, sort of "back of the envelope," just to get an idea of the company's progress two years in the future.[4] To avoid overcomplicating the situation, we adopt a few basic projection assumptions:

TABLE 11–5

ROE performance should be consistent with operating and investment assumptions.

Net Margin	Asset Turnover	Balance Sheet Leverage	ROE
10%	1.0	1.0	10%
5%	2.0	1.0	10%

- Sales grow at the 5 percent rate of inflation.
- Capital expenditures equal depreciation. This assures that the dollar amount of the company's fixed assets is constant over the projection period.
- Net margins remain constant.
- Working capital turnover—working capital to sales—is constant. This assures us the working capital will scale with sales consistent with historical financial performance.

In year 2, the forecast's first year, the company produces $420 million sales, a 5 percent increase. Current assets and liabilities each rise 5 percent, keeping working capital and sales in scale. Fixed assets are unchanged at $500. Return on equity, based upon the year 1 $400 beginning balance sheet, is 15.8 percent. The company has generated $58 in cash, which, for the sake of simplicity, we pay to shareholders as a dividend. Without the dividend, projected future income will contain interest earnings.

In year 3, sales reach $441 and income climbs to $66 as the 5 percent growth trend continues. Working capital rises to $110, still in scale with rising sales. Fixed assets remain constant, in keeping with our original assumptions. PML produces $61 of cash in year 3, which again is dividended to shareholders.

But look what has happened to the ROE. It has risen to 16.3 percent. How, with steady-state assumptions, could the ROE have risen? A rising ROE is particularly distressing since, all else being equal, we would expect competitive pressures to force future returns downward. What has gone wrong here?

The back-of-the-envelope process runs counter to some of this chapter's forecasting principles:

- Constant margins may not properly account for the company's competitive environment. If the actions of competitors force returns on equity downward, net margins will likely follow.
- Fixed asset accounts have not been properly scaled with sales growth, creating a potential imbalance. The result is rising asset turnover. Why, for example, can the company grow sales without changes in its fixed assets? If the company can increase turnover this way, can it do so sustainably? Is management taking special actions to increase efficiency?

If the ROEs are rising because management is starving the business of capital, should an investor pay more for the business? Even though returns have risen, how has value been created? Valuation methods, under these conditions, are likely to produce flawed results (Table 11–6).

- A sustainable ROE will be overestimated, producing too much abnormal income, or
- Cash investment needs will be underestimated, resulting in too high a free-cash flow, or
- Investors are likely to apply too high a multiple to earnings or book value.

FINANCIAL MODEL DESIGN: TRICKS AND TRAPS

Most financial professionals have, from time to time, created financial forecasting models in spreadsheet systems like Excel, but equity analysts must live with their creations every day. To an equity analyst, a financial model is a tool, and that tool's design and quality critically affects the quality of his or her work. As a working analyst, I developed a number of model design rules, mostly through painful trial and error. This may seem like simple stuff, but believe me, it was hard won.

■ **Trick**   Capture as much financial history as you can. Several years of quarterly data are very helpful in resolving consistency issues like those we discussed above.

■ **Trick**   Forecast the current year by quarters, and the following years by the full year. Most analysts "quarterize" next years' forecast late in the current year. If you quarterize too early, revisions are difficult and time-consuming. Time you don't usually have.

■ **Trick**   Model what the company reports, in the format it reports. This is a huge timesaver. Earnings and other financial releases can be immediately incorporated into the model, without your trying to remember what accounts were consolidated into which line of the model. It is also far easier to talk numbers to management in their own language. This rule may require the analyst to write models "from scratch" rather than use prepackaged modeling systems. That's why they pay you the big bucks.

TABLE 11–6

Simple modeling assumptions can produce unexpected (and unwarranted) results.

	Year 1	Year 2E	Post-dividend Year 2E	Year 3E	Post-dividend Year 3E
Income Statement					
Sales	400	420		441	
Net income	60	63		66	
Net margin	15%	15%		15%	
Inflation rate	5%	5%		5%	
Balance Sheet					
Cash		58	—	61	—
Current assets	200	210	210	220	220
Fixed assets	300	300	300	300	300
Total assets	500	568	510	581	520
Current liabilities	100	105	105	110	110
Equity	400	463	405	471	410
Total	500	568	510	581	520
Working capital	100	105		110	
Common dividend			58		61
Return on Beginning Equity			15.8%		16.3%
Net margin			15.0%		15.0%
Asset turnover			0.84		0.86
Balance sheet leverage			1.25		1.26
Return on Ending Equity			15.6%		16.1%
Net margin			15.0%		15.0%
Asset turnover			0.82		0.85
Balance sheet leverage			1.26		1.27

■ **Trick**   It may be necessary to model financial details that the company does not report, for example, product level sales and prices. This is great for keeping a forecast honest, but realize that this portion of your model can drift far from reality.

■ **Trick**   Finally, always try to capture every piece of data the company does release. It may seem like unnecessary effort, but it is worth it in the end.

Uncouple Quarterly and Annual Forecasts

Consider the hypothetical forecast in Table 11–7, made at the beginning of 1999. Sales growth and net margin are assumed to be 10 percent and 100 shares are outstanding.

You will save yourself much pain if you design your models so that

- The FY 1999 forecast is the sum of the four quarters, rather than independently determined.
- The FY 2000 forecast is not produced by growing the FY 1999 forecast, but is again independently determined, even "hard-wired" by entering numbers rather than formulas into the spreadsheet.

It is very tempting, but unwise, to write formulas like

$$\text{Sales}_{\text{FY 2000}} = \text{sales}_{\text{FY 1999}} * (1 + \text{growth rate}) \qquad (11.5)$$

The flaw in such formulas is that, as actual quarterly results are reported

TABLE 11–7

Typical earnings forecast will contain quarterly and annual projections.

	1QE	2QE	3QE	4QE	FY 1999	FY 2000
Sales	100	105	110	115	430	473
Net income	10.0	10.5	11.0	11.5	43.0	47.3
EPS	$0.10	0.11	0.11	0.12	0.44	$0.47

and entered into the model, the changes propagate into future years, sometimes without the analyst's noticing. You don't want this to happen because changing earnings forecasts is a big deal. You want to make changes deliberately, not automatically. Perhaps you still believe that FY 2000 EPS will be $0.47, in spite of some quarterly fluctuations in FY 1999. After the 1999 first quarter is reported, for example, your model will look like Table 11–8. The effects of the actual first quarter are reflected in the FY 1999, where forecasted sales have risen to $432 from $430 and EPS from $0.44 to $0.45, but FY 2000 is unaltered. This may or may not be the pattern of earnings you wish to forecast, but at least with this system you can make alterations consciously.

■ **Trick**   Uncouple current quarterly and future annual forecasts. Make changes directly to future years' forecasts rather than permitting fluctuations in the current year to impact the following year's projections.

Uncouple Detail and Financial Statement Models

Separate financial models into a top-down forecast section and a bottom-up detail section because, as usual, it saves time, as shown in Figure 11–1.

It is tempting to write formulas like

Total top-down sales

$$= \text{sum of bottom-up segment/product sales} \quad (11.6)$$

Don't do it. It is much too slow and it destroys valuable analytic insights.

TABLE 11–8

Entry of actual results can alter both current and future years' projections.

	1QA	2QE	3QE	4QE	FY 1999	FY 2000
Sales	102	105	110	115	432	473
Net income	11.0	10.5	11.0	11.5	44.0	47.3
EPS	$0.11	0.11	0.11	0.12	0.45	$0.47

FIGURE 11-1

Spreadsheets may contain both top-down forecasts and
bottom-up product or segment detail.

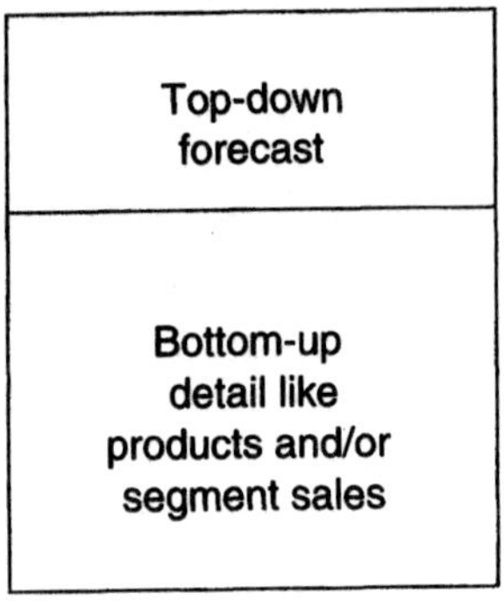

```
+--------------------+
|                    |
|     Top-down       |
|     forecast       |
|                    |
+--------------------+
|                    |
|    Bottom-up       |
|    detail like     |
|  products and/or   |
|   segment sales    |
|                    |
+--------------------+
```

- Product- or segment-level detail, if it is reported at all, can
  frequently be included in "analysts' supplements," which
  appear after initial earnings releases.
- But even if segment detail is available immediately, the analyst
  often needs to alter the top-down section of the model, which
  contains the projected financial statements, as rapidly as
  possible without thinking about the fine details. With four or
  five earnings releases sometimes occurring within minutes of
  one another, speed is critical.
- Even if you have bottom-up detail and enter it into the model,
  you must still forecast future performance from the product,
  rather than the financial statement level. This is very slow, and
  it diverts attention from developing financial trends.

Keeping top-down and bottom-up forecasts separate permits the analyst to match financial trends, revealed in growth rates and margins,
with product-level trends, through a *variance box*. Analysts can then
think about whether their top-down, financial statement models can actually be realized at the product level.

Consider again the hypothetical forecast in Table 11–7. Suppose
we have independently developed product-level detail supporting the
income statement projection, as shown in Table 11–9. Then when the
first-quarter actual results are reported, a variance with our original product-level expectations is immediately evident. This variance is a valuable

TABLE 11-9

Product-level detailed forecasts mirror top-down projections.

Sales	1QE	2QE	3QE	4QE	FY 1999	FY 2000
Product A	50	52	55	58	215	235
Product B	25	27	28	29	109	120
Product C	25	26	27	28	106	118
Total	100	105	110	115	430	473

signal that unexpected issues are arising at the product level, as shown in Table 11–10.

■ **Trick**   Develop top-down financial statement projections and bottom-up product/segment/divisional forecasts independently. A variance box built into the model can then signal important areas of disagreement between the two (Figure 11–2). This is useful both in reporting actual results and in the development of the model itself.

STARTING A FINANCIAL MODEL: DELL COMPUTER

We begin here the development of a financial model for Dell Computer, which will be our running example through the entire modeling process, with a discussion of base case assumptions for the model's most important drivers, like sales growth and gross margin. In Appendix 11–1, we have captured six years of DELL historical financial statements. In this example, we will not, for simplicity's sake, develop quarterly projections.

TABLE 11-10

If product- and top-level forecasts are independent, actual top-down results will create a useful variance.

Sales	1Q	2QE	3QE	4QE	FY 1999	FY 2000
Top down	102	105	110	115	432	473
Bottom up	100	105	110	115	434	473
Variance	2	—	—	—	2	—

FIGURE 11–2

A "variance box" can illustrate useful differences between
product-level assumptions and actual top-down results.

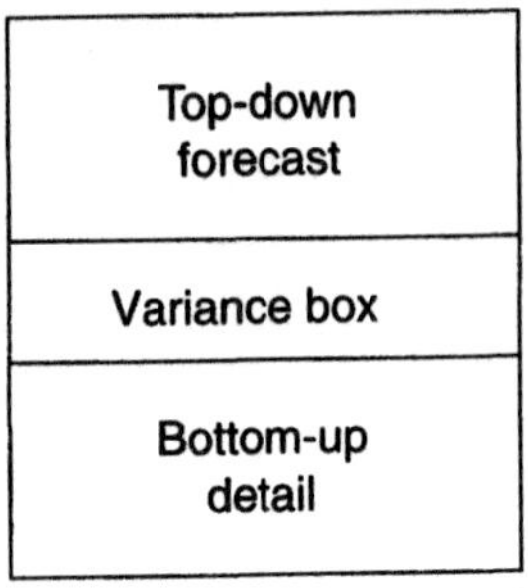

Top-down forecast
Variance box
Bottom-up detail

Because the company discloses relatively little product-level detail, we
will also not do a bottom-up forecast. However, working DELL analysts
probably do attempt bottom-up forecasting as a "reality check" on their
financial expectations.

As in all financial modeling, the DELL model is not prophecy but
the presentation of an opinion. In this model, I take a relatively conservative stance, forecasting the gradual moderation of growth and margins
but continued high asset efficiency. Another analyst might have taken a
more aggressive stance. The important thing is to take a position and
support it with argument.

■ **Trick**   Financial models are expressions of investment opinion,
not predictions of the future. Always take a clear position on the company's future prospects.

Model Structure

Notice first the model's structure. The first three financial statements,
income statement, statement of cash flows, and balance sheet, are modeled in the form they are reported by the company. The exception is the
SOCF, which is presented in a slightly rearranged "total cash flow" format, which we'll discuss in Chapter 13.

Following the financial statements is a "Supporting calculations"
section. This section provides further detail of fixed asset, shareholders'
equity, and particularly interest income and expense. This detail will be
useful in forecasting.

Finally, the "Financial analysis" section presents common-sized income statements and a variety of ratio families. It is in this section that the principal assumptions of our DELL forecast are developed.

Sales As the Forecast Driver

Like many financial models of commercial and industrial companies, DELL sales is the forecast driver. All other accounts, both income statement and balance sheet, must therefore scale correctly as sales change. But how are sales likely to change?

From a reading of the annual reports and the ratio analysis of both Gateway and Dell in Chapter 7, we learned a number of facts about the personal computer industry in the mid-to-late 1990s:

- The industry experienced increasing pricing—and margin—pressure as consumer tastes shifted toward lower-priced systems, particularly the sub-$1000 machines. Both companies responded to this challenge. Gateway diversified its revenue sources and began a marketing push. Dell placed more emphasis on sales of higher priced notebook and corporate enterprise systems, actively sought new markets and products, and worked to advance its technology—particularly in the enterprise area.
- Although both Gateway and Dell continued to grow more rapidly, the personal computer industry sales grew at a much lower, 10 to 15 percent, rate. The very dominance of these two strong marketing companies signals a maturing of the PC market.

Strong unit volume growth, combined with weakening price, was apparent in data presented in the fiscal 1999 Dell annual report. Unit sales volume growth averaged 62 percent in fiscal 1998 and fiscal 1999, with enterprise and notebook systems growing at 100 percent plus rates. But average revenue per unit was flat to down, as shown in Table 11–11.

In fact, although no unambiguous trend is apparent, the company's sales growth slowed to 48 percent in 1999 from an average of 53 percent in the three previous years. In keeping with the heightened competitive environment and maturing of the industry, then, let's project a gradual sales growth reduction for Dell through 2003, as shown in Table 11–12.

TABLE 11–11

Dell's unit volume increased sharply in 1998 to 1999, but pricing showed signs of pressure. (Years ending February 1 and January 29, respectively)

Unit Sales Volume	1998	1999
Total	60%	64%
Enterprise systems	256%	130%
Notebooks	66%	108%
Desktop systems	55%	55%
Average revenue per unit	0%	(10)%

Source: Dell financial reports.

TABLE 11–12

Dell sales projection anticipates declining growth as personal computer industry and company mature.

	1998	1999	2000E	2001E	2002E	2003E
Sales growth	58.9%	48.0	45.0	45.0	40.0	35.0%

Gross Margin and SGA

Dell has shown steadily improving gross margins, as the company has adjusted to rising competitive pressure in consumer desktop systems by shifting sales emphasis to higher-margin enterprise and notebook systems. But given the maturing PC market, a conservative expectation might be a gradual margin decline through 2003, as shown in Table 11–13. In keeping with the conservative stance of the projection, we allow SGA as a percentage of sales to creep upward from the 9.8 percent level in 1998 to 1999 to 10.5 percent by 2003.

Cash Conversion Cycle

Turnover projections are the model's driver of Dell's working capital and cash conversion cycle. The company's asset turnovers have improved in

TABLE 11-13

Projected margins also illustrate increasing competitive pressure.

	1998	1999	2000E	2001E	2002E	2003E
Gross margin	22.1%	22.5	22.5	21.8	21.0	20.0%
SGA	9.8%	9.8	10.0	10.3	10.5	10.5%

recent years, and there seems no good reason to break this trend, even in light of more difficult competitive conditions. Dell's operational strategy—made to order, direct sales of PC systems—should continue to produce high cash flow efficiency, especially since unit volumes continue to be robust and component pricing, like PC pricing, is likely to continue to fall.

The slight projected rise in inventory turnover and fall in payables turnover reflects a continuation of trends established in the 1994 to 1999 period (Table 11–14). The resulting rise in the cash conversion cycle, from (10) to (18) days, also mirrors the 1994 to 1999 trend, as shown in Appendix 11–1.

A PARTIAL REALITY CHECK

How accurate did these DELL base case assumptions, actually done in late 1999, prove to be? It won't surprise you to know that they were wrong, although their direction was right. Rather than declining to 45

TABLE 11-14

Cash conversion cycle projections show improvement.

	1998	1999	2000E	2001E	2002E	2003E
Receivables turnover	8.3	8.7	8.7	8.7	8.7	8.7
Inventory turnover	41.2	51.8	55.0	55.0	55.0	55.0
Payables turnover	5.8	5.9	5.5	5.5	5.5	5.5
Cash conversion cycle	(10)	(13)	(18)	(18)	(18)	(18)

percent in 2000 from 48 percent in 1999, DELL fiscal 2000 sales growth actually dropped to 38 percent. The company's fiscal 2000 growth gross margin fell to 20.7 percent rather than holding steady at the projected 22.5 percent. Asset efficiency did remain high, however, with the actual (19) day cash conversion cycle bettering the projected (18) days. In the wake of the now-slowing U. S. economy, the company's fiscal 2001 year is looking evern gloomier. Nine-month sales growth through October 2000 was 26 percent, well below the forecast 45 percent, and its gross margin reached 21 percent, somewhat below the projection's 21.8 percent. At this writing, analysts are cutting DELL 2002 earnings estimates in anticipation of weakening personal computer demand and competitive pricing pressures.[5]

The point of this reality check is not to prove my skill as a forecaster, although that would be nice, but to demonstrate the necessity of taking a firm position. In fact, my base case missed some critical economic developments. The forecast did not incorporate the slowing of the U.S. economy in the wake of the aggressive Federal Reserve interest rate increases of 1999 and 2000. Nor did it anticipate the immediate impact on margins of increasing PC price competition. Undoubtedly, it also missed a variety of other important financial drivers. What the forecast did do, though, was to present a conservative analysis of DELL's future prospects. The position, rather than its details, is the more important element of the forecast.

NOTES

[1] At this point, as discussed further in Chapter 20, it's often helpful to write a one-page summary of your investment thesis. This summary not only can guide financial modeling but can assist the arrangement of your research data in some logical order. The summary can suggest information gaps, where more work is needed, or information gluts, where more appendixes are needed.

[2] Krishna G. Palepu, Victor L. Bernard, and Paul M. Healy, *Introduction to Business Analysis and Valuation*, South-Western College Publishing, 1996, p. 5-3.

[3] Ibid. p. 5-6.

[4] Ibid., suggested by a discussion question on p. 5-22.

[5] "Dell's Earnings Estimates Are Cut on Fears About Industry Outlook," *The Wall Street Journal* Interactive Edition, January 9, 2001.

Dell Computer Corporation Consolidated Statement of Income

(January fiscal year end)

	1994	1995	1996	1997	1998	1999	2000E	2001E	2002E	2003E
Consolidated Statement of Income										
Net revenue	2,873	3,475	5,296	7,759	12,327	18,243	26,452	38,356	53,698	72,493
Cost of revenue	2,440	2,737	4,229	6,093	9,605	14,137	20,501	30,013	42,422	57,994
Gross margin	433	738	1,067	1,666	2,722	4,106	5,952	8,342	11,277	14,499
Selling, gen, admin expenses	423	424	595	826	1,202	1,788	2,645	3,931	5,638	7,612
Research & development	49	65	95	126	204	272	397	575	805	1,087
Total operating expenses	472	489	690	952	1,406	2,060	3,042	4,507	6,444	8,699
Operating income	(39)	249	377	714	1,316	2,046	2,910	3,836	4,833	5,799
Financing and other	—	(36)	6	33	52	38	93	138	203	289
Income before tax, extraordinary loss	(39)	213	393	747	1,368	2,084	3,003	3,973	5,035	6,089
Provision for income tax	(3)	64	111	216	424	624	901	1,192	1,511	1,827
Income before extraordinary loss	(36)	149	272	531	944	1,460	2,102	2,781	3,525	4,262
Extraordinary loss, net of tax			—	(13)	—	—	—	—	—	—
Net income	(36)	149	272	518	944	1,460	2,102	2,781	3,525	4,262
Preferred stock dividends	(4)	(9)	(12)	—	—	—	—	—	—	—
Net available to common	(40)	140	260	518	944	1,460	2,102	2,781	3,525	4,262
Diluted EPS	$ (0.53)	$ 0.79	$ 0.33	$ 0.66	$ 1.28	$ 0.53	$ 0.76	$ 1.02	$ 1.31	$ 1.60
Diluted common shares		189.3	790	782	758	2,772	2,769	2,737	2,699	2,657
Effective tax rate	7.7%	30.0%	28.2%	28.9%	31.0%	29.9%	30.0%	30.0%	30.0%	30.0%
Interest expense	9	12	15	7	3	19				
EBITDA	(8)	282	415	761	1,383	2,149	3,063	4,056	5,135	6,201

Statement of Cash Flows

	1994	1995	1996	1997	1998	1999	2000E	2001E	2002E	2003E
Net Income	(36)	149	272	518	944	1,460	2,102	2,781	3,525	4,262
Adjustments to reconcile net income to net cash										
Depreciation and amortization	31	33	38	47	67	103	154	220	302	401
Other, net	4	33	22	66	188	455	(60)	(90)	(132)	(188)
Interest expense less interest income, net	—	23	(4)	(21)	(34)	(25)				
Subtotal	35	89	56	92	221	533	93	131	171	213
Cash flow before working capital, interest	(1)	238	328	610	1,165	1,993	2,195	2,912	3,695	4,476
Cash flow effects of working capital										
Working capital	97	(11)	(195)	622	365	367	344	444	596	791
Net non-current assets, liabilities	17	39	38	109	28	51	159	228	294	360
Subtotal	114	28	(157)	731	393	418	503	671	890	1,151
Cash flow before interest	113	266	171	1,341	1,558	2,411	2,698	3,583	4,585	5,627
Interest expense, net		(23)	4	21	34	25	60	90	132	188
Cash flow from operations	113	243	175	1,362	1,592	2,436	2,758	3,673	4,717	5,815
Cash flow effects of long-term assets										
Marketable securities purchases	(2,588)	(4,644)	(4,545)	(9,538)	(12,305)	(16,459)	(1,121)	(1,727)	(2,445)	(2,482)
Marketable securities maturities, sales	2,335	4,464	4,442	8,891	12,017	15,341				
Capital expenditures	(48)	(64)	(101)	(114)	(187)	(296)	(407)	(511)	(632)	(763)
Subtotal	(301)	(244)	(204)	(761)	(475)	(1,414)	(1,528)	(2,238)	(3,077)	(3,245)
Free cash flow	(188)	(1)	(29)	601	1,117	1,022	1,230	1,435	1,640	2,570
Dividends	(2)	(9)	(14)		(1)					(725)
Free cash flow after dividends	(190)	(10)	(43)	601	1,116	1,022	1,230	1,435	1,640	1,845
Cash flow effects of financing										
Purchase of common stock				(495)	(1,023)	(1,518)	(1,230)	(1,435)	(1,640)	(1,845)
Repurchase of 11.5% notes				(95)						
Issuance of common stock	22	35	48	57	88	212				
Proceeds from long-term debt	97	14				494				
Repayment of long-term debt	(59)	(1)								
Cash from sale of options					38					
Proceeds from preferred stock	120									
Subtotal	180	48	48	(533)	(897)	(812)	(1,230)	(1,435)	(1,640)	(1,845)
Foreign exchange effects	(2)	2	7	(8)	(14)	(10)				
Net Change in Cash	(12)	40	12	60	205	200	(0)	(0)		0

Balance Sheet

	1994	1995	1996	1997	1998	1999	2000E	2001E	2002E	2003E
Current assets										
Surplus funds							1,121	2,848	5,293	7,775
Cash		43	55	115	320	520	520	520	520	520
Marketable securities		484	591	1,237	1,524	2,661	2,661	2,661	2,661	2,661
Accounts receivable		538	726	903	1,486	2,094	3,041	4,409	6,172	8,332
Inventory		293	429	251	233	273	373	546	771	1,054
Other		112	156	241	349	791	1,323	1,918	2,685	3,625
Subtotal (excl SF)		1,470	1,957	2,747	3,912	6,339	7,917	10,053	12,809	16,193
Property, plant, and equipment, net		117	179	235	342	523	776	1,068	1,397	1,759
Other assest		7	12	11	14	15	16	17	18	19
Total assets		1,594	2,148	2,993	4,268	6,877	9,830	13,986	19,517	25,745
Current liabilities										
Necessary to finance							—	—	—	—
Accounts payable		403	466	1,040	1,643	2,397	3,727	5,457	7,713	10,544
Accrued and other		349	473	618	1,054	1,298	1,889	2,740	3,836	5,178
Subtotal (excl NTF)		752	939	1,658	2,697	3,695	5,617	8,197	11,549	15,722
Long-term debt		113	113	18	17	512	512	512	512	512
Deferred revenue on warranty contracts		68	116	219	225	349	509	738	1,033	1,394
Other		9	7	13	36	—	—	—	—	—
Total liabilities (excl NTF)		942	1,175	1,908	2,975	4,556	6,638	9,446	13,093	17,629
Put options				279	—					
Shareholders equity										
Preferred stock		120	6	—						
Common stock		242	430	195	747	1,781				
Retained earnings		311	570	647	607	606				
Other		(21)	(33)	(36)	(61)	(66)				
Total shareholders equity		652	973	806	1,293	2,321	3,193	4,539	6,424	8,117
Total liabilities and net worth		1,594	2,148	2,993	4,268	6,877	9,830	13,986	19,517	25,745

	1994	1995	1996	1997	1998	1999	2000E	2001E	2002E	2003E
Supporting Calculations										
Fixed assets and depreciation										
PPE		208	374	374	509	775	1,182	1,693	2,325	3,088
– Accumulated depreciation		(91)	(113)	(139)	(137)	(252)	(406)	(626)	(928)	(1,330)
PPE, net		117	179	235	342	523	776	1,068	1,397	1,759
Rate of depreciation		15.9%	10.2%	12.6%	13.2%	13.3%	13.0%	13.0%	13.0%	13.0%
Inventory components										
Production materials		262	390	223	189	234				
Work in process and finished goods		31	39	28	44	39				
Total inventory		293	429	251	233	273				
Shareholders equity/share repurchase										
Beginning equity			652	973	806	1,293	2,321	3,193	4,539	6,424
+ Net income			272	518	944	1,460	2,102	2,781	3,525	4,262
– Dividends			(14)	—	(1)	—	—	—	—	(725)
– Share repurchases			—	(495)	(1,023)	(1,518)	(1,230)	(1,435)	(1,640)	(1,845)
+ Share issuance			48	57	88	212	—	—	—	—
+ Other			15	(247)	479	874	—	—	—	—
Ending equity			973	806	1,293	2,321	3,193	4,539	6,424	8,117
Book value per share						$ 0.91	$ 1.27	$ 1.83	$ 2.63	$ 3.39
Average share repurchase price							$ 41.00	$ 41.00	$ 41.00	$ 41.00
Average share issuance price							$ 41.00	$ 41.00	$ 41.00	$ 41.00
Dividend per share							$ —	$ —	$ —	$ (0.30)
Beginning common shares outstanding							2,543	2,513	2,478	2,438
– Share repurchases							(30)	(35)	(40)	(45)
+ Share issuance							—	—	—	—
Ending common share outstanding						2,543	2,513	2,478	2,438	2,393
Average common stock outstanding						2,531	2,528	2,496	2,458	2,416
Balance factor						241	241	241	241	241
Weighted average diluted shares						2,772	2,769	2,737	2,699	2,657

	1994	1995	1996	1997	1998	1999	2000E	2001E	2002E	2003E
Cash flow items										
Tax rate applied to financing cost	35.0%	35.0%	35.0%	35.0%	35.0%	35.0%	35.0%	35.0%	35.0%	35.0%
Cash flow excl interest–capex	65	202	70	1,227	1,371	2,115	2,291	3,072	3,953	4,864
Working capital (excluding cash)		191	372	(263)	(629)	(537)	(881)	(1,324)	(1,920)	(2,711)
Other assets, net		(70)	(111)	(221)	(247)	(334)	(493)	(721)	(1,015)	(1,375)
Change in working capital			181	(635)	(366)	92	(344)	(444)	(596)	(791)
Change in other assets, net			(41)	(110)	(26)	(87)	(159)	(228)	(294)	(360)
Change in invested funds, excl cash		484	107	646	287	1,137	1,121	1,727	2,445	2,482
Change in funded debt		113	—	(95)	(1)	495	—	—	—	—
Change in cash		43	12	60	205	200	—	—	—	—
Interest income and expense										
Cash		43	55	115	320	520	520	520	520	520
Marketable securities		484	591	1,237	1,524	2,661	2,661	2,661	2,661	2,661
Surplus funds		—	—	—	—	—	1,121	2,848	5,293	7,775
Total invested funds		527	646	1,352	1,844	3,181	4,302	6,029	8,474	10,956
Estimated pre-financing cost cash flow							2,133	2,845	3,641	4,448
Interest rate							3.0%	3.0%	3.0%	3.0%
Interest income							129	174	239	326
Beginning long-term debt			113	113	18	17	512	512	512	512
New long-term debt		113	—	—	—	494	—	—	—	—
Repayment of long-term debt			—	(95)	—	—	—	—	—	—
Other changes in long-term debt			—	—	(1)	1	—	—	—	—
Ending long-term debt		113	113	18	17	512	512	512	512	512
Necessary to finance						—	—	—	—	—
Total borrowed funds		113	113	18	17	512	512	512	512	512
Estimated pre-financing cost cash flow										
Borrowing rate							6.9%	6.9%	6.9%	6.9%
Interest expense							36	36	36	36
+ After-tax operating income							2,037	2,685	3,383	4,060
+ Changes in working capital, other							503	671	890	1,151
– Capital expenditures, other							(407)	(511)	(632)	(763)
Estimated pre-financing cash flow							2,133	2,845	3,641	4,448
Net interest income (expense)	—	(36)	6	33	52	38	93	138	203	289

Financial Analysis

	1994	1995	1996	1997	1998	1999	2000E	2001E	2002E	2003E
Common sized income statement										
Net revenue	100.0%	100.0%	100.0%	100.0%	100.0%	100.0%	100.0%	100.0%	100.0%	100.0%
Cost of revenue	84.9%	78.8%	79.9%	78.5%	77.9%	77.5%	77.5%	78.3%	79.0%	80.0%
Gross margin	15.1%	21.2%	20.1%	21.5%	22.1%	22.5%	22.5%	21.8%	21.0%	20.0%
Selling, gen, admin expenses	14.7%	12.2%	11.2%	10.6%	9.8%	9.8%	10.0%	10.3%	10.5%	10.5%
Research & development	1.7%	1.9%	1.8%	1.6%	1.7%	1.5%	1.5%	1.5%	1.5%	1.5%
Total operating expenses	16.4%	14.1%	13.0%	12.3%	11.4%	11.3%	11.5%	11.8%	12.0%	12.0%
Operating income	-1.4%	7.2%	7.1%	9.2%	10.7%	11.2%	11.0%	10.0%	9.0%	8.0%
Financing and other	0.0%	-1.0%	0.1%	0.4%	0.4%	0.2%	0.4%	0.4%	0.4%	0.4%
Income before tax, extraordinary loss	-1.4%	6.1%	7.4%	9.6%	11.1%	11.4%	11.4%	10.4%	9.4%	8.4%
Provision for income tax	-0.1%	1.8%	2.1%	2.8%	3.4%	3.4%	3.4%	3.1%	2.8%	2.5%
Income before extraordinary loss	-1.3%	4.3%	5.1%	6.8%	7.7%	8.0%	7.9%	7.3%	6.6%	5.9%
Extraordinary loss, net of tax	0.0%	0.0%	0.0%	-0.2%	0.0%	0.0%	0.0%	0.0%	0.0%	0.0%
Net income	-1.3%	4.3%	5.1%	6.7%	7.7%	8.0%	7.9%	7.3%	6.6%	5.9%
Preferred stock dividends	-0.1%	-0.3%	-0.2%	0.0%	0.0%	0.0%	0.0%	0.0%	0.0%	0.0%
Net available to common	-1.4%	4.0%	4.9%	6.7%	7.7%	8.0%	7.9%	7.3%	6.6%	5.9%
Apparent tax rate	7.7%	30.0%	28.2%	28.9%	31.0%	29.9%	30.0%	30.0%	30.0%	30.0%
Dividend payout	5.0%	6.4%	5.4%	0.0%	0.1%	0.0%	0.0%	0.0%	0.0%	17.0%
Returns										
Return on average equity			32.0%	58.2%	89.9%	80.8%	76.2%	71.9%	64.3%	58.6%
Return on beginning equity			39.9%	53.2%	117.1%	112.9%	90.6%	87.1%	77.7%	66.3%
Return on beginning assets (unadjusted)			16.3%	24.1%	31.5%	34.2%	30.6%	28.3%	25.2%	21.8%
Pretax operating return on beg assets			43.3%	33.2%	44.0%	47.9%	42.3%	39.0%	34.6%	29.7%
Return on beginning total capital (adjusted)			36.8%	49.3%	114.8%	112.4%	74.2%	75.1%	69.8%	61.4%
EBITDA/beginning total capital			54.2%	70.1%	167.8%	164.0%	108.1%	109.5%	101.7%	89.4%
Growth										
Net revenue		21.0%	52.4%	46.5%	58.9%	48.0%	45.0%	45.0%	40.0%	35.0%
Operating income			41.1%	38.0%	47.7%	46.5%	47.7%	48.2%	43.0%	35.0%
Net income (before extra items)			82.6%	95.2%	77.8%	54.7%	44.0%	32.3%	26.7%	20.9%
Diluted EPS				100.0%	93.9%	-58.6%	43.2%	33.9%	28.5%	22.9%
Total assets			34.8%	39.3%	42.6%	61.1%	42.9%	42.3%	39.6%	31.9%
Shareholder's equity			49.2%	-17.2%	60.4%	79.5%	37.6%	42.2%	41.5%	26.3%

	1994	1995	1996	1997	1998	1999	2000E	2001E	2002E	2003E
Value Drivers (not adjusted for interest expense)										
Net profit margin	−1.3%	4.3%	4.9%	6.7%	7.7%	8.0%	7.9%	7.3%	6.6%	5.9%
× Asset turnover			3.32	3.61	4.12	4.27	3.85	3.90	3.84	3.71
= Return on beginning assets			16.3%	24.1%	31.5%	34.2%	30.6%	28.3%	25.2%	21.8%
× Financial leverage			2.44	2.21	3.71	3.30	2.96	3.08	3.08	3.04
= Return on beginning equity			39.9%	53.2%	117.1%	112.9%	90.6%	87.1%	77.7%	66.3%
Asset turnover										
Current asset turnover		2.4	2.7	2.8	3.2	2.9	3.3	3.8	4.2	4.5
Current liabilities turnover		4.6	5.6	4.7	4.6	4.9	4.7	4.7	4.6	4.6
Working capital turnover		4.8	5.2	7.1	10.1	6.9	11.5	20.7	42.6	154.2
Accounts receivable turnover		6.5	7.3	8.6	8.3	8.7	8.7	8.7	8.7	8.7
Inventory turnover		9.3	9.9	24.3	41.2	51.8	55.0	55.0	55.0	55.0
Other asset turnover		31.0	33.9	32.2	35.3	23.1	20.0	20.0	20.0	20.0
Accounts payable turnover		6.8	9.1	5.9	5.8	5.9	5.5	5.5	5.5	5.5
Days in receivables		57	50	42	44	42	42	42	42	42
Days in inventories		39	37	15	9	7	7	7	7	7
Days in payables		54	40	62	62	62	66	66	66	66
Cash conversion cycle		42	47	(5)	(10)	(13)	(18)	(18)	(18)	(18)
Sales/capital expenditures		54.3	52.4	68.1	65.9	61.6	65.0	75.0	85.0	95.0
Sales/cash and market securities		6.6	8.2	5.7	6.7	5.7	8.3	12.1	16.9	22.8
Sales/Def revenue on warranty contracts		51.1	45.7	35.4	54.8	52.3	52.0	52.0	52.0	52.0
PPE turnover		29.7	29.6	33.0	36.0	34.9	34.1	35.9	38.4	41.2
Leverage and coverage										
Liabilities to equity		2.60	1.21	2.37	2.30	1.96	2.08	2.08	20.4	2.17
Debt to equity		0.17	0.12	0.02	0.01	0.22	0.16	0.11	0.08	0.06
Debt to capital		0.15	0.10	0.02	0.01	0.18	0.14	0.10	0.07	0.06
Warranty liabilities/equity		0.10	0.12	0.27	0.17	0.15	0.16	0.16	0.16	0.17
Interest coverage		21	25	102	439	108				
Operating cash flow/total liabilities	(4)	0.14	0.15	0.71	0.54	0.53	0.42	0.39	0.36	0.33
Cash flow characteristics										
Net income/cash flow from operations		0.58	1.49	0.38	0.59	0.60	0.76	0.76	0.75	0.73
CFO/capital expenditures		3.80	1.73	11.95	8.51	8.23	6.78	7.18	7.47	7.62
Depreciation/capital expenditures		0.52	0.38	0.41	0.36	0.35	0.38	0.43	0.48	0.53
Sustainable growth rate										
ROE			39.9%	53.2%	117.1%	112.9%	90.6%	87.1%	77.7%	66.3%
Dividend payout			5.4%	0.0%	0.1%	0.0%	0.0%	0.0%	0.0%	17.0%
Sustainable growth rate			37.7%	53.2%	117.0%	112.9%	90.6%	87.1%	77.7%	55.1%

CHAPTER 12

Financial Modeling: The Income Statement and Balance Sheet

- Sales forecasts usually drive the operating portion of the income statement.

- Interest income and expense, on the other hand, are not sales driven but are cash flow driven and a function of corporate financial policies. Since interest is dependent both on beginning and ending balance sheet accounts, the analyst needs to "close the balance sheet" to calculate it. But, of course, without knowing interest amounts, one cannot calculate net income, which one needs to close the balance sheet. There are ways to avoid this common and annoying circularity.

- Like much of the income statement, sales forecasts can drive the bulk of the balance sheet. Turnover ratios can determine working capital accounts. It's also perfectly sensible to scale fixed assets upward (or downward) with sales levels. Existing maturity schedules set funded debt amounts. The final levels of cash or debt are determined when the balance sheet is closed.

- Taxes are a difficult forecasting problem both on the income statement and balance sheet. Historical tax patterns are helpful, but security analysts rarely have the information necessary to precisely model a company's tax situation. In my own experience, company guidance can be important in successfully modeling taxes.

All financial models must begin with the expression, contained in the model's basic assumptions, of an opinion about the company's future prospects. Once the analyst has taken a position, the income statement and balance sheet forecasts are the next steps. In the Dell model, we've chosen sales as the scaling factor, the most common choice in commercial and industrial companies. Most income statement line items, and a surprising amount of the balance sheet, can be projected by combining the projected sales with a forecasted ratio to sales, like a margin or a turnover. The statement line items that do not scale with sales, such as interest expense, taxes, or excess cash, need to be handled separately.

With the income statement and balance sheet completed, the analyst can develop the statement of cash flows (SOCF). Techniques for projecting the SOCF follow in Chapter 13.

THE INCOME STATEMENT: THE EQUITY ANALYST'S LODESTONE

The income statement projection is the starting point—and unfortunately often the ending point—of equity analysts' financial models.

The Sales-Driven Portion of the Income Statement

Most income statement models are scaled by net sales, meaning that

- The analyst makes a sales forecast, projecting future full year's sales from the most current actual.
- Most remaining income statement line items then fall out through the application of margin forecasts. For example, the company's projected gross profit is the product of projected sales and projected gross margin.

Spreadsheet programs will then contain formulas like

$$\text{Sales}_T = (1 + \text{sales growth rate}_T) * \text{sales}_{T-1} \qquad (12.1)$$

$$\text{Gross profit}_T = \text{sales}_T * \text{GP margin}_T \qquad (12.2)$$

This procedure works well through the operating profit line, but it begins to break down with financing costs and taxes. Financing costs are cash flow and balance sheet, rather than sales, driven. Projected taxes can be calculated only when financing costs have been projected.

Dell Projected Income Statement

Our Dell base case assumptions for sales growth and margins takes the financial model through the operating income line, as shown in Appendix 11–1. Projected sales rise to $72.5 billion in fiscal 2003 from $18.2 billion in fiscal 1999, showing the effects of our slowing, but still very strong, growth assumptions. Seeing the remarkable $72 billion sales figure, in fact, I'm very comfortable with more conservative growth assumptions.

Projected operating income rises from $2,046 million in 1999 to $5,799 million in 2003, an annual compound growth rate of about 30 percent. This is a considerable slowdown from the 69 percent annual 1995 to 1999 compound rate, which seems a completely appropriate, but still quite respectable, showing. It also seems reasonable that operating profit growth should trail sales growth, given the maturing of the industry and competitive acceleration. Again, the operating profit projection feels right.

From operating income on, however, the income statement projection becomes more complex. In fact, we need to construct a balance sheet before completing the income statement:

■ Financing costs, in particular, require beginning and ending debt levels, which we do not yet have.

■ The tax provision requires both a pretax income and tax rate projection. Pretax income must be delayed until we have determined financing costs.

Taxes: Always an Analytic Stumbling Block

Although we cannot calculate the tax provision yet, we can at least, perhaps, decide upon a projected tax rate. The tax issue is always an analytical stumbling block. Few analysts attempt a detailed projection of the company's tax obligations unless the issue is highly material—for example, if tax loss carryforwards can be used to lower the tax provision. The reason for this is simple—analysts generally do not have, and companies do not disclose, enough detail to perform a precise tax calculation.

■ **Trick**   Don't waste time on income statement tax calculations unless you absolutely have to. The added detail is often not material.

So what to do? In the absence of a detailed model, we have two choices.

- Use the historical tax rate pattern. If the company's differently taxed income sources remain in relatively the same proportion, for example, the income statement tax rate itself can be relatively stable. Sometimes we get lucky.
- If the historical tax rate pattern is not stable, management guidance might be the only other alternative. Companies conduct tax planning several years into the future, and management should be able to help (subject to Regulation FD, of course).

With Dell, We Got Lucky

Fortunately, with the exception of the 1994 operating loss year, Dell's historical income statement tax rate is stable. In response, we chose a constant 30 percent forecast over the projection period. The "apparent tax rate" is the tax provision divided by the pretax income, as shown in Table 12–1. This result may be, in fact, no more than luck, since, according to the company's 1999 10-K, the components of the tax rate in 1998 and 1999 were themselves not particularly stable, as shown in Table 12–2.

TABLE 12–1

Dell tax rate shows stability.

	1994	1995	1996	1997	1998	1999
Apparent tax rate	7.7	30.0	28.2	28.9	31.0	29.9

TABLE 12–2

But Dell tax rate components are more variable.

	1998	1999
U.S. statutory rate	35.0	35.0
Foreign income taxed at different rates	(4.6)	(7.0)
Other	0.6	2.0
Effective tax rate	31.0	30.0

THE BALANCE SHEET: OVERCOMING CIRCULARITY

We've taken the income statement projection as far as we can without a balance sheet, which we now must build. Fortunately, like the income statement, much of the balance sheet can be constructed using sales-based scaling. The exceptions are tax-related items and financing. Finally, we need a way to "close" the balance sheet without circularity.

Sales-Driven Balance Sheet Accounts

Much of the current and noncurrent balance sheet structure is conveniently sales driven. Working capital accounts are the most straightforward:

$$\text{Accounts receivable}_T = \frac{\text{sales}_T}{\text{receivables turnover}_T} \qquad (12.3)$$

$$\text{Inventory}_T = \frac{\text{cost of goods sold}_T}{\text{inventory turnover}_T} \qquad (12.4)$$

$$\text{Accounts payable}_T = \frac{\text{cost of goods sold}_T}{\text{payables turnover}_T} \qquad (12.5)$$

It should be clear now why I recommended, in Chapter 7, that turnover ratios be calculated with ending balance sheet amounts, rather than beginning or average levels. Calculated in this way, Equations 12.3, 12.4, and 12.5 produce appropriate year-end balance sheet amounts.

Even accounts like cash and short-term debt can be sales driven because we will close the balance sheet by using two new accounts, surplus funds and necessary to finance. One can think of sales-driven cash and debt balances as required operating levels, with the two new accounts providing any excess levels.

Fixed Assets Sales-Driven Forecast

To forecast fixed asset balances using sales projections, one needs first to determine the appropriate drivers of capital expenditures and depreciation expense. First, find a historical pattern, if you can, by looking at

$$\text{Capex turnover}_T = \frac{\text{sales}_T}{\text{capital expenditures}_T} \qquad (12.6)$$

$$\text{Depreciation rate}_T = \frac{\text{depreciation expense}_T}{\text{gross PPE}_T} \qquad (12.7)$$

It seems reasonable that capital expenditures, which drive the company's physical plant, scale roughly with sales, which determine its operations level.

Note that the depreciation rate uses year-end PPE balances, not average or beginning. Then, it's a simple matter to calculate capital expenditures and depreciation:

$$\text{Capital expenditures}_T = \frac{\text{projected sales}_T}{\text{capex turnover}_T} \qquad (12.8)$$

$$\text{Gross PPE}_T = \text{gross PPE}_{T-1} + \text{capital expenditures}_T \qquad (12.9)$$

$$\text{Depreciation expense}_T = \text{gross PPE}_T * \text{depreciation rate}_T \qquad (12.10)$$

Equation 12.9 presumes, of course, that there are no asset sales in the projection. The balance sheet account, net PPE, then falls easily out of the formulas:

$$\text{Accumulated depreciation}_T = \text{accumulated depreciation}_{T-1}$$
$$+ \text{depreciation expense}_T \qquad (12.11)$$

$$\text{Net PPE}_T = \text{gross PPE}_T - \text{accumulated depreciation}_T \qquad (12.12)$$

An advantage of this method is that both capital expenditures and depreciation, two accounts required when we construct the SOCF, become available. These are certainly situations, particularly in startup companies, where sales-driven capital expenditure projections may be inappropriate. Questioning management might be the answer in these circumstances.

Dell

As noted in the "Supporting calculations" section of the model, Dell's depreciation rate varied between 15.9 and 13.3 percent, and fell between 12.6 and 13.3 percent in 1997 to 1999. I projected a 13 percent depreciation rate through 2003, implying an average useful life of 7.7 years (1/13 percent).

Capital expenditures turnover ranged from 52.4 to 68.1 historically, as noted in the model's "Financial analysis/asset turnover" section, but they have generally increased in 1995 to 1999. As a result, I projected a rise to 95.0 by 2003. Given the low capital intensity of the PC assembly process, increasing fixed asset efficiencies do not seem unreasonable, as shown in Table 12–3, especially in light of working capital efficiencies

TABLE 12–3

Dell capex turnover improves (anticipating economies in manufacturing scale).

	1998	1999	2000E	2001E	2002E	2003E
Capex turnover	65.9	61.6	65.0	75.0	75.0	95.0

projected in Chapter 11. In addition, with sales growth slowing, anticipating capital spending that may be in the historical record could decline in importance.

Perhaps most importantly, holding turnover at 65.0 produces $1.1 billion of 2003 capital expenditures, which feels too high given the historical growth pattern.

This projection of increasing capex efficiency may, of course, be seriously flawed, especially given potentially rising competitive pressure. However, the projected capital expenditure amounts, which according to the SOCF range from $407 to $763 million over the forecast period, are relatively insignificant compared to operating cash flow of $2.8 billion to $5.8 billion over the same period. If there is an error, it is probably not disastrous.

Balance Sheet Tax Accounts: Ugh!

Taxes again! This is, fortunately for us all, not a text on calculating or accounting for taxes. But for modeling purposes, the two most common balance sheet tax items, deferred tax (DT) liability and taxes payable, are determined with the following formulas, which are easy to enter into a spreadsheet:

$$\text{Ending DT liability} = \text{beginning DT liability}$$
$$+ \text{tax provision}$$
$$\text{(from the income statement)}$$
$$- \text{DT currently payable} \qquad (12.13)$$

$$\text{Ending taxes payable} = \text{beginning taxes payable}$$
$$+ \text{DT tax currently payable}$$
$$- \text{taxes paid} \qquad (12.14)$$

If you're forced to model these two accounts, here's a suggested method. In the deferred tax liability, the "DT currently payable" is conceptually similar to the depreciation of a fixed asset. You may be able to calculate the rate at which deferred taxes are amortized by examining historical data. For example, first find the gross deferred tax, which is the analog of gross fixed assets:

$$\text{Gross deferred tax}_T = \text{deferred tax}_{T-1} + \text{tax provision}_T \quad (12.15)$$

Then, calculate the deferred tax amortization rate, corresponding to the fixed asset depreciation rate:

$$\text{DT amortization rate}_T = \frac{\text{DT currently payable}_T}{\text{gross DT liability}_T} \quad (12.16)$$

If this amortization rate is stable and can be reliably projected, then Equation 12.3, for ending deferred tax liability, is fully determined.

Modeling income tax payable liability is more challenging because it requires an estimate of taxes paid. Companies are required to disclose paid taxes in their annual 10-K filings with the SEC, so it might be possible to use a similar "amortization rate" reasoning to forecast what portion of gross taxes payable are actually paid each year. It is not reasonable, on the other hand, for an equity analyst to attempt to re-create a company's actual tax filing—from which taxes paid are actually driven.

■ **Trick** To avoid mind-numbing complexity in tax calculations, you might consider using a simple sale-based scaling to project both the deferred tax liability (or asset) and taxes payable.

Dell Lets Us Off the Hook, Again

Another stroke of luck. Dell's balance sheet does not specifically disclose either deferred taxes or taxes payable. Actually, the company carries a deferred tax asset because of the accounting for deferred revenue on warranty contracts.

The model, therefore, uses simple sales scaling on other current assets, accrued and other liabilities, and deferred revenue. The appropriate turnover rates are determined in the model's "Asset turnover" section. The projections are a best guess, given each turnover's historical behavior, as shown in Table 12–4. The associated balance sheet accounts then fall out easily:

$$\text{Balance sheet account}_T = \frac{\text{projected sales}_T \text{ or costs}_T}{\text{turnover}_T} \quad (12.17)$$

TABLE 12-4

Projections of other Dell asset and liability turnovers anticipate relative stability.

	1998	1999	2000E	2001E	2002E	2003E
Other current assets	35.3	23.1	20.0	20.0	20.0	20.0
Accrued liabilities	11.7	14.1	14.0	14.0	14.0	14.0
Deferred revenue	54.8	52.3	52.0	52.0	52.0	52.0

CLOSING THE BALANCE SHEET: AVOIDING CIRCULARITY

Closing the balance sheet, making both sides total to the same amount, can be the source of substantial analytic tail-chasing. The problem is that without a closed balance sheet, net income, which contains financing costs, cannot be determined. But without net income, the balance sheet cannot be closed because net income is necessary to calculate shareholders' equity.

$$\text{Shareholders' equity}_T = \text{shareholders' equity}_{T-1}$$
$$+ \text{ net income}_T - \text{dividends}_T$$
$$+ \text{ shares issued}_T$$
$$- \text{ shares repurchased}_T + \text{other} \quad (12.18)$$

Most modern spreadsheet software can live with circularity, using an iterative process to resolve it. Nevertheless, circularity in financial models is a bad thing. The reason is that circular models are unstable, and small changes or errors in the model can cause the iteration process, which resolves the circularity, to blow up.

■ **Trap**   Financial models are inherently circular, but circular models are problematic.

You can avoid circularity by adding two new accounts to the balance sheet, "surplus funds" on the asset and "necessary to finance" on the liability side. These are the accounts that the spreadsheet will use to balance the balance sheet[1]:

■ If, at the end of the balancing process, liabilities and net worth exceed assets, the model adds the difference to surplus funds.

■ On the other hand, if assets exceed liabilities, the model adds
the difference to necessary to finance.

Step 1. Calculate the Beginning Balances

Calculate the beginning balances for interest-bearing assets and liabilities, including the two new accounts. In the first year of the forecast (the
last year in which actual results are available), surplus funds and necessary to finance are zero. The last actual balance sheet closes without
them.

$$\text{Interest-bearing assets} = \text{surplus funds} + \text{cash}$$
$$+ \text{ marketable securities} \quad (12.19)$$

$$\text{Interest-bearing liabilities} = \text{necessary to finance}$$
$$+ \text{ short-term debt}$$
$$+ \text{ current maturities of long-term debt}$$
$$+ \text{ long-term debt} \quad (12.20)$$

Step 2: Calculate Preinterest Cash Flow

Preinterest cash flow is simply the company's existing prefinancing cash
flow adjusted for after-tax interest expense and income.

$$\text{Preinterest cash flow} = \text{existing prefinancing cash flow}$$
$$+ \text{ after-tax interest expense}$$
$$- \text{ after-tax interest income} \quad (12.21)$$

Another route to preinterest cash flow begins with operating income:

$$\text{Preinterest cash flow} = \text{operating income} * (\ 1 - \text{tax rate}\ )$$
$$+ \text{ changes in working capital}$$
$$- \text{ capital expenditures} \quad (12.22)$$

Either method, used consistently, is acceptable.

Step 3. Calculate Interest Income and Expense

Preinterest cash flow (PICF) contributes either to interest-bearing assets
or liabilities, depending on its sign. If PICF is positive, interest-bearing
assets increase. If PICF is negative, interest-bearing liabilities increase.

The formula below then calculates interest income and expense[2]:

$$\text{Interest income, expense} = (I + 0.5 * I^2)$$
$$* \text{ (beginning balance}$$
$$+ 0.5 * \text{PICF)} \qquad (12.23)$$

where I is the interest rate. Where does this formula come from? Well, if preinterest cash flows evenly over the period, then the second enclosed term in Equation 12.23 is the average balance—either assets or liabilities:

$$\text{Average balance} = \text{beginning balance}$$
$$+ 0.5 * \text{preinterest cash flow} \qquad (12.24)$$

The first enclosed term of 12.23, on the other hand, calculates interest amounts. Multiplying the average balance by I, the interest rate, calculates the interest amount on the balance:

$$\text{Interest on average balance} = I * \text{average balance.} \qquad (12.25)$$

Multiplying the average balance by $0.5 * I^2$ calculates the interest on the interest:

$$\text{Interest on interest} = 0.5 * I^2 * \text{average balance} \qquad (12.26)$$

Clearly, one could carry the calculation—actually a series expansion— to as many terms as he or she likes. I've always found that contributions become very small after the second term.

■ **Trick**   Carry the interest calculation to two terms only. Higher-order terms make minimal contributions to most financial models.

Step 4. Close the Balance Sheet

Adding interest expense and income amounts to the income statement projection permits us to calculate net income. To find the appropriate balancing item, the spreadsheet then must determine surplus funds and necessary to finance:

Surplus funds

$$= \text{MAX (liabilities + shareholders' equity} - \text{assets, 0)} \qquad (12.27)$$

Necessary to finance

$$= \text{MAX (assets} - \text{liabilities} - \text{net worth, 0)} \qquad (12.28)$$

where the MAX function determines the greater of the balance sheet difference and zero. Total liabilities and assets in the MAX function exclude necessary to finance and surplus funds.

■ **Trick**   To close the balance sheet, calculate total assets and liabilites excluding surplus funds and necessary to finance.

Dell Projections Overflow with Surplus Funds
The balance sheet closing tactic discussed above leaves Dell awash in surplus funds. Holding both cash and marketable securities at their year-end 1999 levels, surplus funds reach $7.8 billion by 2003. In fact, by 2003 cash resources exceed shareholders' equity by a considerable margin, as shown in Table 12–5.

If this forecast is even close to true, DELL management faces major financial decisions over the next few years. The temptations will be many: acquisitions, diversification, share repurchases. The question, as always, is whether management can find investment projects for these newly generated funds as attractive as its basic business. If, in fact, the PC business is maturing, future investment requirements will likely also decline, forcing management further afield. This is not a bad problem to have, of course, but that doesn't make it easy.

ALTERNATIVE BALANCE SHEET CLOSERS

The surplus funds/necessary to finance method adds the appropriate balancing item to permit us to close the balance sheet. But suppose instead

TABLE 12–5

Dell projections produce substantial excess funds.

	1999	2000E	2001E	2002E	2003E
Surplus funds	—	1,121	2,848	5,293	7,775
Cash	520	520	520	520	520
Marketable securities	2,661	2,661	2,661	2,661	2,661
Cash resources	3,181	4,302	6,029	8,474	10,956
Shareholders' equity	2,321	3,193	4,539	6,424	8,117

that management wished to issue equity to finance expansion, or to maintain a target leverage or coverage ratio. Our closing methodology can be modified to model these changes. Having said that, a trial-and-error process, in which the analyst tests the impact of new debt and equity issuance, is probably easier and more revealing than hard-wiring corporate financial policies into the model.

But if you want to model a corporate financial policy, like the maintenance of maximum balance sheet leverage or minimum interest coverage, try this.

Step 1. Determine the Financial Limitation

Suppose you wish the model to issue equity so that a minimum cash flow from the operations/funded debt ratio is maintained. Use the basic closing method to calculate interest amounts, calculate net income, and arrive at a cash flow from operations estimate. Calculate projected funded debt in the model then:

$$\text{Projected funded debt} = \frac{\text{CFO}}{\text{minimum cash flow coverage ratio}} \quad (12.29)$$

Calculating funded debt this way will immediately run it to the maximum level.

Step 2. Use Equity to Close the Balance Sheet

In the event that liabilities are insufficient to close the balance sheet, issue equity as the balancing item:

Required equity issuance

$$= \text{MAX (assets} - \text{liabilities} - \text{shareholders' equity, 0)} \quad (12.30)$$

Or the two closing methods, issuing debt or equity, could be combined. The model could issue debt until total interest-bearing assets reached a preset maximum, then begin issuing equity. This would be neat, but, in my mind, overly complicated. I prefer to play with the model.

■ **Trick**   Rather than hard-wiring corporate financial policies into a financial model, test the effect of alternative financing strategies iteratively. Computers are very fast these days.

TABLE 12-6

Given excess cash generation, Dell model includes a share repurchase module.

	2000	2001	2002	2003
Shares repurchased	30	35	40	45
Share price	$41	41	41	$41
Repurchase amount	1,230	1,435	1,640	1,845

OTHER FINANCIAL MODEL FEATURES

Especially for companies like Dell, with projected excess cash generation, a share repurchase module is a revealing addition to the financial
model, and I have included share repurchase in this chapter's calculations. The repurchase module connects to the shareholders' equity formula, Equation 12.18, and the earnings-per-share calculation. I generally
hard-wire the number of shares repurchased and the repurchase price in
each year of the projection, although it is possible to program a dollar
repurchase amount. Which route you take may depend upon the details
of the company's particular share repurchase authorization.

Dell's Share Repurchase Module

The Dell share repurchase module is a useful feature in a company with
such a powerful cash generating capacity. In the "Supporting calculations" section, the model repurchases stock in each of the 2000 to 2003
forecast years at a price of $41 per share, as shown in Table 12-6. In
spite of annual repurchases in excess of $1 billion, the company still
accumulates projected surplus funds of $7.8 billion by year-end 2003.

NOTES

[1] The surplus funds/necessary to finance methodology is taught in the J.P. Morgan Securities Equity Research Analyst Training Program, but the basic idea has been in use
at Morgan since the 1970s, when financial models were run from punch cards on a
mainframe computer.

[2] Thanks go to insurance expert Michael Conn for suggesting this method.

CHAPTER 13

Financial Modeling: The Statement of Cash Flows

- Model the statement of cash flows (SOCF) last. Although it is often thought mysterious, in fact the SOCF is the simplest of the financial statements. It is just an elaborated collection of balance sheet differences.

- The SOCF is most often presented in the "indirect" form, in which net income is adjusted and combined with working capital changes to yield cash flow from operations. There is, however, a "direct" SOCF form, often described as the *cash-on-cash* or *checkbook format,* which expresses operational flows in terms of actual cash moving in and out of the firm.

- I recommend that analysts adopt the *total-cash-flow form* of the SOCF. The total-cash-flow format is a rearrangement of the indirect format, and it is designed to highlight cash flow adequacy at every stage of the company's operations and to isolate more clearly the company's cash sources and uses.

Cash flow statements were always a mystery to me. Add back noncash items. Subtract some things, add others, but who knew the right sign? In fact, the statement of cash flows (SOCF) is the simplest of the financial statements to model. It is derived principally from year-to-year differences in balance sheet accounts. Occasionally, income statement detail is substituted for the balance sheet differences. The result is the SOCF in the familiar indirect form flowing from net income to changes in cash.

The SOCF can be presented—but usually is not—in a direct format, which attempts to deal with cash items rather than with net income. This is the cash flow form we might derive if we could look into the company's checkbook, tracking the sources and destinations of cash movements. Again, there is nothing mysterious about the direct format; in fact, it is only a rearrangement of the same elements presented in the indirect format.

Finally, the indirect SOCF rearranged into the total-cash-flow format can clarify cash sources and uses, as well as suggest some interesting cash-based ratio analysis that mirrors the more familiar margin analysis of the income statement. It is sometimes helpful to state margins in cash rather than in accrual form.

A word of caution: This is not an accounting text and the discussion here avoids substantial accounting detail in the preparation of the SOCF. This chapter is meant to be only a guide for the construction and understanding of SOCF statements as a part of financial models. But this is the general idea.

THE ORIGINS OF THE SOCF

The SOCF is a simple rearrangement of balance sheet differences. Thought of this way, the SOCF's components, and particularly their signs, arise from arithmetic rather than arcane accounting rules—like adding back noncash items. In addition, modeling the SOCF as balance sheet differences guarantees that the statement will "balance" in the end, as long as the balance sheet itself adds correctly. This inherent crosscheck can save lots of analytical pain, although in practice, the SOCF can be more painful to model than its income statement and balance sheet cousins. It never seems to be correct the first time around.

The Financial Accounting Standards Board Statement of Financial Accounting Standard 95 specifies the current SOCF formats in use, and we'll follow those formats in this discussion.[1]

Balance Sheet Differences

The SFAS 95 SOCF format arises almost automatically from year-to-year balance sheet differences, as shown in Table 13–1. Begin with a simplified balance sheet. If we subtract last year's balance sheet from this year's, line by line, the resulting line item differences, denoted by a Δ symbol, remain in balance; that is, total assets still equal total liabilities and net worth:

TABLE 13–1

Balance sheet differences are the basis of the SOCF.

Assets	Liabilities and Net Worth
Cash and cash equivalents	Short-term debt
Other current assets	Other current liabilities
Total current assets	Total current liabilities
Property, plant, and equipment	Long-term debt
Other assets	Other liabilities
	Shareholders' equity
Total assets	Total liabilities and net worth

$$\Delta\text{cash} + \Delta\text{other current assets} + \Delta\text{PPE}$$
$$+ \;\Delta\text{other assets} = \Delta\text{short-term debt}$$
$$+ \;\Delta\text{other current liabilities} + \Delta\text{long-term debt}$$
$$+ \;\Delta\text{other liabilities}$$
$$+ \;\Delta\text{shareholders equity} \qquad (13.1)$$

Some simple algebra rearranges Equation 13.1 to yield

$$\Delta\text{shareholders' equity}$$
$$- \;\Delta \text{ (other current assets} - \text{other current liabilities)}$$
$$- \;\Delta \text{ (other assets} - \text{other liabilities)}$$
$$- \;\Delta\text{PPE}$$
$$+ \;\Delta\text{short-term debt}$$
$$+ \;\Delta\text{long-term debt}$$
$$= \Delta\text{cash} \qquad (13.2)$$

This is beginning to look familiar, but it's still not complete without a little more work. Note, for example, that Δshareholders' equity, the change in shareholders' equity, can be expanded:

$$\Delta\text{shareholders' equity} = \text{net income} - \text{dividends}$$
$$+ \text{ shares issued}$$
$$- \text{ shares repurchased} \qquad (13.3)$$

Changes in property, plant, and equipment, ΔPPE, can also be written in its component parts:

$$\Delta PPE = \text{capital expenditures} - \text{cost of property sold}$$
$$- \text{depreciation expense} \qquad (13.4)$$

But

$$\text{Proceeds of property sold} = \text{cost of property sold}$$
$$+ \text{gain on property sale} \qquad (13.5)$$

Therefore, substituting Equation 13.4 into Equation 13.3:

$$\Delta PPE = \text{capital expenditures} - \text{proceeds of property sold}$$
$$+ \text{gain on property sales} - \text{depreciation expense} \quad (13.6)$$

Substituting for shareholders' equity and PPE in Equation 13.2, a much more familiar format emerges:

Net income
+ depreciation
− gain on property sales
− Δ (other current assets − other current liabilities)
− Δ (other assets − other liabilities)
− capital expenditures
+ proceeds of property sold
− dividends
+ shares issued
− shares repurchased
+ Δshort-term debt
+ Δlong-term debt
= Δcash   (13.7)

Equation 13.7 is the indirect form of the SOCF. Under SFAS 95, the statement is divided into three principal parts: the operating, investing, and financing sections.

Cash Flow from Financing Activities

The cash flow from financing contains cash inflows and outflows to capital providers, both lenders and owners. In Equation 13.7, everything from dividends and below is financing cash flow:

$$
\begin{aligned}
&- \text{ dividends} \\
&+ \text{ shares issued} \\
&- \text{ shares repurchased} \\
&+ \text{ } \Delta\text{short-term debt} \\
&+ \text{ } \Delta\text{long-term debt} \\
&= \text{ cash flow from financing activities} \qquad (13.8)
\end{aligned}
$$

This SOCF section contains both cash inflow and outflow.[2] Inflows consist principally of proceeds from the issuance of debt or equity instruments. Outflows are dividends, share repurchases, and the repayment of principal to lenders. Interestingly, interest expense, which seems to me to be a "financing" flow, is not part of the financing SOCF section, but remains part of operations.

Cash Flow from Investing Activities

The "Cash flow from investing" section of the SOCF contains the cash consequences of purchasing or disposing of assets, businesses, or companies[3]:

$$
\begin{aligned}
&- \text{ Capital expenditures} \\
&+ \text{ proceeds of property sold} \\
&= \text{ cash flow from investing activities} \qquad (13.9)
\end{aligned}
$$

One element is missing from our simplified derivation of the SOCF "Investing section." The "Investing" section contains the cash inflows and outflows associated with the purchase of debt or equity instruments held as investments. In addition, the acquisition of companies often appears as a separate "Investing section" line:

$$
\begin{aligned}
&- \text{ Capital expenditures} \\
&- \text{ purchases of assets held as investments} \\
&+ \text{ sales or maturities of assets held as investments} \\
&+ \text{ proceeds of property sold} \\
&- \text{ acquisition price of companies} \\
&= \text{ cash flow from investing activities} \qquad (13.10)
\end{aligned}
$$

Cash Flow from Operations

Every SOCF line item not included in either the "Financing" or "Investing" sections becomes part of the "Operations" section. Cash flow from operations is literally a grab bag of line items that fit nowhere else on the SOCF:

Net income
+ depreciation
− gain on property sales
− Δ (other current assets − other current liabilities)
− Δ (other assets − other liabilities)
= cash flow from operations (CFO)   (13.11)

CFO is, essentially, the cash flow equivalent of net income and receives almost as much attention. There are some curious things about CFO:

- Net income contains financing costs like interest expense which, perhaps, more properly belong in the SOCF financing section. However, the presence of financing costs in operational cash flows does focus the analyst on coverage issues, which is beneficial.

- Depreciation is added to CFO as if it were producing cash, which of course it is not. Depreciation is in fact a balancing item that permits the cash effects of investment to be presented in the SOCF investment section. The direct cash flow format can eliminate this potential confusion by presenting only true cash items.

- Gains on property sales is another (potentially) nonoperating flow appearing in the CFO. Its negative sign implies that it is a use of operating cash, but it is not. It is in fact another balancing item created by the "Investing" section presentation.

- Any increase in other assets, in excess of an increase in other liabilities, is an operating cash outflow. In the case of working capital line items, this makes reasonable sense. But "other" assets and liabilities may or may not be truly operational. The CFO in effect acts as a catch-all for balance sheet changes that do not have a home elsewhere on the SOCF.

- Analysts often view CFO as superior to net income because it isn't subject to distortion or manipulation. After all, cash is cash, isn't it? Either it's there, or it's not. True enough, but CFO is not free of nonrecurring items. One-time cash events, like recoveries from lawsuits or tax disputes, impact the CFO. Unusual fluctuations in working capital or other assets cause one-off CFO changes.

THE DIRECT SOCF FORMAT

Equity analysts don't get access to companies' checkbooks, but they can rearrange financial statements to simulate a checkbook's cash inflows and outflows. In this "direct" SOCF format, operating cash collections and payments are traced to their sources, as shown in Equation 13.12:

> Cash collections from customers
> − cash payments for production inputs
> − cash payments for expenses
> − cash payments for taxes, interest
> = net cash flow from operations   (13.12)

The technique is to adjust income statement items to reflect cash, rather than accrual, amounts by combining them with the appropriate balance sheet accounts. For example, collections from customers equal net sales less any increase in accounts receivable from net sales, plus any increase in deferred revenue.

> Net sales
> − increase in accounts receivable
> + increase in deferred revenue
> = cash collections from customers   (13.13)

Cash payments for inputs combines cost of goods sold with trade accounts payable. Because I can think of no better place for it, I usually account for depreciation and amortization in payments for inputs:

> Cost of goods sold
> − increase in trade accounts payable
> − depreciation and amortization
> = cash payments for inputs   (13.14)

Tax payments, as a final example, are a bit more complex. The balance sheet or income statement may contain other tax-related items, which also need to be included. The "taxes paid" derived here should equal the tax payments disclosed in the company's 10-K—but, GAAP accounting being what it is, it probably won't. This simply means there are tax items in the company's accounts that you've missed, possibly because they aren't broken out separately:

Tax provision
 − increase in taxes payable
 − increase in deferred tax liability (asset)
= taxes paid　　　　　　　　　　　　　(13.15)

America Online, Inc.

The contrast between the indirect and direct SOCF forms can be startling, as illustrated in Tables 13–2 and 13–3.

In truth, the AOL's CFO, in the indirect format, says very little. We know that in 1997 the company lost $499 million and that $622 million of adjustments resulted in a $123 million cash inflow. The adjustments flowed from a variety of operating and working capital items. Perfectly correct, but not very helpful.

Now look at the direct format. AOL collected $1.9 billion from its customers in 1997. It had several prominent cash outflows:

- Cash payments for inputs equaled $1.1 billion. AOL inputs consist primarily of communications and programming costs of its online systems.
- Marketing expenditures were huge at $480 million. The company's rapid growth required substantial spending.
- Product development costs were $86 million.
- General and administrative overhead consumed $51 million.
- And finally, a series of special charges consumed about $80 million.

The direct SOCF format allows a comparison of income statement margins with their cash flow analogs. For example, income statement gross profit margin is

$$\text{Gross profit margin} = \frac{\text{gross profit}}{\text{net sales}} \qquad (13.16)$$

Cash gross profit margin, on the other hand, flows from the direct CFO:

TABLE 13-2

AOL's 1997 cash flow from operations in the indirect format is correct but not very informative.

Indirect Format	1997
Net income	(499,347)
Adjustments to reconcile net income to net cash provided	
Write-off of subscriber acquisition costs	385,221
Noncash restructuring charge	22,478
Depreciation and amortization	64,572
Amortization of subscriber acquisition costs	59,189
Changes in assets and liabilities, net of effects of acquisitions and dispositions	
Trade accounts receivable	(16,418)
Other receivables	2,083
Prepaid expenses	(44,394)
Deferred subscriber acquisition costs	(130,229)
Other assets	(38,902)
Trade accounts payable	(36,944)
Accrued personnel costs	2,979
Other accrued expenses and liabilities	139,134
Deferred revenue	214,097
Deferred income taxes	—
Other liabilities	(470)
Total adjustments	622,396
Cash flow from operations	123,049

$$\text{Cash gross profit margin} = \frac{(\text{cash collections} - \text{payments for inputs})}{\text{cash collections}} \tag{13.17}$$

AOL's income statement operating is calculated before $97.3 million in 1997 nonrecurring charges, but includes the subscriber acquisition costs write-off. Interestingly, the company's cash gross margin is actually higher than its income statement cousin, primarily because of the $199.8 million increase in deferred revenue, which increases cash collections. (See Table 13–4.)

Because of the $385.2 million write-off in deferred subscriber acquisition costs, AOL's income statement operating and net margins are both negative. After removal of this noncash item, the cash operating and net margins offer a clearer picture of the company's profitability.

TABLE 13-3

In the direct format, AOL's 1997 cash flow from operations is more informative.

Cash Collections		
Total revenues		1,685,228
Trade accounts receivable	(16,418)	
Other receivables	2,083	
Deferred revenue	214,097	199,762
Total collections		1,884,990
Cash Payments to Suppliers and Employees		
Cost of revenues		(1,040,762)
Amortization of goodwill		(6,549)
Trade accounts payable	(36,944)	
Depreciation and amortization	64,572	
Prepaid expenses	(44,394)	(16,766)
Payments for inputs		(1,064,077)
Marketing Costs		(409,260)
Write-off of deferred subscriber acquisition costs		(385,221)
Write-off of acquisition costs	385,221	
Amortization of acquisition costs	59,189	
Change in acquisition costs	(130,229)	314,181
Marketing payments		(480,300)
Product development costs		(58,208)
Change in capitalized development costs	(28,168)	(28,168)
Product development costs		(86,376)
General and administrative expenses		(193,537)
Accrued personnel costs	2,979	
Other accrued expenses and liabilities	139,134	142,113
General and administrative costs		(51,424)
Restructuring charge		(48,627)
Contract termination charge		(24,506)
Settlement charge		(24,204)
Other income (expense)		6,299
Provision for taxes		—
Noncash restructuring charge	22,478	
Other assets	(10,734)	
Other liabilities	(470)	11,274
Other payments and taxes		(79,764)
Cash flow from operations		123,049

TABLE 13–4

AOL's 1997 cash and income statement margins show
some differences.

	Income Statement	Cash
Gross margin	38.2%	43.6%
Operating margin	(24.2)%	10.8%
Net margin	(29.6)%	6.5%

TOTAL CASH FLOW FORMAT

The SOCF in total-cash-flow (TCF) format, a rearrangement of the indirect presentation, is a powerful tool for isolating cash sources and uses,
and for judging a company's cash flow adequacy at a number of critical
points[5]:

> Operating cash flow before working capital, interest
>> − increase in working capital
>
> = operating cash flow before interest
>> − after-tax interest expense (income)
>
> = Cash flow from operations
>> − cash flow from investing activities
>
> = cash flow before financing and dividends
>> − dividends
>
> = cash flow before financing activities
>> + cash flow from investing activities
>
> = change cash and cash equivalents   (13.18)

The TCF format isolates the operational cash flow implications of working capital, interest expense (and income), and dividends, increasing the
number of cash flow "checkpoints":

> *Checkpoint 1.* Cash flow before WC, interest/Increase in working
> capital. The TCF format suggests a cash-based "working capital
> turnover," which measures how adequately the company's
> operations fund working capital needs. Just the isolation of the

increase in working capital as a distinct use (or source) of cash is very useful. A higher turnover is better.

Checkpoint 2. Cash flow before interest/after-tax interest expense. This cash flow coverage ratio measures the actual cash available to pay interest expense.

Checkpoint 3. Net income/CFO. The ratio of accrual income to operational cash flow can be used as a measure of earnings quality. A ratio above 1, suggests lower-quality earnings. The analyst might ask, what is causing cash and earnings to differ? Nonrecurring items, one-time events, aggressive accounting, or perhaps company life cycle issues? Does the ratio change over time, and in the expected direction? Is the ratio consistent with the firm's competitive strategy? From the comparative cross-sectional analysis of the computer industry in Chapter 8, it's clear that most industry players have high earnings quality by this measure (Figure 13–1.)

Checkpoint 4. Cash flow from operations/capital expenditures. This looks like another turnover, measuring the adequacy of operational cash flows to meet investment needs. This ratio is likely to be highly dependent on company life cycle, as discussed in Chapter 8. From the cross-sectional analysis, the strength of Dell's cash flow stands out, although HP and GTW show very strong coverage of fixed expenditures. Silicon Graphics posted negative CFO in 1998. (See Figure 13–2.)

FIGURE 13–1

The net income/CFO ratio shows relatively high quality earnings in the computer industry.

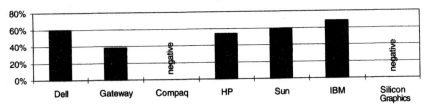

Net income/cash flow from operations is a rough measure of earnings quality.

FIGURE 13–2

Many computer makers generate substantially more cash than is required to support capital expenditures.

CFO/fixed investment measures self-financing capacity.

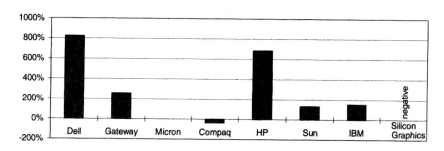

Checkpoint 5. Free-cash flow/dividends. Does the company have the cash to pay its dividends? If not, and dividends are funded with external financing, the company could have very serious trouble maintaining its dividend.

Dell Computer

Let's run through the cash flow checkpoints for Dell's SOCF in total-cash-flow format, shown in Appendix 11–1.

In every year except 1995 and 1996, Dell actually produced cash from working capital and had no need to fund WC investment through operations. Even in 1996, the company's net $195 million WC increase was more than covered by $328 million of cash flow before WC.

The company's cash flow before interest dwarfs interest payments in every year. It seems very unlikely that Dell's ability to meet interest payments will be compromised any time soon.

Since 1997, Dell's CFO substantially exceeded net income, on its face a suggestion of high earnings quality (Table 13–5). The company's strong cash generation from working capital, a product of its made-to-order direct-sales strategy, is the principal source of the difference.

Dell's extraordinary operational cash generation dwarfs its relatively modest capital expenditure requirements since 1994 (Table 13–6).

TABLE 13–5

Dell's CFO exceeded net income in 1994 to 1999 (in $ millions).

	1994	1995	1996	1997	1998	1999
Net income	(36)	149	272	518	944	1,460
CFO	113	243	175	1,362	1,592	2,436
NI/CFO	(32)%	61	155	38	59	60%

TABLE 13–6

Dell's capital expenditures are small relative to CFO
(in $ millions).

	1994	1995	1996	1997	1998	1999
CFO	113	243	175	1,362	1,592	2,436
Capex	48	64	101	114	187	296
CFO/capex	2.35	3.80	1.73	12.0	8.51	8.23

Cash coverage of dividends is a moot point since Dell pays none.

NOTES

[1] Gerald I. White, Ashwinpaul C. Sondhi, and Dov Fried, *The Analysis and Use of Financial Statements,* Wiley, New York, 1997, p. 88.

[2] Ibid., p. 96.

[3] Ibid., p. 95.

[4] Ibid., p. 65.

[5] Krishna G. Palepu, Victor L. Bernard, and Paul M. Healy, *Introduction to Business Analysis & Valuation,* South-Western College Publishing, Cincinnati, Ohio, 1996.

PART FOUR

Equity Valuation

CHAPTER 14

Valuation: Foundations and Fundamentals

- The discounted-cash-flow (DCF) technique is the most familiar and arguably the most rigorous of equity valuation techniques. Unfortunately, in the real world of equity analysis, it is among the most infrequently used—rightly so, in my view.
- The DCF model has a number of potentially serious limitations. It is poorly suited for comparative valuations, lacks the solid intuitive basis of accounting earnings, and is subject to whatever difficulties the capital asset pricing model (CAPM) itself may have.
- Equity analysts often value stocks using accounting-, not cash flow-, based quantitative measures, although accounting numbers expose the valuation process to all the distortions of the GAAP accounting system.
- In spite of the potential distortions, there is a compelling logic to accounting-based techniques. The notion, which I have mentioned before, is that value is created when it is earned, rather than when cash is received. Accounting techniques, however imperfect they may be, are an attempt to measure that earning power.
- The valuation multiple, like price/earnings (P/E) and price/ book value (P/BV), is the most common accounting-based technique. Cross-sectional comparable stock analysis often, but not always, reveals regular patterns in the behavior of valuation multiples. Such regularities, which tie the firm's financial performance to its stock price, can be the basis of a simple target price model.

- Less familiar hybrid valuation techniques, which combine discounting with accounting-based earnings measures, permit the analyst to determine the growth assumptions inherent in a stock price and provide an excellent cross check to DCF and multiple techniques.

The familiar DCF valuation technique is the most complete and rigorous equity valuation method. Unfortunately, in the real world of equity analysis, it is among the most infrequently used, often losing out to accounting-based valuation methods. Why should this be, given what we now know about the distortions introduced by standard accounting rules, as well as potentially incorrect or misleading decisions by management? Have analysts lost their minds, or are they just lazy?

In practice, of course, DCF, based on a forecast of future cash flows, uses essentially the same projection assumptions as an accounting-based technique. Analysts naturally frame the projection argument in accounting terms, forecasting a firm's basic income statement and balance sheet, and then derive a cash flow statement from the two. Projected cash flows therefore have no special claim to forecasting accuracy and in fact likely contain whatever misjudgments were present in the income projection itself.

Beyond the accuracy issue, accounting-based techniques are natural, intuitive, and less complex than their cash flow cousins. If, ultimately, a firm's value is based on its future earnings power, it makes sense to begin with some measure, however flawed, of that earnings power. If the analyst can do that, the entire DCF process, of unraveling the company's operations into cash flows and then rolling the cash flows up into a valuation, is circumvented.

This chapter does not attempt an exhaustive treatment of the DCF technique, a subject admirably discussed elsewhere. My attempt is only to raise some of the DCF issues that particularly interest me, the investment assumptions in free-cash flow, the nature of terminal values, and the frequent tendency of DCF to misestimate actual stock prices.

COMBAT FINANCE

The stock valuation methods that working analysts actually use must be driven by the tremendous time demands of the analysts' world. Nevertheless, many finance writers and teachers begin and end the subject of equity valuation with the discounted-cash-flow technique. There is nothing wrong with DCF. It is certainly rigorous, complete, and familiar. And, at least for the companies they actually cover, most equity analysts already maintain detailed, multi-year financial models that could support DCF valuations. For me, this "coverage" was at times up to 30 companies, with 15 to 20 more typical (and even that is probably too many).

But what about the valuations of all the other industry stocks? Although I covered 20 companies actively, I monitored up to 50 others, for which I maintained no financial models. How can the valuation of these "comparable" companies be understood with a DCF technique? More importantly, how can the information in their stock prices be used without individual DCF models? The fact is that DCF is a fine behind-the-lines method that works well, one company at a time out of the heat of battle. But the working analyst needs "combat finance" techniques that

- Work quickly,
- Can accommodate large numbers of stocks,
- And are framed in the market's valuation multiple language, but nevertheless
- Tie the firm's financial performance to its stock valuation.

Instead of discounting projected cash flows, working analysts and many professional investors rely instead on accounting-based valuation techniques (see Figure 14–1). We will discuss two accounting valuation techniques, relative/multiple valuation (Chapter 15) and hybrid valuation (Chapter 16).

FIGURE 14–1

Equity valuation can be based both on cash-flow and accounting techniques.

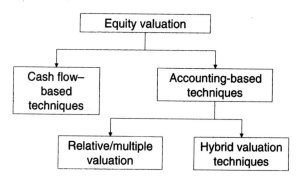

Relative valuation techniques use the stock trading patterns of comparable company groups to connect valuation to underlying financial performance. This is a "relative" technique because individual stocks are judged relative to the group's valuation, versus some absolute standard— if indeed such a standard exists.

We've already had a preview of hybrid valuation in Chapter 2. Hybrid valuations combine

- The discounting technique of the DCF methodology
- Accounting measures of abnormal profit

to arrive at stock valuation conclusions.

ACCOUNTING IS SOMETIMES ANNOYING, BUT IT IS NOT FATALLY FLAWED

The choice to use accounting rather than cash flow data seems, on its face, to be foolish. It is well established, and certainly seems intuitively correct, that there is no direct mapping of earnings data into cash flow data.[1] The two data sets can, and often do, follow very different patterns. So, if cash flow is the correct pattern for valuation, how can earnings-based valuations possibly be valid? Earnings data do not account for the timing of cash flow receipts. They contain no measures of working capital or fixed capital investment necessary to support the assumed level of operations. Accounting data, as we now know, are subject to distortions both from accounting rules themselves and from decisions made in the preparation of financial statements. Finally, and perhaps most tellingly, accounting data contain a variety of noncash items, like depreciation and reserve additions, which cannot possibly affect the company's stock price. Or can they?

- Accounting numbers, on the other hand, are natural and intuitive. It is natural, for example, for investors to focus upon the earning power of a company, rather than its cash flow. Ultimately, the ability to generate profits is the driver of stock value. Of course, if cash is never generated by a company's operations, its stock is unlikely to be a very good investment. The quality of the company's earnings, as we discussed in Chapter 6, should be understood well before a valuation is attempted, regardless of the technique used.

- Accounting techniques, especially hybrid techniques, focus analytic attention on abnormal earnings as the generator of value in a way that cash flow techniques do not.
- Accounting techniques are practical and fast. It is impractical to keep detailed cash flow models for all the companies that the individual analyst must monitor. Some more rapid method of monitoring valuation is needed. This is where accounting-based valuation proves itself.
- Finally, accounting-based relative valuations are economical in that they make use of the information already in stock prices. Prices already contain the market's assessments of risk and future company performance. Why waste this information, even if you do believe DCF is the only valid valuation method? Depending on your position on the market efficiency argument, you may also believe that stock prices contain irrational elements and "investor sentiment." Accounting-based hybrid methods can measure the reasonableness of imbedded financial performance expectations.

DISCOUNTED-CASH-FLOW VALUATION

The DCF technique usually requires the determination of three variables: the cash flows themselves, the discount rate, and the terminal value. As in financial models, after the inputs, the process is fairly mechanical. The principal problem in cash flow projection, in my view, is maintaining consistency between the operational assumptions made—sales, margins, and growth—and the investment assumptions – working capital and fixed investment. The discount rate is usually determined by CAPM techniques. The question is, does CAPM capture all the variables that might affect equity valuation? Since so much (often 70 percent or more) of the value generated by DCF models is contained in the terminal value, an understanding of the assumptions inherent in the terminal value is critical to accurate valuation.

The Structure of the DCF Model

DCF calculations are not inherently difficult, and DCF models have a simple structure. Projected cash flows to equity, the basis for a valuation of the firm's equity alone, are calculated after deduction of non-common-equity capital costs such as after-tax interest or preferred stock dividends. Cash flow to the firm, on the other hand, contains the same operational and investment assumptions as the cash flow to equity but without the removal of capital costs. In the equity valuation, k is the cost of equity capital, usually determined by a CAPM process. In the firm value calculation, the discount rate is the weighted-average cost of capital (WACC), which contains both the cost of equity and the costs of other capital such as debt:

$$\text{Value of equity} = \sum_{i=1}^{\infty} \frac{(\text{CF to equity})_i}{(1 + k)^i} \qquad (14.1)$$

$$\text{Value of the firm} = \sum_{i=1}^{\infty} \frac{(\text{CF to the firm})_i}{(1 + \text{WACC})^i} \qquad (14.2)$$

Cash Flow Confusion

Projected cash flow to common equity is generally calculated by deducting expected capital expenditures and required debt service from cash flow from operations, which already contains a deduction of after-tax interest costs. Pretty simple, but there are some subtleties:

Cash flow to equity = cash flow from operations
                      − appropriate level of capital expenditures
                      − preferred dividends
                      − debt repayments
                      + proceeds of new debt issuance   (14.3)

First, buried within the cash flow from operations are two components, the cash generated before working capital investment and the working capital investment itself:

Net income
  ± Noncash items in income
      Cash flow before working capital investment   (14.4)
  (Increase)/decrease in working capital
      Cash flow from operations

Projected net income contains assumptions about the level of the company's operations and its projected growth. It is reasonable to expect that an investment in working capital might be needed to support the expected level of operations. This is the first place where a consistency between the operational assumptions in the model, contained primarily in the net income projection, and the investment assumptions must be maintained.

My students often ask what level of capital expenditures (capex) to assume in a cash flow projection. Recommendations on this question vary. Some say capital expenditures sufficient to maintain existing operations are the appropriate choice. Or perhaps that level of capex should be adjusted for inflation. I believe that, once cash flow from operations is determined, a level of fixed investment, appropriate to the growth and production assumptions, is also determined. This is the second operational/investment consistency. The driving assumption is the future scale of the company's operations, perhaps measured by sales. Investment assumptions, both working and fixed, must be determined by that basic scale choice. Analysts often are guided to capital expenditure assumptions by management. If management guidance on capex is used, then the analyst's operational scale assumptions are bounded. That is, the productive capacity implied in management's capital expenditure plans limits sales growth and operational scale assumptions. Unless that limitation is observed, the company's cash flow generating capacity could be seriously misstated.

What scale assumption is appropriate? Essentially, any scale assumption the analyst feels comfortable with. In the absence of any direct statement from management, I believe that the market values most common stocks as if (1) the company is run by pretty much the same people in pretty much the same way and (2) operations continue pretty much as they have in the recent past. Whether it is reasonable to expect such continuity is the analyst's principal dilemma.

Cash Flow to the Firm

Instead of a valuation of the common equity alone, the DCF model is often—perhaps most often—used to value the entire capital base of the firm. In this case, all capital charges such as dividends and interest must be eliminated from the cash flow:

Cash flows to the firm = cash flow from operations
+ interest expense * (1 − tax rate)
− appropriate level of capital expenditures

(14.5)

TERMINAL VALUES ARE A BIG DEAL

Terminal values are arguably the most important component of the DCF calculation, since they often produce 70 percent or more of the final valuation. It's critical to understand what you're doing with terminal values.[2]

Terminal values arise, of course, because analysts cut off the infinite DCF series at a time T. The value of equity is then the present value of T cash flows plus the present value of the firm's value at time T—the terminal value.

$$\text{Value at time } 0 = \sum_{i=1}^{T} \frac{\text{FCF}_i}{(1 + k)^i} + \sum_{i=T+1}^{\infty} \frac{\text{FCF}_i}{(1 + k)^i} \qquad (14.6)$$

$$= \sum_{i=1}^{T} \frac{\text{FCF}_i}{(1 + k)^i} + \frac{\text{TV}_T}{(1 + k)^T}$$

where FCF is the free-cash flow to equity, and TV is the terminal value:

$$\sum_{i=T+1}^{\infty} \frac{\text{FCF}_i}{(1 + k)^i} = \left[\frac{1}{(1 + k)^T} \right] * \sum_{i=1}^{\infty} \frac{\text{FCF}_i}{(1 + k)^i} \qquad (14.7)$$

$$= \frac{\text{TV}_T}{(1 + k)^T}$$

Choosing *T*

Things get much simpler if T is the point competitive equilibrium, where rival companies force investment returns on incremental projects to the normal rate. New investment projects can then add no value to the firm, no matter their size, and can safely be ignored. Chapter 2 demonstrated the equivalence of the growth and investment formulations:

- Value stops growing when cash flow (or abnormal earnings) growth ends.
- Equivalently, value growth stops when returns on incremental investment equal the normal rate, ROE = k.

Since growth beyond the point of competitive parity adds no value, it can also be ignored, reducing the growth projection problem to the time period 0 to T. This is very good, provided that T is not too long since analysts can safely ignore long-term growth rates, which no one can accurately forecast anyway. But how long is T?

The FLH "Christmas tree" of Chapter 5 suggests that above- and below-average earners begin to perform alike in five to seven years, supporting the common DCF assumption that $T = 5$ years. But I particularly like the Gray/Cusatis/Woolridge (GCW) "1-5-7-10 rule" for picking T[3]:

■ Set $T = 1$ year for "boring companies" which (1) operate in highly competitive, low-margin industries and (2) "have nothing particular going for them."

■ Set $T = 5$ years for "decent companies" with reasonable reputations and prospects.

■ Set $T = 7$ years for "good companies" with good growth potential, brand names, marketing channels, consumer recognition, or some other recognizable competitive advantage.

■ Set $T = 10$ years for "great companies" with substantial, persistent competitive advantages like strong marketing power, brand names, or technology.

GCW recommend that no company be given an "excess return period" longer than 10 years, and they're probably right. If, after making reasonable operating assumptions, you must extend cash flow growth 10 years to justify an equity valuation, something is probably very wrong.

Calculating the Terminal Value

If cash flow growth beyond year T does not contribute to value, then the terminal value reduces to a very simple expression:

$$
\frac{TV_T}{(1 + k)^T} = \sum_{i=T+1}^{\infty} \frac{FCF_i}{(1 + k)^i}
$$

$$
= \left[\frac{FCF_{T+1}}{(1 + k)^T} \right] * \sum_{i=1}^{\infty} \frac{1}{(1 + k)^i}
$$

$$
= \frac{(FCF_{T+1}/k)}{(1 + k)^T} \tag{14.8}
$$

Therefore, the terminal value is simply the next period's free-cash flow capitalized at the cost of equity k:

$$
TV_T = \frac{FCF_{T+1}}{k} \tag{14.9}
$$

Returns on Existing Projects

By placing T at the point of competitive parity, the firm's incremental investment projects earn only the normal rate. Further growth adds no value. But what about the firm's existing investment projects? What return do they earn? As Chapter 2 also proves, existing projects continue to earn abnormal returns forever![4] Aside from the mathematics, we know this because

- The firm has a nonzero value at time T equal to TV_T. Since new investment projects produce no value, existing projects produce this value. Existing projects must therefore continue to earn nonnormal returns. If $TV_T = 0$, the firm's existing investments produce only the normal return. A zero terminal value is a very rare assumption in DCF analyses running up to 10 future years (except, perhaps, in valuations of capital projects with limited lives).
- The projects that produce value at time T must be those started prior to time T since cash flow growth stops at time T.

Upon first reading this conclusion, I was shocked by its apparent lack of conservatism. Won't even existing investment projects also be subject to competitive attack and eventually suffer declining returns? Worse yet, won't DCF analyses produce values that are far too high because of this apparent perpetuity of abnormal returns? Maybe, but that's how DCF works. The theory implies that the firm as a whole does not continue to earn abnormal returns. The firm's aggregate ROE approaches a normal rate asymptotically as projects earning the normal return come increasingly to dominate the firm's investments—not a terribly outrageous assumption. In reality, of course, old investments have a finite life and beyond the T point are probably replaced by new investments earning the normal return.

Overcoming Terminal Value Anxiety

It isn't surprising, because of their importance, that terminal values have been surrounded by a number of strict taboos, leading to substantial analytic anxiety. Anxiety in an analyst may be a professional necessity, but there are some terminal values issues that deserve demystification.

Growth and Terminal Values

Even though, beyond point T, further cash flow growth does not increase value, I often see terminal values with a growth component (the derivation of Equation 14.10 is the same as that of Equation 2.15 in Chapter 2):

$$\text{TV}_T = \frac{\text{FCF}_{T+1}}{(k - g)} \qquad \checkmark \qquad (14.10)$$

The only legitimate use of growth after point T, in my view, is to maintain the projected physical scale of the firm versus its nominal scale. Without g, the terminal value maintains only the dollar amount of cash flows. If, on the other hand, g equals something like a long-term inflation rate, then the terminal value maintains the company's physical scale at T. Either may be correct, depending on the anticipated competitive conditions in the industry.

If g is anything larger than long-term inflation, then something completely different is going on. Growth beyond T in excess of inflation means that incremental investment projects earn positive abnormal returns and contribute to value in perpetuity. If T is close to the competitive parity point, perpetual abnormal returns are illogical. If you find it necessary to add an excessive growth factor to the terminal value, then several problems may exist:

- Post-T cash flows are too low because projected growth prior to T is too slow.
- The cost of equity k is in error; the principal culprits here are the risk factor β and the market premium assumption in the capital asset pricing formulation of the cost of equity:

  $\checkmark \quad k = \text{risk-free rate} + \beta * \text{equity market premium}$
- The stock itself is overpriced.
- T is not, in fact, a point of equilibrium.

Exit Multiples

In spite of their apparent circularity, using "exit multiples" to calculate terminal value is very common in practice:

$$\text{TV}_T = \frac{P}{E} \text{ exit multiple} * E_{T+1} \qquad (14.11)$$

The terminal value is an estimate of the stock's price at time T. But how can we know the value of the stock at time T when it is the value of the stock we are trying to calculate? Good question. The answer usually is that some comparable group of stocks suggests an appropriate exit multiple. How we can use comparable stocks to find valuation multiples is the subject of Chapter 16. But if a public sale of the stock is contemplated at time T, the method has some logic.

What should the exit multiple be? If T is really the competitive equilibrium point, then, applying Equation 2.18 from Chapter 2, P/E must be $1/k$, where k equals the cost of equity:

$$\frac{P_T}{E_{T+1}} = \frac{1}{k} + \left(\frac{1}{E_{T+1}}\right)$$
$$* \left[\sum_{i=T+1}^{\infty} \frac{(\text{abnormal earnings})_i}{(1 + k)^i} - \frac{\text{abnormal earnings}_{T+1}}{k} \right] \quad (14.12)$$

If abnormal earnings are zero beyond point T, then P/E equals k and the terminal value is the capitalized earnings in time $T + 1$. Just as with the growth factor, too high an exit multiple violates the competitive parity assumption, suggesting other problems with the valuation.

$$\mathrm{TV}_T = \frac{E_{T+1}}{k} \quad (14.13)$$

Especially in initial public offerings of new companies, T is not the competitive parity point but the time of the anticipated IPO. What then? In that case, one might anticipate that abnormal earnings will continue beyond T, and P/E could greatly exceed $1/k$. Analysts often use P/E multiples of recent comparable IPOs as a guide.

DELL COMPUTER

A DCF valuation of Dell, using the financial model developed in Chapters 11 to 13, illustrates the process (Table 14–1). This example values the entire firm, and cash flows to the firm therefore exclude after-tax interest (both expense and income). For example, the $2,291 million estimated 2000 cash flow to the firm equals the $2,698 million cash flow before interest in the SOCF, less capital expenditures of $407 million. Our Dell financial model ends in 2003, and cash flows thereafter grow at an assumed 20 percent annually, a fairly aggressive assumption, I think. I use a 10-year projection, following the 1-5-7-10 rule, because I think Dell falls into the "great company" category.

TABLE 14–1

Dell discounted-cash-flow value is $91.5 billion, based on a 10-year projection horizon (in $ millions).

	Cash Flow to the Firm	Growth in Cash Flows	Present Value of Cash Flows
2000	2,291	—	2,047
2001	3,072	34.1%	2,453
2002	3,953	28.7%	2,821
2003	4,864	23.0	3,102
2004	5,873	20.0	3,327
2005	7,004	20.0	3,568
2006	8,405	20.0	3,826
2007	10,086	20.0	4,103
2008	12,103	20.0	4,400
2009	14,524	20.0	4,718
2010/terminal value			57,191
Total value			91,556

The cost of equity equals 11.9 percent, calculated by the standard CAPM methodology. The risk-free rate estimate is 5.00 percent, which equals a 6.25 percent 30-year government bond rate adjusted downward by 125 basis points, compensating for the bond's own beta. An equity market premium of 5 percent is a typical estimate. Dell's beta at this time was 1.37:

Cost of equity = risk-free rate + β * equity market premium

= (6.25% − 1.25%) + 1.37 * 5.00%

= 11.9%

Strictly speaking, we ought to use a weighted-average cost of capital (WACC) in this valuation, calculated with the market values of debt and equity:

WACC = % equity capital cost of equity
+ % debt capital * cost of debt

But realistically, the value of the company's equity so greatly exceeds its $512 million (book value) debt that it is safe, I think, to ignore the debt contribution to the WACC, given the margin of error of the entire exercise.

The terminal value is the 2010 cash flow, $17,429, capitalized at 11.9 percent, assuming a 2 percent long-term inflation rate:

$$\text{Terminal value} = \frac{\$17,429}{(11.9\% - 2.0\%)}$$
$$= \$176,046$$

Notice that the $57,191 terminal value present value is 62 percent of the $91,556 total value estimate, even though the terminal value falls 10 years out. With a shorter valuation period, terminal values can produce an even greater part of total value.

The company's DCF value must be (1) reduced by the market value of funded debt and (2) increased by the company's $2,661 million in marketable securities to arrive at the value of equity. We will use the $512 million book value of long-term debt as a proxy for market value:

Value of equity = value of total capital
            − value of debt + value of marketable securities
       = $91,556 − $512 + $2,661
       = $93,705

The add-back of the value of marketable securities is the reason that interest income is eliminated from cash flow estimates. Given the 2,543 million common shares outstanding, we arrive at a $36.81 estimate of Dell's value per share.

Interestingly, On October 24, 1999, when I presented this example to one of my Columbia Business School MBA classes, the actual Dell stock price was $40 1/8. At the January 31, 1999, end of the company's fiscal year (to which we have technically discounted), the stock stood at $50 per share.

The result, that DCF valuation underestimates the stock price, was familiar during the 1990s. Our model's cash flow estimates don't seem overly conservative—10 years of 20 percent plus annual growth is very strong, especially given the personal computer industry's increasing competitiveness about which we have spoken.

It is possible, and many have argued, that a 5 to 7 percent equity market risk premium is too high, and that 2 to 4 percent is more appropriate. A 3 percent risk premium reduces the cost of equity to 9.1 percent, raising the DCF value estimate to about $56 per share. Clearly, the risk premium assumption can have a significant effect upon the DCF result.

Or, perhaps, Dell stock at this time was truly overvalued. However, since the end of 1998 the stock spent most of its time north of $40. From late 2000, the stock fell steadily before bouncing back in January 2001 to about $25.00. If the DCF indicates overvaluation, then the overvaluation was remarkably persistent (see Figure 14.2).

The Dell example illustrates the principal difficulties with the DCF methodology[5]:

- Long-term cash flow projections are subject to substantial error. To recognize Dell's superior competitive position, a 10-year projection horizon seems appropriate. But the accuracy of such long-term projections is suspect, to say the least.

- The choice of the horizon, the point of competitive equilibrium, is itself uncertain. The longer cash flow continues to grow, the higher the DCF valuation. Perhaps the DCF's underestimation of Dell's stock price implies that the market, rationally or irrationally, expects a longer horizon. Or, perhaps not.

- The terminal value, coming as it does at the end of a long-term projection, is subject to the highest error. Unfortunately, it

FIGURE 14–2

Dell spent substantial time above its estimated $37 DCF value.

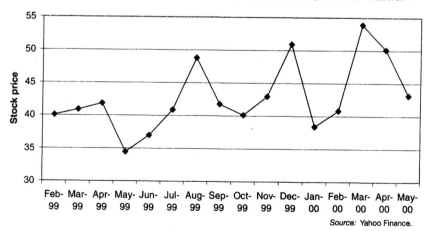

Source: Yahoo Finance.

is also the largest contributor to the DCF value, 62 percent in the Dell case.

■ The cost of capital itself is uncertain, as the Dell result shows. Small changes in market premium assumptions make large value differences. Further, capital costs can be altered by capital structure assumptions. In fairness, capital cost calculations introduce potential errors into other valuation methods, particularly the hybrid techniques discussed in Chapter 16.

NOTES

[1] See, for example, Alfred Rappaport, *Creating Shareholder Value,* rev. and updated, The Free Press, New York, 1998, ch. 2, "The Shortcomings of Accounting Numbers."

[2] See the excellent discussion of terminal values in Krishna G. Palepu, Victor L. Bernard, and Paul M. Healy, *Introduction to Business Analysis & Valuation,* South-Western College Publishing, Cincinnati, Ohio, 1996, ch. 6, pp. 6–1 to 6–24.

[3] Gary Gray, Patrick J. Cusatis, and J. Randall Woolridge, *Streetsmart Guide to Valuing a Stock,* McGraw-Hill, New York, 1999, p. 48.

[4] Palepu, Bernard, and Healy, *Introduction to Business Analysis & Valuation,* p. 6–6.

[5] Robert F. Reilly and Robert P. Schweihs, *The Handbook of Business Valuation,* McGraw-Hill, New York, 2000, p. 331.

CHAPTER 15

Combat Finance: Relative Methods and Companion Variable Models

- A stock's current valuation multiples should be a function of its expected future financial performance.
- Each valuation multiple has an associated companion financial performance variable. For example, the price/book value multiple is associated with the firm's return on equity.
- The valuation multiple/companion variable connection can be established by examining the trading patterns of groups of comparable companies, using a simple regression technique. In this context, *comparable* means companies, likely in the same industry, whose cash flow characteristics and investment risk are sufficiently similar to permit the companion variable regularities to emerge.
- Because it relies on the prices of comparable company stocks, this valuation methodology can specify a single stock's valuation only relative to the group—hence the term *relative valuation*. If the group as a whole is mispriced, then the valuations suggested by the methodology itself will also be inaccurate. Of course, all valuation methods, even DCF, suffer from this problem.
- The relative valuation method provides a systematic technique for predicting a stock's target price. Once established, the empirical connection between valuation and performance leads directly to predictions of future valuation multiples, and therefore to target prices.

"Hot Prospects Ltd. (HPL) has superior management, product development, and marketing within its industry group. Yet, its price/earnings ratio is 15, well below the industry average of 20. We therefore expect the company's valuation to rise over the next 12 months, as its competitive strength is revealed, and set a target price of $40.00, or 20 times our $2.00 per share earnings forecast." Have you ever heard or read a similar statement from an equity analyst? The analyst has used a group of companies that he or she regards as comparable to Hot Prospects to establish a valuation benchmark. Feeling that HPL is a better-than-average company, he or she concludes that it is undervalued relative to the group and predicts an expansion of its multiple. Using the predicted expanded multiple, he or she sets a 12-month target price using his or her own earnings forecast. Seems reasonable, doesn't it?

As a junior analyst, I too encountered lots of verbal and written arguments like this one. But what bothered me then, and still bothers me, about this kind of reasoning is its imprecision. I became engaged in a vendetta against averages. What is there exactly about HPL that makes it better than average? Why, for example, if Hot Prospects is really superior, does it trade at only a 15 P/E? Is it really "cheap" because its multiple is below the industry average? What, exactly, about the company's financial performance will change in the next 12 months to support the multiple expansion? Or does the multiple expand independent of underlying financial performance?

There are, in fact, often underlying regularities in the stock valuations of comparable companies. These regularities are revealed through a simple regression model that ties a company's financial performance, as the independent variable, to a variety of valuation multiples, such as stock price/earnings and price/book value. Discovery of these regularities permits the analyst to introduce substantially more rigor into target prices, which all too often appear to be drawn from thin air.

THE THEORY, AS USUAL

The connection between stock valuation and financial performance can be illustrated by returning to our trusted ally from Chapter 2, the dividend discount model (DDM). Clearly, the DDM builds a bridge between stock price and company performance, in this case its dividend performance:

$$P_0 = \sum_{i=1}^{\infty} \frac{D_i}{(1 + k)^i} \qquad (15.1)$$

where, once again, P_0 is the stock price at time 0, D_i the dividend in the ith period, and k the cost of equity. The DDM is of course in every way correct, but unfortunately it is not very helpful. In the first place, it does not connect the most-used measures of financial performance, like earnings or return on equity, directly to stock price. And it requires a multiyear model for each valuation considered.

A simpler version of the DDM, the Gordon growth model, assumes that dividends grow at a constant rate g from time period 1:

$$P_0 = \sum_{i=1}^{\infty} \frac{D_i}{(1 + k)^i}$$

$$= \sum_{i=1}^{\infty} \frac{D_1 * (1 + g)^{i-1}}{(1 + k)^i}$$

$$= \frac{D_1}{(k - g)} \tag{15.2}$$

The Gordon growth model does not have universal application. It is clear, for example, that should the growth rate g exceed the cost of capital k, the model breaks down. In such cases, it simply cannot be used. The Gordon growth format is used here only because it suggests a direction for research into the connection between value and performance. Sometimes the directions suggested are fruitful, and sometimes, unfortunately, they are not.

Notice that Equation 15.2 expresses the stock price in terms of three variables:

- *Next year's dividend, D_1*. This provides the theory with a "prospectiveness" that is essential to bear in mind. It is next year's performance, not last year's, that drives valuation. Prospectiveness is not a matter of fashion but a mathematical requirement.
- *The cost of equity, k.*
- *The long-term rate of growth, g*. Growth is the most problematic and difficult of the three variables because analysts rarely have sufficient insight to predict such long-term variables. The high sensitivity of the model to the growth variable amplifies the difficulty.

The Dividend Yield

Dividend yield is the first valuation metric to fall out of the Gordon model. After some simple algebra, Equation 15.2 can be rearranged into the following form:

$$\frac{D_1}{P_0} = (k - g) \qquad (15.3)$$

The dividend yield D_1/P_0 is in prospective form, that is, next year's dividend divided by today's stock price. Notice also that if the dividend yields of multiple companies were to be plotted on a graph versus projected long-term growth, the plot should reveal an inverse linear relationship. (See Figure 15–1.)

If the cost of equity k were to differ among the group of companies chosen for the graph, some of the companies might fall far from the line plotted. The trick is to pick a comparable group that minimizes deviations sufficiently to allow the underlying relationship to emerge. Whether

FIGURE 15–1

The dividend yield is inversely proportional to the long-term dividend growth.

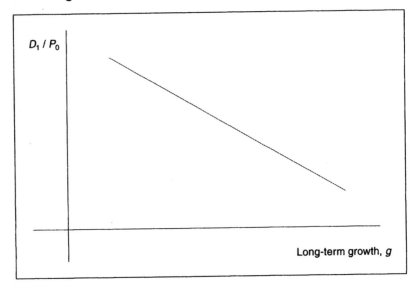

it is easily visible or not, however, dividend yield in general should be inversely proportional to long-term growth. Although this is a mathematical certainty, the inverse relationship between dividends and growth also has a qualitative logic. One would not expect rapidly growing companies, early in their life cycles, to pay dividends but rather to reinvest their cash resources in building their businesses.

The Price/Earnings Ratio

Beginning again with Gordon growth, and dividing both sides of the equation by first-period earnings E_1, Equation 15.2 can again be modified:

payout ratio $b = \dfrac{D_1}{E_1} \times 100$

= Discount rate or stock

= Cost of Capital

$$\frac{P_0}{E_1} = \frac{(D_1/E_1)}{(k - g)}$$

$$= \frac{b}{(k - g)} \qquad (15.4)$$

where b is the dividend payout ratio, D_1/E_1. The P/E is connected in Equation 15.4 to the company's growth, dividend policy, and cost of equity:

- The P/E multiple is formed from today's stock price P_0 and next year's expected earnings. That is, P/E is inherently forward looking. Remember from Chapter 2 the difficulties with backward-looking P/E ratios.
- It is probably more helpful to think of P/E as driven by payout policy, b, not by individual dividends. The higher the payout, the higher the P/E, all else being equal. The concept of payout policy can be generalized to include share repurchases without spoiling the logic of the model.
- P/E is inversely proportional to long-term growth, but unfortunately the relationship is not linear since g appears in the denominator of Equation 15.4. This nonlinearity may not be a huge problem in comparable industry groups where variations in growth patterns are more limited.

The broader implications of the payout factor b reveal themselves through the clean surplus relationship in Equation 15.5:

$$BV_0 + E_1 - D_1 = BV_1 \qquad (15.5)$$

Rearranging 15.5:

$$D_1 = E_1 - (BV_1 - BV_0) \qquad (15.6)$$

The company's dividend can be expressed in terms of its earnings and other book value changes, which could include share repurchases. I myself like to think of the variable b as a measure of the total cash return to shareholders.

Right from the start, the P/E companion variable model is in trouble. From Chapter 2, it is clear that P/E is driven only by growth in abnormal earnings, not actual earnings, sales, assets, or any other financial variable. The P/E rises only with growth under conditions of competitive advantage (that is, where actual returns on equity exceed capital costs). It isn't at all clear, for example, that the consensus earnings growth estimates in Equation 15.4 will produce useful results.

The Price/Book Value Multiple

Again, we can modify the Gordon growth model in Equation 15.2 by dividing both sides of the equation by the book value BV_0:

$$\frac{P_0}{BV_0} = \frac{(D_1/BV_0)}{(k - g)}$$

$$= \frac{(b * E_1/BV_0)}{(k - g)}$$

$$= \frac{b * ROE_1}{(k - g)} \qquad (15.7)$$

where ROE_1 equals E_1/BV_0, the return on equity in period 1, and b equals D_1/E_1, the first-period dividend payout. As with the dividend yield and price/earnings ratio, the price/book value multiple has a connection to company performance:

- P/BV is directly proportional to next year's ROE, not last year's. It is an inherently prospective concept, like the related D/P and P/E multiples. Any model suggested by these results must be forward looking to have a hope of success. Returns on equity must therefore be formed from projected, not historical, earnings.

- The variables b, k, and g are also drivers of the P/BV multiple. Like the P/E, higher growth companies and those with substantial cash payouts to shareholders ought to have higher P/BV multiples.

Other Valuation Multiples

Let's form some other valuation multiples and look at their drivers. Using the same logic as before, we can form the valuation multiples from prospective sales S_1 and existing assets A_0. The price/sales ratio is particularly revealing:

$$
\frac{P_0}{S_1} = \frac{(D_1/S_1)}{(k - g)}
$$

$$
= \frac{(b * E_1/S_1)}{(k - g)}
$$

$$
= \frac{(b * \text{net margin on sales})}{(k - g)} \tag{15.8}
$$

where the net margin on sales is formed from next year's projected earnings E_1 and projected sales S_1. One of the problems with the price/sales ratio is, in fact, that it should be formed from next year's (actually the next 12 month's) sales. Although individual analysts may have their own sales forecasts, there are often no market-wide estimated sales consensus figures. As a result, P/S multiple is calculated with historical sales, a procedure that is almost bound to produce difficulties, especially when sales growth rates are changing rapidly.

Look out for the valuation formula using total assets A_0, however, because it contains a logical inconsistency. Total assets are funded by the company's total capital structure, not the common equity alone. The stock price P_0 bears no direct relationship to the total assets A_0, unlike the total common equity BV_0. This is a problem similar to the cash flow confusion that plagues the DCF system. Only the cash flow that is specific to the capital being valued can be appropriately included in a DCF model. Equity cannot be valued using total cash flow to the entire capital structure, for example. Neither can a valid valuation multiple for common equity be formed from financial measures, like total assets, that are supported by all elements of capital.

In fact, there is some question about the price/sales ratio itself. Since the company's sales are supported by all its capital, not just common equity, isn't a more valid valuation metric firm value/sales, not stock price/sales? The answer is probably yes. Nevertheless, because sales is intimately connected to earnings through the income statement, the potential inconsistency is frequently tolerated.

The Pattern Emerges

These few examples suggest that each of the valuation measures has associated with it a unique "companion variable," as well as the common variables of cash payout policy b and cost of equity k, as shown in Table 15–1.

Beyond the dividend yield and the price/earnings ratio, which seem uniquely to be driven by the growth rates, valuation multiples formed from other financial measures seem to be related to returns on those measures. For example, the price/book value multiple is related to the return on equity (ROE). Price/sales, on the other hand, is driven by the net margin, the return on sales. With the caveat above about potential inconsistencies, a valuation multiple formed from any financial metric ought to be directly proportional to the return on that metric. This conclusion holds for purely financial measures like book value, and for physical measures of performance like production levels, the number of customers, or number of machines in an installed base.

TABLE 15–1

Each equity valuation measure has a unique companion independent variable.

	Companion Variable	Other Variables
D/P	Long-term growth, g	k
P/E	Long-term growth, g	b, k
P/BV	ROE	b, k, g
$P/$sales	Net margin on sales	b, k, g
$P/$other	Return on other	b, k, g

It is perfectly possible to predict an appropriate valuation multiple for any stock by using the equations above. But the stock market has done the calculation already, with the result contained in the current stock price. Is there a way to extract that valuation information? We might, for example, gather the appropriate data for all traded stocks in the market and construct a giant linear regression model in the form

Predicted valuation multiple $= A_0 + A_1 *$ (return)

$$+ A_2 * \text{(payout)}$$
$$+ A_3 * \text{(cost of equity)}$$
$$+ A_4 * \text{(long-term growth)} \quad (15.9)$$

where A_i are the coefficients generated by the multiple regression technique. Then with the specification of the four independent variables—return, dividend payout, cost of equity, and long-term growth—it is possible to predict the appropriate valuation multiple for any stock in the market.[1] This prediction closes the circle, drawing the connection between performance and value. Although some of the relationships are not in fact linear, models like this have been successfully developed.

Unfortunately, for the equity analyst, more often than not an industry specialist, a model like this is unsatisfactory, for a number of reasons:

- A full-market model is much too coarse for industry analysis. Economic and competitive forces far beyond the industry of interest influence its predictions, and it can at best provide a vague idea of specific company-level valuations. Such models do, however, demonstrate the conceptual power of the Gordon Growth analysis.

- The multiple regression model is inconvenient for the equity analyst. First, it involves collection of multiple data points for each stock in the analysis, which is a great deal of trouble if nothing else. This remark is not motivated by intellectual sloppiness. Speed is the essence of analysis. Unnecessary data gathering is as damaging to good analysis as insufficient data gathering. If the analyst can usefully get away with less, my view is get away with less.

But can we get away with less? This is an empirical, not a theoretical, issue. Consider, for example, a model with only one independent variable, the companion variable:

Predicted valuation multiple $= A_0 + A_1 *$ (companion variable)

$$(15.10)$$

Such a model might provide a satisfactory prediction of any company's valuation provided that the variables it excludes, like dividend payout or cost of equity, explain little of the valuation multiple's variation. But this is precisely the effect of forming regression analyses from *comparable* companies, usually in the same industry. We have in fact discovered an operational definition of comparable: Comparable companies share enough investment risk, cash flow, and perhaps even growth characteristics so that the principle differences in their valuations are created by the companion variable. For example, consider a model for the price/ book value multiple, P/BV, containing the companion variable ROE:

$$\text{Predicted } P/BV = A_0 + A_1 * (\text{ROE}) + A_2 * (\text{payout})$$
$$+ A_3 * (\text{cost of equity}) \qquad (15.11)$$
$$+ A_4 * (\text{long-term growth})$$

If the model were to consider all traded stocks, for example, differences in payout, cost of equity, and growth must very likely be significant and probably contribute substantially to the variation in P/BV. But with comparable companies within a particular industry, such differences may be much smaller. Companies may share investment risk, payout, and even growth. If these variables do not contribute significantly to differences in valuation, then a model containing only the companion variable ROE should work reasonably well:

$$\text{Predicted } P/BV = A_0 + A_1 * (\text{ROE}) \qquad (15.12)$$

Reducing the analysis to the industry level, in effect, introduces a bias into the analysis that, we hope, permits us to eliminate all independent variables except the companion variable. As I said, this is a hope, not a theoretical requirement. We need to check these models to see if they work.

Just a word about statistical rigor: Very often industry analyses might involve relatively small numbers of companies. Perhaps only a few industry players are publicly traded. Or maybe the analyst is focusing on a submarket of the industry with only a few competitors. In such a case, the regression analysis probably has relatively few data points. Even with a single independent variable, so few data points could very well render the analysis statistically suspect. (For example, a low degree of freedom makes it more difficult to be confident in the statistical significance of the regression coefficients.) My reaction to this issue is, so what? If I had only two publicly traded comparable stocks, and I were trying to value a third (perhaps an IPO), I would use the two existing stocks' valuations as a guide. In fact, referring to Equation 15.12, if the IPO company's ROE were between the ROE's of the comparables A and B, I'd be inclined to place its predicted P/BV multiple on the line drawn between them, regardless of the statistics. (See Figure 15–2.)

I suggest this procedure because I believe that this is the way the market is likely to arrive at its own valuation of the IPO. But again, I regard this as an empirical issue. Let's see what the data say.

THE COMPUTER INDUSTRY

Let's test a couple of the companion variable models. As a first example, consider 12 computer/electronics manufacturers listed in the July 1999

FIGURE 15–2

Using companion variables, two publicly traded stocks can suggest the valuation of a third.

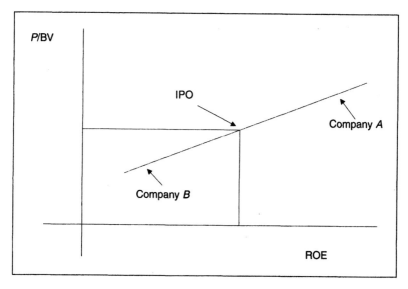

issue of *Upside* magazine, shown in Table 15–2. Stock price and estimated earnings data appeared in the magazine. Book value per share
relies upon data from the most recent company financial statements. Dividends appear because they are later used in the sustainable growth calculation.

The Price/Book Value Model Works Well . . .

The computer industry price/book value multiple is remarkably success-
ful. The model's companion variable is return on beginning book value
(ROBBV), calculated with estimated earnings and current book value.
Taking data from Table 15–2, for example, IBM's P/BV multiple and
ROBBV are

$$P/\text{BV multiple for IBM} = \frac{\$113.75}{\$10.03}$$

$$= 11.3 \qquad (15.13)$$

$$\text{ROBBV for IBM} = \frac{\$3.27}{\$10.03}$$

$$= 32.6\% \qquad (15.14)$$

The computer industry is unusual because of its very high returns
and P/BV multiples (Table 15–3). Companies with projected net losses
are eliminated from the analysis. The valuation multiple/companion variable pattern is obvious from Figure 15–3, and the regression equation
shows a very high R^2 of 92 percent:

$$\text{Predicted } P/\text{BV} = 35.4 \text{ ROBBV} - 1.2 \qquad (15.15)$$

An R^2 of 50 percent or less is more typical of the P/BV-ROE
regression. The correlation is so high in this case because of the very
wide range of the data, from a 30.2 P/BV and 85.7 percent ROE for
Dell down to 2.8 and 7.8 percent for NCR. Data points at either end of
the range tend to act, statistically, as the end points of a line and produce
the very high strong fit shown. In other words, such a high R^2 is partially
a statistical artifact rather than a real-life test of the model's predictive
power. Nevertheless, in keeping with long-standing analytic tradition, I
take full credit for the wonderful result.

TABLE 15-2

Basic computer industry data supports a relative valuation of the group.

	Ticker	6/2/99 Stock Price	Predicted 1999 Earnings	Book Value per Share	Annual Dividend per Share
Apple Computer	AAPL	46.56	4.23	$14.93	—
Compaq	CPQ	23.38	0.47	6.90	$0.08
Data General	DGN	14.38	(0.33)	8.12	—
Dell	DELL	33.50	0.95	1.11	—
Gateway	GTW	59.19	2.14	9.05	—
Hewlett-Packard	HWP	89.75	2.84	17.96	—
IBM	IBM	113.75	3.27	10.03	0.44
NCR	NCR	39.25	1.09	13.92	—
Silicon Graphics	SGI	12.56	(0.45)	7.12	—
Sun Microsystems	SUNW	56.69	2.73	10.25	—
Tandem	TAN	81.25	2.25	5.31	$0.80
Unisys	UIS	$38.00	$1.03	$5.29	—

Source: *Upside* Magazine and company financial statements.

TABLE 15-3

The computer industry shows a wide variation in returns and *P/BV* multiples.

	ROBBV	P/BV
AAPL	28.3%	3.12
CPQ	6.8	3.39
DELL	85.7	30.2
GTW	23.6	6.54
HWP	15.8	5.00
IBM	32.6	11.3
NCR	7.8	2.82
SUNW	26.6	5.53
TAN	42.3	15.3
UIS	19.5%	7.19

FIGURE 15-3

Return on beginning book value strongly influences computer industry *P/BV* multiples.

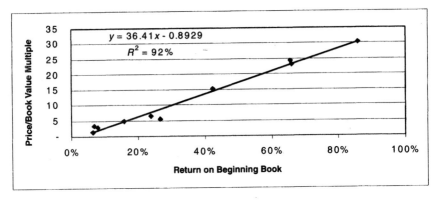

. . . The Price/Earnings Model Does Not

Emboldened by the success of both the *P*/BV, we might expect the price/ earnings model, formed with some measure of earnings growth as the companion variable, to be equally successful. For argument's sake, we'll use two earnings growth measures, the sustainable growth and the Institutional Brokerage Estimate System (I/B/E/S) median long-term growth consensus. (See Table 15–4.) For most of the computer companies, the sustainable growth equals ROBBV since they pay no dividends. I've again eliminated companies with negative estimated earnings.

Unfortunately, as we might have suspected, the *P/E* model is not very robust. With sustainable growth as the independent variable, the model's R^2 is a barely visible 2 percent, and, in fact, there is little evidence of a pattern in the data. (See Figure 15–4.) The situation is not, unfortunately, much improved with the long-term growth estimate as the independent variable. (See Figure 15–5.)

Perhaps the failure of the *P/E* model is unique to the computer industry, although it isn't clear why this should be. Let's look at similar analyses for the food, diversified chemical, and pharmaceutical industries.

OTHER INDUSTRY VALUATION MODELS

A repetition of the same *P*/BV and *P/E* companion variable analysis in three other industries—food, diversified chemicals, and pharmaceuticals—yields results similar to the computer industry. In general, the

TABLE 15–4

Computer industry *P/E* multiples are more tightly grouped, but
estimated growth varies widely.

	P/E	Sustainable Growth	I/B/E/S Long-Term Growth
AAPL	11.0	28.3%	15.0%
CPQ	49.7	5.7	20.0
DELL	35.3	85.7	35.0
GTW	27.7	23.6	24.0
HWP	31.6	14.0	15.0
IBM	34.8	28.2	12.7
NCR	36.0	7.8	20.0
SUNW	20.8	26.6	18.0
TAN	36.1	27.3	17.0
UIS	36.9	19.5%	18.0%

FIGURE 15–4

Computer industry *P/E* multiples show no apparent relationship
to estimated sustainable growth.

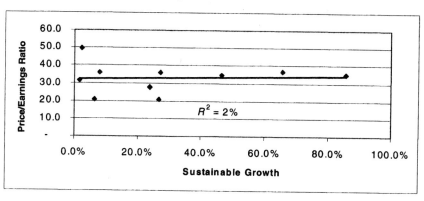

I/B/E/S system provided estimated earnings and long-term consensus
growth for each company. The book value per share is calculated using
company financial data.

FIGURE 15–5

Substituting long-term for sustainable growth doesn't
strengthen the computer industry *P/E* model's explanatory
power significantly.

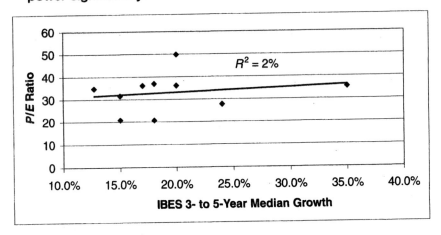

*P/*BV-ROBBV Models Again Perform Well

*P/*BV-ROBBV models again work remarkably well in the three new
industries. For nine companies in the food industry, R^2 is high because
of the "straight-line effect" seen in the computer companies. But unlike
the computer companies, the food industry effect happens because of the
industry's highly leveraged capital structures that generate very large
ROBBVs. General Mills and Campbell Soup Co., for example, show very
high ROBBVs because of substantial debt financing. R^2 for the chemical
and pharmaceutical industries are more typical 34 and 57 percent, respectively—lower but still excellent. (See Figure 15–6.) However, even
if we eliminate General Mills and Campbell, dropping the two highest
ROBBV companies, the food model continues to work very well. (See
Figures 15–7, 15–8, and 15–9.)

P/E—Growth Models Yield Mixed Results

Changing industries does not solve the *P/E* problem. *P/E* remains ill
behaved, showing no apparent companion variable pattern with sustainable growth as the independent variable. The I/B/E/S consensus growth
yields no better results.

FIGURE 15–6

Like the computer industry, the food industry P/BV model works well.

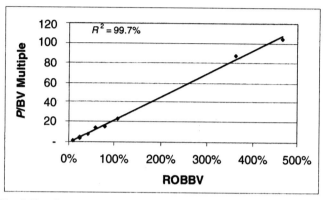

Companies: Nabisco Holdings, Sara Lee Corp., H.J. Heinz, Best Foods, Kellogg, Conagra, Ralston Purina, General Mills, Campbell Soup Co.

FIGURE 15–7

Even without outliers, the food industry P/BV model shows strong explanatory power.

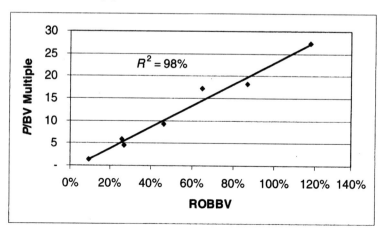

FIGURE 15-8

The diversified chemical industry *P*/BV model is more typical of the technique's results.

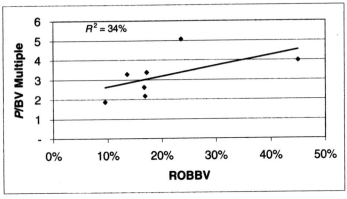

Companies: Dow Chemical, DuPont, Rohm & Haas, Union Carbide, Air Products, Hercules, and Olin

FIGURE 15-9

The pharmaceutical industry *P*/BV model, like the chemical industry, shows a strong valuation pattern.

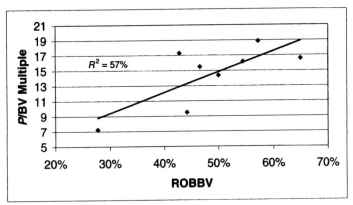

Companies: Eli Lilly, Pfizer, Merck, Abbott, Bristol-Myers, Schering-Plough, American Home Products, Warner Lambert

The food industry, for example, shows relatively little trend, but there may be a weak but discernible rise with increasing sustainable growth. The graph again eliminates General Mills and Campbell Soup because of outlying sustainable growth rates. *P/E* might rise with growth, for example, if firms were investing at returns in excess of their capital costs. (See Figure 15–10.)

Perhaps equity-only valuation models like *P/E*-growth are really unsuitable when companies, like many of the food companies, are capitalized mostly with debt. But then why does the *P/BV*-ROBBV model work so well? It is, in fact, the *P/E* that misbehaves, not the industry data, in my view.

The *P/E*-growth model for the diversified chemical industry works considerably better, but with a strange twist, as shown in Figure 15–11.

The *P/E* multiple falls with increasing growth, suggesting that the faster a diversified chemical company grows, the less it is worth. If these companies were investing capital at rates below their capital costs, then more investment and/or growth would naturally destroy value.

With the pharmaceuticals, very little pattern is evident (Figure 15–12). Pfizer, for example, produces a 29 percent sustainable growth and a 40.4 *P/E*. Abbott, on the other hand, generates a similar 28 percent growth rate but carries only a 21.5 *P/E*. In the pharmaceutical industry, similar growth creates very different valuations, suggesting that some

FIGURE 15–10

Food industry *P/E*s may rise weakly with increasing sustainable growth.

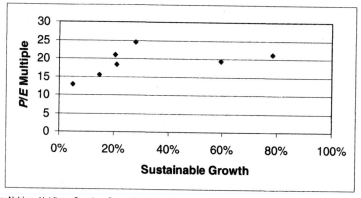

Companies: Nabisco Holdings, Sara Lee Corp., H.J. Heinz, Best Foods, Kellogg, Conagra, and Ralston Purina.

FIGURE 15–11

Diversified chemical industry *P/Es*, on the other hand, seem to decline with increasing growth.

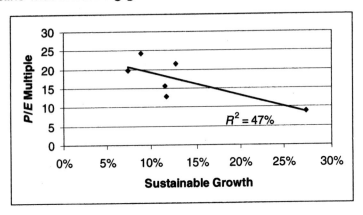

FIGURE 15–12

Pharmaceutical industry *P/Es* show little relationship to growth.

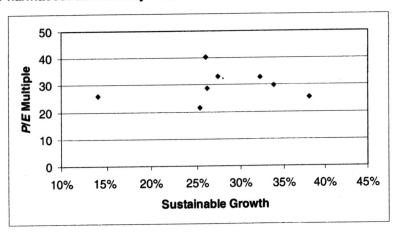

companies grow profitably, but others do not. More on the behavior of *P/E* in Chapter 17.

CHEAP STOCKS

The relative valuation regression technique can add considerable precision to the issue of what stocks are "cheap." The procedure is simple:

- Using the regression model and the companion variable for each company in the group, calculate the valuation multiple predicted by the formula.
- Compare the prediction to the company's actual valuation.
- Cheap stocks are those that trade at multiples below those predicted by the regression equation. Likewise, expensive stocks sell at multiples above those predicted by the model.

For example, Gateway's 23.6 percent return on book value produces a 7.75 times predicted P/BV multiple:

$$\text{Predicted } P/BV = 35.4 * \text{return on book value} - 1.2$$
$$= 35.4(23.6\%) - 1.2$$
$$= 7.15 \tag{15.16}$$

The company's actual P/BV is 6.54 times or below the 7.15 prediction. In this case, GTW is considered undervalued by 8 percent:

$$\% \text{ Over(under)valuation} = \frac{(\text{actual } P/BV - \text{predicted } P/BV)}{(\text{actual } P/BV)}$$
$$= \frac{(6.54 - 7.15)}{6.54}$$
$$= (9\%) \tag{15.17}$$

I performed a similar analysis for all the companies in the group and arranged the results from most under- to most overvalued. (See Figure 15–13.)

The model suggests that at the time Sun Microsystems and Gateway were undervalued, and NCR and Compaq overvalued, based upon a relative valuation standard. Is this really true? Are these stocks really mispriced to this extent? There are a number of possible explanations for the results, other than mispricing of the stocks:

- Perhaps other variables, like risk or growth, which the companion variable model eliminates, can explain the apparent deviation of these stocks from prediction. If additional variables do explain the differences, then the stocks are not mispriced.
- It may be that market expectations beyond one year are sufficiently negative or positive to cause the valuation

FIGURE 15–13

Computer industry stocks form a clear pattern of under- and overvaluation, using the *P/BV* model results.

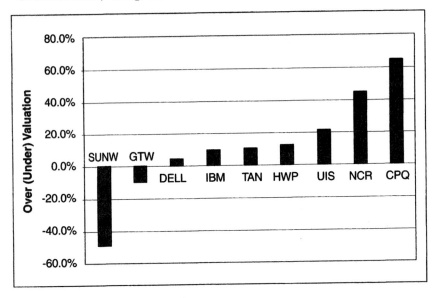

differences noted. The companion variable model has only a one-year prospective reach.

■ Or it may be that there are qualitative differences between the companies that explain their valuation. Management quality, marketing expertise, new product development and research, the appearance of a strong competitor or technology, could all cause the market to revalue a company.

Regardless of the reason for the deviation, at the very least Figure 15–13 is highly suggestive. It suggests further questions, causes the analyst to dig deeper, and provides a strong starting point for further inquiry. Whether, finally, we decide that these apparent valuation discrepancies are real or not, at least we know that they exist.

COMPANION VARIABLES AND TARGET PRICES

The companion variable regression technique is the basis of target prices. The process is straightforward, illustrated for the *P/BV-ROBBV* system in Figure 15–14. From a comparable group of companies, the analyst develops a companion variable regression model. The regression model generates a *P*/BV multiple if given an actual—or predicted—ROBBV. From his or her financial model of the company under study, the analyst draws a prediction of future ROBBV and BV. When inserted into the companion variable model, the predicted ROBBV produces a predicted valuation multiple *P*/BV. Multiplying the predicted *P*/BV by the projection of future BV, the analyst produces a target price.

There are, of course, some assumptions buried in this method:

- Setting future target prices using current stock trading patterns presumes that overall market conditions remain relatively the same. Remember that this is a relative valuation method. It has nothing to say about the absolute valuation of the group. If, for example, a decline in interest rates causes the market—and the comparable group—to rise in value, then value predictions of the current companion variable model will be consistently too low.

- Setting target prices with a companion variable model implies that the general character of the company's business remains similar to the comparable group over the estimation period. If management changes, product development, acquisitions, or competition alters the company's fundamentals, then the companion variable model will mispredict future value. It is relatively easy to slip into this error, since the analyst's financial model of the company may well anticipate such

FIGURE 15–14

Relative valuation models, like *P*/BV-ROE, can form a rigorous basis for target prices.

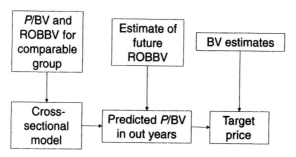

future events. Unfortunately, the companion variable model cannot.

■ Target prices will contain the same valuation errors found in the current comparable group, a particularly difficult issue. If, for example, the companion variable model suggests a stock was overvalued, a simple application of the model to future value drivers will likely include the same overvaluation. The analyst must decide whether the valuation signals given by the model are valid before blindly applying it to future performance.

Dell Computer "Valuation Box"

In Chapters 11 to 13, we developed a five-year model for Dell. What changes in the company's stock price can we expect as its financial performance develops in future years? Consider the year 2001 in which our model projected a year-end book value of $1.83 per share. Year 2002 predicted EPS to be $1.31, producing a projected year-end 2001 ROBBV of 71.6 percent:

$$\frac{EPS_{2002}}{BV_{2001}} = \frac{\$1.31}{\$1.83}$$
$$= 71.6\% = ROBBV \tag{15.18}$$

The companion variable model Equation 15.16 suggests that a 71.5 percent ROBBV should be valued at 24.1 times book: *return on begining BV*

$$Predicted\ P/BV_{2001} = 35.4\ ROBBV - 1.2$$
$$= 35.4\ (71.6\%) - 1.2$$
$$= 24.1 \tag{15.19}$$

Our year-end 2001 target price is then about $44, using the 2001 ending book value prediction:

$$Target\ price_{2001} = \$1.83 * 24.1$$
$$= \$44.18 \tag{15.20}$$

A similar method can be applied to any year for which we have Dell projections, forming a "valuation box," illustrated in Table 15–5. Predictions of future ROBBV and BV come from the Dell financial

TABLE 15–5

Dell valuation box predicts a $56 2002 target price.

	Stock price	P/BV	Book Value	ROBBV	P/E
Current	$33.50	30.2	$1.11	85.7%	35
YE2000	$34.58	27.2	$1.27	80.3%	34
YE2001	$44.18	24.1	$1.83	71.6%	34
YE2002	$53.48	20.3	$2.63	60.8%	33

model. Predictions of P/BV are the product of the companion variable model.

This may strike many as excessively mechanical. But we can learn something from the mechanism. For example, the Dell financial model predicts a declining ROBBV, from 85.7 percent at the beginning of the analysis to 60.8 percent by 2002. The companion variable model, in this case, generates a contracting P/BV multiple. If our predicted returns decline, and yet we still have expectations of an expanding valuation multiple, the model makes an interesting point. How can multiples expand when returns are contracting? Maybe there's a way, but at least the question arises.

Referring to Figure 15–13, the companion variable model implies that, at a 30.2 P/BV multiple, Dell is very nearly correctly priced.

$$\text{Predicted } P/BV_{\text{Dell}} = 35.4 \text{ ROBBV} - 1.2$$
$$= 35.4 \ (85.7\%) - 1.2$$
$$= 29.1 \qquad\qquad (15.21)$$

This strong agreement is to some extent a statistical artifact since Dell's returns and valuation are so much larger than others of the comparable group. The valuation box will, therefore, contain the assumption that the stock is about correctly priced, all else being equal. But is this really so, given the statistical issues in the relative valuation model? And can we expect this fair pricing—if it really exists—to persist in the future? Again, it is the mechanism, as rigid as it may be, that raises these questions.

The P/E implications of the target price model appear in the table. Although they play no direct role in the calculations, P/E predictions are a useful crosscheck of the valuation logic.

TIME SERIES MODELS

Companion variable relative valuation models are "cross sectional" in that they use a cross section of companies captured at a particular time. But company valuations change in time as well as relative to peers. Can we develop a model, for example, that tracks the valuation of a single company over a period of time? What does it mean, exactly, that stocks are "interest rate sensitive"? Exactly how do interest rates drive stock values over time? The key to such a model lies in the cost-of-capital variable, k.

The Theory (Sigh)

Returning to the expression for P/E in Equation 15.4, notice that the formula contains the cost-of-capital k in the denominator:

$$\frac{P_0}{E_1} = \frac{b}{(k - g)} \qquad (15.22)$$

Standard CAPM theory expresses k as a combination of a risk-free rate and market premium:

$$k = \text{risk-free rate} + \beta * \text{market premium} \qquad (15.23)$$

Substituting 15.23 into Equation 15.4, the P/E becomes an inverse function of the risk-free interest rate:

$$\frac{P_0}{E_1} = \frac{b}{(\text{risk-free rate} + \beta * \text{market premium} - g)} \qquad (15.24)$$

Since the interest rate changes over time, we might try a time-dependent P/E model with the risk-free rate (RFR) as the independent variable:

$$\text{Predicted } \frac{P_0}{E_1} = A_0 + A_1 * \left(\frac{1}{\text{RFR}}\right) \qquad (15.25)$$

If a relationship like Equation 15.25 can be found for a particular stock, then a prediction of future interest rates produces a prediction of the stock's future P/E, all else being equal. This is one precise expression of interest rate dependence, with the coefficient A_1 being the "bond beta" of the stock.

Often, instead of interest rates, the time dependence of valuation multiples is expressed using a market index P/E like the S&P 500:

$$\text{Predicted } \frac{P_0}{E_1} = B_0 + B_1 * (\text{S\&P 500 } P/E \text{ index}) \quad (15.26)$$

In this case, a prediction of the future S&P 500 index level generates a predicted P/E multiple for the stock. Equation 15.26 has less theoretical basis than the interest rate–based formula Equation 15.25. However, if risk, cash flow, and growth relationships between a single company and the broader market are relatively constant, then a stable relationship like Equation 15.26 may in fact exist. In any event, such relationships are widely used by analysts.

The Allstate Corporation

The Allstate Corporation is an appropriate candidate to test this theory because, as a financial stock, we might expect it to show both strong interest rate and strong broader market dependence. In fact, for the period January 1995 to October 1998, the company's P/E was correlated far more strongly with the broader market, as represented by the S&P 500 composite P/E, than to interest rates, represented by a composite inter-mediate-term government bond yield:

$$\text{Predicted } P/E = 0.49 + 0.61 * (\text{S\&P 500 composite } P/E) \quad (15.27)$$

$$\text{Adjusted } R^2 = 75.7\%$$

$$\text{Predicted } P/E = 2.80 + 0.57 * \left(\frac{1}{\text{intermediate bond yield}}\right) \quad (15.28)$$

$$\text{Adjusted } R^2 = 16.2\%$$

This period of relatively constant interest rates produces, as expected, relatively constant predictions for ALL's P/E in the 10 to 14 times range over most of the period. However, the company's actual P/E rose steadily over the period, reaching nearly 16 before falling to 12 to 14 by period end. ALL's rising P/E mirrored the rising market P/E. But, at the end of the period, the company's valuation deviates from both predictions. Falling interest rates drive a sharp rise in predicted P/E in the interest rate model. Steady S&P valuations, on the other hand, suggested that the company's valuation should remain relatively unchanged. However, the prospect of increasing competitiveness in the company's basic auto insurance markets likely produced the nasty decline in ALL's P/E. In these results lie several lessons (see Figure 15–15):

FIGURE 15–15

Interest rates or the S&P 500 *P/E* index can predict an
individual stock's valuation behavior over time.

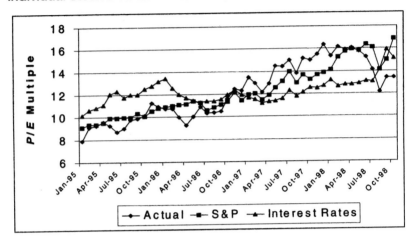

- The interest rate and market valuation sensitivities suggested
  by these models are not immutable. Changes in the underlying
  profitability, strategy, and market risks of the company can
  alter its valuation independent of the movement of interest
  rates and the broader market. Just as with the valuation box,
  blind application of time series models can produce wildly
  inaccurate predictions. On the other hand, deviations from time
  series model predictions can suggest some underlying
  fundamental change.

- Time series models point out the flaws in reasoning from time
  averages, just as companion variable models do with cross-
  sectional averages. "Company *X*'s *P/E* is below its historical
  average, and we therefore expect it to rise." But the question
  is, why is the stock trading below its historical averages? If the
  analyst hasn't controlled for changes in interest rates and
  broader market valuations, historical time averages are, in a
  word, useless.

NOTES

[1] See, for example, Aswath Damodaran, *Damodaran on Valuation,* Wiley, New York,
1994, chs. 10–12.

CHAPTER 16

Hybrid Valuation Techniques

- Hybrid valuation methods combine discounting, generally associated with free-cash flow valuation techniques, with accounting earnings.

- The same return on equity, cost of equity, and growth rate are consistent with a wide range of stock values. The sustainability of profitable growth is the final variable necessary to completely specify the value of the firm.

- The price/book value valuation multiple is a function of the level of future abnormal earnings, but the price/earnings multiple is more complex and driven by abnormal earnings growth.

The Stern Stewart EVA technique is an informative addition to financial performance measures like net income and net cash flow from operations, but, in its usual form, it is less appropriate to the analyst concerned principally with the value of common stocks. Beginning with a common dividend discount valuation model, an equity valuation analog of EVA can be derived, with many of the attractive features of the Stern Stewart construct and in a much more convenient form for equity analysts. This equity model is driven by the firm's abnormal earnings (AE) and is effectively a hybrid of cash flow–based and earnings-based valuation techniques. The AE model permits the calculation of equity values for any combination of return on equity (ROE), cost of equity (k), growth rate (g), and period of profitable growth. In concert with the relative valuation techniques of Chapter 15, the model can make specific estimates of the stock market's growth expectations for any stock—a helpful

check on the reasonableness of valuation. Finally, the equity-only formulation permits a rigorous examination of the drivers of both the price/
book value (P/BV) and price/earnings multiples (P/E), illustrated but
not proven in Chapter 2.

AN EQUITY REFORMULATION

The common dividend discount model can be transformed into an AE
format that is the analog of the Stern Stewart EVA formulation. The
advantages of such a model can be substantial for the equity analyst.[1]

The analysis begins with the familiar dividend discount valuation
model:

$$V_0 = \sum_{i=1}^{\infty} \frac{D_i}{(1 + k)^i} \qquad (16.1)$$

where V_0 is the stock price and D_i is the annual dividend in year i.

The derivation requires that the "clean surplus relationship" shown
in Equation 16.2 be true. The clean surplus relationship demands that
dividends and earnings be the sole source of equity book value changes.
Dividends can be thought of in a more general sense as cash flows to
(and from) investors and might include share buybacks, for example.
Under GAAP accounting, the clean surplus relationship isn't always true.
Often adjustments are made directly to the equity account, bypassing the
income statement (an example of this is the accounting for marketable
securities under SFAS 115). However, past accounting for equity book
value is irrelevant to the derivation; in fact, all that matters is that the
clean surplus relationship apply prospectively. Most analysts probably
project financial statements on this basis already:

$$\text{BV}_i = \text{BV}_{i-1} + E_i - D_i \qquad (16.2)$$

The derivation requires two additional definitions, shown in Equations
16.3 and 16.4:

$$E_i = \text{ROE}_i * \text{BV}_{i-1} \qquad (16.3)$$

$$\frac{\text{BV}_i}{(1 + k)} = \text{BV}_i - \frac{k * \text{BV}_i}{(1 + k)} \qquad (16.4)$$

Equation 16.3 states that earnings E_i are generated by applying a return
on equity ROE_i to the book value at the beginning of period i (the end

of the period $i - 1$). The formulation is therefore inherently prospective; earnings are generated by the investment of the beginning book value. Equation 16.4 is an identity, which can be proven by a little algebra (for everyone's sake, not shown).

Substituting the clean surplus relationship into the dividend discount model in Equation 16.1:

$$V_0 = \sum_{i=1}^{\infty} \frac{D_i}{(1 + k)^i}$$
$$= \sum_{i=1}^{\infty} \frac{[E_i - (BV_i - BV_{i-1})]}{(1 + k)^i} \tag{16.5}$$

Now let's look at an expansion of the first two terms of the series generated by 16.5:

$$V_0 = \frac{[E_1 - (BV_1 - BV_0)]}{(1 + k)} + \frac{[E_2 - (BV_2 - BV_2)]}{(1 + k)^2} \tag{16.6}$$
$$+ \cdots + \frac{E_n - (BV_n - BV_{n-1})}{(1 + k)^n} + \cdots$$

Using the relationships in Equations 16.3 and 16.4, the first two terms become

$$V_0 = BV_0 + \frac{(E_1 - k * BV_0)}{(1 + k)} + \frac{(E_2 - k * BV_1)}{(1 + k)^2}$$
$$- \frac{BV_2}{(1 + k)^2} + \sum_{i=3}^{\infty} \frac{[E_i - (BV_i - BV_{i-1})}{(1 + k)^i} \tag{16.7}$$

The third term $BV_2/(1 + k)^2$ is eliminated in the further expansion of the series. In fact, Equation 16.7, in the limit, reduces to a very familiar form:

$$V_0 = BV_0 + \sum_{i=1}^{\infty} \frac{(E_i - k * BV_{i-1})}{(1 + k)^i}$$
$$= BV_0 + \sum_{i=1}^{\infty} \frac{[(ROE_i - k * BV_{i-1})]}{(1 + k)^i} \tag{16.8}$$

If $AE_i = (ROE_i - k) * BV_{i-1}$ is the abnormal earnings attributable to equity in period i, the Equation 16.8 is the analog of Equation 2.11

in Chapter 2 and Equation 10.6 in Chapter 10. But this time, we value only the firm's equity rather than its total capital:

$$V_0 = BV_0 + \sum_{i=1}^{\infty} \frac{AE_i}{(1 + k)^i} \tag{16.9}$$

The AE formulation in Equation 16.9 looks a lot like a discounted-cash-flow analysis and can even be converted into the familiar terminal-value format. For example, suppose our planning horizon extends to time T. Equation 16.9 breaks down into the beginning book value BV_0, the present value of abnormal earnings through time T, and the present value of abnormal earnings after time T:

$$V_0 = BV_0 + \sum_{i=1}^{T} \frac{AE_i}{(1 + k)^i} + \sum_{i=T+1}^{\infty} \frac{AE_i}{(1 + k)^i} \tag{16.10}$$

V_T, the stock value at time T, can be written as the sum of the time T book value BV_T and the present value of future abnormal earnings. Multiplying every term in the summation by $(1 + k)^T$ permits the series to begin at time $T + 1$ instead of time 1. Solving the equation for the summation term yields Equation 16.11.

$$V_T = BV_T + (1 + k)^T * \sum_{i=T+1}^{\infty} \frac{AE_i}{(1 + k)^i} \tag{16.11}$$

$$\sum_{i=T+1}^{\infty} \frac{AE_i}{(1 + k)^i} = \frac{(V_T - BV_T)}{(1 + k)^T} \tag{16.12}$$

Substituting the expression in Equation 16.12 into Equation 16.10, the abnormal earnings formulation takes on a somewhat more familiar form[2]:

$$V_0 = BV_0 + \sum_{i=1}^{T} \frac{AE_i}{(1 + k)^i} + \frac{(V_T - BV_T)}{(1 + k)^T} \tag{16.13}$$

Unlike a DCF valuation, in which the terminal value equals the equity value of the firm at time T, the terminal value in an AE formulation equals the *equity value added* ($V_T - BV_T$) at time T, generally a smaller number. *Equity value added* is the analog of the Stern Stewart "market value added" concept, and it simply equals the company's stock price at time T minus its book value. DCF terminal values often contain a high percentage (up to 70 percent is not uncommon) of firm value; on the other hand, the AE format places far less weight on the terminal value because much of the firm's equity value is already contained in its beginning book value BV_0.

SELF-CORRECTING VALUATIONS

Note also that Equations 16.9 and 16.13 contain only accounting earnings, not cash flows or dividends. The only assumption made in their derivation is that the clean surplus relationship holds. How is it that accounting earnings, subject to all the now-infamous distortions of economic reality, can produce an accurate valuation of the firm? We know, for example, that

- GAAP principles and management discretion sometimes distort accounting representations of economic reality.
- Earnings-based valuation makes no provision for the timing of cash flows from earnings.
- The AE format fails to account for the timing of capital expenditures.

On the issue of accounting distortions, the AE format is uniquely *self-correcting*[3]. For example, suppose a particular accounting principle causes earnings to be economically understated. The earnings understatement also causes equity book value to be understated, which in turn reduces the equity charge $k * BV$ applied to future earnings. As earnings under- or overstatements reverse (as they eventually must) over time, abnormal earnings $E - k * BV$ compensate for the understatement of accounting earnings.

For example, consider an earnings understatement X in period 1 which is reversed in period 2, as shown in Table 16–1. For simplicity, ignore the beginning book value at time $t = 0$.

Note that the present value of period 2 abnormal earnings is just large enough to offset the period 1 earnings distortion. As a general rule, GAAP and management distortions of reported earnings should not affect AE valuations, provided that valuation time horizons permit the reversal process described above to occur. Clearly, if the analyst is unaware of potential distortions, or if distortions do not reverse during the planning horizon T, then AE valuations will be incorrect. Errors are equally likely to occur in discounted-cash-flow (DCF) calculations when earnings are systematically over- or understated. This is because, in truth, most DCF

TABLE 16-1

Hybrid valuation methods can compensate for accounting-based distortions.

	1	2
Earnings	$-X$	$+X$
Beginning book value		$-X$
Abnormal earnings	$-X$	$X - k * (-X) = X + k * X$
PV (abnormal earnings)	$-X$	$(X + k * X)/(1 + k) = X$

analyses begin with an earnings projection. Relatively few are from a direct, cash-on-cash analysis. Cash flow may very well accurately reflect historical economic reality, but cash flow projections are not inherently superior to earnings projections, in my view. Aside from the issue of accuracy, the advantages of the AE format can be considerable:

■ AE valuations force the analyst to consider the company's investment opportunities and their potential returns; the investment viewpoint places natural limits on the company's profitable growth, and therefore on its value.

■ Reported earnings, whatever their inherent faults, are at least reported. Cash flow is often not, although this may be changing.

■ Earnings-based valuations can be adjusted rapidly for changes in familiar value drivers, like return on investment and growth; DCF formulations, on the other hand, are more complex to alter.

As to the question of the model's failure to account for cash flow timing, the AE formulation is, absent distortions, the exact equivalent of an investment cash flow analysis, as demonstrated in Chapter 2. The timing of cash flows is "wrapped up" in the expected investment returns—this is, in fact, how the returns are generated.

THE GROWTH CONTENT OF STOCK PRICES

In the Chapter 15 discussion of relative equity valuation techniques, we noted that, in the stock groups chosen, actual P/BV multiples differed, often substantially, from the predictions of the simple regression models. There are many possible explanations for these differences: over- or undervaluation, poor choice of the comparable group, individual company variations, and many others. The AE valuation technique can help frame this question in a more systematic way. Specifically, the formulation permits the characterization of these deviations from predicted valuations as variations in the market's estimate of the sustainability of individual company growth.

Relative techniques effectively predict individual company valuations based on the average expected growth of the chosen comparable company group. The market, on the other hand, may have different profitable growth expectations for individual companies, and AE analysis can determine those expectations. By considering the growth content of individual stocks in light of what we know about their competitive situations, we can begin to judge the reasonableness of individual company stock valuations. For example, if we found 8 to 10 years of profitable growth embedded in the valuation of a company with little competitive advantage in an intensely competitive industry, we might suspect that the stock is overvalued (at the time of the analysis).

To demonstrate the technique, consider a group of comparable property/casualty insurers, as shown in Table 16–2. I chose the property/casualty insurance industry because I happen to know it well and because, like many financial service industries, P/BV multiple valuation models have substantial explanatory power. Table 16–2 presents the return on beginning book value and the P/BV multiple for 13 property/casualty insurers on April 21, 1999. Return on equity is the next 12 months' consensus First Call earnings per share estimate divided by the company's current equity book value per share, as reported. Price/book value is the current stock price divided by the reported equity book value per share. Long-term growth is the I/B/E/S analysts' median growth estimate. Sustainable growth, on the other hand, is the product of the firm's ROE and earnings retention ratio (not shown).

The simple regression technique introduced in Chapter 15, with return on book value as the independent and P/BV as the dependent variable, produces a regression equation, shown in Figure 16–1, which explains 43 percent of the variation in P/BV, quite a strong result. Nevertheless, individual companies' valuations can differ substantially from the regression analysis prediction. For example, ACE Limited (ACL), a Bermuda-based specialty insurer with a $6 billion market capitalization,

TABLE 16–2

P/E and P/BV valuations of property/casualty insurance stocks showed strong similarities in April 1999.

	P/E	Long-Term Growth	P/BV	Return on Equity	Sustainable growth
ACL	12.9	13.0	1.49	11.5	9.7
AGII	14.1	NA	0.80	5.6	0.4
CB	13.8	11.4	1.69	12.3	8.6
FMT	9.4	13.1	1.41	15.0	12.6
HGIC	9.6	10.7	1.06	11.1	8.3
OC	8.9	11.4	1.09	12.3	9.6
ORI	8.8	11.0	1.12	12.8	10.5
REL	6.5	12.0	0.68	10.4	7.6
SIGI	9.4	10.0	0.83	8.8	6.2
SPC	10.9	10.3	1.03	9.4	5.7
TAP	10.3	12.4	1.52	14.7	12.6
XL	12.1	12.8	1.30	10.8	6.7
ZNT	13.6	NA	1.14	8.3	3.4
Average	10.8	—	1.17	11.0	7.8

NA = Not Available

FIGURE 16–1

P/BV-return on book value model for property/casualty insurers shows typical predictive power.

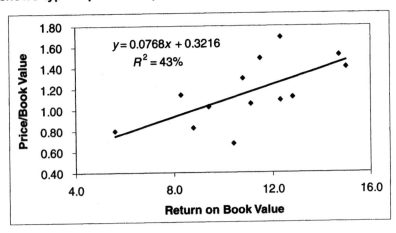

$y = 0.0768x + 0.3216$

$R^2 = 43\%$

posted an actual P/BV multiple of 1.49 but a predicted multiple of 1.20. Why?

A couple of possible explanations of the deviation from prediction might apply:

- ACL may be inappropriately classed with this group of comparable property/casualty companies. This is possible but unlikely, given ACL's exclusively property/casualty business, large size (bringing it closer to industry averages, all else equal), and product diversification (ensuring that one product line is not likely to overly influence the multiple).

- The company is overvalued. Again, this is possible but difficult to prove under any circumstances.

- ACL's risk is substantially lower than average. In fact, the opposite is true; ACL insures some of the world's most volatile risks. Its beta does not differ substantially from other insurers.

- There is a hidden variable that, if specified, could explain the difference from prediction.

If there is a hidden variable, what is it? Of the basic value drivers—return on equity, growth, and cost of capital—growth is the likely candidate. The regression model already contains ROE, so return differences are accounted for. The cost of capital is, in a mature industry like property/casualty insurance, unlikely to differ substantially from company to company. In fact, by picking a comparable industry group, we are attempting to limit the variation of capital costs among the companies in the group. What exactly about growth could explain the prediction error? It could, of course, be the absolute level of growth. Or it could be the sustainability of growth, which is the variable we'll explore further.

The AE method helps specify growth sustainability as a component of valuation. As illustrated in Chapter 2, Equation 16.8 is an infinite series that can be extended to any number of terms from $i = 1, ..., \infty$, depending on the number of years of profitable growth that the company can sustain.[4] Each additional year of profitable (unprofitable) growth produces a slightly higher (lower) stock price. For example, in the limit of perpetual profitable growth of g, the stock value V_0 reaches

$$V_0 = (\text{ROE} - g) * \frac{BV_0}{(k - g)} \qquad (16.14)$$

where ROE and g are constant for all years.

If the firm were to generate three years of profitable growth, after which abnormal earnings remained constant, its stock value would be

$$
\begin{aligned}
V_0 = BV_0 &+ (ROE - k) * \frac{BV_0}{(1 + k)} \\
&+ (ROE - k) * \frac{BV_1}{(1 + k)^2} \\
&+ (ROE - k) * \frac{BV_2}{(1 + k)^3} \\
&+ (ROE - k) * \frac{BV_3}{k * (1 + k)^3}
\end{aligned}
\tag{16.15}
$$

Assuming that later years' book values can be determined by growing the beginning book value, as in $BV_1 = (1 + g) * BV_0$, dividing both sides of Equation 16.15 by BV_0, and substituting the more familiar P_0 for V_0:

$$
\begin{aligned}
\frac{P_0}{BV_0} = 1 &+ \frac{(ROE - k)}{(1 + k)} \\
&+ (ROE - k) * \frac{(1 + g)}{(1 + k)^2} \\
&+ (ROE - k) * \frac{(1 + g)^2}{(1 + k)^3} \\
&+ (ROE - k) * \frac{(1 + g)^3}{k * (1 + k)^3}
\end{aligned}
\tag{16.16}
$$

In fact, a similar expression can be derived for any number of years of profitable growth, out to the perpetuity limit shown in Equation 16.14. Each additional year produces a different value, and these values can be plotted to demonstrate the range into which the company's P/BV might fall. The series ends at the year when competitive equilibrium is reached and competitive forces finally drive returns on equity ROE down to the cost of equity k. By matching the firm's actual P/BV multiple to those produced in the series expansion, we can determine the number of years of profitable growth embedded in the valuation.

Before looking at the valuation range, let's consider exactly what rate of growth is appropriate for Equation 16.16. The sustainable growth rate is a good candidate for the job. The sustainable growth rate is the product of the firm's ROE and dividend retention ratio, and measures the rate at which book value can grow without outside financing. The principal advantages of the sustainable rate are (1) it can be calculated easily and consistently for most companies; (2) it is specifically tied to book value growth, which is what the analysis requires; and (3) it is an inherently sensible estimate of any company's near-term growth potential. For ACL, the appropriate variables are

$$ROE = 11.5\%$$

$$k = 8.7\%$$

$$g = 9.7\%$$

ACL's sustainable rate is the product of the company's 11.5 percent ROE and its dividend retention ratio 84.5 percent. ACL generates a 2.8 percent (11.5 percent − 8.7 percent) positive spread between ROE and k and can be expected to trade above book value, which of course it does. Figure 16–2 presents the range of potential ACL P/BV multiples between 1 and 20 years of profitable growth.

Note that, to sustain a 1.49 times P/BV multiple, the market must assume that ACL can grow profitably for about 6 years. The 1.20 predicted P/BV multiple, on the other hand, can be achieved with less than 1 profitable year.

FIGURE 16–2

In April 1999, ACE's actual P/BV multiple contained an estimated six years of profitable growth.

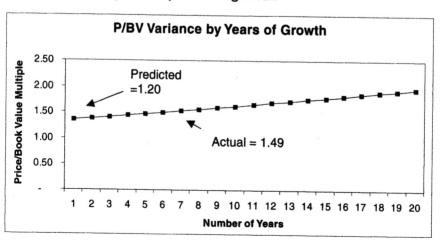

But why is the prediction of the regression analysis so low? Embedded in the regression analysis is the market's estimate of the comparable group's average profit sustainability. The market apparently believes that, on average, the property/casualty insurance industry was, at this time, capable of little profitable growth. To check this, consider the average insurance company from Table 16–2:

$$\text{ROE} = 11.0\%$$

$$g = 7.8\%$$

$$P/BV = 1.17$$

According to the AE analysis of the average insurer in Figure 16–3, less than one year of profitable growth is necessary to sustain a P/BV of 1.17 times, indicating the market's (justifiably) low expectations for the industry at the time.

Note that in both the ACL and average insurer, the growth rate g exceeds the cost of capital k, making the perpetuity expression Equation 16.4 inapplicable. It seems reasonable in the shorter term that firms might be able to reinvest all earnings (less dividends) profitably; but in the longer run, competition is likely to make this impossible. The growth rate g used in perpetuity is very likely much smaller than the near-term sustainable rate. It is, in fact, probably closer to the long-term growth in the overall economy.

FIGURE 16–3

P/BV multiple of the average P/C insurer in April 1999 contained less than one year of profitable growth.

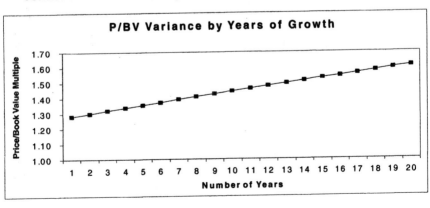

THE COMPLETE SPECIFICATION OF VALUATION MULTIPLES

Chapter 2 hinted at the answer, but now we can demonstrate rigorously what drives both the P/BV and P/E ratios. Price/book value is a function of the level of future abnormal earnings, which explains why return on book value is a powerful predictor of valuation multiples. P/E, on the other hand, is a more complex function of the growth in future abnormal earnings. The dependence of P/E on the growth in abnormal, rather than reported earnings, explains the frequent difficulty in modeling P/E multiples.[5]

P/BV Multiple Is the Simple One

The P/BV multiple is a function of the level of future abnormal earnings. In the following equations the stock's price P_0 appears in place of value V_0. Strictly speaking, of course, these equations predict stock value rather than price multiples. Returning to Equation 16.9, and again using P_0 in place of V_0:

$$P_0 = BV_0 + \sum_{i=1}^{\infty} \frac{AE_i}{(1 + k)^i}$$

and dividing both sides by BV_0, the beginning book value:

$$\frac{P_0}{BV_0} = 1 + \left(\frac{1}{BV_0}\right) * \sum_{i=1}^{\infty} \frac{AE_i}{(1 + k)^i} \tag{16.17}$$

The P/BV multiple is a direct function of the present value of future abnormal earnings. If abnormal earnings are positive, the P/BV ratio exceeds 1. Negative future abnormal earnings drive the P/BV below one. Companies with zero abnormal earnings trade at one times book value. Clearly, any nonreversing distortions in reported earnings could cause actual valuations to differ from these predictions.

P/E Is Driven by Growth

Growth in future abnormal earnings is the driver of the price/earnings multiple. To see this, divide both sides of Equation 16.9 by E_1, the earnings during period 1:

$$\frac{P_0}{E_1} = \left(\frac{BV_0}{E_1}\right) + \sum_{i=1}^{\infty} \frac{(AE_i/E_1)}{(1 + k)^i} \tag{16.18}$$

Equation 16.18 can be simplified by a bit of algebraic manipulation, beginning with the identities $AE_1 = (ROE_1 - k) * BV_0$ and $E_1 = ROE_1 * BV_0$:

$$AE_1 = (ROE_1 - k) * BV_0$$

$$= E_1 - k * BV_0 \tag{16.19}$$

Solving for BV_0 and dividing the solution by E_1, Equation 16.19 becomes

$$\frac{BV_0}{E_1} = \left(\frac{1}{E_1}\right) * \frac{(E_1 - AE_1)}{k} \tag{16.20}$$

$$= \frac{1}{k} - \left(\frac{1}{E_1}\right) * \frac{(AE_1)}{k}$$

Substituting the 16.20 expression for BV_0/E_1 into Equation 16.18:

$$\frac{P_0}{E_1} = \frac{1}{k} + \left(\frac{1}{E_1}\right) * \sum_{i=1}^{\infty} \left[\frac{AE_i}{(1 + k)^i} - \frac{AE_1}{k}\right] \tag{16.21}$$

The price/earnings ratio, according to Equation 16.21, is a function of the amount by which the present value of future abnormal earnings exceeds current abnormal earnings (capitalized at k, the cost of equity). As Chapter 2 demonstrated, the P/E cannot expand beyond $(1/k)$, even if a firm's abnormal earnings are positive and reported earnings are growing, unless future abnormal earnings levels exceed current levels.

For mature industries unable to build abnormal earnings, P/E should show relatively little dependence upon long-term growth, regardless of how fast that growth is. Consider, for example, the 13 property/casualty companies listed in Table 16.2. The cross-sectional graph in Figure 16–4, plotting each company's P/E multiple versus its sustainable growth rate (the product of ROE and the earnings retention rate), illustrates the point.

As expected, little discernible relationship between sustainable growth and the P/E ratios of the companies seems to emerge. In fact, the same growth rates appear very compatible with a number of P/E

FIGURE 16–4

Property/casualty stock *P/E*s generally decline with increasing growth.

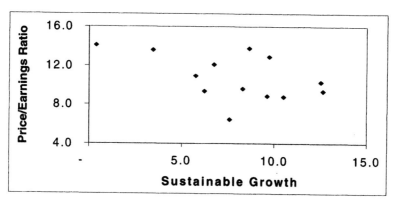

multiples. Like the diversified chemical group in Figure 15.11, the property/casualty companies appear to show declining *P/E* with growth.

VALUATION MULTIPLES AND COMPANY PERFORMANCE

The results above can explain the often puzzling behavior of *P*/BV and *P/E* multiples. It is not true, for example, that "good" companies ought to have both a high *P/E* and *P*/BV. Valuation multiples are dependent on both the level and growth of abnormal earnings.

In fact, there are at least four distinct value multiple combinations worthy of discussion, as illustrated in Table 16.3.[6] Companies with both

TABLE 16–3

The level and growth of expected future abnormal earnings signal the market's view of company prospects, and in turn control valuation multiples.

AE Levels/AE Growth	Slow	Fast
Low	Limited prospects	Turnaround
High	Maturing companies	High flyers

low and slowly growing future abnormal earnings levels are likely to have both a low P/BV multiple and a low P/E multiple. These companies have limited performance prospects. At the other end of the spectrum, "high flyers" with high and rapidly growing abnormal earnings levels have high P/E and P/BV multiples and strong performance prospects. Between these two extremes are firms with high but slowly growing AE levels, showing high P/BV and low P/E multiples. These are likely to be successful but maturing companies facing stiffening competition. Low but rapidly growing AE levels produce low P/BV and high P/E multiples. Companies in this situation may be experiencing a "turnaround" from a period of earnings pressure.

NOTES

[1] Gerald I. White, Ashwinpaul C. Sondhi, and Dov Fried, *The Analysis and Use of Financial Statements,* Wiley, New York, 1997, p. 1063. The AE derivation follows WSF, who refer to this model as the "Edwards-Bell-Ohlson (EBO) model."

[2] Ibid, p. 1065.

[3] See, for example, Krishna G. Palepu, Victor L. Bernard, and Paul M. Healy, *Introduction to Business Analysis and Valuation,* South-Western College Publishing, Cincinnati, Ohio, 1997, p. 7-7, or White, Sondhi, and Fried, *The Analysis and Use of Financial Statements,* p. 1067.

[4] Palepu, Bernard, and Healy, *Introduction to Business Analysis,* p. 7-3. PBH call this a "shortcut" approach that can serve as a good "sanity check" because of the tendency of more complex models—and DCF valuations—to contain inconsistencies and unreasonable assumptions, about which I spoke at some length in Chapter 14.

[5] White, Sondhi, and Fried, *The Analysis and Use of Financial Statements,* p. 1069.

[6] Ibid., pp. 1071–1072.

CHAPTER 17

The Quirky
Price/Earnings Ratio

- Although one of the most widely used valuation measures, the price/earnings ratio is also one of the most problematic. Driven by the growth of future abnormal earnings, the P/E's of companies within the same industry often show no discernible pattern.

- The complexity of the P/E ratio seems to be absent in the Gordon growth model, creating considerable confusion about the ratio's behavior. In fact, the Gordon growth model is completely consistent with the more robust expression for P/E from Chapter 16.

- The P/E-to-growth ratio is an often-used valuation rule of thumb, but it too is sometimes ill behaved. The expected one-to-one relationship between P/E and growth is not theoretically supported and, unfortunately, occurs only by chance.

The P/E ratio was, for a long time, a deep, personal puzzlement to me. Unlike the more mundane, and less frequently used, P/BV multiple, P/E multiples for comparable companies often show no apparent pattern. When P/E does show a pattern, it is likely to be industry dependent. In this chapter, we'll explore in more depth why P/E multiples are so problematic.

Analysts' reliance upon the P/E-to-growth ratio (PEG) is understandable, but it suffers from many of the same ills as the P/E ratio itself. Unlike relative valuation techniques, which indicate over- or undervaluation of comparable stocks relative to each other, the PEG potentially allows the analyst to step out of the circle and judge what a stock is "really" worth, in an absolute sense. Would it were so. The problem with the PEG ratio is that it is a function of the company's expected growth rate. Companies in different life cycle positions, from the high growth emerging to the slower growth mature stage, can be expected to have varying PEG ratios. To know what PEG "really" should be, the analyst must make a judgment about the company's future prospects for profitable growth. This, unfortunately, returns him or her firmly to the central problem of valuation, competitive positioning, and foils the escape into a purer world of absolute valuations. This is not to say that the PEG ratio is not useful. It is simply not infallible.

THE DRIVERS OF THE *P/E* MULTIPLE

A simplification of Equation 16.21 for the *P/E* multiple can shed some light on the behavior of this relatively complex valuation multiple:

$$\frac{P_0}{E_1} = \frac{1}{k} + \left(\frac{1}{E_1}\right) * \sum_{i=1}^{\infty} \left[\frac{AE_i}{(1+k)^i} - \frac{AE_1}{k}\right] \qquad (17.1)$$

Consider the case of constant abnormal earnings growth. This assumption requires a perpetuity growth rate g that is likely much lower than the sustainable growth rates used in the text.[1] The summation term in Equation 17.1 can be simplified:

$$\sum_{i=1}^{\infty} \left[\frac{AE_i}{(1+k)^i}\right] = \sum_{i=1}^{\infty} \left[\frac{AE_1 * (1+g)^{i-1}}{(1+k)^i}\right]$$

$$= \frac{AE_1}{(k-g)} \qquad (17.2)$$

Equation 17.1 then becomes

$$\frac{P_0}{E_1} = \left(\frac{1}{k}\right) + \frac{(AE_1/E_1)}{(k-g)} - \frac{(AE_1/E_1)}{k}$$

$$= \left(\frac{1}{k}\right) * \left\{1 + \left(\frac{AE_1}{E_1}\right) * \left[\frac{g}{(k-g)}\right]\right\} \qquad (17.3)$$

Depending on the sign and value of the term (AE_1/E_1), a graph of *P/E* versus the growth rate g could have a number of shapes. If on average $AE_1 = 0$, for a cross section of comparable companies, *P/E* multiples for the group should show little or no correlation to growth rates and be clustered around the line $1/k$:

$$\frac{P_0}{E_1} = \left(\frac{1}{k}\right) \tag{17.4}$$

This is very like Figure 16–4 for the property/casualty insurers implying that, on average, the companies generate little abnormal income. The property/casualty group shows an average cost of equity of 9.00 to 9.50 percent, implying a P/E of 10.5 to 11.1, very close to the actual 10.8 industry average. (See Figure 17–1.)

For the pharmaceutical group, on the other hand, P/E shows a similar flat graph but with P/E clustered around 30.0 times, with a spread of 20.0 to 40.0. This result implies strongly that abnormal earnings growth for the group is nonzero but that individual company growth rates can differ substantially.

If, on the other hand, (AE_1/E_1) were positive, indicating positive abnormal earnings (we'll ignore the case in which both E and AE are negative since P/E under those circumstances is meaningless), P/E should increase at an accelerating pace with higher growth g. Conversely, if (AE_1/E_1) is negative, P/E should decline with higher growth. (See Figure 17–2.)

In practice, of course, any single industry might contain some firms generating positive AE and others zero or negative AE. In that case, cross-sectional $P/E - g$ plots may very well show little apparent pattern. The best solution to this dilemma is to avoid P/E valuation formulations

FIGURE 17–1

In the absence of abnormal earnings growth, *P/E* multiples will cluster around 1/*k*, the reciprocal of the cost of equity.

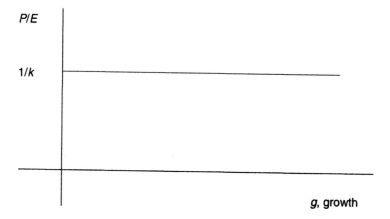

FIGURE 17–2

With nonzero abnormal earnings, *P/E* multiples of comparable groups can follow a variety of patterns.

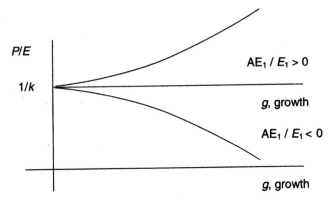

altogether. Failing that, it may be possible to abandon growth as an independent variable and substitute AE, each firm's expected abnormal earnings, perhaps in the form $(ROE - k)$ or ROE/k. Companies in a cross-sectional analysis might then cluster around the line in Figure 17–3.

Or, as much as I hate to admit it, the industry average *P/E* may, in some cases, be the best available indicator of individual firm value, especially in more mature industries where abnormal earnings are low.

FIGURE 17–3

In place of growth, *P/E* multiples might be plotted against abnormal earnings $(ROE - k)$.

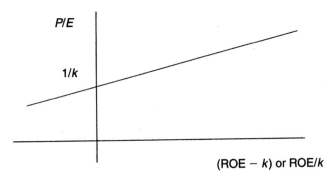

GORDON GROWTH AND THE *P/E* RATIO

The simple expression Equation 15.4 for P/E derived in Chapter 15 from the Gordon growth model is in fact completely consistent with the more robust form of the P/E in Equation 17.3. The more robust expression for P/E can often be a better guide to the ratio's actual behavior because it incorporates variation in the abnormal earnings power among the companies in a relative valuation exercise.

Beginning with the dividend discount model, the Gordon growth model provides a simple expression for the stock price based upon the next period's expected dividend and long-term growth rate:

$$P_0 = \frac{D_1}{(k - g)} \qquad (17.5)$$

From that simple expression, we can construct a simple formula for the P/E ratio of the company:

$$\frac{P_0}{E_1} = \frac{b}{(k - g)} \qquad (17.6)$$

where b is the company's expected dividend payout ratio.

If the clean surplus ratio (17.7) holds, the dividend payout ratio can be written as Equation 17.8:

$$D_1 = (BV_0 + E_1 - BV_1) \qquad (17.7)$$

$$b = \frac{(BV_0 + E_1 - BV_1)}{E_1} \qquad (17.8)$$

where D_1 is the expected dividend payment in period 1.

Realizing that $g * BV_0 = BV_1 - BV_0$, Equation 17.8 can be rearranged:

$$b = \frac{(E_1 - g * BV_0)}{E_1}$$

$$= \frac{1 - g * BV_0}{E_1}$$

$$= 1 - \left(\frac{g}{k}\right) * \left(\frac{k * BV_0}{E_1}\right) \qquad (17.9)$$

where, in the second term, both multiplying and dividing by k, the cost of equity, leaves the entire expression unchanged. But $k * BV_0$ is simply the normal earnings of the company during period 1 and can therefore be rewritten as:

$$k * BV_0 = E_1 - AE_1 \qquad (17.10)$$

where E_1 is the reported earnings in period 1, and AE_1 the abnormal earnings in the same period. Substituting this new expression Equation 17.10 into the formula for b, Equation 17.9, we arrive at Equation 17.11 after a little algebra:

$$
\begin{aligned}
b &= 1 - \left(\frac{g}{k}\right) * \left(\frac{k * BV_0}{E_1}\right) \\
&= 1 - \left(\frac{g}{k}\right) * \left[\frac{(E_1 - AE_1)}{E_1}\right] \\
&= 1 - \left(\frac{g}{k}\right) * \left(\frac{1 - AE_1}{E_1}\right) \\
&= \left(\frac{1}{k}\right) * \left[k - g + g * \left(\frac{AE_1}{E_1}\right)\right] \qquad (17.11)
\end{aligned}
$$

Returning to Equation 17.6, the Gordon growth expression for P/E, we substitute Equation 17.11 for b:

$$
\begin{aligned}
\frac{P_0}{E_1} &= \frac{b}{(k - g)} \\
&= \left(\frac{1}{k}\right) * \left[\frac{k - g + g * \left(\dfrac{AE_1}{E_1}\right)}{(k - g)}\right] \\
&= \left(\frac{1}{k}\right) * \left\{1 + \left(\frac{AE_1}{E_1}\right) * \left[\frac{g}{(k - g)}\right]\right\} \qquad (17.12)
\end{aligned}
$$

which is precisely the expression presented in Equation 17.3.

The more complex P/E expression in Equation 17.3 helps explain why P/E-to-growth formulations, which we take up next, are sometimes unsatisfactory. Variations in abnormal earnings seem quite natural even within a comparable group of companies, which is likely to contain both an industry's leaders and laggards. Such variations can obscure any obvious relationship between P/E and the rate of growth.

THE *P/E*-TO-GROWTH RATIO: ANOTHER CASUALTY

The *P/E*-to-growth (PEG) ratio is a very popular valuation rule of thumb, generally pegged at 1.0 or more for rapidly growing, successful firms. Firms with *P/E* ratios below their growth rates—and we have yet to define what "growth rate" we mean—are, in this scheme, considered undervalued. Unfortunately, the PEG is another casualty of our analysis, failing, like its cousin the *P/E*, to show regular behavior. In fact, using long-term growth estimates, PEG will probably on average equal or exceed 2.0 times for firms in competitive equilibrium and those making profitable investments (whose returns exceed the cost of equity). But when PEG is calculated using nearer-term expected growth rates, which may be higher than longer-term rates, it will depend critically on the assumed number of future profitable growth years. In highly competitive industries, PEG can readily fall below 1.0. Like the *P/E* multiple itself, the near-term growth form of the PEG, often employed in newer, more rapidly growing companies, should be used with some care.

Assuming a long-term growth rate *g*, the *P/E* ratio formula is Equation 17.3:

$$\frac{P_0}{E_1} = \left(\frac{1}{k}\right) * \left\{ 1 + \left(\frac{AE_1}{E_1}\right) * \left[\frac{g}{(k-g)}\right]\right\}$$

with a cost of equity *k*, abnormal earnings AE, and reported earnings *E*. The PEG ratio is therefore:

$$PEG_1 = \left(\frac{1}{kg}\right) * \left\{ 1 + \left(\frac{AE_1}{E_1}\right) * \left[\frac{g}{(k-g)}\right]\right\}$$

$$= \frac{1}{kg} + \frac{1}{kg}\frac{AE_1}{E_1}\frac{g}{k-g} \qquad (17.13)$$

The Long-Term PEG Exceeds 1.0

$$= \frac{1}{kg} + \frac{1}{k}\frac{AE_1}{E_1}\frac{1}{k-g}$$

Suppose that, on average, abnormal earnings are zero, as they would be in competitive equilibrium, that the long-term growth rate is 4 to 6 percent, and that the cost of equity is about 8.75 percent, consistent with a long treasury bond rate of about 6 percent and a beta of 1.00. The PEG ratio in this case will vary between 1.9 and 2.9 times, expressing the growth rate in absolute rather than percentage terms:

$$
\begin{aligned}
PEG_1 &= \left(\frac{1}{kg}\right) \\
&= \left(\frac{1}{8.75\%}\right) * \left(\frac{1}{4 \text{ to } 6}\right) \\
&= 1.9 \text{ to } 2.9 \text{ times}
\end{aligned}
$$

Clearly, the PEG will exceed this level if anticipated abnormal earnings are positive, and fall short if abnormal earnings are negative. Notice that a PEG of 2.0 does not, in this case, mean that the firm is "overvalued."

Near-Term Growth Rates Complicate the PEG

Long-term growth rates are notoriously difficult to estimate and cannot vary much from the underlying economic growth, at least for more mature companies. To avoid such estimation difficulties, the PEG ratio is often calculated with near-term growth estimates, especially with newer, faster growing companies. In this case, the value of PEG will depend on the expected number of years of profitable growth. For example, consider a firm with a 20 percent return on equity (ROE) and an earnings retention rate of 85 percent. Assuming no external financing, the company can grow at a sustainable rate of 17 percent (85 percent * 20 percent). A firm with a 20 percent ROE might very well have a beta of greater than 1.00, so for the sake of argument we assume a 1.10 beta, producing about a 9.2 percent cost of equity:

$$
\begin{aligned}
k &= \text{risk-free rate} + \beta * \text{market premium} \\
&= (6.00\% - 1.25\%) + 1.10 * (4.00\%) \\
&= 9.2\%
\end{aligned}
$$

This company clearly generates a substantial 10.8 percent excess return (20 percent − 9.2 percent), and, with its 17 percent sustainable growth rate, should support a fairly robust P/E. However, the PEG ratio is reduced by the high expected growth rate and varies from 0.7 to 2.9 times, assuming between 1 and 20 years of profitable growth. The predicted P/E itself falls between 11.9 times and 49.6 times over the same period. (See Figure 17–4.)

FIGURE 17–4

When calculated with near-term growth, the PEG ratio is a function of the expected number of future profitable years.

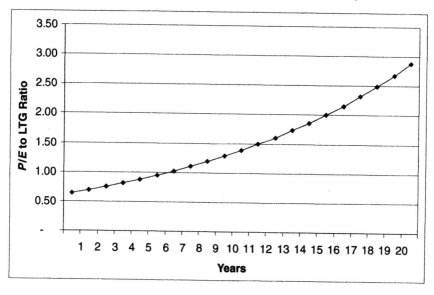

Interestingly, the PEG remains below 1.0 for about 5 years in this example. Even for our profitable and rapidly growing hypothetical firm, strong competitive forces, capable of eliminating abnormal profit within 5 years, will push PEG below 1.0. If the firm carried a P/E multiple between 20 and 30 times, about where the S&P average P/E lies at this writing, its PEG is 1.2 to 1.8 times, below the 1.9 to 2.9 equilibrium range but in excess of the 1.0 times rule of thumb. In this example, 20 to 30 times the P/E multiple is equivalent to about 8 to 13 years of profitable growth, qualifying our hypothetical example as a "great company" under the GCW rules of Chapter 14. Nevertheless, in neither the high- nor the low-growth case is the company misvalued, in spite of the divergence of PEG from 1.0. In this example, PEG equals 1.0 at around 6 years of profitable growth, corresponding to P/Es between 16 and 18 times.

As a measure of relative value, the PEG ratio suffers from the same ambiguities as the P/E multiple itself:

■ Even within an industry, companies may show wide variations in the level and sustainability of abnormal earnings, potentially obscuring any obvious pattern in both the P/E and PEG multiples.

■ The PEG ratio is a function of the rate of growth g itself and will vary with companies' growth rates. Using a PEG industry average as a valuation yardstick will be flawed if these variations are substantial.

■ As with any relative valuation method, variations in risk can impact capital costs and obscure valuation patterns. The use of "comparable companies" in relative valuation is intended to mitigate this problem but, of course, not eliminate it. The PEG ratio is subject to the same uncertainties.

P/E AND THE FRANCHISE FACTOR

A rearrangement of Equation 17.3 offers another revealing view of the P/E ratio as a function of the firm's growth opportunities and its "franchise factor."[2]

$$\frac{P_0}{E_1} = \left(\frac{1}{k}\right) + \frac{(AE_1/E_1)}{(k-g)} - \frac{(AE_1/E_1)}{k}$$

$$= \frac{1}{k} + \frac{g}{(k-g)} * \frac{AE_1}{k * E_1} \qquad (17.3)$$

Notice that the term $(AE_1)/(k * E_1)$ can be rewritten as:

$$\frac{(AE_1)}{(k * E_1)} = \frac{(ROE_1 - k) * BV_0}{(k * E_1)}$$

$$= \frac{(ROE_1 - k)}{(k * ROE_1)}$$

So Equation 17.3 takes the form of Equation 17.14.

$$\frac{P_0}{E_1} = \left(\frac{1}{k}\right) + \frac{g}{(k-g)} * \frac{(AE_1)}{(k * E_1)}$$

$$= \frac{1}{k} + \frac{g}{(k-g)} * \frac{(ROE_1 - k)}{k * ROE_1} \qquad (17.14)$$

In Equation 17.14, the P/E ratio is a combination of three factors:

- A base P/E equal to $1/k$,
- The present value of growth opportunities, $g/(k - g)$, and
- The franchise factor, $(\text{ROE}_1 - k)/(k * \text{ROE}_1)$

We know from earlier in the chapter that, in the absence of abnormal earnings, the P/E multiple will not exceed $1/k$. But Equation 17.14 adds another twist to the P/E story. The factors that raise P/E above its base depend upon both the presence of future growth/investment opportunities and the company's ability to achieve a competitive advantage.

The growth factor $g/(k - g)$ is a measure, in present value terms, of the impact of future growth/investment opportunities. The franchise factor $(\text{ROE}_1 - k)/(k * \text{ROE}_1)$, on the other hand, measures the impact on P/E of the firm's competitive advantage, its ability to generate above average returns on investment.

So, when considering whether a stock deserves a premium P/E multiple, we are led back to the fundamental questions raised by competitive and strategic analysis. Does the firm have opportunities to invest, and therefore to grow, profitably? Can the firm create a competitive advantage over its rivals? The franchise factor formulation does not, however, address the critical third fundamental analytic question, how long can the firm sustain its competitive advantage? To answer that question, the hybrid valuation techniques of Chapter 16 are more useful.

NOTES

[1] Financial theory calls for the use of long-term, not sustainable, growth as the P/E companion variable. Perhaps, then, the failure of sustainable growth, probably a much higher number, to explain the variation of P/E in Chapter 15 is understandable. But long-term growth itself is another problem with the P/E ratio. Long-term growth rates are notoriously difficult, if not actually impossible, to predict accurately. Further, small errors in the estimates can result in large valuation differences, likely contributing to the absence of discernible patterns in P/E versus long-term growth plots.

[2] This discussion is drawn principally from Robert A. Taggart, Jr., *Quantitative Analysis for Investment Management,* Prentice Hall, Englewood Cliffs, N.J., 1996, pp. 59–69.

CHAPTER 18

Valuation of Speculative Stocks

- Speculative stocks are defined here as those for which a substantial portion of the value is based, in the words of Graham and Dodd, "on projection, conjecture, extrapolation, hopes, and even dreams,"[1] not on any significant historical record.

- Relative valuation methods, which measure the value relationship among a group of speculative comparable stocks, can be useful. However, as in all relative valuations, the method leaves disturbingly open the major issue of the absolute valuation of the group itself. That is, even if individual stocks seem rightly valued versus their peers, the group itself may be grossly misvalued.

- In speculative situations, it should be possible to discover the performance expectations inherent in the stock's valuation, even in the absence of current earnings or cash flow. It is then the analyst's task to judge whether these expectations seem reasonable. As always, analysts must inevitably return to the basics of the competitive process, which no amount of analytic sophistication seems to replace.

- It is not within the scope of this book to resolve the difficult issue of stock market efficiency, if indeed it can be resolved within the current financial theoretical framework. Nevertheless, it may very well be that speculative stocks, in particular, spend substantial periods of time far from their "fair value." In this case, the pressures of supply and demand may outweigh, at least temporarily, fundamental financial expectations, a situation that cannot, by definition, occur in efficient markets.

In an efficient stock market, it is not possible for supply and demand forces to systematically cause stocks to deviate from their fair values. Prices in an efficient market can certainly differ from fair value, but such differences are random and short lived. This is because there is always enough competitive arbitrage to rapidly correct price imbalances. But suppose conditions, such as a strong market trend or the absence of borrowable stock, interfere with the market's natural competitive forces. Speculative stocks especially, for which there are already substantial uncertainties about future financial performance, might then depart from "fair value" by large amounts, and for long periods. Traditional financial theory does require that arbitrage adjust for stock mispricing, but how quickly? The boom-and-bust behavior of the technology-driven Nasdaq market from 1998 to 2000 suggests, to me at least, that price imbalances may be persistent.

In speculative stocks, of course, the issue of fair value itself is problematic. New, rapidly growing companies often have no current earnings. Assessment of sales and margin prospects may make prediction of future cash flows highly uncertain. So how is it possible to say anything useful about the price of speculative issues? One possibility is relative valuation techniques. Although they leave aside the absolute value question, relative techniques offer some possibility of identifying *outliers,* those stocks that seem over- or undervalued relative to their peers.

But these relative techniques will not be persuasive to investors who, regardless of the relative valuations within the group, have no confidence in the group's collective value. For example, relative techniques may suggest that Company *X*'s 100 times *P/E* ratio should more appropriately be 75 times. These techniques have nothing to say about the appropriateness of the 75 to 100 *P/E* range itself.

Although it may not be possible to reliably place a fair value on speculative issues through traditional valuation techniques, it should be possible, by using those same techniques, to extract the market's own performance expectations built into the stock's price. Then it is the analyst's task, based on his or her knowledge of the firm's products, markets, competition, and management, to form judgments about the reasonableness of those expectations. This technique reverses the usual analytic process, which first forms expectations of future performance upon which a valuation is built. Nevertheless, turning the analytic process on its head has advantages:

- It is "real." A stock's price is its price. It does not involve the formulation of what may, to an investor, seem like unrealistic performance expectations (either too optimistic or too pessimistic).
- Historical experience can be used. Perhaps not the experience of the company being valued, which may have no experience, but that of other companies and markets further along in their development.
- The investor can specify his or her own return expectations, another "real" number, not the result of theoretical musings.

In the end, of course, these techniques will not tell the analyst what the stock is "really" worth. But with future potential and return expectations placed within the analyst's comfort zone, the technique can tell the analyst what the stock is not worth, and that can be just as valuable a piece of information.

REVERSE ENGINEERING SPECULATIVE STOCKS

Beginning, as always, with the dividend discount model (DDM), we assume that because of current rapid growth and investment, a company is not expected to pay dividends until after time T:

$$
\begin{aligned}
\text{Value of equity}_0 &= \sum_{i=1}^{\infty} \frac{(\text{dividend})_i}{(1 + k)^i} \\
&= \sum_{i=T+1}^{\infty} \frac{(\text{dividend})_i}{(1 + k)^i} \\
&= \frac{\text{value of equity}_T}{(1 + k)^T} \qquad (18.1)
\end{aligned}
$$

where k is the cost of equity. Equation 18.1 simply says that, in the absence of dividends for the first T periods, the value of the company at time 0 equals the value at time T, discounted over the intervening T periods.

Without current earnings or cash flow, valuations of speculative stocks are often expressed with other "metrics" such as book value, sales, physical volume, number of customers, number of installed units, or growth. Equation 18.1 should provide a means to tie current valuations, expressed in an appropriate metric, to the future financial performance of the company. For example, our company may have no current earnings prospects, but it does have current and expected future sales, permitting us to form a price/sales ratio:

$$\text{Value}_0 = \frac{\text{value}_T}{(1 + k)^T}$$

$$\frac{\text{Value}_0}{\text{Sales}_1} = \left(\frac{\text{value}_T/\text{sales}_1}{(1 + k)^T}\right) \tag{18.2}$$

But $\text{sales}_{T+1} = \text{sales}_1 * (1 + g)^T$, where g is the expected average sales growth rate through time T. Let's again make the substitution of the stock's price for its value. Substituting into Equation 18.2:

$$\frac{\text{Price}_0}{\text{Sales}_1} = \frac{(\text{Price}_T/\text{Sales}_{T+1}) * (1 + g)^T}{(1 + k)^T} \tag{18.3}$$

Equation (18.3) ties the current price/sales multiple of the company to a future price/sales multiple. But, suppose further that, by time T, the company is able to generate earnings E_{T+1}. It should be possible to frame the company's future performance in more comfortable price/earnings ratio terms. Equation 18.4 is a simple identity created by simultaneously multiplying and dividing by E_{T+1}:

$$\left(\frac{\text{Price}_T}{\text{Sales}_{T+1}}\right) = \left(\frac{\text{Price}_T}{E_{T+1}}\right) * \left(\frac{E_{T+1}}{S_{T+1}}\right) \tag{18.4}$$

Substituting into Equation 18.3:

$$\frac{\text{Price}_0}{\text{Sales}_1} = \left(\frac{\text{Price}_T}{E_{T+1}}\right) * \left(\frac{E_{T+1}}{S_{T+1}}\right) * \frac{(1 + g)^T}{(1 + k)^T} \tag{18.5}$$

Notice that the term $(E_{T+1}/\text{Sales}_{T+1})$ is simply the company's net margin on sales at time $T + 1$:

$$\frac{\text{Price}_0}{\text{Sales}_1} = \left(\frac{\text{Price}_T}{E_{T+1}}\right) * \frac{\text{Net margin}_{T+1} * (1 + g)^T}{(1 + k)^T} \tag{18.6}$$

AMAZON.COM

On September 2, 1999, the Amazon.com (AMZN) price/sales ratio was about 5.6 times, based on an expected next 12 months' sales of $1.7 billion, a share price of $58.81, and 161.4 million shares outstanding:

$$\frac{\text{Price}_0}{\text{Sales}_1} = \frac{(\$58.81)}{(\$1.7 \text{ billion}/161.4 \text{ million shares})} = 5.6 \text{ times}$$

The question is, with what sort of future financial performance is such a valuation consistent? To answer that question, Equation 18.6 requires four variables: a time T at which AMZN produces expected profits, a future P/E expectation, a projected net margin on sales, and the intervening sales growth rate.

Net Margin

In what range will AMZN's net margin on sales ultimately settle? Hard to say, given the range of potential profit margins displayed by successful marketing firms at the time, as shown in Table 18–1.

As a compromise position, we choose 5 percent as the company's future net margin. The higher the projected net margin, the higher the justifiable current price/sales ratio.

P/E Multiple

Valuations of technology stocks in late 1999 remained relatively high, as data from the September 1999 issue of *Upside* magazine indicate, and as shown in Table 18–2. At the same time, P/E multiples for retailers were somewhat lower, as shown in Table 18–3. Again, as a compromise, we choose a future P/E multiple of 50 times. As with the net margin,

TABLE 18–1

Technology companies show wide variation in net margin.

	Net Margin
Quality mass retailers (Home Depot, Wal-Mart)	3–4%
PC manufacturers (Dell, Gateway, and Apple)	5–8%
The Gap	8–9 %
Networking companies (Cisco, Oracle)	14–18%
Intel	24–25%
Microsoft	40–41%

Source: Recent company financial reports.

TABLE 18–2

Technology *P/E* multiples also vary widely.

	Average *P/E*
Wired networks (Nextel, Vodafone)	28
Computer systems (Dell, Gateway)	46
Software (Microsoft, Oracle)	72
Content (3DO, Electronic Arts)	98
Semiconductors (Applied Materials)	114

Source: Upside Magazine.

TABLE 18–3

Retailer's *P/E* multiples vary somewhat less than those of technology companies.

	P/E Multiples
Borders	12
Barnes & Noble	24
The Gap	34
Wal-Mart	48
Home Depot	54

the higher the projected future multiple place upon earnings, the higher the justifiable current stock price.

THE CALCULATION

To complete our inputs, we choose three years as the onset of profitability in AMZN. Substituting these data into Equation 18.6:

$$50 * 5.0\% * \frac{(1 + g)^3}{(1 + k)^3} = 5.6 \tag{18.7}$$

Equation 18.7 still contains two unknowns, the sales growth rate *g* and the required rate of return k. If we choose to specify k, then the required growth rate for AMZN can be forced out:

$$(1 + g)^3 = \left[\frac{5.6}{(50 * 5.0\%)} \right] * (1 + k)^3 \qquad (18.8)$$

Suppose we choose a required rate of return over the three years of between 15 and 50 percent. The 15 percent return may seem low—especially at the time, but we include it to test a potential lower end of AMZN future performance.

Solving Equation 18.8 for g, assuming k of 15, 30, 40, and 50 percent, permits specification of the required AMZN financial performance in 2003, the year of assumed profit onset, as shown in Table 18–4.

In the third quarter of 1999, AMZN posted a loss of $0.26 per share, or $1.04 annualized. In order for investors to earn annual returns between 15 and 50 percent, AMZN must generate between $1.79 and $3.98 in EPS by 2003, valued at a 50 P/E. Sales growth must average between 50 and 97 percent over the three-year period. For the top 50 percent return, AMZN must have reached a price of $199 by 2002 year end. At this writing (in early 2001), AMZN stood at $18¹⁵⁄₁₆. Its last reported quarterly EPS (September 2000) was a $0.25 loss.

Was AMZN too expensive in September 1999? Or was it fairly valued? Or perhaps even undervalued? The reverse technique demonstrated here permits these questions to be clarified and restated. The

TABLE 18–4

AMZN's required future financial performance varies with the investor's desired rate of return.

$k =$	15%	30%	40%	50%
$(1 + g)^3$	3.4	4.9	6.2	7.6
Annual sales growth, g	50%	70	84	97%
Sales ($ billion)	5.8	8.4	10.4	12.9
Earnings ($ million)	290	418	522	643
EPS	$1.79	2.59	3.23	$3.98
Share price 2002	$90	130	162	$199

question really is, does the financial performance embedded in the current AMZN price seem attainable, given the investor's return expectations for the stock? Earnings turnarounds of the type shown here may seem unreasonable to some, understated to others.

Sustained sales growth rates north of 50 percent may seem fanciful, even for high-growing technology companies. But lest high performance seem outrageous, consider once again Dell Computer, our running example for modeling and valuation.

DELL COMPUTER

In early September 1999, Dell Computer (DELL) stood at $40.19 with a prospective price/sales ratio of about 3.40 times. Sales growth since 1995 averaged about 50 percent annually. Knowing this, what would you have paid for Dell in 1995?

Turning to Equation 18.6, the P/S ratio in late 1994 is fully specified, once we insert our return expectations:

$$\frac{P}{S_{1995}} = 3.4 * \left[\frac{(1 + 0.50)^4}{(1 + k)^4} \right] \tag{18.9}$$

Let's again consider a 15 percent to 50 percent range of required returns. Estimating that 1995 Dell sales per share were about $2.00, Equation 18.9 provides a range of potential prices, as shown in Table 18–5.

To earn a very respectable 50 percent annual return for four years, an investor could have paid as much as $7 for a Dell share at year-end 1995. But adjusted for splits in September 1998 and March 1999, Dell's actual September 1994 share price was about $0.60![2]

The Dell example, surprising as it is, only emphasizes a basic truth about speculative stocks: The uncertainties about future financial performance are very high.

TABLE 18–5

To earn returns of 15 to 50 percent, investors should have purchased Dell at $8 to $23 per share in 1995.

$k =$	15%	30%	40%	50%
P/S_{1995}	9.8	6.0	4.5	3.4
Share price	$20.00	$12.00	$9.00	$7.00

RELATIVE VALUATION TECHNIQUES FALTER

Relative valuation techniques are driven by companion variables, pairs consisting of a valuation measure and a financial performance measure (Table 18–6). The problem with many speculative stocks is that often one member of the pair is missing.

Companies with no current or near-term projected future earnings have no ROE or net margin. The P/E multiple, relying as it does on long-term earnings growth and abnormal earnings performance, is unlikely to bear a simple relationship to earnings growth, even if the comparable group of stocks does have earnings. In speculative stocks, P/E is even less helpful.

Perhaps a mix-and-match strategy, using a valuation measure with any available companion variable (not its own), might gain us some ground. Unfortunately, as illustrated in Figure 18–1 of 10 Internet stocks in early September 1999, the results are less than satisfactory. The graph matches a price/sales ratio with First Call growth estimates.

Price/sales shows a general increase with earnings growth estimates but not a consistent rise, with some serious outliers like Yahoo and Amazon.com. I would be reluctant to assume that any pattern at all exists in the data. This is not surprising since the method has no sound theoretical base.

ANOTHER RULE OF THUMB: HOPE SPRINGS ETERNAL

Rules of thumb for the valuation of speculative stocks are also problematic. The difficulties with the PEG ratio should now be apparent from Chapter 17's discussion. The PEG is unstable, varying with life cycle development of the company and its remaining years of profitable

TABLE 18-6

Relative valuation methods often rely on companion variables containing earnings estimates.

Valuation Measure	Companion Variable
P/E multiple	Earnings growth
P/BV multiple	Return on equity
P/S multiple	Net margin on sales

FIGURE 18-1

A *P/E*-growth valuation of Internet stocks in September 1999 shows some pattern, but with significant outliers like AMZN.

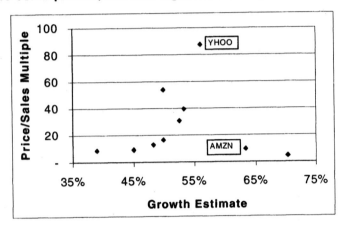

growth. Another related rule, a derivative of some of the analysis in this chapter, also presents difficulties:

$$\frac{\text{Price}}{\text{Sales}} = \text{growth rate} * \text{net margin} \qquad (18.10)$$

The correct relationship between the price/sales multiple and the net margin on sales is given in Equation 18.6:

$$\frac{\text{Price}_0}{\text{Sales}_1} = \left(\frac{\text{Price}_T}{E_{T+1}}\right) * \text{net margin}_{T+1} * \frac{(1 + g)^T}{(1 + k)^T}$$

For the rule in Equation 18.10 to work, a couple of fortunate circumstances must be present:

- The *P/E* ratio must be roughly equal to the growth rate used. This is, of course, possible (and it is often assumed to be so), as demonstrated in Chapter 17, but it is certainly not required. Stated another way, if the stock's *P/E* is greater than the growth rate used, the rule of thumb will produce a *P/S* ratio that is too low, perhaps leading to the conclusion that the stock is overvalued.

- The growth rate g and the required return k must also be roughly the same. This also may be true, but maybe not. If required returns exceed the sales growth rate, then the formula will specify a P/S multiple that is too high, leading to the erroneous conclusion that the stock is undervalued.

- The growth rate g necessary for the formula to work is of course the sales, not the earnings, growth. To the extent that they differ, use of an earnings growth rate—the one most often specified in consensus forecasts, for example—could also result in errors in the rule-of-thumb use.

HIGH GROWTH STOCKS: THE SIEGEL CALCULATOR

The Siegel Calculator, a valuation technique suggested by the recent writings of Professor Jeremy Siegel of the Wharton School, provides a check on the reasonableness of high valuation multiples without resorting to rules of thumb.[3] Consider a company, for example, which produces an expected 50 percent near-term earnings growth. Using the PEG rule, investors might apply a 50.0 P/E multiple to the company's trailing $1.00 EPS and pay $50.00 for the stock. The question is, how long must the company sustain the 50 percent growth track to justify the $50 stock price? Just how much pressure have we placed on future performance by paying 50 times earnings? Assuming a 15 percent discount rate, a 20.0 P/E exit multiple, no dividends, and up to 7 years of 50 percent growth, the Siegel Calculator suggests an answer. The notion behind the 20 times exit multiple is that, when its extraordinary growth spurt ends, the company's multiple returns to a more typical market level.

If, in fact, the company's 50 percent growth regime continues for only 3 years, at the end of which its P/E falls to 20 times, then the PEG price of $50 is too high (Table 18.7). The company is worth only about $44. On the other hand, with a 5-year growth horizon, $50 looks like an excellent price. In the 5-year scenario, investors could expect to see analysts' 12-month target prices north of $86. The striking aspect of these results is the stock's high sensitivity to the assumed growth horizon. Extending the growth horizon only two years makes the difference between a disappointing investment and a home run. With a 7-year growth horizon, investors might even have paid 100 times current earnings and still expected almost a 50 percent return (given the $147.73 target price)

TABLE 18.7

If 50 percent growth continues for 3 years or less, the stock is
overpriced at $50.

Growth Horizon	3 years	5 years	7 years
Current stock value	$44.38	75.51	$128.46
12-month target price	$51.04	86.84	$147.73

TABLE 18–8

The Siegel Calculator format reveals the impact of changing
growth horizons.

Year	Growth	Earnings	P/E	Stock Price
0		$1.00	50.0	$50.00
1	50%	1.50		
2	50%	2.25		
3	50%	3.38	20.0	$67.50
4	50%	5.06		
5	50%	7.59	20.0	$151.88
6	50%	11.39		
7	50%	$17.09	20.0	$341.72

over 12 months. With a 3-year horizon and a $100 stock price, however,
investors might justifiably fear about a 50 percent drop in the stock over
12 months.

A 3-year horizon doesn't seem unreasonable, but does 7 years of
50 percent growth make sense? Maybe, but it is likely to be quite a rare
performance. Assuming high flyers eventually return to earth, a P/E
multiple 50 times or more places extraordinary (perhaps unrealistic) demands on future financial performance, regardless of the near-term
growth outlook.

Although I've argued that absolute valuation rules of thumb do not
exist, the Siegel Calculator comes close. If 7 years of sustained, extraordinary growth is rare, the Calculator places a reasonable upper limit on
P/E, given a near-term growth outlook, a discount rate, and an exit multiple (Table 18–8). In the current case, for example, even paying 50 times

trailing earnings for 50 percent near-term growth is risky, and paying more than that may be foolish.

NOTES

[1] Sidney Cottle, Roger F. Murray, and Frank E. Block, *Graham and Dodd's Security Analysis,* 5th ed., McGraw-Hill, New York, 1988, p. 545.

[2] Yahoo.finance.com.

[3] See, for example, Jeremy J. Sigel, "Big-Cap Tech Stocks Are a Sucker Bet," *The Wall Street Journal,* March 14, 1998.

CHAPTER 19

Equity Analysis and Business Combinations

- No other corporate event demands higher analytic skepticism than a merger and acquisition (M&A) transaction.
- Research evidence suggests that mergers and acquisitions transactions do not on average create value for the acquiring company's shareholders.[1]
- In the absence of value creation, other considerations, such as the maintenance of competitive parity through scale or the use of free-cash flow, may drive deals.[2]
- Synergies common among bidders in an M&A auction, such as the reduction of duplicative overhead expenses, are unlikely to create value for the winner. This is because the auction price is likely to rise to include the common value of those synergies. To create value, the winning bidder must have synergies that are rare and costly for competitors to duplicate.[3]
- Earnings accretion and dilution, a much-watched M&A indicator, is a function, among other things, of the comparative price/earnings ratios of the target and acquiring firm.
- The criteria for the accretion of shareholder value and earnings accretion in the acquiring firm are not the same.

Given the stock market's tremendous interest in M&A, one would like to believe that M&A are viable managerial tools for the creation of shareholder value in the acquiring company. Sadly, it appears it is not. Most transactions seem to leave the bulk of the value of potential synergies in the selling shareholder's hands. Acquirers appear to systematically underestimate the difficulty of realizing synergies in highly competitive production and labor markets, pay too high a purchase premium, and then fail to realize expected returns—regardless of how smoothly the "transition" is managed. Nevertheless, M&A can preserve competitive parity in consolidating industries, where survival, rather than value addition, is the principal issue. Finally, earnings accretion seems to have little to do with the addition of shareholder value. Analysts should approach M&A transactions with substantial skepticism.

THE UNFORTUNATE VALUE STORY

Making an M&A deal work is much harder than successfully blending two, often distinct, corporate cultures, although that is certainly hard enough.[4] The acquiring company must first meet performance expectations contained in the predeal price of its stock and in the stock of the target company. Then management must achieve the efficiencies necessary to justify any premium paid over the target's predeal price. But these efficiencies may still not be enough because the more common synergies, like administrative and overhead savings, are often shared by other bidders for the target company and incorporated into the purchase price. True value-adding synergies, which must be uncommon and costly to duplicate, are rare in competitive industries (that's why these industries are competitive). And finally, to gain the opportunity to do all this, the acquirer must pay up front.

Digging a Hole with the Purchase Premium

As Sirower[5] makes painfully clear, a substantial purchase premium in an M&A deal can dig a very deep value hole, placing pressure on the post-acquisition performance of the combined entity. The dilemma is illustrated well by the abnormal earnings value formulation. There exists some AE level that can justify the price P_{post} paid for a target company's stock:

$$P_{post} = BV + \sum_{i=1}^{\infty} \frac{AE_i}{(1 + k)^i} \qquad (19.1)$$

where BV is the book value of equity, AE_i the postacquisition abnormal earnings, and k the cost of equity of the target company. Postacquisition abnormal earnings should equal the sum of the target's expected preacquisition earnings and any additional earnings anticipated as a result of the acquisition:

$$AE_i = AE_i(\text{preacq}) + AE_i(\text{incremental}) \qquad (19.2)$$

So Equation 19.1 becomes

$$P_{\text{post}} = BV + \sum_{i=1}^{\infty} \frac{AE_i(\text{preacq})}{(1 + k)^i}$$

$$+ \sum_{i=1}^{\infty} \frac{AE_i(\text{incremental})}{(1 + k)^i} \qquad (19.3)$$

The preacquisition abnormal earnings AE_i (preacq) already contain the market's growth and profitability expectations for the target company. The transaction must therefore, at least, preserve the target company's existing performance outlook before relying on incremental earnings AE_i (incremental), which are the deal's "synergies." Note that the first two terms of Equation 19.3 equal the target company's preacquisition stock price P_{pre}:

$$P_{\text{post}} = P_{\text{pre}} + \sum_{i=1}^{\infty} \frac{AE_i(\text{incremental})}{(1 + k)^i} \qquad (19.4)$$

Some of the earnings improvements AE_i (incremental) could be generated within the acquiring company. For example, the target company may provide expanded distribution channels for the acquirer's products, generating increased acquirer sales. This fact does not fundamentally alter the analysis. By simultaneously subtracting and dividing by P_{pre} on both sides of Equation 19.3, the expression can be reduced to

$$\left(\frac{P_{\text{post}} - P_{\text{pre}}}{P_{\text{pre}}} \right) = \left[\frac{RPI}{P_{\text{pre}}} \right] * \sum_{i=1}^{\infty} \frac{1}{(1 + k)^i} \qquad (19.5)$$

where RPI is the required performance improvement, AE_i (incremental), assuming equal annual improvements:

$$RPI = AE_i \text{ (incremental)} \qquad (19.6)$$

The left side of Equation 19.5 is simply the percentage premium paid over the preacquisition price of the target company:

$$\% \text{ acquisition premium} = \frac{(P_{\text{post}} - P_{\text{pre}})}{P_{\text{pre}}} \qquad (19.7)$$

Rearranging Equation 19.5 and assuming an N year planning horizon (synergies are expected to be produced for N years, beginning in year 1):

$$\frac{RPI}{P_{pre}} = \frac{\% \text{ acquisition premium}}{\displaystyle\sum_{i=1}^{N} \frac{1}{(1+k)^i}} \qquad (19.8)$$

Why limit the duration of synergies to N years? Because competition catches on quickly, and very likely it will not suffer supernormal earnings to continue indefinitely. Performance improvements are measured a percentage of the target's preacquisition stock price.

Figure 19–1 illustrates the performance improvement necessary to justify purchase premiums of 25, 35, 50, and 75 percent if profitability improvements last for up to seven years, beginning in the first year and assuming a 10 percent cost of equity. For example, a 50 percent purchase premium requires a 13 percent performance improvement each year if improvements last for five years. And this is just to break even and earn back the cost of capital! To earn excess returns, performance improvements must be even greater.

To recognize the difficulty of achieving full incremental earnings in the first year of the combination, i can be set to successively higher years. For example, calculating Equation 19.8 for $i = 2$ through N means that incremental earnings begin only in the second year of the combination and continue until year N.

In Figure 19–2, N equals 7 years and needed improvements are illustrated for beginning years up to 5. Surprisingly large improvements

FIGURE 19–1

Required performance improvement rises sharply with the premium paid in mergers and acquisitions transactions.

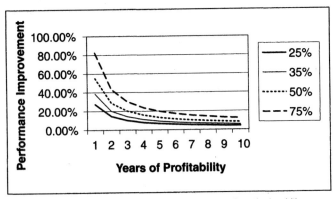

FIGURE 19-2

If performance improvements are delayed by one to five years, substantially larger subsequent improvements are necessary.

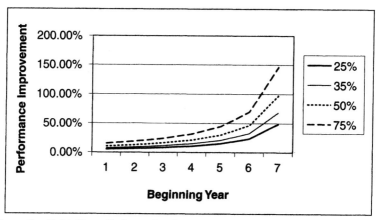

Source: From Mark L. Sirower, *The Synergy Trap: How Companies Lose the Acquisition Game.* Copyright © 1997 by Mark L. Sirower. Reprinted with the permission of The Free Press, a Division of Simon & Schuster, Inc.

(as a percentage of the target's preacquisition stock price) are needed for a variety of acquisition premiums and starting years, again assuming a 10 percent cost of equity.

A 35 Percent Purchase Premium

For example, a transaction completed at a 35 percent premium to the target company's predeal stock price, where synergies begin in year 1 and persist for five years, requires about a 9 percent performance improvement. Now, 9 percent may not seem like a lot, but consider the level of abnormal earnings necessary to produce such an upside. In Equation 19.8:

$$RPI = (ROE - k) * BV \qquad (19.9)$$

The required performance improvement equals the target company's book value times the difference between return on equity ROE and the cost of equity k. ROE in this case is the return associated with the synergies produced by the acquisition. Rearranging Equation 19.9 assuming the 9 percent improvement, the required spread between ROE and k is revealed:

$$\frac{(\text{ROE} - k) * \text{BV}}{P_{\text{pre}}} = 9\%$$

$$\text{(19.10)}$$

$$\text{ROE} - k = \frac{9\% * P_{\text{pre}}}{\text{BV}}$$

If, for example, the target company's preacquisition P/BV multiple were 3.0 times, Equation 19.20 implies that the deal's synergies must produce returns 27 percentage points *in excess of equity costs*, or roughly 37 percent at the example's 10 percent cost of equity. A 37 percent return on equity is a tall order, and the necessary returns rise rapidly as the purchase premium increases. If improvements do not begin until year 2 (not an unusual circumstance), the required ROE jumps to 46 percent (3.0 * 12.1 percent + 10 percent).

Competition and Synergies

If acquisition premiums dig acquiring companies into a financial hole, synergies must dig them out. Unfortunately, synergies are often not equal to the task.

As Equation 19.3 points out, before synergies can provide any help, acquirers must preserve the preacquisition values already built into the target company's stock (assuming, of course, that the acquisition premium was positive). At the same time, they must preserve the predeal values built into their own stocks. Managers therefore need to run harder to achieve hoped-for synergies and competitive advantage, while taking care that none of these efforts undermine the existing performance of either company. This process is like driving a car down the highway, accelerating to 100 miles per hour while tinkering with the engine.[6]

Even if successful at preserving existing values, the synergies built into the purchase price need to be achieved. In competitive M&A markets, however, available synergies are likely to be more limited than acquirers realize[7]:

- In an arguably efficient stock market, exploiting "undervalued" target companies may be difficult, even if acquirers were able to correctly value their targets, because of the potential for competing bids.
- Finding operational synergies in efficient production markets is likely to be difficult. Competition should have forced

exploitation of any obvious opportunity for efficiency in the target company.

- Finally, it is not clear that acquirers can profit from "undermanagement." Again, efficient labor markets may have bid away any apparent opportunities.

Even if some synergies survive in imperfectly competitive markets, their value might be incorporated into the target's price, especially in an auction process. Obvious efficiencies, like reduction of administrative expenses and overhead, are broadly achievable and are therefore unlikely to add value for the winning bidder.[8] For a synergy to add value, it must be uncommon among bidders and costly for others to duplicate. The presence of uncommon synergies is the real meaning of "fit" in M&A transactions.

So let's summarize. Before an acquisition can add value to the winning bidder, management must leap a number of hurdles:

- The preacquisition value of the target, which contains the market's expectations (perhaps for above-normal returns) before the deal, must be preserved, while management attempts to exploit available synergies.

- Simultaneously, none of management's actions can be permitted to damage the predeal value of the acquiring company.

- Finally, management must achieve at least those synergies common to other bidders since the final purchase price very likely already reflects these synergies' value. When all this is done, incremental efforts may add value to shareholders.

The Winner's Curse

It may be even worse; successful bidders may suffer from the "winner's curse."[9] First documented in studies of Gulf of Mexico oil drilling rights auctions, winning bidders were consistently disappointed with their returns on investment, even though plenty of oil was found. Strong evidence exists that winnning bidders overpaid for properties, even though they knew (or should have known) better.

Rational markets do not make such errors. It is reasonable for rational bidders to assume that the most optimistic and aggressive bid is likely to win, jeopardizing subsequent investment returns. Knowing this, bidders should lower their bids to adjust for the presence of other bidders. Unfortunately, they don't. Repeated experimental and field data suggest that, although the average bid may actually be lower than the target's value, winning bidders repeatedly overpay. No acquisition synergies are sufficient to compensate the acquirer who overpays.

Given the apparent reality of the winner's curse, Thaler speculates about stock valuations themselves.[10] If the most aggressive and optimistic bidders win, and such bidders systematically overpay, one might expect to see the pattern of return reversal ("reversion to the mean") actually observed in stock prices. Initial returns are high as stocks rise above intrinsic value, and then fall (or actually become negative) as the overpayment takes its toll. Of course, in a rational market, participants would be aware of the winner's curse and would sell/short stocks that are in the process of such overshoot. As described in Chapter 5, the debate on these issues continues.

DEALS HAPPEN ANYWAY

In spite of the evidence, mergers and acquisitions transactions continue to captivate Wall Street. Suppose that on average, M&A deals do not add value to the acquiring shareholders. There may still be reasons to do these deals.[11]

A Matter of Survival

An M&A transaction may not add value, but it still may be worth doing to preserve existing values. For example, in a consolidating industry, participants may grow through acquisition in order to achieve the production efficiencies necessary to stay competitive. Acquirers therefore act to preserve their existing industry position, knowing that deals are unlikely to provide value boosts and to maintain their existing (presumably attractive) returns. Permitting competitors to capture scale or technology from acquired firms could place a firm in permanent secondary industry status or jeopardize its survival. Even if a transaction destroys some value, management may view it as superior to the alternative—to lose all value.

Such an acquisition strategy, unfortunately, may doom acquirers to mediocrity. As companies grow in size without adding value, operations move closer and closer to industry averages. The result is competitive convergence, against which Porter warned at some length in Chapter 4. In an industry in which participants act principally to keep pace or stay a little ahead, superior returns are difficult to achieve.

Analysts should be very wary of consolidating industries, in my view. The very consolidation process may erode the potential for superior long-term returns. Unless one can identify the target firms ahead of the market, available returns to the shareholder may be disappointing. The winner's curse operates again.

Burning a Hole

If a company generates free-cash flow, management may see its duty to invest, even if returns on investment do not exceed capital costs. After all, such a strategy will increase the company's size without harming shareholders, who still receive their required return. Management may well believe such a strategy is superior to returning funds to shareholders, and normal returns don't look so bad anyway. Of course, shareholders may prefer to redeploy returned funds into businesses capable of generating returns in excess of capital costs.

It's All Management's Fault

Then there are the inevitable "agency" problems, in which management acts in its own interests rather than the shareholders'. Management may see clear advantages, for example, in a large, diversified company, even if such diversification does not add value for shareholders (who could have achieved the diversification on their own, perhaps at lower cost). Large companies have lower bankruptcy risks, increasing management's job security. The volatility of a diversified company's earnings and stock may be lower, keeping Wall Street happier, management more secure, and stock options in the money.

Kidding Yourself

Finally, there is my personal favorite explanation for M&A transactions, managerial "hubris." After all, even if M&A deals generate no value on average, no management team thinks it's average. It may see opportunities to exploit the "undermanagement" of the target firm. In many deals, however, management must be very good indeed since they likely paid a premium for the chance to prove their worth, and they paid that premium up front.

Even if the evidence is that undervalued, inefficient, and under-managed target companies are rarely identified and, if identified, cannot be bought at prices low enough, M&A deals are not likely to stop.

EARNINGS ACCRETION AND VALUE ADDITION

Judging the value of an M&A transaction is never easy, but, unfortunately, earnings accretion and dilution, much-watched indicators of deal success, have little to do directly with shareholder value. Accretion results if the acquirer's postacquisition earnings per share (EPS) are greater than the preacquisition EPS. The relationship between pre- and postacquisition EPS is governed largely by the price/earnings ratios of the two companies. Value, on the other hand, is added if incremental postacquisition abnormal earnings exceed those sufficient to compensate for the purchase premium.

Conditions for Earnings Accretion

The acquiring company's EPS accretes if

EPS of the consolidated firm

$$> \text{the acquirer's preacquisition EPS} \quad (19.11)$$

The postacquisition EPS of the consolidated company is a function of the earnings of the two original companies with a number of adjustments. Assume that the transaction is accounted for as a purchase:[12]

$$E_C = E_A + E_T - \text{GWA} - I * (1 - \text{TR}) \pm E_O \quad (19.12)$$

where E_C = prospective earnings of the consolidated company
E_A = prospective earnings of the acquiring company
E_T = prospective earnings of the target company
GWA = annual goodwill amortization (perhaps on its way out)
I = incremental interest expense of the consolidated company (if any)
TR = corporate tax rate of the consolidated company

E_O = earnings effects of fair market value adjustments + cost and revenue synergies − new preferred stock dividends ± other adjustments

E_C must contain any costs associated with net incremental financing taken on to pay for the acquisition. The costs of existing financing are already included in the earnings of the acquiring and target companies. The interest expense I in Equation 19.22 will also include interest income lost because of acquisition cash payments.

The earnings effects E_O of purchase accounting can be complex, and are beyond our scope here. The requirement to record acquired assets at fair value, for example, might have significant subsequent income effects. For example, a target company using the FIFO (first in, first out) method for inventory valuation might carry inventory at low historical costs. A write-up to fair value causes subsequent increases in cost of goods sold and reduces reported earnings. For simplicity, E_{adj} combines all the earnings adjustments in Equation 19.12:

$$E_{adj} = \text{GWA} + I * (1 - \text{TR}) \pm E_o \qquad (19.13)$$

If the combined EPS are not diluted, then it must be true that the combined per share income is at least equal to the preacquisition EPS of the acquirer:

$$\frac{E_C}{(N_A + \Delta N_A)} \geq \frac{E_A}{N_A}$$

$$\frac{(E_A + E_T + E_{adj})}{(N_A + \Delta N_A)} \geq \frac{E_A}{N_A}$$

$$E_A * \left(\frac{\Delta N_A}{N_A}\right) \leq E_T + E_{adj} \qquad (19.14)$$

where N_A = total preacquisition common shares of the acquirer
ΔN_A = incremental common shares issued by the acquirer

For simplicity, assume an all-stock transaction in which the acquiring company issues new stock to purchase the target. The target's purchase price equals its price/earnings multiple (when the price is set) times its prospective earnings E_T. Dividing the purchase price by the stock price of the acquiring company produces the number of new shares it must issue:

$$\text{Purchase price} = \text{PE}_T * E_T \qquad (19.15)$$

$$\Delta N_A = \frac{(\text{PE}_T * E_T)}{P_A} \qquad (19.16)$$

where P_A is the acquirer's stock price and PE_T is the target company's price earnings multiple at the deal price. Substituting Equation 19.16, the expression for ΔN_A into Equation 19.14 yields, after some algebra:

$$\text{PE}_T \le \text{PE}_A * \left[\frac{(E_T + E_{\text{adj}})}{E_T} \right] \qquad (19.17)$$

In purchases where earnings adjustments E_{adj} are small (synergies offset financing costs and goodwill amortization, for example) or in pooling transactions, earnings accrete if the price earnings multiple of the acquiring company exceeds that of the target:

$$\text{PE}_A \ge \text{PE}_T \qquad (19.18)$$

A common criticism of pooling accounting, and perhaps one of the reasons for its probable demise, is that management can manipulate annual earnings per share by mergers with lower-valued companies. At any rate, Equation 19.17 expresses the general conditions under which earnings accretion occurs. The principal drivers are the relative price earnings multiples of the two companies, the earnings of the target, and adjustments to earnings flowing from purchase accounting rules and synergies.

Earnings Accretion with a 35 Percent Price Premium

Following the example above, consider the acquisition of Company T by Company A at a 35 percent price premium with the following values for the principal price and earnings variables:

$$P_T, \text{preacquisition} = \$100$$

$$P_T = \$135$$

$$E_T = \$5$$

$$E_{\text{adj}} = \$1$$

Company T's preacquisition P/E ratio of 20 rises to 27 with the 35 percent purchase premium:

$$\frac{P_T, \text{ preacquisition}}{E_T} = \frac{\$100}{\$5} = 20$$

$$\frac{P_T}{E_T} = \frac{\$135}{\$5} = 27$$

For the deal to be earnings accretive, the inequality in Equation 19.17 must hold:

$$\text{PE}_T \leq \text{PE}_A * \left[\frac{(E_T + E_{\text{adj}})}{E_T}\right]$$

$$27 \leq \text{PE}_A * \left[\frac{(5.00 + 1.00)}{5.00}\right] \tag{19.19}$$

Or expressed in terms of Company A's P/E ratio:

$$\text{PE}_A \geq 22.5$$

Provided Company A's stock sells at a 22.5 P/E or greater, the transaction will be earnings neutral or accretive. The deal may, but need not, meet incremental abnormal earnings or other value conditions.

Conditions for Value Accretion

The critical difference between the conditions for earnings accretion and those for value accretion is that value accretion is not a function of the market valuation of the acquirer. Rather, it is driven by the level of supernormal earnings generated by the deal in excess of those already incorporated into the target's preacquisition price.

A modification of Equation 19.4 expresses the basic value accretion condition. The price paid for the target company cannot exceed the target's preacquisition price plus the present value of incremental supernormal earnings:

$$P \leq P_{\text{pre}} + \sum_{i=1}^{\infty} \frac{\text{AE}_i \text{ (incremental)}}{(1 + k)^i} \tag{19.20}$$

Dividing both sides of Equation 19.19 by E_T, the predeal earnings of the target company, and assuming that equal annual supernormal earnings are generated over an N-year planning horizon, the value accretion condition becomes

$$\mathrm{PE}_T \le \frac{P(\mathrm{preacq})}{E_T} + \left(\frac{\mathrm{AE}}{E_T}\right) * \sum_{i=1}^{N} \frac{1}{(1 + k)^i} \qquad (19.21)$$

The value accretion condition Equation 19.20 is easier to meet as AE— the incremental supernormal earnings generated by the transaction— increases. The condition becomes more difficult to meet as N, the planning horizon, declines and the starting year rises from 1.

The value accretion conditions, presented in Equation 19.21, and the earnings accretion from Equation 19.17 have no apparent connection. Although it is certainly possible that earnings accretion results from a deal in which value is added, it seems equally possible that the opposite is true. Of what use, then, is the earnings accretion calculation, and why does the stock market seem so focused on the answer? Earnings accretion may provide the market clues about value, even if it contains no answers:

- The earnings drag created by financing costs and the amortization of goodwill may provide the market clues about the investment returns of the acquisition. The larger the earnings drag, the higher the target's price relative to earnings, and the lower the potential investment returns. It is those returns, and their relation to capital costs, which actually determine the acquisition's value added.

- The willingness of acquiring management to pay a high price for an acquisition (relative to current earnings) may communicate information to the market about the acquirer's industry view and financial judgment. Substantial earnings dilution, for example, could indicate serious overpayment, or, alternatively, a positive view of the target's longer-term earnings prospects.

- Frequent disruption of earnings patterns by acquisitions could signal a growing complexity in the acquirer's financial statements, making analysis and insight more difficult. Small or slightly accretive earnings effects may reassure the market that the company still remains transparent analytically.

- It is unfortunately true that bad financial news is often followed by more bad financial news. Severe earnings dilution may trigger the market's natural wariness, increasing the company's perceived (if not its true) risk and lowering its stock price.

Value Accretion with a 35 Percent Purchase Premium

The previous example noted that Company A's P/E ratio must exceed 22.5 times if the transaction is to produce earnings accretion in the combined companies. But under what conditions will the acquisition produce incremental *value*? Unlike earnings accretion, the answer depends not on Company A's P/E but on the deal's synergies, the incremental abnormal earnings produced by the transaction, as shown in Equation 19.20.

Like the first example above, we assume that the deal's synergies begin in year 1 and last for 5 years, with a 10 percent cost of capital:

$$i = 1$$

$$N = 5$$

$$k = 10\%$$

Equation 19.20 then reduces to

$$PE_T \leq \frac{P(\text{preacq})}{E_T} + \frac{AE}{E_T} \sum_{i=1}^{N} \frac{1}{(1 + k)i}$$

$$27 \leq 20 + \left(\frac{AE}{\$5}\right) * 3.79$$

$$AE \geq (27 - 20) * \frac{\$5}{3.79}$$

$$AE \geq \$9.23 \tag{19.22}$$

This is a rather astonishing result, given that Company T's preacquisition earnings were only $5.00, but it is perfectly consistent with the roughly 9 percent required performance improvement of the Sirower formula of Equation 9.8:

$$\frac{RPI}{P_{\text{pre}}} = \frac{\$9.23}{\$100} = 9.23\%$$

Whether such a stiff performance improvement requirement can be met in this acquisition is unclear, and it is certainly not obvious from the earnings accretion calculation.

A simple way to fool one's self about the required level of synergy is to assume that incremental abnormal earnings persist indefinitely. Instead of equaling 3.79, then, the summation term in Equation 19.20 actually reaches 10.00, with $k = 10$ percent:

$$\sum_{i=1.00}^{\infty} \frac{1.00}{(1.00 + 0.10)^i} = 10.00$$

Under these conditions, the required performance improvement in the Company A–Company C transaction falls from \$9.23 to \$3.50, an apparently more manageable number.

$$AE \geq (27 - 20) * \frac{\$5}{10.0}$$

$$AE \geq \$3.50$$

But remember, AE is not reported incremental earnings but earnings in excess of capital costs, making even the perpetual synergy case seem much less jolly.

NOTES

[1] See, for example, Richard H. Thaler, *The Winners' Curse: Paradoxes and Anomalies of Economic Life,* Princeton University Press, Princeton, N.J., 1992, p. 59; Jay B. Barney, *Gaining and Sustaining Competitive Advantage,* Addison-Wesley Publishing Company, Reading, Mass., 1997, pp. 437–473; or Mark L. Sirower, *The Synergy Trap,* The Free Press, New York, 1997.

[2] Barney, *Competitive Advantage,* pp. 448–452.

[3] Ibid., p. 452. Barney applies the VRIO method to the analysis of mergers and acquisitions.

[4] The material in this section is drawn from Sirower, *Synergy Trap.*

[5] Ibid.

[6] Ibid., p. 36.

[7] Thaler, *Winners' Curse,* p. 59.

[8] Barney, *Competitive Advantage,* p. 459.

[9] Thaler, *Winners' Curse,* pp. 50–62.

[10] Ibid., footnote 9 on p. 60.

[11] Barney, *Competitive Advantage,* pp. 448–452.

[12] As mentioned in Chapter 2, at this writing, the Financial Accounting Standards Board has issued no final standard for accounting for business combinations and goodwill.

PART FIVE

Getting It Down on Paper

CHAPTER 20

Financial Writing: Don't Bury the Lead

- Don't bury the lead! Financial writing has far more in common with journalism than with scientific writing. Conclusions always come first.

- Financial analytic reports need five sections: recommendation and summary, earnings forecast, valuation, elaboration, and detail. This is a law of nature. The order is important. You can reverse the earnings and valuation, but the recommendation always comes first, and the detail last.

- Financial writing is persuasion, not description. All components of the report are driven by the investment argument. Always ask, does this material contribute meaningfully to the argument? If not, take it out. If you can't bear its loss, put in an appendix.

- Give the reader a break. Don't make him or her dig for conclusions or critical information. The harder you make it on the reader, the less likely he or she is to read your work.

- Analysts should commit the *Elements of Style*[1] to memory, literally. In general, analytic writing should be in the active voice; contain mostly positive, concrete statements; and, most importantly, be brief.

- Logical traps can sink an otherwise strong investment argument. Avoid chained logic, in which a number of conditions must be met for the argument to succeed. If one condition is successfully challenged, the entire argument is lost.

Don't bury the lead! I repeat this before, during, and after every writing assignment in my equity analysis courses, but breaking the "scientific" writing style is very difficult for most of us. The measured and logical scientific progression, from methodology to data to discussion to conclusion, is exactly wrong for financial analytic reports. Unlike finance professors, investors don't read a financial analysis because they have to, and they don't read it as they would a scientific paper. They read it as they would read a newspaper. Investors scan the headlines. If they are intrigued, they may read a little deeper, always searching for critical information up front. If they have to dig or wait to see the point, they likely will stop reading, and the report will fail.

A financial analysis should contain five sections: summary and conclusion, earnings forecast, valuation, elaboration, and detail. Every securities house has its own style, and analysts can fool with the order a bit, but conclusions are always first and detail is always last. The report becomes more detailed from front to back. Wading through elaboration on the way to a conclusion will discourage most readers instantly. This order applies not only to the report as a whole but to each subsection. The conclusions of the valuation section come first, for example, and the elaboration next. Any element of the report that catches the reader's eye, like a table, chart, or graph, must be self-explanatory. Charts that are titled "Sales from 1990 to 1999" will, I assure you, be ignored. Who knows what such a chart means, and why should the reader care?

Financial writing is about persuasion, not description. It is the analysts's first job to present an investment argument. It is not financial information, but the meaning of financial information in the argument's context that is important. The analyst must therefore present his or her interpretation of data, not simply list it. If data do not contribute to the argument, then why are they in the report? Analysts, being overly fond of detail, have difficulty giving up any datum. That's what appendixes are for.

THE STRUCTURE OF AN ANALYTIC REPORT

From front to back, an analytic report evolves from summary to fine detail. Using the financial analysis and valuation material from previous chapters, I try to illustrate what the principal sections of a hypothetical Dell Computer analytic report might look like.

Recommendation and Summary

A financial report is best written from front to back. After finishing all the background analytic work, I suggest completing the recommendation and summary page first, before any other section of the report. Not only is this an excellent way to organize your own thoughts, but also the summary page dictates the direction taken by the rest of the report. In supporting the principal investment arguments presented in the summary, you essentially write the entire report. I strongly advise against the "data dump" method of report creation, in which the analyst begins by writing everything he or she knows about the firm, in no particular order, in the hope of "fixing it up" later. It might be possible to convert a data dump to a disciplined investment argument, but it isn't probable. To write a summary, ask yourself, as you will probably someday be asked, "Tell me in 30 seconds why I should (or shouldn't) buy this stock."

■ **Tip**   Avoid the data dump report writing style. First do the thinking and then do the writing.

At J. P. Morgan Securities, where I learned the trade, the first page of each analytic report contained the investment recommendation, a brief summary of the report's argument, and a table of statistics. The need for brevity and clarity is intense in such a small space. Arguably, this is the report's most important page.

■ **Trick**   Write the recommendation and summary page before starting the rest of the report.

First page formats differ widely among securities houses. Most present the reader with as complete a snapshot of the stock and the report itself as can be fit on a single page. Some houses provide statistical data on earnings, market capitalization, valuation, revenues, growth, and a variety of other numbers; others begin with text. But everyone uses the report's first page to grab the reader, often through a provocative subtitle. Page 1 is the analyst's best chance of pulling in the reader, and most brokerage reports lead with their best stuff.

Pulling together my rather cautious views of Dell Computer in 1999, my first draft of the summary page of a hypothetical Dell report might sound like this:

Dell Computer is and will remain the personal computer industry's premier growth company, and should handily weather hardening industry competitive conditions, unit pricing pressure, and slowing industry growth. Although Dell could be tested if PC markets turn unexpectedly sour, the company's skilled management, powerful business model, superior product offerings, and financial strength should maintain its strong competitive position. I recommend further accumulation of DELL and rate it a Buy with a fiscal 20001 target price of $44.

However, Dell's powerful historical growth trends are likely to moderate through 2003. Slowing sales performance and declining margins reduce DELL's projected annual EPS growth to 43 percent in fiscal 2000, producing EPS of $0.76 compared with 66 percent growth and $0.53 in 1999. Sales growth, which averaged 51 percent annually in 1996–1999, declines to an expected 31 percent in 2000 and then, gradually, to 23 percent by 2003. Projected gross margin, also suffering from intensified industry competition, ends its 1996–1999 rise, reaching only the 22.5 percent 1999 level in fiscal 2000 and returning to about the 1996 level of 20 percent by 2003.

Slowing earnings growth and narrowing investment opportunities in the maturing PC industry will probably reduce DELL's return on equity and therefore its valuation multiples over the forecast period. From the current 30 times, the company's projected price/book value ratio falls to about 24 times at fiscal 2001 year end, producing a $44 target price (compared with $33.50 currently) on a projected $1.83 book value per share. DELL's P/E ratio falls to a projected 33 times from the current 35 over the same period."

This argument, of course, immediately raises concerns. I've recommended that investors buy DELL, but forecasted deteriorating business conditions. Although I very likely would have taken this position in 1999, this is a high-risk strategy that is vulnerable to unexpected events, especially in the out years of the forecast. I chose to walk the tightwire, and I would have eventually fallen. DELL did in fact reach the $50 to $60 range in early 2000, but its most recent ending price (1/26/01) was actually $26.50, well below the $44 forecast (DELL's 2001 fiscal year ended February 2, 2001).

These are exactly the sorts of issues that the summary page is designed to reveal, and one of the reasons it pays to write it first. And the dilemma is a common one. I am clearly uneasy about DELL's outlook but have not committed to a truly nasty financial projection, for which there was no obvious justification at the time. As a result, the valuation box in Chapter 15 supports a "soft landing" for DELL at a higher $44 target price in 2001.

Investment Thesis

The investment thesis is the report's first layer of detail. If the summary and recommendation answers the 30-second question about the stock as a whole, the investment thesis devotes 30 seconds to the recommendation's principal arguments.

Each investment thesis is a more detailed version of the report's summary, often supplemented by a short company description and risk factors. Just as the investment thesis fleshes out the summary, each following section of the report is an elaboration of material presented earlier. As the reader moves through the report, topics are discussed in greater detail, finally reaching the appendixes with their dizzying collections of numbers.

I have always considered the "Risks" section, sometimes included in the investment thesis, to be problematic. Given investors' concentration on return, its very presence appears to undermine the investment argument. The temptation, therefore, is to present mitigating factors along with risks. Of course, if the principal risks are mitigated, why mention them at all? In general, it is probably true that equity analytic reports deal clumsily with risk, failing to define it in nearly the detail devoted to the investment return argument. But the notion that investors will forgive a failed stock recommendation because its cause was mentioned in a "Risks" section is, in my view, whimsical.

The investment thesis is an increasingly popular addition to many brokerage reports. It's a great opportunity to remind the investor (and the analyst him- or herself) why this investment recommendation makes sense. Some analysts use the investment thesis to present a broader, macro discussion of overall economic and sector trends driving investment recommendations. This is fine, it seems to me, as long as the reader can find supporting material somewhere else in the report.

In the DELL case, I might have written the following:

Investment Thesis

- *Skilled Management*—Dell management has proven to be highly adaptive in an increasingly difficulty industry environment, positioning the company for global and enterprise system growth as retail markets harden.

- *Strong Business Model*—Despite the maturing of the PC industry, DELL should maintain superior earnings growth because of the efficiency of its build-to-order business model.

- *Superior Product Line*—DELL's superior desktop, laptop, and server product offerings are well diversified and guard against selective market downturns.
- *Financial Strength*—The company's strong cash flow and balance sheet are a significant competitive advantage in more difficult pricing environments and should allow it to overcome weaker competitors.

Risks

- *Maturing PC Market*—Slowing PC industry growth will harden competitive conditions and exert continuing pricing pressure. DELL must continue to shift its product mix toward higher margin laptop and server markets.
- *Vulnerability to General Downturn*—In a slower growth environment, DELL could be more vulnerable to a general economic slowdown in the United States. The company will continue to build its global sales effort.

Earnings Outlook

The earnings outlook presents a summary of the income statement forecast through a discussion of the forecast's principal economic drivers. This is not a line-by-line analysis of projected earnings. Rather, it is focused on the most important of the analyst's base case assumptions, those that reflect his or her fundamental judgments about the firm's future potential. Revenue growth, operating margins, and capital investment requirements probably qualify as fundamental, but other variables might also.

■ **Tip**   Use the earnings outlook section to present the base case assumptions driving your financial model.

Because of the variation in company economics, brokerage formats, and analyst styles, it's difficult to generalize about earnings models. But arguably, the earnings model is the heart of any analytical report since it is here that qualitative conclusions about the company's and/or industry's future are given numerical substance. At issue is the power of the analyst's vision to generate future earnings. Most earnings sections therefore make a strong effort to tie the principal investment drivers, perhaps as summarized in the investment thesis, directly to future earnings. In fact, I wonder if an investment driver that has no earnings consequences is an investment driver at all.

In this section of the hypothetical DELL report, I follow the themes introduced in the report's summary and concentrate on sales growth and gross margin, actually picking up part of the first sentence of the summary paragraph.

> Although Dell's earnings per share grew at an 82 percent average annual rate in 1996–1999, moderating sales growth and declining margins will likely reduce its annual earnings rise to 43 percent in fiscal 2000, producing EPS of $0.76, compared with 66 percent growth at $0.53 in 1999. Thereafter, I expect annual earnings growth to fall gradually to about 22 percent in 2003 (see Table X).
>
> Dell's unit sales should continue their strong growth, led by enterprise (workstations and servers) and laptop systems, but expected revenue per system will be under pressure. Revenue per unit has declined steadily since 1995, while unit sales growth remained robust, as shown in Table Y.

TABLE X

DELL's projected EPS growth gradually declines as sales and margin growth slow.

	1999	2000E	2001E	2002E	2003E
Net revenue ($billions)	$18.2	26.5	38.4	53.7	$72.5
% revenue growth	48.0%	45.0	45.0	40.0	35.0%
Gross margin	22.5%	22.5	21.8	21.0	20.0%
EPS	$0.53	0.76	1.02	1.31	$1.60
% EPS growth	65.6%	43.4	34.2	28.4	22.1%

TABLE Y

DELL's unit sales growth is strong, but average system revenues are declining.

	1995	1996	1997	1998	1999
Unit sales growth	8%	48	55	60	64
Average revenue per unit	$2,900	2,850	2,700	2,600	$2,350

I expect annual unit sales growth to decline from 60 percent to 50 percent over the forecast period, with annual 10 percent drops in average revenue per unit.

Declining revenue per unit will likely be offset by falling component costs and a continuing shift to higher margin laptop and enterprise systems, moderating the impact on gross margin. Nevertheless, some margin pressure is likely, and I forecast a gradual gross margin decline from the 22.5 percent level in 1999 to an estimated 20.0 percent in 2003.

Valuation

The objective of the valuation section is the presentation of the analyst's target price argument. The "valuation box" technique of Chapter 15 is a useful discipline here because it contains both the value driver (earnings growth or return on equity) and valuation multiple assumptions. Rising multiples are, for example, harder to justify with falling growth or returns staring one in the face. Further, the valuation box attaches a time period to the target price—robbing the analyst of the wiggle room a vague time period might provide.

■ **Trick**   The valuation argument builds upon the earnings outlook by using the financial model's specific predictions as the basis of the projected target price.

Of course, the analyst needs some technique to tie performance to value, and we discussed such techniques in Chapters 14 to 18. My own prejudice toward multiple-based valuation methods, both relative and hybrid, should be clear at this point, but any logical valuation process is acceptable.

Often part of a valuation analysis, a milestones and catalysts topic discusses events that are likely to move the stock. Target prices are all very well, but investors will probably ask why, exactly, does the stock move from its current price to the target (catalysts) and what are the appropriate indicators of the investment recommendation's success (milestones).

■ **Trick**   Include milestones and catalysts in the valuation discussion so that investors will have tangible indicators of the investment thesis's success (or failure).[2]

Milestones and catalysts also provide a basis for returning to the stock periodically to update both investors and salespeople. Any excuse for talking is a good excuse.

Like earnings models, valuation arguments vary with the company and the analyst. In my experience, most Wall Street analytic reports seem to employ a relative valuation methodology using the valuation multiples of comparable companies, although they may use other valuation methods as well. Many equity analysts are, in fact, also industry sector specialists, and they think in terms of the valuation of a group of stocks. Institutional investors may also have industry specialties, again making relative valuation relevant. But ultimately, I think relative valuation methods are popular because they are persuasive. A DCF analysis, relying on analyst-generated cash flows and discount rates, may or may not be accurate, but stock prices are always stock prices. Valuations based upon the trading of comparable stocks therefore have a special substance lacking in less connected methods. Linked to comparable valuations, target prices driven by projected performance improvements seem more credible. Not only that, but projected performance improvements themselves can be compared to the operations of competitors—another reality check. One danger in relative valuation analysis, of course, is that the process does not catch a company's divergence from its comparable group because, for example, of technological innovation or product market shifts. When the comparables no longer compare, relative valuation must yield to more fundamental techniques like hybrid analysis or DCF. An even more important danger, especially with speculative companies or industries, is that the comparable group itself is mispriced. Use of relative valuation in such circumstances is like redecorating a burning house.

The computer industry relative valuation analysis from Chapter 15 might appear in the Dell analysis in the following way:

From its current $33.50 price, DELL should rise to an estimated $44 by fiscal year end 2001 because of strong earnings and capital generation, offset partially by falling valuation multiples. I expect the company's return on equity to fall gradually from about 86 percent in 1999 to 61 percent in 2003, driven by slowing earnings growth. Falling returns on equity carry DELL's price/book value multiple from its current 30.2 times level to 20.3 times by 2003, as shown in Table Z.

Dell generates substantial additional capital through 2002; its book value per share rises to $2.63 from $1.11 currently. However, return levels steadily fall as earnings fail to keep pace with capital growth. As a result, I expect DELL's *P*/BV multiple to drop from the current 30.2 level to 20.3 at fiscal year end 2002. *P/E* shows a similar, but less dramatic decline.

TABLE Z

In the DELL valuation box, falling returns on equity produce a
gradual decline in both *P/BV* and *P/E* over the forecast period.

	Stock Price	P/BV	Book Value per Share	Return on Equity	P/E
Current	$33.50	30.2	$1.11	85.7%	35
2000E	34.58	27.2	1.27	80.3	34
2001E	44.18	24.1	1.83	71.6	34
2002E	$53.48	20.3	$2.63	60.8%	33

The key to Dell's forecasted stock price rise lies in the company's ability to maintain unit sales growth, in the face of a continuing fall in average system prices. Investors should be watchful of business or economic conditions that reduce unit growth, especially in the company's rapidly expanding (and very profitable) enterprise system market. Any substantial cutback in business spending for computer systems could be a serious negative for DELL.

This valuation discussion focuses investors' attention on unit growth, particularly on the enterprise system market, as the principal catalyst for further stock price increases. Milestones could include periodic measures of business capital spending, consumer demand for computers, or the company's own estimates of enterprise system growth. With continuing forecasted pricing pressure, unit growth will be a closely watched indicator.

Elaboration

The objective of the report's elaborative sections is to present the competitive and strategic analysis that supports the investment arguments made earlier. The summary, earnings outlook, and valuation sections told the reader *what* the analyst expects to happen. The elaborative sections tell the reader *why*. This is the place to present the nature-nurture competitive arguments of Chapters 4 and 5.

Elaborative material must address itself to the principal investment theses. Nothing, it seems to me, is more potentially distracting to the reader than to wonder, "Why am I reading this?" If the elaborative material is a recognizable continuation of the report's principal investment theses, the question does not arise.

■ **Tip**   The elaborative sections of an analytical report present the competitive and strategic arguments supporting the analyst's investment theses.

There is no magic to this business segment organization. Elaboration can be structured around products, markets, customers, technologies, or practically any other topic. But the themes of the investment theses, earnings projections, and valuation must be supported by elaboration.

You can elaborate on other themes, of course, but be careful about their relevance. The reader will likely be confused by cluttering the report with a mass of information that is off point. As analysts, we are, of course, abnormally fond of detail. If you simply can't live without some data in the report, put it in an appendix. The body of the report must follow the investment logic.

In the Dell report, given our focus on sales and margin growth, I'd expect to see a market-by-market elaboration of sales, pricing, and profit trends. The idea is to build the product/market level support for Table Y in the earnings section (actually reconciling market level detail to the table would be helpful). Preparing this section would likely take considerable analytic legwork, since the company discloses little of this data. To support the catalyst/milestone argument in the valuation section, some discussion of macroeconomic drivers of Dell growth is probably essential. The effort here is to correlate Dell's performance to broader indicators of consumer and business spending, retail sales, and economic growth. Given that international sales might have to offset domestic weakness, extending the economic discussion abroad is probably essential.

In addition, the elaboration section usually presents some discussion of and comparisons to the company's leading competitors. We have already conveniently completed this task in Chapter 7's cross-sectional ratio analysis.

Detail

The full force of the report's detail, especially the financial model, should be confined to appendixes, leaving the body free to describe and elaborate upon the investment theses. I am aware of the pain analysts suffer seeing their cherished data banished to the report's outer fringes. The idea, however, is to create a tight, logical argument in the report's body for the benefit of the reader, not a monument to the knowledge of the analyst.

■ **Tip**   If you can't live without it, put information peripheral to the report's principal investment thesis in an appendix.

My sense is that most securities houses and equity analysts "get it" when it comes to detail. Pages of industry and company facts seem to be giving way to investment arguments. Increasingly well informed readers, who sometimes have industry knowledge rivaling that of the analyst, may drive this. Sophisticated investors need to know how the analyst interprets the facts, and that's where analytic reports must focus.

In our Dell report, at the very least, the appendixes will present our Dell financial model. But we might also include an appendix containing the full cross-sectional ratio analysis of the computer industry and the detail of the computer industry relative valuation model.

GIVING THE READER A BREAK

The burden of proof and clarity in an analytic report lies with the analyst. Readers will not, and cannot be expected to, search your writing for its logic and information. You must make the logic immediately accessible. Here are some ideas.

Don't Bury the Lead

Readers approach financial analytic reports as they would a newspaper. They skip through the report like a stone across water, stopping occasionally to focus. To accommodate this reading style, the analyst must be sure that, at every level of the report, summary precedes detail and conclusions precede explanation. The report's first page summarizes the report, the first sentence of a major subsection summarizes that section, the first sentence of a paragraph summarizes the paragraph, and so on. The reader always knows where he or she is going and can make sense of the document at any level, from headlines down to individual paragraphs.

Notice in the hypothetical Dell report that the first sentences of the summary, earnings, and valuation sections summarize the conclusions of that section. In fact, the first sentences, if read together, tell much of the story:

> Dell Computer is and will remain the personal computer industry's premier growth company, and should handily weather hardening industry competitive conditions, unit pricing pressure, and slowing industry growth. However, Dell's powerful historical growth trends are likely to moderate through 2003. From its current $33.50 price, DELL should rise to an estimated $44 by fiscal year end 2001, driven by strong earnings and capital generation, offset partially by falling valuation multiples.

Be Ruthless About Detail

The single most important question, which you must answer for the reader everywhere in the document, is "Why is this material here?" When deciding whether and where to use material, ask yourself the same question.

Make Sense of Charts and Tables

Ever run across a chart or table titled something like "Sales from 1990 to 1995"? What are we supposed to make of that? It may describe accurately what's in the chart, but the reader has no idea what it means because very likely *he or she has not read the surrounding text.* And it is the analyst's job to present meaning, in the context of an investment thesis, not just information. If sales from 1990 to 1995 is interesting but doesn't contribute much to the investment argument, why is the chart there in the first place? If I were the reader, I probably wouldn't stop one second to look at that chart.

In the hypothetical DELL report, the titles of Tables X, Y, and Z themselves form a reasonably coherent argument:

> DELL's projected EPS growth gradually declines as sales and margin growth slow (Table X). DELL unit sales growth is strong, but average system revenues are declining (Table Y). In the Dell valuation box, falling returns on equity produce a gradual decline in both *P*/BV and *P/E* over the forecast period (Table Z).

A reader, scanning the report by reading chart and table titles, could get a good idea of the investment argument being presented.

STYLE AND ITS ABUSE

Like any profession, equity analysis has its own lingo. Without repeating *The Elements of Style,* let me mention a few of the most irritating constructions I see in financial writing.

Avoid the Passive Voice

In spite of its authoritative sound, the passive voice stinks. Avoid it. Passive voice constructions always sound to me like an attempt to shift responsibility away from the writer. Unfortunately, as an analyst, you cannot escape.

Don't Say:	Do Say:
■ "It is thought . . ."	■ "I think . . ."
■ "It is projected that . . ."	■ "I project . . ."
■ "Sales are projected to grow 5 percent."	■ "Projected sales grow at 5 percent."

Be Positive

Readers generally want to know what is rather than what is not.

Don't Say:	Do Say:
■ "Management was not expecting the order to be cancelled."	■ "Management was surprised by the order's cancellation."
■ "The company has not produced sales growth."	■ "The company has failed to increase sales."
■ "We do not expect the company to meet its growth target."	■ "The company's projected growth falls short of the target."

Be Concrete

Do not, through vague writing, raise more questions than you answer. This is a sure way to stop readers in their tracks.

Don't Say:	Do Say:
■ "A period of slow earnings growth set in."	■ "Earnings growth slowed to 5 percent for two years."

Be Brief

Enough said.

Don't Say:	Do Say:
■ "The reason that expense growth accelerated is that . . . ."	■ "Expense growth accelerated because . . ."
■ "The fact that management has not succeeded in its efforts to . . ."	■ "Management's failure to . . ."
■ "The company's sales are expected to grow going forward."	■ "The company's expected sales grow."

THE CHAINED-LOGIC TRAP

Support your investment theses with independent points rather than chained logic. In chained logic, the success of any investment argument depends on those preceding it. For example, imagine you are pitching the purchase of ABC stock to an investor with the following argument:

> ABC Inc.'s potential acquisition of XYX Ltd. should permit the combined companies to expand their distribution, allowing cross selling of products and leading to accelerated earnings growth.

Before you can finish the sentence, the investor says, "Cross selling doesn't work." I hope you have another idea, because that one is dead. I kept a top hat and cane in my briefcase in case I needed to dance out of a client's office after such a showstopper.

Instead of chained logic, present individual, free-standing investment arguments. Such arguments could include an attractive valuation, robust industry growth, strong competitive position, or potential earnings acceleration.

In the Dell investment thesis, I can argue the merits of each of the points separately. If an investor rejects one, it isn't good, but at least there is something left to talk about.

- Skilled Management
- Strong Business Model
- Superior Product Line
- Financial Strength

In the long run, Dell's financial strength and the quality of its product line, for example, are obviously connected. But, in the shorter term, these investment arguments can be made relatively independently of the skills of management or the business model.

NOTES

[1] William Strunk and E. B. White, *The Elements of Style,* 3rd ed., MacMillan Publishing, New York, 1979.

[2] I must thank my first director of research, John Conti of J. P. Morgan Securities, for always insisting on milestones and catalysts. John's concern was not only where the stock might be going but also how it was likely to get there.

Bibliography

FINANCIAL STATEMENT ANALYSIS

Bernstein, Leopold A. *Analysis of Financial Statements.* New York: Irwin, 1993.
———, and John J. Wild. *Financial Statement Analysis: Theory, Application, and Interpretation.* New York: Irwin/McGraw-Hill, 1997.
Fridson, Martin S. *Financial Statement Analysis: A Practitioner's Guide.* New York: Wiley, 1996.
Gibson, Charles H. *Financial Statement Analysis: Using Financial Accounting Information.* Cincinnati, Ohio: South-Western College Publishing, 1998.
Hirst, D. Eric, and Mary Lea McAnally. *Cases in Financial Reporting: An Integrated Approach With an Emphasis on Earnings Quality and Persistence.* Englewood Cliffs, N.J.: Prentice-Hall, 1998.
Ittelson, Thomas. *Financial Statements: A Step-by-Step Guide to Understanding and Creating Financial Reports.* Franklin Lakes, N.J.: Career Press, 1998.
Schoenebeck, Karen P. *Interpreting and Analyzing Financial Statements.* Englewood Cliffs, N.J.: Prentice-Hall, 1998.
Stickney, Clyde P. *Financial Reporting and Statement Analysis: A Strategic Perspective.* Forth Worth, Tex.: The Dryden Press, 1996.
White, Gerald I., Ashwinpaul C. Sondhi, and Dov Fried. *The Analysis and Use of Financial Statements.* New York: Wiley, 1998.

SECURITY ANALYSIS

Benninga, Simon Z., and Oded H. Sarig. *Corporate Finance: A Valuation Approach.* New York: McGraw-Hill, 1997.
Coggin, T. Daniel, and Frank J. Fabozzi, editors. *Applied Equity Analysis.* New Hope, Penn.: Frank J. Fabozzi Associates, 1999.

Cottle, Sidney, Roger F. Murray, and Frank E. Block. *Graham and Dodd's Security Analysis.* New York: McGraw-Hill, 1988.

Fischer, Donald, E., and Ronald J. Jordan. *Security Analysis and Portfolio Management.* Englewood Cliffs, N.J.: Prentice-Hall, 1995.

Fuller, Russell J., and James L. Farrell, Jr. *Modern Investments and Security Analysis.* New York: McGraw-Hill, 1987.

Hackel, Kenneth S., and Joshua Livnat. *Cash Flow and Security Analysis.* New York: Irwin, 1996.

Jacobs, Bruce I., and Kenneth N. Levy. *Equity Analysis: Quantitative Analysis for Stock Selection.* New York: McGraw-Hill, 2000.

Klein, Peter J. *Getting Started in Security Analysis.* New York: Wiley, 1998.

Lowe, Janet. *The Rediscovered Benjamin Graham.* New York: Wiley, 1999.

Palepu, Krishna G., Victor L. Bernard, and Paul M. Healy. *Introduction to Business Analysis and Valuation.* Cincinnati, Ohio: South-Western Publishing, 1997.

Rees, Bill. *Financial Analysis.* Englewood Cliffs, N.J.: Prentice-Hall, 1995.

Shim, Jae K., and Joel G. Siegel. *Handbook of Financial Analysis, Forecasting, and Modeling.* Englewood Cliffs, N.J.: Prentice-Hall, 1988.

Suutari, Raymond K. *Business Strategy and Security Analysis: The Key to Long-Term Investment Profits.* New York: Irwin, 1996.

VALUATION

Coggin, T. Daniel, and Frank J. Fabozzi. *Applied Equity Valuation.* New Hope, Penn.: Frank J. Fabozzi Associates, 1999.

Copeland, Tom, Tim Koller, and Jack Murrin. *Valuation: Measuring and Managing the Value of Companies.* New York: Irwin, 1993.

Damodaran, Aswath. *Damodaran on Valuation: Security Analysis for Investment and Corporate Finance.* New York: Wiley, 1994.

———. *Investment Valuation: Tools and Techniques for Determining the Value of Any Asset.* New York: Wiley, 1996.

Ehrbar, Al. *EVA: The Real Key to Creating Wealth.* New York, Wiley, 1998.

Grant, James L. *Foundations of Economic Value Added.* New Hope, Penn.: Frank J. Fabozzi Associates, 1997.

Gray, Gary, Patrick J. Cusatis, and J. Randall Woolridge. *Valuing a Stock: The Savvy Investor's Key to Beating the Market.* New York: McGraw-Hill, 1999.

Hooke, Jeffrey C. *Security Analysis on Wall Street: A Comprehensive Guide to Today's Valuation Methods.* New York: Wiley, 1998.

Lease, Ronald C., Kose John, Avner Kalay, Uri Lowenstein, and Oded H. Sarig. *Dividend Policy: Its Impact on Firm Value.* Boston, Mass.: Harvard Business School Press, 2000.

Madden, Bartley J. *CFROI Investing: A Total System Approach to Valuing the Firm.* Newton, Mass.: Butterworth-Heinemann, 1999.

Rappaport, Alfred. *Creating Shareholder Value: The New Standard for Business Performance.* New York: The Free Press, 1997.

Smithers, Andrew, and Stephen Wright. *Valuing Wall Street: Protecting Wealth in Turbulent Markets.* New York: McGraw-Hill, 2000.

Stewart, G. Bennett. *The Quest for Value.* New York: Harper Business, 1991.

ECONOMICS

Campbell, John Y., Andrew W. Lo, and A. Craig MacKinlay. *The Econometrics of Financial Markets.* Princeton, N.J.: Princeton University Press, 1997.

Thaler, Richard H. *The Winner's Curse: Anomalies and Paradoxes of Economic Life.* Princeton, N.J.: Princeton University Press, 1992.

STRATEGY

Barney, J. B. *Gaining and Sustaining Competitive Advantage.* Reading, Mass.: Addison-Wesley, 1997.

Besanko, David, David Dranove, and Mark Shanley. *The Economics of Strategy.* New York: Wiley, 1996.

Bovet, David, and Joseph Martha. *Value Nets: Breaking the Supply Chain to Unlock Hidden Profits.* New York: Wiley, 2000.

Brandenburger, Adam M., and Barry J. Nalebuff. *Co-opetition.* New York: Doubleday, 1996.

Day, George S., and David J. Reibstein, editors. *Wharton on Dynamic Competitive Strategy.* New York: Wiley, 1997.

Dixit, Avinash K., and Barry J. Nalebuff. *Thinking Strategically: The Competitive Edge in Business, Politics and Everyday Life.* New York: W. W. Norton, 1991.

Foss, Nicolai J., editor. *Resources, Firms & Strategies.* New York: Oxford University Press, 1997.

Ghemawat, Pankaj. *Commitment: The Dynamic of Strategy.* New York: The Free Press, 1991.

Grant, Robert M. *Contemporary Strategy Analysis.* Malden, Mass.: Blackwell Publishers, 1998.

Norman, Richard, and Rafael Ramirez. *Designing Interactive Strategies: From Value Chain to Value Constellation.* New York: Wiley, 1998.

Oster, Sharon M. *Modern Competitive Analysis.* New York: Oxford University Press, 1994.

Parolini, Cinzia. *The Value Net: A Tool for Competitive Strategy.* New York: Wiley, 1999.

Pitts, Robert A., and David Lei. *Strategic Management: Building and Sustaining Competitive Advantage.* Cincinnati, Ohio: South-Western College Publishing, 2000.

Porter, Michael E. *Competitive Advantage.* New York: The Free Press, 1985.

———. *Competitive Strategy.* New York: The Free Press, 1980.

———. *On Competition.* Boston: Harvard Business Review of Books, 1998.

Segev, Eli. *Business Unit Strategy.* New York: Wiley, 1997.

Tuominen, Kari. *Managing Change: Practical Strategies for Competitive Advantage.* Milwaukee, Wisc.: American Society for Quality Press, 2000.

ACCOUNTING

Beaver, William H. *Financial Reporting: An Accounting Revolution.* Englewood Cliffs, N.J.: Prentice-Hall, 1998.

Mulford, Charles W., and Eugene E. Comiskey. *Financial Warnings: Detecting Earnings Surprises, Avoiding Business Troubles, Implementing Corrective Strategies.* New York: Wiley, 1996.

Schilit, Howard M. *Financial Shenanigans: How to Detect Accounting Gimmicks and Fraud in Financial Reports.* New York: McGraw-Hill, 1993.

INVESTMENTS

Bernstein, Peter L., and Aswath Damodaran. *Investment Management.* New York: Wiley, 1998.

Bernstein, Peter L., and Frank J. Fabozzi, editors. *Streetwise: The Best of the Journal of Portfolio Management.* Princeton, N.J.: Princeton University Press, 1997.

Bodie, Zvi, Alex Kane, and Alan J. Marcus. *Investments.* New York: Irwin, 1996.

Coggin, T. Daniel, Frank J. Fabozzi, and Robert D. Arnott, editors. *The Handbook of Equity Style Management.* New Hope, Penn.: Frank J. Fabozzi Associates, 1997.

Elton, Edwin J., and Martin J. Grubar. *Modern Portfolio Theory and Investment Analysis.* New York: Wiley, 1995.

Fabozzi, Frank J. *Investment Management.* Englewood Cliffs, N.J.: Prentice-Hall, 1999.

Fisher, Philip A. *Common Stocks and Uncommon Profits.* New York: Wiley, 1996.

Fridson, Martin S. *Investment Illusions: A Savvy Wall Street Pro Explodes Popular Misconceptions About the Market.* New York: Wiley, 1993.

Maginn, John L., and Donald L. Tuttle. *Managing Investment Portfolios: A Dynamic Process.* Boston, Mass.: Warren Gorham and Lamont, 1990.

Taggart, Robert A. *Quantitative Analysis for Investment Management.* Englewood Cliffs, N.J.: Prentice-Hall, 1996.

Warwick, Ben. *Searching for Alpha: The Quest for Exceptional Investment Performance.* New York: Wiley, 2000.

Whitman, Martin J. *Value Investing: A Balanced Approach.* New York: Wiley, 1999.

MARKET EFFICIENCY

Gladwell, Malcolm. *The Tipping Point: How Little Things Can Make a Big Difference.* Boston, Mass.: Little Brown, 2000.

Haugen, Robert A. *Beast on Wall Street: How Stock Volatility Devours Our Wealth.* Englewood Cliffs, N.J.: Prentice-Hall, 1999.

———. *The Inefficient Stock Market: What Pays Off and Why.* Englewood Cliffs, N.J.: Prentice-Hall, 1999.

———. *The New Finance: The Case Against Efficient Markets.* Englewood Cliffs, N.J.: Prentice-Hall, 1995.

Jacobs, Bruce I. *Capital Ideas and Market Realities: Option Replication, Investor Behavior, and Stock Market Crashes.* Malden, Mass.: Blackwell Publishers, 1999.

Kindleberger, Charles P. *Manias, Panics and Crashes: A History of Financial Crises.* New York: Wiley, 1997.

Lo, Andrew W., and A. Craig MacKinlay. *A Non-Random Walk Down Wall Street.* Princeton, N.J.: Princeton University Press, 1999.

Lowenstein, Roger. *When Genius Failed: The Rise and Fall of Long-Term Capital Management.* New York: Random House, 2000.

Scheifer, Andrei. *Inefficient Markets: An Introduction to Behavioral Finance.* New York: Oxford University Press, 2000.

Shiller, Robert J. *Irrational Exuberance.* Princeton, N.J.: Princeton University Press, 2000.

———. *Market Volatility.* Boston, Mass.: The MIT Press, 1999.

Tvede, Lars. *The Psychology of Finance.* New York: Wiley, 1999.

OTHER

Benninga, Simon. *Financial Modeling.* Cambridge: The MIT Press, 1998.

Cornell, Bradford. *The Equity Risk Premium: The Long-Run Future of the Stock Market.* New York: Wiley, 1999.

Damodaran, Aswath. *Applied Corporate Finance.* New York: Wiley, 1999.

Fritzman, Mark P. *Puzzles of Finance.* New York: Wiley, 2000.

Kurtz, Howard. *The Fortune Tellers: Inside Wall Street's Game of Money, Media, and Manipulation.* New York: The Free Press, 2000.

Pratt, Shannon P. *The Cost of Capital.* New York: Wiley, 1998.

Sahlman, William A., Howard H. Stevenson, Michael J. Roberts, and Amar Bhide. *The Entrepreneurial Venture.* Boston: Harvard Business School Press, 1999.

Sirower, Mark L. *The Synergy Trap: How Companies Lose the Acquisition Game.* New York: The Free Press, 1997.

Stern, Joel M., and Donald H. Chew. *The Revolution in Corporate Finance.* Malden, Mass.: Blackwell Publishers, 1998.

Tryfos, Peter. *Methods for Business Analysis and Forecasting: Text & Cases.* New York: Wiley, 1998.

Index

About the Author

James English is currently an adjunct assistant professor of finance at Columbia University School of Business. He spent twenty years with JP Morgan serving in many positions, including managing director of JP Morgan Capital, the firm's venture capital unit. In his over quarter-century career in finance, English's experience extends to virtually every one of the field's subspecialties: commercial banking and credit analysis, corporate treasury and foreign exchange, capital markets, mergers & acquisitions, venture capital, and sell-side equity analysis.